Xamarin Blueprints

CW00500705

Leverage the power of Xamarin to create stunning
cross-platform and native apps

Michael Williams

PUBLISHING

BIRMINGHAM - MUMBAI

Xamarin Blueprints

Copyright © 2016 Packt Publishing

All rights reserved. No part of this book may be reproduced, stored in a retrieval system, or transmitted in any form or by any means, without the prior written permission of the publisher, except in the case of brief quotations embedded in critical articles or reviews.

Every effort has been made in the preparation of this book to ensure the accuracy of the information presented. However, the information contained in this book is sold without warranty, either express or implied. Neither the author, nor Packt Publishing, and its dealers and distributors will be held liable for any damages caused or alleged to be caused directly or indirectly by this book.

Packt Publishing has endeavored to provide trademark information about all of the companies and products mentioned in this book by the appropriate use of capitals. However, Packt Publishing cannot guarantee the accuracy of this information.

First published: September 2016

Production reference: 1270916

Published by Packt Publishing Ltd.
Livery Place
35 Livery Street
Birmingham
B3 2PB, UK.
ISBN 978-1-78588-744-4

www.packtpub.com

Credits

Author

Michael Williams

Reviewer

Engin Polat

Commissioning Editor

Amarabha Banerjee

Acquisition Editor

Larissa Pinto

Content Development Editor

Prashanth G

Technical Editor

Shivani K. Mistry

Copy Editor

Safis Editing

Project Coordinator

Ulhas Kambali

Proofreader

Safis Editing

Indexer

Tejal Daruwale Soni

Graphics

Jason Monteiro

Production Coordinator

Melwyn Dsa

About the Author

Michael Williams is an Insightful, results-driven full stack developer with notable experience in cross-platform development using Xamarin and native languages for multiple platforms. He also builds and researches server-side architecture using CQRS and event-sourcing. He shares his knowledge on his personal blog at (`www.imobservable.com`).

Also an entrepreneur, the owner of Flush Arcade, a company involved in developing creative, innovative, and ideative games (`www.flusharcade.com`).

About the Reviewer

Engin Polat has been involved in many large and medium-scale projects on .NET technologies as a developer, architect, and consulting and has won many awards since 1999.

Since 2008, he has been giving training to many large enterprises in Turkey about Windows development, Web development, distributed application development, software architecture, mobile development, cloud development, and so on. Apart from this, he organizes seminars and events in many universities in Turkey about .NET technologies, Windows platform development, cloud development, Web development, game development, and so on.

He shares his experiences on his personal blog (http://www.enginpolat.com). He has MCP, MCAD, MCSD, MCDBA, and MCT certifications.

Since 2012 he has been recognized as a Windows Platform Development MVP (Most Valuable Professional) by Microsoft. Between 2013 and 2015, he was recognized as a Nokia Developer Champion; very few people in the world are given this award.

Since 2015 he also recognized as a Microsoft Regional Director by Microsoft.

www.PacktPub.com

Did you know that Packt offers eBook versions of every book published, with PDF and ePub files available? You can upgrade to the eBook version at www.PacktPub.com and as a print book customer, you are entitled to a discount on the eBook copy. Get in touch with us at customercare@packtpub.com for more details.

At www.PacktPub.com, you can also read a collection of free technical articles, sign up for a range of free newsletters and receive exclusive discounts and offers on Packt books and eBooks.

https://www2.packtpub.com/books/subscription/packtlib

Do you need instant solutions to your IT questions? PacktLib is Packt's online digital book library. Here, you can search, access, and read Packt's entire library of books.

Why subscribe?

- Fully searchable across every book published by Packt
- Copy and paste, print, and bookmark content
- On demand and accessible via a web browser

Table of Contents

Preface 1

Chapter 1: Building a Gallery Application 7

    Create an iOS project 8

    Creating a UIViewController and UITableView 9

    Customizing a cell's appearance 12

    Creating an Android project 16

    Creating an XML interface and ListView 17

    Shared projects 19

    Custom row appearance 21

    Bitmap functions 26

    The ALAssetLibrary 29

    Adding the iOS photo screen 33

    Adding the Android photo screen 37

    Summary 40

Chapter 2: Building a SpeechTalk Application 41

    Cross-platform development with Xamarin.Forms 42

        So how would this look in Xamarin.Forms? 43

    Setting up platform projects 44

        So what is happening here? 47

    Setting up the SpeechTalk.iOS project 47

    Setting up the SpeechTalk.Droid project 49

    Xamarin.Forms, Windows Phone, and Visual Studio 49

        What can we see here? 52

    Inversion of Control (IoC) with Xamarin.Forms 55

        So why should we use it? 56

        So how do we benefit from this? 56

    Autofac 57

    iOS text-to-speech implementation 59

    Bindings 65

    Android text-to-speech implementation 68

    Setting up IoC with Android 70

    WinPhone text-to-speech implementation 71

    IoC with Windows Phone 72

    Platform independent styling 73

Summary	74
Chapter 3: Building a GPS Locator Application	75
Core location and GPS	76
Project setup	76
Navigation with Xamarin.Forms	78
Why would we do this?	78
Building the navigation control	80
View model navigation	82
Integrating Google Maps using Xamarin.Forms.Maps	86
Reactive Extensions	89
Core location with iOS and the CLLocationManager library	90
Handling location updates	94
Android and the LocationManager	100
Creating an exit point	105
Creating an API key for Android	107
Creating our Windows project	110
Core Location Services with Windows Phone	112
The Application class	116
Web services and data contracts	118
What about data contracts?	118
Creating another API key for geocoding	120
Creating GeocodingWebServiceController	121
Newtonsoft.Json and Microsoft HTTP client libraries	125
ModernHttpClient and client message handlers	127
Feeding JSON data into the IObservable framework	130
More Reactive Extensions	132
Resource (RESX) files	132
Using GeocodingWebServiceController	134
OnNavigatedTo and OnShow	135
Pythagoras equirectangular projection	139
How are we going to calculate the closest position?	140
Summary	145
Chapter 4: Building an Audio Player Application	147
Solution setup	148
Inversion of control with MVVMCross	149
View-models with Xamarin native	150
Creating the bindings	153
NSLayoutContraints	154

MVVMCross setup inside the PCL 156
Setting up MVVMCross with iOS 157
Setting up MVVMCross with Android 159
The SoundHandler interface 161
Implementing the iOS SoundHandler using the AVAudioPlayer
framework 162
The Mvx IoC container 165
The audio player 166
A cleaner code approach to NSLayout 169
Creating AudioPlayerPageViewModel 173
Implementing the Android SoundHandler using the MediaPlayer
framework 180
XML and Mvx bindings 184
MvxActivities 185
Summary 192

Chapter 5: Building a Stocklist Application 193
Understanding the backend 194
Creating an ASP.Net Web API 2 project 195
Building an API controller 198
Setting up the mobile projects 200
Building core mobile projects 201
Improving app performance 202
Creating a global App.xaml 208
Theming with ControlTemplates 210
Updating the MainPageViewModel 214
Creating the Stocklist web service controller 217
ListViews and ObservableCollections 219
Value converters 225
Adding a DataTemplate to the global resource dictionary 226
Styles 227
Further optimization with XAML 229
Creating StockItemDetailsPage 230
Custom renderers 233
Adding styles for custom elements 236
Creating StockItemDetailsPageViewModel 236
Setting up the native platform projects 239
Hosting the Web API project locally 240
Summary 245

Chapter 6: Building a Chat Application   247

    The Model-View-Presenter (MVP) pattern   249
        So why bother with this approach?   249
    Architecture   249
        How do we determine which layers our project needs?   250
    SignalR   251
    Starting with Open Web Interface for .NET (OWIN)   255
        Creating an authorization server using OWIN OAuth 2.0   256
        OAuthAuthorizationServerProvider   256
        Use OAuthBearerAuthentication   258
    Setting up the AuthenticationRepository   259
        Configuring the Web API   261
        Building the AccountController   262
        Configuring OAuth Authentication with our Web API   264
        Building the SignalR Hub   265
    Setting up mobile projects   268
        Creating the SignalRClient   269
        Building the WebApiAccess layer   274
        Application state   278
    Setting up the navigation service   278
        Building the iOS navigation service   279
        Building the Android navigation service   280
        Building the iOS interface   282
    Handling Hub proxy callbacks   284
    Implementing the LoginPresenter   286
    Creating the connection between Presenter and View   289
    Building the LoginActivity   294
    Implementing the ClientsListPresenter   299
    Creating ClientListViewController   304
    The TaskCompletionSource framework   307
    Creating the ClientsListActivity   308
    Overriding the OnBackPressed activity   310
    Building the ListAdapter   311
    Building the ChatPresenter   314
    Building the iOS ChatView   316
    Extending the UIColor framework   320
    Android TableLayouts   323
    Building the Android ChatActivity   324
    Running the server and clients   328

Summary 328

Chapter 7: Building a File Storage Application 329

Project structure setup 330
Building a data access layer using SQLite 331
Building the ISQLiteStorage interface 333
Adding additional threading techniques 334
How do we solve this problem? 334
Creating the AsyncSemaphore 334
Creating the AsyncLock 336
Implementing native setup requirements for SQLite 337
Implementing the IoC container and modules 338
Implementing cross-platform logging 339
Implementing the SQLiteStorage class 341
Introduction to C# 6.0 syntax 341
Handling alerts in view-models 346
Building the IMethods interface 348
Building the ExtendedContentPage 351
Why are we implementing two different techniques for showing alerts? 352
Building a CarouselView using custom layouts 352
Adding scroll control to the CarouselView 356
Building a CustomRenderer for native gestures 358
Building the user interface 368
Using a SynchronizationContext 376
How do we know this context is from the main UI thread? 376
Building the EditFilePage 378
Behaviours 379
Challenge 383
Building the Windows Phone version 383
Summary 385

Chapter 8: Building a Camera Application 387

Solution setup 388
Building the MainPageViewModel class 390
Improving the INotifiedPropertyChanged implementation 390
Creating the custom UI objects 398
Building the FocusView 402
Xamarin.Forms animations 403
Xamarin.Forms compound animations 405
Building the CameraView 408

Building a control for the iOS camera 412
Building the iOS CameraRenderer 426
Integrating the Android Camera2 framework 429
Building the CameraViewRenderer in Android 449
Handling native touch events through the FocusView 451
Using RX to handle events 455
Building a VisualElementRenderer for iOS 455
Building the CustomImageRenderers 456
Building the UIImageEffects class 461
Building the CustomImageRenderer for Android 462
Triggers 468
    Easing.SinIn 471
    Easing.SinOut 471
Platform effects 472
Building the CameraPage 477
Adding native orientation events 491
Challenge 498
Summary 498

Index 499

Preface

Throughout my journey as a mobile developer, I have worked with many different development paradigms and techniques. I have built mobile applications in Java, objective-C, Swift (2 and 3), and C# across all mobile platforms. I've even built entire servers for my mobile applications.

I'm not standing here to brag, or to say that I'm an expert. But I do believe that I have encountered a ton of problems, and built solutions that a lot of mobile developers will require.

My latest work has been around building cross-platform solutions with Xamarin using both native and Xamarin.Forms. I have spent a lot of time narrowing down, what I believe are the best approaches in building any cross-platform mobile application. Building good architecture, structure, and a smooth user experience, whilst sharing as much code as possible.

Enjoy.

What this book covers

Chapter 1, *Building a Gallery Application*, provides you a walkthrough for native development with Xamarin by building an iOS and Android application that will read from your local gallery files and display them into a UITableView and ListView.

Chapter 2, *Build a SpeechTalk Application*, provides you a walkthrough of Xamarin.Forms development by building an iOS, Android and Windows Phone application that will use platform speech services to talk text typed into a text field.

Chapter 3, *Building a GPS Locator Application*, shows you how to build a Xamarin.Forms application that integrates native GPS location services and Google Maps APIs. We will cover more content on IoC containers, the Xamarin.Forms.Maps library, and techniques for C# async and background tasks.

Chapter 4, *Building an Audio Player Application*, in this chapter, we will integrate native audio functions for processing a sound file using the AVFramework in iOS, and MediaPlayer framework in Android.

Chapter 5, *Building a Stocklist Application*, in this chapter we look at detailing our XAML interfaces using CustomRenderers, Styles, and ControlTemplates. We also build a simple web service and setup a JSON feed for our mobile application.

Chapter 6, *Building a Chat Application*, in this chapter our user interface will move away from MVVM design and follow a new paradigm called MVP (Model-View-Presenter). We take another step further into the backend and set up a SignalR hub and client to simulate a chat service, where data will be sent between the server and clients instantly as the messages become available. Another key topic of focus is the project architecture, spending time on separating the project into modules, and creating a nicely tiered structure that will maximize code sharing across different platforms.

Chapter 7, *Building a File Storage Application*, in this chapter we walk through more development using Xamarin.Forms. We look at Behaviors and their use with user interfaces. We also build a custom layout using the Layout <View> framework and build our first SQLite database for storing text files.

Chapter 8, *Building a Camera Application*, our last chapter, will introduce Effects and Triggers. We learn how to apply them to user interfaces and use them with Styles. We also build multiple complex CustomRenderers for native platform cameras, tinting images and receiving touch events.

What you need for this book

Xamarin Studio

To install a copy of Xamarin Studio visit the following link:

```
https://www.xamarin.com/download
```

Building Windows Phone Applications

In order to build windows phone applications, you will need a computer with Windows, Microsoft Visual Studio, and the Universal Windows Platform SDK installed.

Running solutions

You will also need an iOS, android and windows phone device for testing. If you don't have access to devices, you will have to install simulators for each platform.

iOS

Simulators can be installed via XCode. If you haven't got XCode installed, you will need to install a fresh copy.

Android

Please install a copy of **Geny Motion** from the link below:

```
https://www.genymotion.com/
```

Windows Phone

The UWP SDK comes with simulators for Microsoft Visual Studio.

Who this book is for

If you are a mobile developer looking to create interesting and fully featured apps for different platforms, then this book is the ideal solution for you. A basic knowledge of Xamarin and C# programming is assumed.

Conventions

In this book, you will find a number of text styles that distinguish between different kinds of information. Here are some examples of these styles and an explanation of their meaning.

Code words in text, database table names, folder names, filenames, file extensions, pathnames, dummy URLs, user input, and Twitter handles are shown as follows: "Yes, it is our `AppDelegate` file; notice the `.cs` on the end."

A block of code is set as follows:

```
private void handleAssetsLoaded (object sender, EventArgs e)
    {
        _source.UpdateGalleryItems
(_imageHandler.CreateGalleryItems());
        _tableView.ReloadData ();
    }
```

New **terms** and **important words** are shown in bold. Words that you see on the screen, for example, in menus or dialog boxes, appear in the text like this: "To do so, we simply select **File** | **New** | **Solution** and select an **iOS Single View App**."

 Warnings or important notes appear in a box like this.

 Tips and tricks appear like this.

Reader feedback

Feedback from our readers is always welcome. Let us know what you think about this book-what you liked or disliked. Reader feedback is important for us as it helps us develop titles that you will really get the most out of. To send us general feedback, simply e-mail feedback@packtpub.com, and mention the book's title in the subject of your message. If there is a topic that you have expertise in and you are interested in either writing or contributing to a book, see our author guide at www.packtpub.com/authors.

Customer support

Now that you are the proud owner of a Packt book, we have a number of things to help you to get the most from your purchase.

Downloading the example code

You can download the example code files for this book from your account at http://www.packtpub.com. If you purchased this book elsewhere, you can visit http://www.packtpub.com/support and register to have the files e-mailed directly to you.

You can download the code files by following these steps:

1. Log in or register to our website using your e-mail address and password.
2. Hover the mouse pointer on the **SUPPORT** tab at the top.
3. Click on **Code Downloads & Errata**.
4. Enter the name of the book in the **Search** box.

5. Select the book for which you're looking to download the code files.
6. Choose from the drop-down menu where you purchased this book from.
7. Click on **Code Download**.

Once the file is downloaded, please make sure that you unzip or extract the folder using the latest version of:

- WinRAR / 7-Zip for Windows
- Zipeg / iZip / UnRarX for Mac
- 7-Zip / PeaZip for Linux

The code bundle for the book is also hosted on GitHub at `https://github.com/PacktPublishing/Xamarin-Blueprints`. We also have other code bundles from our rich catalog of books and videos available at `https://github.com/PacktPublishing/`. Check them out!

Errata

Although we have taken every care to ensure the accuracy of our content, mistakes do happen. If you find a mistake in one of our books-maybe a mistake in the text or the code-we would be grateful if you could report this to us. By doing so, you can save other readers from frustration and help us improve subsequent versions of this book. If you find any errata, please report them by visiting `http://www.packtpub.com/submit-errata`, selecting your book, clicking on the **Errata Submission Form** link, and entering the details of your errata. Once your errata are verified, your submission will be accepted and the errata will be uploaded to our website or added to any list of existing errata under the Errata section of that title.

To view the previously submitted errata, go to `https://www.packtpub.com/books/content/support` and enter the name of the book in the search field. The required information will appear under the **Errata** section.

Piracy

Piracy of copyrighted material on the Internet is an ongoing problem across all media. At Packt, we take the protection of our copyright and licenses very seriously. If you come across any illegal copies of our works in any form on the Internet, please provide us with the location address or website name immediately so that we can pursue a remedy.

Please contact us at `copyright@packtpub.com` with a link to the suspected pirated material.

We appreciate your help in protecting our authors and our ability to bring you valuable content.

Questions

If you have a problem with any aspect of this book, you can contact us at `questions@packtpub.com`, and we will do our best to address the problem.

1
Building a Gallery Application

This chapter will walkthrough native development with Xamarin by building an iOS and Android application that will read from your local gallery files, and display them in a **UITableView** and **ListView.** The following topics will be covered in this chapter:

Expected knowledge:

- Creating iOS provision certificates
- iOS development
- Objective-C
- Creating keystores
- Android development
- Java

In this chapter you will learn the following:

- Creating an iOS project
- Creating a UIViewController and UITableView
- Customizing a cell's appearance
- Creating an Android project
- Creating an XML interface and ListView
- Shared projects
- Custom row appearance
- Bitmap functions
- The ALAssetLibrary
- Adding the iOS photo screen
- Adding the Android photo screen

Create an iOS project

Let's begin our Xamarin journey; we will start by setting up our iOS project in Xamarin Studio:

1. Start by opening Xamarin Studio and creating a new iOS project. To do so, we simply select **File** | **New** | **Solution** and select an **iOS Single View App**; we must also give it a name and add the bundle ID you want in order to run your application.

 It is recommended that for each project, a new bundle ID is created, along with a developer provisioning profile for each project.

2. Now that we have created the iOS project, you will be taken to the following screen:

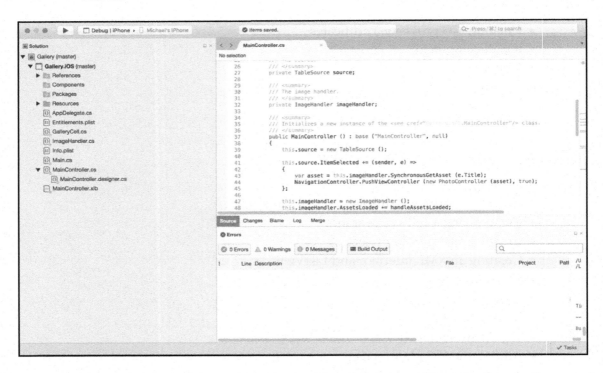

Doesn't this look familiar? Yes, it is our `AppDelegate` file; notice the `.cs` on the end; because we are using C#, all our code files will have this extension (no more `.h` or `.m` files).

Before we go any further, spend a few minutes moving around the IDE, expanding the folders, and exploring the project structure; it is very similar to an iOS project created in XCode.

Creating a UIViewController and UITableView

Now that we have our new iOS project, we are going to start by creating a `UIViewController`. Right-click on the project file, select **Add** | **New File**, and select **ViewController** from the **iOS** menu selection in the left-hand box:

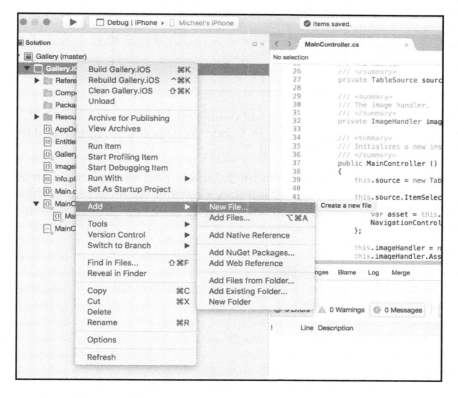

You will notice three files generated, a `.xib`, a `.cs`, and a `.designer.cs` file. We don't need to worry about the third file; this is automatically generated based upon the other two files.

Right-click on the project item and select **Reveal in Finder**,

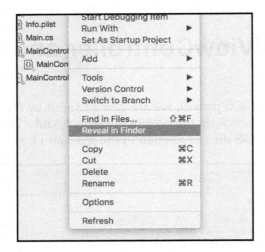

This will bring up the finder where you will double-click on the GalleryCell.xib file; this will bring up the user interface designer in XCode. You should see automated text inserted into the document to help you get started.

Firstly, we must set our namespace accordingly, and import our libraries with using statements. In order to use the iOS user interface elements, we must import the UIKit and CoreGraphics libraries. Our class will inherit the UIViewController class in which we will override the ViewDidLoad function:

```
namespace Gallery.iOS
{
    using System;
    using System.Collections.Generic;

    using CoreGraphics;
    using UIKit;

    public partial class MainController : UIViewController
    {
        private UITableView _tableView;

        private TableSource _source;
```

```
        private ImageHandler _imageHandler;

        public MainController () : base ("MainController", null)
        {
            _source = new TableSource ();

            _imageHandler = new ImageHandler ();
            _imageHandler.AssetsLoaded += handleAssetsLoaded;
        }

        private void handleAssetsLoaded (object sender, EventArgs e)
        {
            _source.UpdateGalleryItems
    (_imageHandler.CreateGalleryItems());
            _tableView.ReloadData ();
        }

        public override void ViewDidLoad ()
        {
            base.ViewDidLoad ();

            var width = View.Bounds.Width;
            var height = View.Bounds.Height;

            tableView = new UITableView(new CGRect(0, 0, width, height));
            tableView.AutoresizingMask = UIViewAutoresizing.All;
            tableView.Source = _source;

            Add (_tableView);
        }
    }
}
```

Our first UI element created is UITableView. This will be used to insert into the UIView of the UIViewController, and we also retrieve width and height values of the UIView to stretch the UITableView to fit the entire bounds of the UIViewController. We must also call Add to insert the UITableView into the UIView. In order to fill the list with data, we need to create a UITableSource to contain the list of items to be displayed in the list. We will also need an object called GalleryModel; this will be the model of data to be displayed in each cell.

Follow the previous process for adding two new .cs files; one will be used to create our UITableSource class and the other for the GalleryModel class. In TableSource.cs, first we must import the Foundation library with the using statement:

```
using Foundation;
```

Now for the rest of our class. Remember, we have to override specific functions for our `UITableSource` to describe its behavior. It must also include a list for containing the item view-models that will be used for the data displayed in each cell:

```
public class TableSource : UITableViewSource
    {
        protected List<GalleryItem> galleryItems;
        protected string cellIdentifier = "GalleryCell";

        public TableSource (string[] items)
        {
            galleryItems = new List<GalleryItem> ();
        }
    }
```

We must override the `NumberOfSections` function; in our case, it will always be one because we are not having list sections:

```
        public override nint NumberOfSections (UITableView tableView)
        {
            return 1;
        }
```

To determine the number of list items, we return the count of the list:

```
        public override nint RowsInSection (UITableView tableview, nint
    section)
        {
            return galleryItems.Count;
        }
```

Then we must add the `GetCell` function; this will be used to get the `UITableViewCell` to render for a particular row. But before we do this, we need to create a custom `UITableViewCell`.

Customizing a cell's appearance

We are now going to design our cells that will appear for every model found in the `TableSource` class. Add a new `.cs` file for our custom `UITableViewCell`.

We are not going to use a `.xib` and simply build the user interface directly in code using a single `.cs` file.

Now for the implementation:

```
public class GalleryCell: UITableViewCell
    {
        private UIImageView _imageView;

        private UILabel _titleLabel;

        private UILabel _dateLabel;

        public GalleryCell (string cellId) : base
(UITableViewCellStyle.Default, cellId)
        {
            SelectionStyle = UITableViewCellSelectionStyle.Gray;

            _imageView = new UIImageView()
            {
                TranslatesAutoresizingMaskIntoConstraints = false,
            };

            _titleLabel = new UILabel ()
            {
                TranslatesAutoresizingMaskIntoConstraints = false,
            };

            _dateLabel = new UILabel ()
            {
                TranslatesAutoresizingMaskIntoConstraints = false,
            };

            ContentView.Add (imageView);
            ContentView.Add (titleLabel);
            ContentView.Add (dateLabel);
        }
    }
```

Our constructor must call the base constructor, as we need to initialize each cell with a cell style and cell identifier. We then add a UIImageView and two UILabels for each cell, one for the filename and one for the date. Finally, we add all three elements to the main content view of the cell.

When we have our initializer, we add the following:

```
public void UpdateCell (GalleryItem gallery)
        {
            _imageView.Image = UIImage.LoadFromData (NSData.FromArray
(gallery.ImageData));
            _titleLabel.Text = gallery.Title;
```

```
                        _dateLabel.Text = gallery.Date;
            }

            public override void LayoutSubviews ()
            {
                base.LayoutSubviews ();

                ContentView.TranslatesAutoresizingMaskIntoConstraints = false;

                // set layout constraints for main view
                AddConstraints
(NSLayoutConstraint.FromVisualFormat("V:|[imageView(100)]|",
NSLayoutFormatOptions.DirectionLeftToRight, null, new
NSDictionary("imageView", imageView)));
                AddConstraints
(NSLayoutConstraint.FromVisualFormat("V:|[titleLabel]|",
NSLayoutFormatOptions.DirectionLeftToRight, null, new
NSDictionary("titleLabel", titleLabel)));
                AddConstraints (NSLayoutConstraint.FromVisualFormat("H:|-10-
[imageView(100)]-10-[titleLabel]-10-|", NSLayoutFormatOptions.AlignAllTop,
null, new NSDictionary ("imageView", imageView, "titleLabel",
titleLabel)));
                AddConstraints (NSLayoutConstraint.FromVisualFormat("H:|-10-
[imageView(100)]-10-[dateLabel]-10-|", NSLayoutFormatOptions.AlignAllTop,
null, new NSDictionary ("imageView", imageView, "dateLabel", dateLabel)));
            }
```

Our first function, UpdateCell, simply adds the model data to the view, and our second function overrides the LayoutSubViews method of the UITableViewCell class (equivalent to the ViewDidLoad function of a UIViewController).

Now that we have our cell design, let's create the properties required for the view-model. We only want to store data in our GalleryItem model, meaning we want to store images as byte arrays. Let's create a property for the item model:

```
namespace Gallery.iOS
{
    using System;

    public class GalleryItem
    {
        public byte[] ImageData;

        public string ImageUri;

        public string Title;
```

```
        public string Date;

        public GalleryItem ()
        {
        }
    }
}
```

Now back to our `TableSource` class. The next step is to implement the `GetCell` function:

```
public override UITableViewCell GetCell (UITableView tableView, NSIndexPath
indexPath)
        {
            var cell = (GalleryCell)tableView.DequeueReusableCell
(CellIdentifier);
            var galleryItem = galleryItems[indexPath.Row];

            if (cell == null)
            {
                // we create a new cell if this row has not been created
yet
                cell = new GalleryCell (CellIdentifier);
            }

            cell.UpdateCell (galleryItem);

            return cell;
        }
```

Notice the cell reuse on the `if` statement; you should be familiar with this type of approach, it is a common pattern for reusing cell views and is the same as the Objective-C implementation (this is a very basic cell reuse implementation). We also call the `UpdateCell` method to pass in the required `GalleryItem` data to show in the cell. Let's also set a constant height for all cells. Add the following to your `TableSource` class:

```
public override nfloat GetHeightForRow (UITableView tableView, NSIndexPath
indexPath)
        {
            return 100;
        }
```

So what is next?

```
public override void ViewDidLoad ()
{
..
table.Source = new TableSource ();
..
```

```
}
```

Let's stop development and have a look at what we have achieved so far. We have created our first `UIViewController`, `UITableView`, `UITableViewSource`, and `UITableViewCell`, and bound them all together. Fantastic!

We now need to access the local storage of the phone to pull out the required gallery items. But before we do this, we are going to create an Android project and replicate what we have done with iOS.

Creating an Android project

Our first step is to create new general Android app:

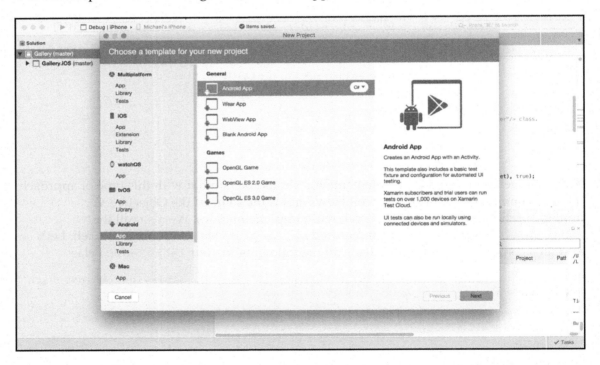

The first screen you will land on is `MainActivity`. This is our starting activity, which will inflate the first user interface; take notice of the configuration attributes:

```
[Activity (Label = "Gallery.Droid", MainLauncher = true, Icon =
"@mipmap/icon")]
```

The `MainLauncher` flag indicates the starting activity; one activity must have this flag set to `true` so the application knows what activity to load first. The `icon` property is used to set the application icon, and the `Label` property is used to set the text of the application, which appears in the top left of the navigation bar:

```
namespace Gallery.Droid
{
    using Android.App;
    using Android.Widget;
    using Android.OS;

    [Activity (Label = "Gallery.Droid", MainLauncher = true, Icon =
"@mipmap/icon")]
    public class MainActivity : Activity
    {
        int count = 1;

        protected override void OnCreate (Bundle savedInstanceState)
        {
            base.OnCreate (savedInstanceState);

            // Set our view from the "main" layout resource
            SetContentView (Resource.Layout.Main);
        }
    }
}
```

The formula for our activities is the same as Java; we must override the `OnCreate` method for each activity where we will inflate the first XML interface `Main.xml`.

Creating an XML interface and ListView

Our starting point is the `main.xml` sheet; this is where we will be creating the `ListView`:

```
<?xml version="1.0" encoding="utf-8"?>
<LinearLayout xmlns:android="http://schemas.android.com/apk/res/android"
    android:orientation="vertical"
    android:layout_width="fill_parent"
    android:layout_height="fill_parent">
    <ListView
        android:id="@+id/listView"
        android:layout_width="fill_parent"
        android:layout_height="fill_parent"
        android:layout_marginBottom="10dp"
        android:layout_marginTop="5dp"
```

```
            android:background="@android:color/transparent"
            android:cacheColorHint="@android:color/transparent"
            android:divider="#CCCCCC"
            android:dividerHeight="1dp"
            android:paddingLeft="2dp" />
</LinearLayout>
```

The `main.xml` file should already be in the **resource | layout** directory, so simply copy and paste the previous code into this file.

Excellent! We now have our starting activity and interface, so now we have to create a `ListAdapter` for our `ListView`. An adapter works very much like a `UITableSource`, where we must override functions to determine cell data, row design, and the number of items in the list.

Xamarin Studio also has an Android GUI designer.

Right-click on the Android project and add a new empty class file for our adapter class. Our class must inherit the `BaseAdapter` class, and we are going to override the following functions:

```
public override long GetItemId(int position);

public override View GetView(int position, View convertView, ViewGroup
parent);
```

Before we go any further, we need to create a model for the objects used to contain the data to be presented in each row. In our iOS project, we created a `GalleryItem` to hold the byte array of image data used to create each `UIImage`. We have two approaches here: we could create another object to do the same as the `GalleryItem`, or even better, why don't we reuse this object using a shared project?

Shared projects

We are going to delve into our first technique for sharing code between different platforms. This is what Xamarin wants us to achieve, and reuse as much code as possible. The biggest disadvantage when developing natively is two different language, and we can't reuse anything.

Let's create our first shared project:

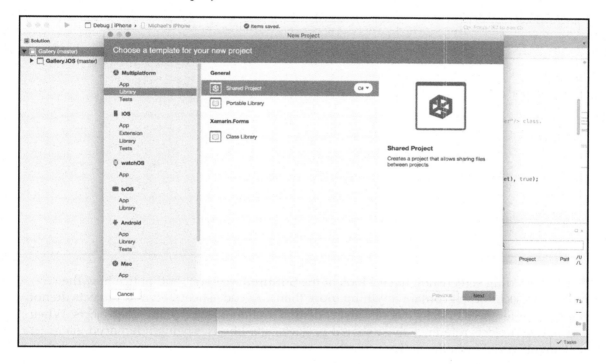

Our shared project will be used to contain the `GalleryItem` model, so whatever code we include in this shared project can be accessed by both the iOS and Android projects:

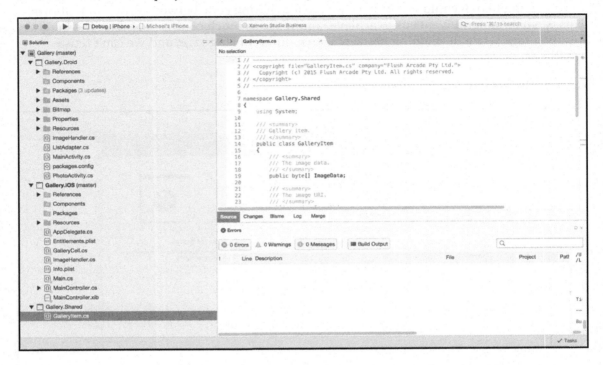

In the preceding screenshot, have a look at the **Solution** explorer, and notice how the shared project doesn't contain anything more than `.cs` code sheets. Shared projects do not have any references or components, just code that is shared by all platform projects. When our native projects reference these shared projects, any libraries being referenced via `using` statements come from the native projects.

Now we must have the iOS and Android projects reference the shared project; right-click on the **References** folder and select **Edit References**:

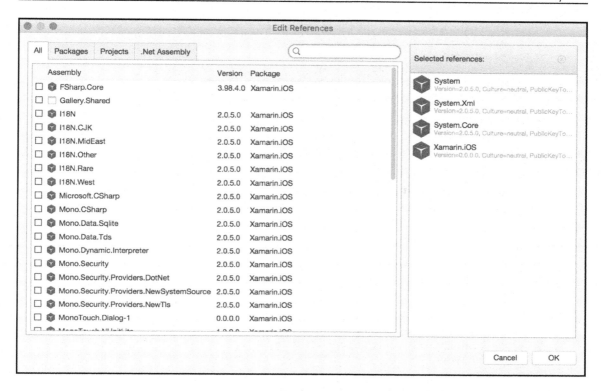

Select the shared project you just created and we can now reference the `GalleryItem` object from both projects.

Custom row appearance

Let's get back to the `ListAdapter` implementation and design our `ListView` row appearance. Open the **Resources | Layout** folder, create a new `.xml` file for the cell appearance, call it `CustomCell.xml`, and copy in the following XML code:

```xml
<?xml version="1.0" encoding="utf-8"?>
<LinearLayout xmlns:android="http://schemas.android.com/apk/res/android"
    android:orientation="horizontal"
    android:layout_width="match_parent"
    android:layout_height="match_parent"
    android:weightSum="4">
    <LinearLayout
        android:orientation="vertical"
        android:layout_width="match_parent"
```

```
android:layout_height="match_parent"
android:layout_weight="1">
<ImageView
    android:id="@+id/image"
    android:layout_width="100dp"
    android:layout_height="100dp"
    android:adjustViewBounds="true" />
</LinearLayout>
<LinearLayout
    android:orientation="vertical"
    android:layout_width="match_parent"
    android:layout_height="match_parent"
    android:layout_weight="3"
    android:weightSum="2">
<TextView
    android:id="@+id/title"
    android:layout_width="wrap_content"
    android:layout_height="wrap_content"
    android:layout_weight="1" />
<TextView
    android:id="@+id/date"
    android:layout_width="wrap_content"
    android:layout_height="wrap_content"
    android:layout_weight="1" />
</LinearLayout>
</LinearLayout>
```

We are creating the same layout as the custom cell made for iOS, but in Android we will use the `ImageView` and `TextView` objects. Now that we have our custom cell, we can implement the the `GetView` function. The `GetView` function is exactly like the `GetCell` function in the preceding `UITableSource` implementation. Open up the `ListAdapter.cs` file and continue with the list adapter implementation:

```
public class ListAdapter : BaseAdapter
    {
        private List<GalleryItem> _items;
        private Activity _context;

        public ListAdapter(Activity context) : base()
        {
            _context = context;
            _items = new List<GalleryItem>();
        }

        public override Java.Lang.Object GetItem (int position)
        {
            return null;
```

```
        }

        public override long GetItemId(int position)
        {
            return position;
        }

        public override int Count
        {
            get
            {
                return items.Count;
            }
        }
    }
```

We override the `Count` property and functions `GetItemId` and `GetItem`, to return the number of gallery items in our list. These override functions are exactly the same as the overrides in Java for any `BaseAdapter` inherited class. Now for the `GetView` function:

```
public override View GetView(int position, View convertView, ViewGroup
parent)
        {
            View view = convertView; // re-use an existing view, if one is
available

            if (view == null)
            {
                // otherwise create a new one
                view =
context.LayoutInflater.Inflate(Resource.Layout.CustomCell, null);
            }

            // set image
            var imageView = view.FindViewById<ImageView>
(Resource.Id.image);
            BitmapHelpers.CreateBitmap (imageView, _items
[position].ImageData);

            // set labels
            var titleTextView = view.FindViewById<TextView>
(Resource.Id.title);
            titleTextView.Text = _items[position].Title;
            var dateTextView = view.FindViewById<TextView>
(Resource.Id.date);
            dateTextView.Text = _items[position].Date;

            return view;
```

```
            }

        private async void createBitmap(ImageView imageView, byte[]
    imageData)
        {
            try
            {
                if (imageData != null)
                {
                    var bm = await
    BitmapFactory.DecodeByteArrayAsync(imageData, 0, imageData.Length);
                    if (bm != null)
                    {
                        imageView.SetImageBitmap(bm);
                    }
                }
            }
            catch (Exception e)
            {
                Console.WriteLine ("Bitmap creation failed: " + e);
            }
        }
    }
```

Notice in the `GetView` function we are using the `CustomCell` layout for each row; we also have a `private` method for creating our bitmaps from each model's byte array.

If we have a look at the current implementation, what do we notice here?

We are creating a bitmap every time the cell requires this data again for the view; is this efficient? No, we should be reusing bitmaps and memory as much as possible.

This tends to be a common issue with Android `ListView`.

What is the most memory efficient way to reuse bitmaps across hundreds of items in a `ListView` while scrolling and staying smooth as we move down the list at various speeds? How can we tackle this problem? Let's have a look at how we can approach this problem.

Firstly, we need to implement an object called `ImageHandler`. This will contain the logic for retrieving byte arrays from all gallery images on an Android device. Create a new file, name it `ImageHandler`, and start importing these namespaces:

```
namespace Gallery.Droid
{
    using System;
    using System.Collections.Generic;

    using Android.Database;
```

```
using Android.Content;
using Android.Provider;

using Gallery.Shared;

public static class ImageHandler
{
}
}
```

This class will include a function, `GetFiles`, which will create gallery items based upon the items pulled from any device's gallery using the `ContentResolver` interface:

```
public static IEnumerable<GalleryItem> GetFiles(Context context)
{
    ContentResolver cr = context.ContentResolver;

    string[] columns = new string[]
    {
        MediaStore.Images.ImageColumns.Id,
        MediaStore.Images.ImageColumns.Title,
        MediaStore.Images.ImageColumns.Data,
        MediaStore.Images.ImageColumns.DateAdded,
        MediaStore.Images.ImageColumns.MimeType,
        MediaStore.Images.ImageColumns.Size,
    };
    var cursor =
cr.Query(MediaStore.Images.Media.ExternalContentUri, columns, null, null,
null);

    int columnIndex = cursor.GetColumnIndex(columns[2]);

    int index = 0;

    // create max 100 items
    while (cursor.MoveToNext () && index < 100)
    {
        index++;

        var url = cursor.GetString(columnIndex);

        var imageData = createCompressedImageDataFromBitmap (url);

        yield return new GalleryItem ()
        {
            Title = cursor.GetString(1),
            Date = cursor.GetString(3),
            ImageData = imageData,
```

```
                    ImageUri = url,
                };
            }
        }
```

Using `ContentResolver` (used to access the content model), we resolve **URIs** to specific content providers. A content provider provides queries to content, in our case image files. We simply create an access query off the main context's `ContentResolver` instance, and we provide an array of columns for the query to retrieve (for example, file titles, file data, file size, and so on). The first parameter is as follows:

```
"MediaStore.Images.Media.ExternalContentUri"
```

This is used for retrieving the URI to each piece of content returned from the query. Finally, we now have a cursor to iterate through, exactly like an `Enumerable`, which will loop to the end until there are no more items, and for each iteration we pull the data and URI columns and create a new `GalleryItem`. You will notice a little trick here with the `yield` keyword: if we call this function, it will actually return the entire `Enumerable` from start to finish. Calling the function starts *for each-ing* over the object; the function is called again until it *yields*. In the return from calling this function, we get an `Enumerable` of all the items retrieved from the query as gallery items with image information and local URI.

Bitmap functions

What about the byte data? First, let's implement our `BitmapHelpers`; these will include two global functions to help with bitmap processing:

```
public static int CalculateInSampleSize(BitmapFactory.Options options, int reqWidth, int reqHeight)
    {
        // Raw height and width of image
        float height = options.OutHeight;
        float width = options.OutWidth;
        double inSampleSize = 1D;

        if (height > reqHeight || width > reqWidth)
        {
            int halfHeight = (int)(height / 2);
            int halfWidth = (int)(width / 2);

            // Calculate a inSampleSize that is a power of 2 - the
decoder will use a value that is a power of two anyway.
            while ((halfHeight / inSampleSize) > reqHeight &&
(halfWidth / inSampleSize) > reqWidth)
```

```
            {
                inSampleSize *= 2;
            }
        }

        return (int)inSampleSize;
    }

    public static async void CreateBitmap(ImageView imageView, byte[]
imageData)
    {
        try
        {
            if (imageData != null)
            {
                var bm = await
BitmapFactory.DecodeByteArrayAsync(imageData, 0, imageData.Length);
                if (bm != null)
                {
                    imageView.SetImageBitmap(bm);
                }
            }
        }
        catch (Exception e)
        {
            Console.WriteLine ("Bitmap creation failed: " + e);
        }
    }
```

Our first function will determine the best sample size by the requested width and height.
This is a very good technique for reducing the resources required to load an image into
memory. Our next function is used to create a bitmap for the ImageView that is passed in
from the byte data.

The next step is to create this image data using the private method
createCompressedImageDataFromBitmap:

```
private static byte[] createCompressedImageDataFromBitmap(string url)
    {
        BitmapFactory.Options options = new BitmapFactory.Options ();
        options.InJustDecodeBounds = true;
        BitmapFactory.DecodeFile (url, options);
        options.InSampleSize = BitmapHelpers.CalculateInSampleSize
(options, 1600, 1200);
        options.InJustDecodeBounds = false;

        Bitmap bm = BitmapFactory.DecodeFile (url, options);
```

```
        var stream = new MemoryStream ();
        bm.Compress (Bitmap.CompressFormat.Jpeg, 80, stream);
        return stream.ToArray ();
    }
```

This method will take the image URI and decode the bitmap options in order to sample the smallest possible size for the dimensions provided.

We have to make sure that we flag `InJustDecodeBounds` so this bitmap is not loaded into memory while we are retrieving the options information. This approach is very useful for reducing images to the size we require, thus saving memory. We then compress the image by 80% into a JPEG and convert the stream into a byte array for our `GalleryItem` model.

Now let's go back to the `adapter` class and add this method to fill in the items of our `ListAdapter`:

```
public ListAdapter(Activity context) : base()
    {
        _context = context;
        _items = new List<GalleryItem>();

        foreach (var galleryitem in ImageHandler.GetFiles (_context))
        {
            _items.Add (galleryitem);
        }
    }
```

 Remember we must have a reference in our list adapter to the main context.

Now for the final piece of the puzzle, connecting the adapter to our list view. Open up the `MainActivity.cs` file and update the code list like so:

```
public class MainActivity : Activity
    {
        private ListAdapter _adapter;

        protected override void OnCreate (Bundle savedInstanceState)
        {
            base.OnCreate (savedInstanceState);

            SetContentView (Resource.Layout.Main);

            _adapter = new ListAdapter (this);
```

```
var listView = FindViewById<ListView> (Resource.Id.listView);
listView.Adapter = adapter;
    }
}
```

And voila! Try running the application and watching the `ListView` update with the images in your device's **Gallery** folder. Congratulations! You have just developed your first `Xamarin.Android` application. Now we must replicate this approach for the iOS version.

 Notice the challenge with context switching when jumping back and forth between Android and iOS; it can get confusing. Luckily, with Xamarin we keep to just one programming language, which helps reduce the complexity.

The ALAssetLibrary

Jumping back into our iOS, we are going to use the `ALAssetsLibrary` class and call the Enumerate function by passing in the group type `ALAssetsGroupType.SavedPhoto`, the enumeration result delegate `GroupEnumerator`, and the error action that will be performed if an exception occurs.

Start by adding in a new `.cs` file for our iOS image handler:

 We are not going to use a static class with this object.

```
namespace Gallery.iOS
{
    using System;
    using System.Threading;

    using UIKit;
    using AssetsLibrary;
    using Foundation;

    /// <summary>
    /// Image handler.
    /// </summary>
    public class ImageHandler
    {
        /// <summary>
        /// The asset library.
```

```
        /// </summary>
        ALAssetsLibrary _assetLibrary;

        /// <summary>
        /// Initializes a new instance of the <see
cref="Gallery.iOS.ImageHandler"/> class.
        /// </summary>
        public ImageHandler ()
        {
                _assetLibrary = new ALAssetsLibrary();
                _assetLibrary.Enumerate(ALAssetsGroupType.SavedPhotos,
GroupEnumerator, Console.WriteLine);
        }
    }
}
```

In our constructor, we create the new instance of the ALAssetsLibrary and call the Enumerate function; now let's add the GroupEnumerator delegate:

```
private void GroupEnumerator(ALAssetsGroup assetGroup, ref bool shouldStop)
        {
                if (assetGroup == null)
                {
                    shouldStop = true;
                    NotifyAssetsLoaded ();

                    return;
                }

                if (!shouldStop)
                {
                    assetGroup.Enumerate(AssetEnumerator);
                    shouldStop = false;
                }
        }

        private void AssetEnumerator(ALAsset asset, nint index, ref bool
shouldStop)
        {
                if (asset == null)
                {
                    shouldStop = true;
                    return;
                }

                if (!shouldStop)
                {
                    // add asset name to list
```

```
                    _assets.Add (asset.ToString());
                    shouldStop = false;
                }
        }

    private void NotifyAssetsLoaded()
        {
            if (AssetsLoaded != null)
            {
                AssetsLoaded (this, EventArgs.Empty);
            }
        }
```

Notice the call to notify our event handler. This signals we have reached the end of the `asset` library, and we have retrieved all `ALAsset` in our gallery. We can now pull out a list of the file names, so we need to add another function that will pull out the `ALAsset` object synchronously:

```
public ALAsset SynchronousGetAsset(string filename)
        {
            ManualResetEvent waiter = new ManualResetEvent(false);
            NSError error = null;
            ALAsset result = null;
            Exception exception;

            ThreadPool.QueueUserWorkItem ((object state) =>
assetLibrary.AssetForUrl (new NSUrl (filename), (ALAsset asset) =>
                {
                    result = asset;
                    waiter.Set ();
                },
                e =>
                {
                    error = e;
                    waiter.Set ();
                }));


            if(!waiter.WaitOne (TimeSpan.FromSeconds (10)))
                throw  new Exception("Error Getting Asset : Timeout,
Asset=" + filename);

            if (error != null)
                throw new Exception (error.Description);

            return result;
        }
```

Finally, we need a public function that will pull all the byte arrays and NSURL into an Enumerable of gallery items that we will use to populate the UITableView.

 As this is only a demo, we are only going to take the first 100 items. If you would like another challenge, remove Take(100), and see if you can adjust the code to load thousands of images more efficiently.

```
foreach (var file in _assets.Take(100))
    {
        using (var asset = SynchronousGetAsset (file))
        {
            if (asset != null)
            {
                var thumbnail = asset.Thumbnail;
                var image = UIImage.FromImage (thumbnail);
                var jpegData = image.AsJPEG ().ToArray ();

                yield return new GalleryItem ()
                {
                    Title = file,
                    Date = asset.Date.ToString(),
                    ImageData = jpegData,
                    ImageUri = asset.AssetUrl.ToString ()
                };
            }
        }
    }
```

Let's look a bit more closely at this function. We use the asset library object to pull out all the filenames we have in our gallery, then for each filename we pull out the ALAsset object, and from this we create a GalleryItem object for each, which takes the image data as a byte array from the ALAsset and the NSURL of the asset. Now let's create an instance of the ImageHandler inside our TableSource:

```
private ImageHandler _imageHandler;

public TableSource (string[] items)
{
    _galleryItems = new List<GalleryItem> ();
    _imageHandler = new ImageHandler ();

    foreach (var galleryItem in imageHandler.GetFiles ())
    {
        _galleryItems.Add (galleryItem);
```

```
        }
    }
```

Excellent! Now we have our gallery items ready to display inside the table.

For the final piece of the iOS project, let's go back to our `AppDelegate.cs` file. We still need to implement the `FinishedLaunching` method. Our root controller is going to be a `UINavigationController`, which will use the `MainController` as the starting `UIViewController`:

```
public override bool FinishedLaunching (UIApplication application,
NSDictionary launchOptions)
        {
                _window = new UIWindow (UIScreen.MainScreen.Bounds);

                MainController mainController = new MainController();

                var rootNavigationController = new UINavigationController();
                rootNavigationController.PushViewController(mainController,
false);

                _window.RootViewController = rootNavigationController;
                _window.MakeKeyAndVisible ();

                return true;
        }
```

We also adjust the window bounds the main screen bounds and call the function on the window at the very end of `MakeKeyAndVisible`.

Adding the iOS photo screen

Now that we have our list page, we want to add another `UIViewController` for displaying selected photos. Let's add a new `UIViewController` and call it `PhotoController`. In `PhotoController`, we are going to build a screen that simply displays the same content in the `PhotoCell`, but a bit larger.

First, let's add the navigation flow from `MainController` to `PhotoController`. We are going to be pushing a new `PhotoController` whenever a row is selected. Open up `TableSource.cs` and add the following; at the top, we need to add an `EventHandler`:

```
public event EventHandler<GalleryItem>
  ItemSelected;
```

Whenever the row is selected we want to fire this event:

```
public override void RowSelected (UITableView tableView, NSIndexPath
indexPath)
        {
            if (ItemSelected != null)
            {
                ItemSelected (this, galleryItems[indexPath.Row]);
            }

            tableView.DeselectRow (indexPath, true);
        }
```

Whenever the row is selected, we want to fire this event and pass the gallery item for the index path row. Now we need to handle this event in the `MainController` class to push a new `PhotoController` on the navigation stack, but before we do this we need to implement `PhotoController`:

```
public partial class PhotoController : UIViewController
    {
        /// <summary>
        /// The image view.
        /// </summary>
        private UIImageView _imageView;

        /// <summary>
        /// The title label.
        /// </summary>
        private UILabel _titleLabel;

        /// <summary>
        /// The date label.
        /// </summary>
        private UILabel _dateLabel;

        /// <summary>
        /// Initializes a new instance of the <see
cref="Gallery.iOS.PhotoController"/> class.
        /// </summary>
        public PhotoController (ALAsset asset) : base ("PhotoController",
```

```
null)
        {
            _imageView = new UIImageView ()
            {
                TranslatesAutoresizingMaskIntoConstraints = false,
                ContentMode = UIViewContentMode.ScaleAspectFit
            };

            _titleLabel = new UILabel ()
            {
                TranslatesAutoresizingMaskIntoConstraints = false,
            };

            _dateLabel = new UILabel ()
            {
                TranslatesAutoresizingMaskIntoConstraints = false,
            };

            _imageView.Image = new
UIImage(asset.DefaultRepresentation.GetFullScreenImage ());
            _titleLabel.Text = asset.DefaultRepresentation.Filename;
            _dateLabel.Text = asset.Date.ToString ();
        }
```

This is very similar to our `GalleryCell` presentation, but this controller will stack the elements vertically and force the image to scale to fit, keeping the image's correct ratio to avoid any warping. Now let's add `ViewDidLoad` to lay out the views:

```
public override void ViewDidLoad ()
        {
            base.ViewDidLoad ();

            View.Add (_imageView);
            View.Add (_titleLabel);
            View.Add (_dateLabel);

            // set layout constraints for main view
            View.AddConstraints
(NSLayoutConstraint.FromVisualFormat("V:|[imageView]-10-
[titleLabel(50)]-10-[dateLabel(50)]|",
NSLayoutFormatOptions.DirectionLeftToRight, null, new
NSDictionary("imageView", imageView, "titleLabel", titleLabel, "dateLabel",
dateLabel)));

            View.AddConstraints
(NSLayoutConstraint.FromVisualFormat("H:|[imageView]|",
NSLayoutFormatOptions.AlignAllTop, null, new NSDictionary ("imageView",
imageView)));
```

```
            View.AddConstraints
(NSLayoutConstraint.FromVisualFormat("H:|[titleLabel]|",
NSLayoutFormatOptions.AlignAllTop, null, new NSDictionary ("titleLabel",
titleLabel)));
            View.AddConstraints
(NSLayoutConstraint.FromVisualFormat("H:|[dateLabel]|",
NSLayoutFormatOptions.AlignAllTop, null, new NSDictionary ("dateLabel",
dateLabel)));
        }
```

There's nothing new here; we are simply adding the three elements and setting our layout constraints accordingly. We stretch all elements to the entire width of the view and stack elements down the pages with the image view on top and a dynamic size based upon the aspect size of the image.

Finally, the last step is to add the event handler whenever a row is selected. We use ImageHandler to fetch ALAsset by the title (filename) in the gallery item, then pass this into the constructor of a new PhotoController and update the constructor of MainController:

```
            public MainController () : base ("MainController", null)
            {
                _source = new TableSource ();

                _source.ItemSelected += (sender, e) =>
                {
                    var asset = _imageHandler.SynchronousGetAsset (e.Title);
                    NavigationController.PushViewController (new
PhotoController (asset), true);
                };

                _imageHandler = new ImageHandler ();
                _imageHandler.AssetsLoaded += handleAssetsLoaded;
            }
```

Excellent! Now run the application and try selecting a few items in the list; you will be navigated to a new PhotoController which will display the selected ALAsset image with its filename and date information.

Adding the Android photo screen

Implementing a photo view for cell selections is very similar, although with Android we will be using an intent to create a new activity, which in turn will inflate a new view to display the image and details. Let's start by adding a new XML called photo_view.xml, and paste in the following code:

```xml
<?xml version="1.0" encoding="utf-8"?>
<LinearLayout xmlns:android="http://schemas.android.com/apk/res/android"
    android:orientation="vertical"
    android:layout_width="match_parent"
    android:layout_height="match_parent"
    android:weightSum="4">
    <LinearLayout
        android:orientation="vertical"
        android:layout_width="match_parent"
        android:layout_height="match_parent"
        android:layout_weight="1">
        <ImageView
            android:id="@+id/image_photo"
            android:scaleType="centerCrop"
            android:layout_width="wrap_content"
            android:layout_height="wrap_content"
            android:adjustViewBounds="true" />
    </LinearLayout>
    <LinearLayout
        android:orientation="vertical"
        android:layout_width="match_parent"
        android:layout_height="match_parent"
        android:layout_weight="3"
        android:weightSum="2">
        <TextView
            android:id="@+id/title_photo"
            android:layout_width="wrap_content"
            android:layout_height="wrap_content"
            android:layout_weight="1" />
        <TextView
            android:id="@+id/date_photo"
            android:layout_width="wrap_content"
            android:layout_height="wrap_content"
            android:layout_weight="1" />
    </LinearLayout>
</LinearLayout>
```

The layout is very much the same as the `custom_cell.xml` sheet, although we are going to stack items vertically and set the following two properties to keep the correct image aspect ratio:

```
android:adjustViewBounds="true"
android:scaleType="centerCrop"
```

Make sure XML sheets do not contain the same IDs as any other XML sheet.

Now that we have our user interface for the `PhotoActivity`, let's add the new activity:

```
[Activity (Label = "Gallery.Droid", Icon = "@mipmap/icon")]
    public class PhotoActivity : Activity
    {
        /// <summary>
        /// Raises the create event.
        /// </summary>
        /// <param name="savedInstanceState">Saved instance state.</param>
        protected override void OnCreate (Bundle savedInstanceState)
        {
            base.OnCreate (savedInstanceState);

            // Set our view from the "main" layout resource
            SetContentView (Resource.Layout.Photo);

            var imageData = Intent.GetByteArrayExtra ("ImageData");
            var title = Intent.GetStringExtra ("Title") ?? string.Empty;
            var date = Intent.GetStringExtra ("Date") ?? string.Empty;

            // set image
            var imageView = FindViewById<ImageView>
(Resource.Id.image_photo);
            BitmapHelpers.CreateBitmap (imageView, imageData);

            // set labels
            var titleTextView = FindViewById<TextView>
(Resource.Id.title_photo);
            titleTextView.Text = title;
            var dateTextView = FindViewById<TextView>
(Resource.Id.date_photo);
            dateTextView.Text = date;
        }
    }
```

Looking at this new activity, what can we see? Notice the attributes at the top:

```
[Activity (Label = "Gallery.Droid", Icon = "@mipmap/icon")]
```

There is no `MainLauncher` tag because this is not our starting activity. We then add the `intent.GetExtras` for the image data and strings required to display on our `Photo` interface.

Now we need to make one addition to the `ListAdapter` class:

```
public GalleryItem GetItemByPosition (int position)
{
    return _items[position];
}
```

When an item in the list is selected, we need to be able to access the selected `GalleryItem`. Our next step is to add the `ItemClick` delegate for the `ListView`. Open up the `MainActivity` class and add the following to the `OnCreate` function:

```
listView.ItemClick += (object sender, AdapterView.ItemClickEventArgs e) =>
        {
            var galleryItem = adapter.GetItemByPosition (e.Position);
            var photoActivity = new Intent(this,
typeof(PhotoActivity));
            photoActivity.PutExtra ("ImageData",
galleryItem.ImageData);
            photoActivity.PutExtra ("Title", galleryItem.Title);
            photoActivity.PutExtra ("Date", galleryItem.Date);
            StartActivity(photoActivity);
        };
```

Place this after we set the list adapter. When an item is clicked, we simply pull out the gallery item from our adapter by the position passed from the `ItemClickEventArgs`. Once we have the gallery item, we create the new `PhotoActivity` intent and pass the extras.

That is all; run the application and play around selecting cells to display the `PhotoActivity`.

Summary

In this chapter, we built a gallery application on both iOS and Android using native development with Xamarin. We learnt how to setup projects in Xamarin Studio and code using the native frameworks in C#. In the next chapter, we will build a text to speech service using `Xamarin.Forms`.

Try improving on this code and make this function asynchronous; the more background processing we have at this stage, the better. These are the small improvements we should take time with, as combining all these small additions can create a real difference to the speed of your application.

As this is only a demo, we are only going to take the first 100 items. If you would like another challenge, remove `Take(100)`, and see if you can adjust the code to load thousands of images more efficiently.

2

Building a SpeechTalk Application

In this chapter, we introduce development with `Xamarin.Forms`. We will build a cross-platform application for iOS, Android, and Windows Phone that integrates native platform speech services to speak text typed from a text field.

Expected knowledge:

- Microsoft Visual Studio.

In this chapter, you will learn the following:

- Cross-platform development with `Xamarin.Forms`
- Setting up platform projects
- Setting up a `SpeechTalk.iOS` project
- Setting up a `SpeechTalk.Droid` project
- `Xamarin.Forms`, Windows Phone, and Visual Studio
- Inversion of Control (IoC) with `Xamarin.Forms`
- AutoFac
- iOS text-to-speech implementation
- Bindings
- Android text-to-speech implementation
- Setting up IoC with Android
- WinPhone text-to-speech implementation
- IoC with Windows Phone
- Platform-independent styling

Cross-platform development with Xamarin.Forms

The key ingredient in cross-platform development with Xamarin is code sharing. Sharing native code is great, but we still have the issue of writing separate user interface code for each platform. The **Windows Presentation Framework (WPF)** is a presentation system which uses an XML-based language known as **Extensible Application Markup Language (XAML)**. Xamarin.Forms uses WPF and the **Model-View-View-Model (MVVM)** paradigm to build native user interfaces from a single C# shared code base, whilst maintaining access to all native APIs on each platform.

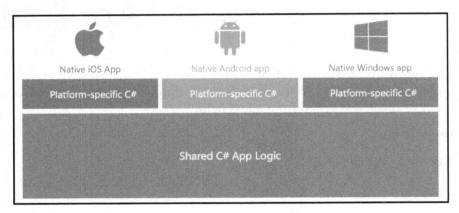

The preceding diagram represents a native architecture. We keep all the sharable code Inside the **Shared C# App Logic** block (normally a shared project) for each platform project to access, i.e. the GalleryItem class would be kept here since it is shared between both projects.

So how would this look in Xamarin.Forms?

Using Xamarin.Forms, since we have the ability to share the user interface screens, we can share the entire view and view model code between all platforms:

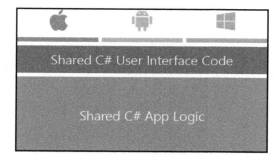

In the preceding diagram, the code contained in the **Shared C# App Logic** block is contained in a **Portable Class Library** (**PCL**), which each native project will import. Xamarin.Forms makes it possible to share up to 85% of code.

Let's now delve into development and setup our first Xamarin.Forms project.

Setting up platform projects

In Xamarin Studio, let's start by setting up the platform projects. Go to **File** | **New Solution** and select a **Xamarin.Forms** app from the cross-platform menu on the left:

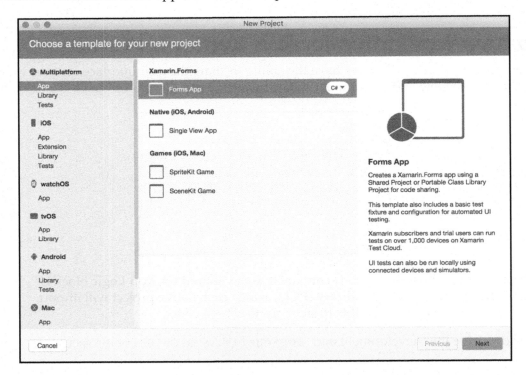

Once the project is created, you will see both an iOS and Android project created along with a PCL.

 Unfortunately, we can't develop our Windows Phone applications through Xamarin Studio; we will be touching on this after the iOS and Android projects.

Let's create our first `ContentPage` in XAML, right-click on the PCL, create a new XAML `ContentPage`, and call it `MainPage`:

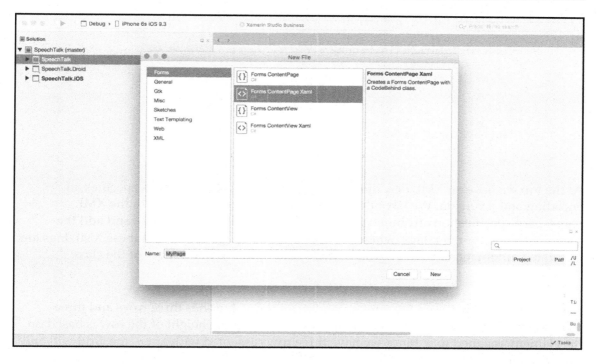

Xamarin.Forms provides the option to build user interfaces entirely in C#, but it is recommended you stick with XAML because it is a very powerful markup language. The code required for a XAML sheet is much smaller than a user interface in C#.

We also want to create a new folder called Pages and add MainPage to this folder.

Our first element on the page is a Grid. A Grid separates a layout by rows and columns based upon the entire size of the screen. Rows work from top to bottom and columns work from left to right; copy the following into the MainPage.xaml sheet:

```xml
<?xml version="1.0" encoding="UTF-8"?>
<ContentPage xmlns="http://xamarin.com/schemas/2014/forms"
    xmlns:x="http://schemas.microsoft.com/winfx/2009/xaml"
    x:Class="SpeechTalk.Pages.MainPage">

    <ContentPage.Content>

    <Grid x:Name="Grid" RowSpacing="0" Padding="10, 10, 10, 10" >
        <Grid.RowDefinitions>
            <RowDefinition Height="Auto"/>
            <RowDefinition Height="Auto"/>
            <RowDefinition Height="Auto"/>
```

```
        </Grid.RowDefinitions>

        <Grid.ColumnDefinitions>
            <ColumnDefinition Width="*"/>
        </Grid.ColumnDefinitions>

    </Grid>

    </ContentPage.Content>

</ContentPage>
```

At the top we have an XML description tag exactly like Android, which specifies an encoding and a version. We have the declaration of a `ContentPage` with the XML namespace specification attribute `xmlns`. We then specify the class name and add the `ContentPage.Content` tags, where we will create the page layout. All these XML tags are generated automatically; the only change we made was the namespace of the class:

```
x:Class="SpeechTalk.Pages.MainPage"
```

The Grid inserted between the `ContentPage.Content` tags has three rows and three columns. Each row definition is assigned `Auto`, meaning the height of the row is based on the element assigned to it. Since we have three rows assigned with `Auto`, the Grid will only fill the height of the contained elements (similar to the `wrap_content` flag in android). The Grid will take up the entire width of the page as its one column definition is set to "*", meaning it will stretch one column to the entire width of the page. We have our basic page layout, so let's leave it there and move back into the project structure.

In `SpeechTalk.PCL`, we have a file called `SpeechTalk.cs`; we should rename this `App.cs` to match the class name. In the `App.cs`, this is the application starting point. In the constructor of the application class, you will see a `MainPage` property automatically set like so:

```
public App ()
    {
        // The root page of your application
        MainPage = new ContentPage {
            Content = new StackLayout {
                VerticalOptions = LayoutOptions.Center,
                Children = {
                    new Label {
                        XAlign = TextAlignment.Center,
                        Text = "Welcome to Xamarin Forms!"
                    }
                }
            }
        }
```

```
    };
  }
```

So what is happening here?

When the project is created, we automatically receive an `App` class with the `MainPage` property set to a new `ContentPage`. The preceding code block is an example of an interface built entirely via c-sharp. We want to replace this with an instantiation of our `MainPage`, and set this new object to the `MainPage` property of the `App` class.

Here is the updated constructor:

```
public App ()
  {
      MainPage = new MainPage ();
  }
```

It's much cleaner, you can already see how messy the code would look like if we were to build complex user interfaces in **C#**.

Setting up the SpeechTalk.iOS project

Let's also have a look at the project setup on the native side for iOS and Android. Open the `AppDelegate.cs` file; it should look like this:

```
[Register ("AppDelegate")]
public partial class AppDelegate :
global::Xamarin.Forms.Platform.iOS.FormsApplicationDelegate
  {
      public override bool FinishedLaunching (UIApplication app,
NSDictionary options)
      {
          global::Xamarin.Forms.Forms.Init ();

          LoadApplication (new App ());

          return base.FinishedLaunching (app, options);
      }
  }
```

Have a look at the super class:

```
global::Xamarin.Forms.Platform.iOS.FormsApplicationDelegate
```

Since Xamarin.Forms 1.3.1 and the updated unified API, all our app delegate should be inheriting is Xamarin.Forms.Platform.iOS.FormsApplicationDelegate. We also have the standard FinishedLaunching function; in here we must call Forms.Init which will initialize Xamarin.Forms, and then call LoadApplication with a new instantiation of the App class. We then return the base class FinishedLaunching function, passing in the app and options objects.

You can see that this FinishedLaunching function is an override of the standard app delegate function.

 We must initialize forms before anything else occurs in this function.

Let's run the iOS application and see what happens:

Fantastic, a blank application. That means we have now successfully run our first iOS Xamarin.Forms project.

Setting up the SpeechTalk.Droid project

Let's do the same for Android and set up Xamarin.Forms accordingly. Inside our Android project, open the MainActivity.cs class and look at the OnCreate function:

```
[Activity (Label = "SpeechTalk.Droid", Icon = "@drawable/icon",
MainLauncher = true, ConfigurationChanges = ConfigChanges.ScreenSize |
ConfigChanges.Orientation)]
    public class MainActivity :
global::Xamarin.Forms.Platform.Android.FormsApplicationActivity
    {
        protected override void OnCreate (Bundle bundle)
        {
            base.OnCreate (bundle);

            global::Xamarin.Forms.Forms.Init (this, bundle);

            LoadApplication (new App ());
        }
    }
```

The MainActivity class must
inherit Xamarin.Forms.Platform.Android.FormsApplicationActivity; we must call the super class OnCreate method before we initialize Xamarin.Forms and load in our new instantiated app class. That's all, we can now run the Android application and see the exact same results, a blank page. Congratulations, you have just shared your first Xamarin.Forms interface.

Xamarin.Forms, Windows Phone, and Visual Studio

Now let's look at sharing our MainPage interface with Windows Phone.

> Not everyone will extend an app onto Windows Phone, so if you are not interested in creating a Windows Phone example you can skip this part.

We are going to be using Microsoft Visual Studio, so open it up and open the SpeechTalk solution file (SpeechTalk.sln) we created in Xamarin Studio. Portability between the two IDEs is very good; watch the solution port directly into Visual Studio and open your PCL file without any issues.

Create a GIT repository to help control the continuous change between Xamarin Studio and Visual Studio, we recommend creating a GIT repository for every chapter.

The iOS and Android projects may not be compatible as we created these in Xamarin Studio.

You can build iOS and Android applications directly in Visual Studio, but running iOS applications will require a mac build host.

Now it's time to create a new Windows Phone project:

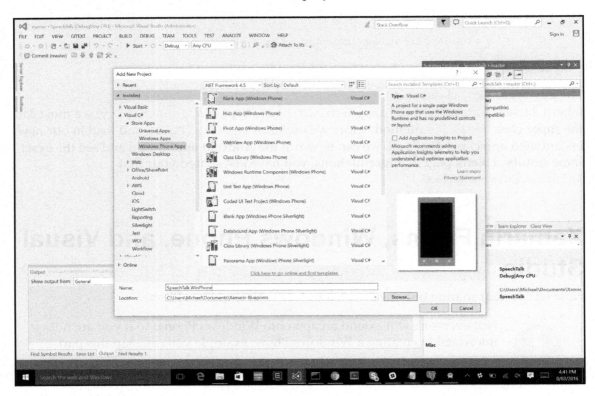

Unfortunately, the automated setup done with iOS and Android will not be done with the Windows Phone project. All the setup will be done manually, but this is good for walking you through the manual setup.

We import the **Xamarin.Forms** nuget package:

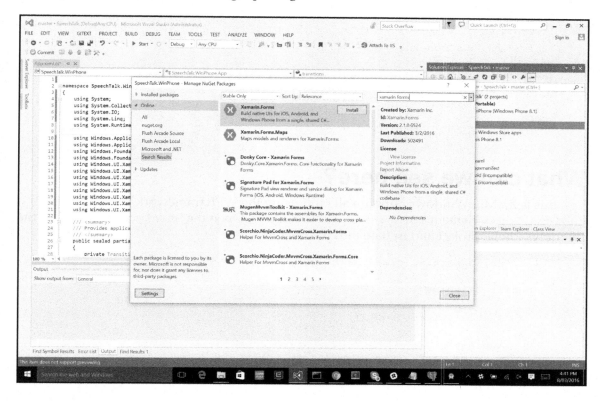

Now its time to look at the `MainPage.xaml` and `MainPage.xaml.cs` files in the **Windows Phone** project.

Wait a minute, haven't we already made one of these?

Now that you are preparing a Windows Phone project, we can see the original WPF structure used in Xamarin.Forms.

Open up `MainPage.xaml` and paste in the following:

```
<forms:WindowsPhonePage
    x:Class="SpeechTalk.WinPhone.MainPage"
    xmlns="http://schemas.microsoft.com/winfx/2006/xaml/presentation"
    xmlns:x="http://schemas.microsoft.com/winfx/2006/xaml"
    xmlns:local="using:SpeechTalk.WinPhone"
    xmlns:forms="using:Xamarin.Forms.Platform.WinRT"
    xmlns:d="http://schemas.microsoft.com/expression/blend/2008"
    xmlns:mc="http://schemas.openxmlformats.org/markup-compatibility/2006"
```

```
    mc:Ignorable="d"
    Background="{ThemeResource ApplicationPageBackgroundThemeBrush}">
    <Grid>
    </Grid>
</forms:WindowsPhonePage>
```

If any lines get underlined, just ignore them; this is an issue in Visual Studio.

What can we see here?

Yes, this is XAML. Windows apps are all built using the WPF framework. We create the `Xamarin.Forms` element `forms:WindowsPhonePage`. Open the `MainPage.xaml.cs` in the Windows Phone project and update the constructor:

```
public sealed partial class MainPage
{
    public MainPage()
    {
        InitializeComponent();

        NavigationCacheMode = NavigationCacheMode.Required;
        LoadApplication(new SpeechTalk.App());
    }
}
```

Project setup is quite simple, but we are not calling `Forms.Init` anywhere. Open up the `App.xaml.cs` file in the **Windows Phone** project and look for this block of code:

```
if (rootFrame == null)
{
    // Create a Frame to act as the navigation context and navigate to the
first page
    rootFrame = new Frame();

    // TODO: change this value to a cache size that is appropriate for your
application
    rootFrame.CacheSize = 1;

    Xamarin.Forms.Forms.Init(e);

    if (e.PreviousExecutionState == ApplicationExecutionState.Terminated)
    {
```

```
        // TODO: Load state from previously suspended application
    }

    // Place the frame in the current Window
    Window.Current.Content = rootFrame;
}
```

We must manually add this line:

```
Xamarin.Forms.Forms.Init(e);
```

Set the cache size to 1:

```
rootFrame.CacheSize = 1;
```

Finally, we now need to reference the **SpeechTalk** PCL project we created in Xamarin Studio earlier:

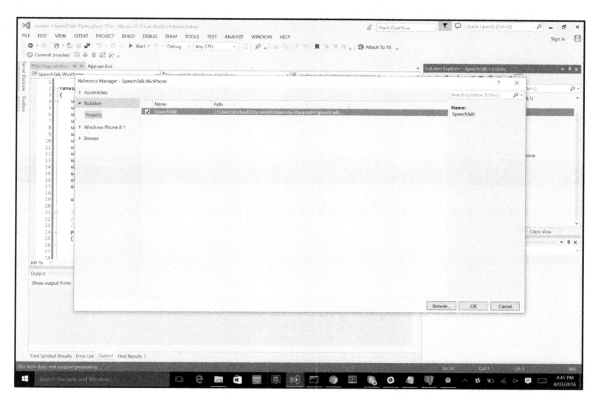

You may run into issues with referencing this project to the targets set by the PCL by default:

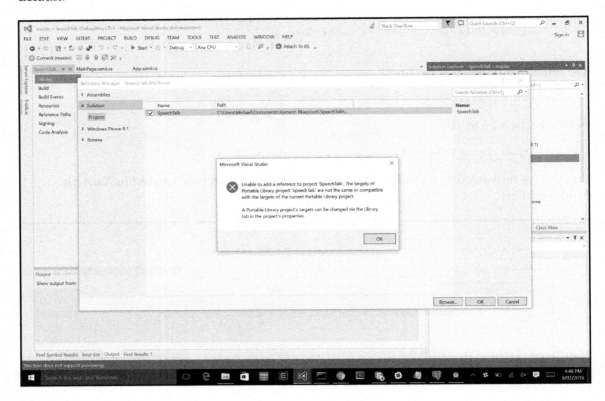

To fix this issue, open the **SpeechTalk** PCL project and update the target configurations in **Properties**:

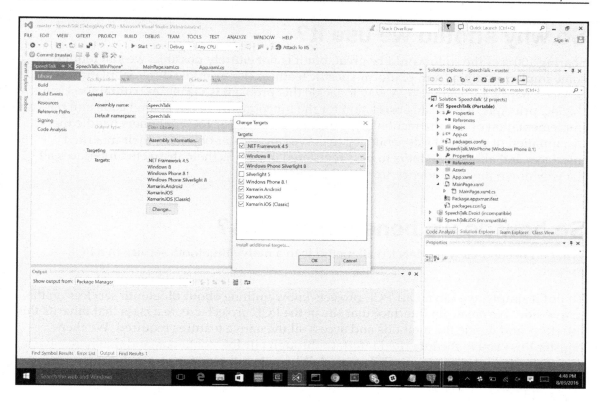

Click on the **Change** button where it says **Targets** and make sure the preceding checkboxes are selected. That's everything; try building and running the application. We should see a blank page like the Android and iOS projects. Gerat we have now made a cross-platform application for all platforms.

Now let's get into the fun stuff with IoC.

Inversion of Control (IoC) with Xamarin.Forms

The **Inversion of Control (IoC)** principle is very a useful technique when writing cross-platform applications.

So why should we use it?

Sharing 100% of the code would be great, but it is not entirely possible; we still require some implementation from platform-specific features (for example different platform services, hardware, cameras). A way to tackle this problem is via an **IoC container**. Using the IoC principle, we use an abstraction for the functionality in our shared code and pass an implementation of the abstraction into our shared code. Our IoC containers handle the instantiation of an object's dependency tree. We can register objects to their inherited interfaces and allow containers to pass registered objects as their abstracted interfaces all the way down the dependency tree (all the way to PCL).

So how do we benefit from this?

What if I needed view models to call methods to a native Bluetooth service in a PCL project?

To put it simply, we can't. Our PCL projects know nothing about Bluetooth services on the native side. We create an interface that sits in the PCL project, create a class that inherits this interface, and define the methods and access all the native features required. We then register this class to the inherited interface through our IoC container, and finally resolve this abstracted interface in our PCL project. When we call functions from this interface down in the PCL, it will be calling the registered class function definitions described on the native side:

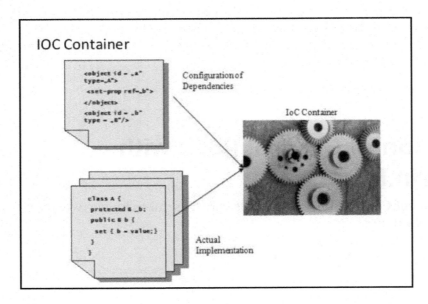

Now back to our `SpeechTalk` application. Because the PCL project cannot share code from the native side text-to-speech services, we will have to use IoC to access the native-side features from our PCL. Let's start by declaring an interface for our text to speech service, creating a new folder called `Services`, and adding a new `ITextToSpeech.cs` file for the interface:

```
public interface ITextToSpeech
{
    void Speak (string msg)
}
```

Autofac

Before we begin implementing the different native sides to this interface, let's first add in our IoC container to handle the abstraction. There are a few IoC containers that are free online; for this example we are going to use **Autofac**. Let's add the NuGet packages for the PCL, iOS, and Android projects:

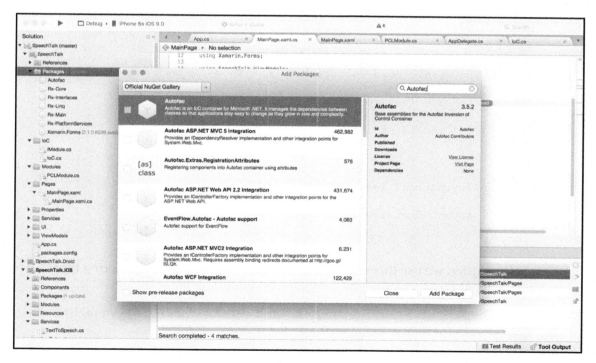

Now that we have our IoC container, let's build the iOS implementation. For each platform, we want to create objects called **Modules** for registering abstracted interfaces. Let's add a new folder called IoC to the PCL project and add a new file called `IoC.cs`:

```
public static class IoC
{
    public static IContainer Container { get; private set; }

    private static ContainerBuilder builder;

    public static void CreateContainer()
    {
        builder = new ContainerBuilder();
    }

    public static void StartContainer()
    {
        Container = builder.Build();
    }

    public static void RegisterModule(IModule module)
    {
        module.Register (builder);
    }

    public static void RegisterModules(IEnumerable<IModule> modules)
    {
        foreach (var module in modules)
        {
            module.Register (builder);
        }
    }

    public static T Resolve<T>()
    {
        return Container.Resolve<T> ();
    }
}
```

Looking at this closer, we use this static class for registering modules, registering types, resolving registered types, creating the container, and building the container.

The `ContainerBuilder` must be built after all types have been registered.

We must register and start this container before we initialize the application. Open up your AppDelegate.cs file and update the FinishedLaunching function:

```
public override bool FinishedLaunching (UIApplication app,
NSDictionary options)
    {
        global::Xamarin.Forms.Forms.Init ();

        InitIoC ();

        LoadApplication (new App ());

        return base.FinishedLaunching (app, options);
    }

private void InitIoC()
    {
        IoC.CreateContainer ();
        IoC.RegisterModule (new IOSModule());
        IoC.RegisterModule (new PCLModule());
        IoC.StartContainer ();
    }
```

The InitIoC function will first create the container, register the modules, and build the IoC container.

> Our container must be created before we can start registering, and our container builder must be built before we can start resolving.

Each module has register functions that will use the created ContainerBuilder to register types.

iOS text-to-speech implementation

Each module will retrieve the current container used throughout the entire lifetime of your application. Inside the register function is where we register the class implementation of the text to speech interface. This will be done at the very start of the application before we load anything else.

Let's start first with adding the iOS module. Add a new folder in the iOS project called **Modules**, create a new file called iOSModule.cs, and paste in the following:

```
public class IOSModule : IModule
{
    public void Register(ContainerBuilder builer)
    {
        builer.RegisterType<TextToSpeech> ().As<ITextToSpeech>
().SingleInstance ();
    }
}
```

The next step is to add the iOS text to speech service. Add a new folder called Services and add a new file called TextToSpeech.cs. In this file, we are going to access the iOS AVSpeechSynthesizer:

```
public class TextToSpeech : ITextToSpeech
{
    public void Speak (string msg)
    {
        var speechSynthesizer = new AVSpeechSynthesizer ();

        var speechUtterance = new AVSpeechUtterance (msg)
        {
            Rate = AVSpeechUtterance.MaximumSpeechRate / 4,
            Voice = AVSpeechSynthesisVoice.FromLanguage ("en-US"),
            Volume = 0.5f,
            PitchMultiplier = 1.0f
        };

        speechSynthesizer.SpeakUtterance (speechUtterance);
    }
}
```

Looking closely at this class, we are going to use the speech synthesizer to produce a SpeechUtterrance object, which contains the text to speak. We also set the language, volume, and speech rate.

Notice how we inherit the interface we are going to register through the IoC container?

As we are coding this class on the native side, we are able to access all native iOS features, so back in the PCL when we call the function Speak in the interface, the preceding code will execute.

Our next step is to implement the view model principles for our pages. Create a new folder called `ViewModels` and add two new files, `ViewModelBase.cs` and `MainPageViewModel.cs`. The `ViewModelBase` class will be the base call for all view models for handling property change events with any view model's properties:

```
public abstract class ViewModelBase : INotifyPropertyChanged
    {
        #region Public Events

        public event PropertyChangedEventHandler PropertyChanged;

        #endregion

        #region Methods

        protected virtual void OnPropertyChanged([CallerMemberName] string
propertyName = null)
        {
            PropertyChangedEventHandler handler = this.PropertyChanged;

            if (handler != null)
            {
                handler(this, new PropertyChangedEventArgs(propertyName));
            }
        }

        #endregion
    }
```

Let's look a bit closer. The first property defined is `PropertyChanged EventHandler`, which will fire on any property data change. Notice the use of the # define statements; these are useful for breaking up blocks of coding and navigating through your code sheets.

 These are particularly useful when we have big code sheets.

The class inherits the `INotifyPropertyChanged` interface, meaning we have to define the `OnPropertyChanged` function. This function is used to fire the `PropertyChanged` event to signal that a property within this class has changed data. Now let's implement the `MainPageViewModel`.

How do we use the `OnPropertyChanged` principle with our `MainPageViewModel`?

With each property in the `MainPageViewModel`, we have to call the `OnPropertyChanged` function to fire the `EventHandler`, thus notifying of a data change for a particular property. Let's begin by creating the `MainPageViewModel` with its private properties and constructor:

```
public class MainPageViewModel : ViewModelBase
    {
        #region Private Properties

        private readonly ITextToSpeech _textToSpeech;

        private string _descriptionMessage = "Enter text and press the
 'Speak' button to start speaking";

        private string _speakEntryPlaceholder = "Text to speak";

        private string _speakText = string.Empty;

        private string _speakTitle = "Speak";

        private ICommand _speakCommand;

        #endregion

        #region Constructors

        public MainPageViewModel (ITextToSpeech textToSpeech)
        {
            _textToSpeech = textToSpeech;

            _speakCommand = new Command ((c) => _textToSpeech.Speak
(this.SpeakText));
        }

        #endregion
    }
```

This is the first time we are going to access the `Systems.Windows.Input` library. **Commands** are used for our `Button` object on the `ContentPage`; we will set up a binding on the button so whenever a press event occurs, this command will execute, running the action it is assigned in the constructor. Notice how we are passing the `TextToSpeech` interface; this is where things will get trickier with the IoC container.

Now we add the public properties of the view model, which call the `OnPropertyChanged` function:

```
#region Public Properties

        public string DescriptionMessage
        {
            get
            {
                return _descriptionMessage;
            }

            set
            {
                if (value.Equals(_descriptionMessage))
                {
                    return;
                }

                _descriptionMessage = value;
                OnPropertyChanged("DescriptionMessage");
            }
        }

        public string SpeakEntryPlaceholder
        {
            get
            {
                return _speakEntryPlaceholder;
            }

            set
            {
                if (value.Equals(_speakEntryPlaceholder))
                {
                    return;
                }

                _speakEntryPlaceholder = value;
                OnPropertyChanged("SpeakEntryPlaceholder");
            }
        }

        public string SpeakText
        {
            get
            {
                return _speakText;
```

```
        }

    set
    {
        if (value.Equals(_speakText))
        {
            return;
        }

        _speakText = value;
        OnPropertyChanged("SpeakText");
    }
}

public string SpeakTitle
{
    get
    {
        return _speakTitle;
    }

    set
    {
        if (value.Equals(_speakTitle))
        {
            return;
        }

        _speakTitle = value;
        OnPropertyChanged("SpeakTitle");
    }
}

public ICommand SpeakCommand
{
    get
    {
        return _speakCommand;
    }

    set
    {
        if (value.Equals(_speakCommand))
        {
            return;
        }

        _speakCommand = value;
```

```
                OnPropertyChanged("SpeakCommand");
        }
    }

    #endregion
```

That's it! We have our first view model. Notice the `get` and `set` methods for each property; they are exactly the same as functions, just with a nicer presentation. Every time we retrieve the data inside a `public` property, it will pull the data contained in the `private` property, and every time we set the `public` property, if the value is different to the current value, we will set the `private` variable contained and call the `OnPropertyChanged` function to fire the `EventHandler` in the base class. When this event fires, it will update whatever view is bound to it.

Bindings

Back in the PCL project, we are going to run through the concept of binding view models to views, displaying view model data, and propagating data changes through the `INotifyPropertyChanged` interface.

Let's begin with our `MainPage.cs` and complete the rest of the user interface for this page:

```xml
<?xml version="1.0" encoding="UTF-8"?>
<ContentPage xmlns="http://xamarin.com/schemas/2014/forms"
    xmlns:x="http://schemas.microsoft.com/winfx/2009/xaml"
    x:Class="SpeechTalk.Pages.MainPage"
    BackgroundColor="White">

    <ContentPage.Content>

    <Grid x:Name="Grid" RowSpacing="10" Padding="10, 10, 10, 10"
VerticalOptions="Center">
        <Grid.RowDefinitions>
            <RowDefinition Height="Auto"/>
            <RowDefinition Height="Auto"/>
            <RowDefinition Height="Auto"/>
        </Grid.RowDefinitions>

        <Grid.ColumnDefinitions>
            <ColumnDefinition Width="*"/>
        </Grid.ColumnDefinitions>

        <Label x:Name="DesciptionLabel" Font="Arial, 20" Grid.Row="0"
Grid.Column="0"/>
```

```
        <Entry x:Name="SpeakEntry" Grid.Row="1" Grid.Column="0"/>

        <Button x:Name="SpeakButton" Grid.Row="2" Grid.Column="0"/>
    </Grid>

    </ContentPage.Content>

  </ContentPage>
```

We now have a Label, Entry, and Button; each has the x:Name, Grid.Row, and Grid.Column properties assigned.

Notice how we relate the rows and columns to the definitions section previously?

We have also set, on the bounding Grid, padding values for left, up, right, and down; set the vertical options to Center; and set a row spacing of 10. The Padding will place gaps around the entire bounds of the Grid and the ContentPage.

Padding works exactly like margins in HTML.

The RowSpacing property will set the gaps between each row; as each element is placed in a new row, they will be stacked vertically with a pixel spacing of 10 between each. Since we only have 1 column, this column width will take up the entire width of the **Grid**, so each element will be at the full width of the Grid.

Finally, setting the VerticalOptions of the Grid to Center will position all elements to the center of the Grid. Now let's set up the binding between the MainPage and MainPageViewModel.

Create a new file, add it to the modules folder called PCLModule.cs, and paste in the following:

```
public class PCLModule : IModule
{
    public void Register(ContainerBuilder builer)
    {
        builer.RegisterType<MainPageViewModel> ().SingleInstance();
        builer.RegisterType<MainPage> ().SingleInstance();
    }
}
```

Hold on... why are we registering our pages and view models in the container?

We don't need to abstract these.

Registering both views and view models in the container allows us to add our related view models in the constructor; as we only ever need one instance of both the view and view model throughout the entire lifetime of the application, we can set up the `MainPage.xaml.cs` file like this:

```
public partial class MainPage : ContentPage
    {
        public MainPage ()
        {
            InitializeComponent ();
        }

        public MainPage (MainPageViewModel model)
        {
            BindingContext = model;
            InitializeComponent ();
        }
    }
```

The instance of the `MainPageViewModel` that was created in the container when registered will be pulled out of the `MainPage` constructor on creation. This is the same technique used with the instance of the `MainPageViewModel`, where we place the `ITextToSpeech` abstraction in the constructor; it will pull out the instance registered on the native side, and in turn we can now use this object to start calling the functions that will run the `native-side` code.

Now back to the `MainPage.xaml` sheet, let's set up the property bindings; update the label, entry, and button to the following:

```
<Label x:Name="DesciptionLabel" Text="{Binding DescriptionMessage}"
Font="Arial, 20" Grid.Row="0" Grid.Column="0"/>

<Entry x:Name="SpeakEntry" Placeholder="{Binding SpeakEntryPlaceholder}"
Text="{Binding SpeakText, Mode=TwoWay}" Grid.Row="1" Grid.Column="0"/>

<Button x:Name="SpeakButton" Text="{Binding SpeakTitle}" Command="{Binding
SpeakCommand}" Grid.Row="2" Grid.Column="0"/>
```

We have set up bindings for the text on the label and entry properties; notice the two-way binding mode set on the entry text property?

What this means is if we change the data from the user interface (as it is a text box, will we will be changing the data on the UI front) or the view model, both endpoints will receive the data change accordingly. We have also set up a binding with the command on the button; now, whenever we press this button on the page, it will run the action assigned to it in the view model.

Now that all the coding is done, let's run the application; try typing in text and pressing the **Speak** button and have a listen:

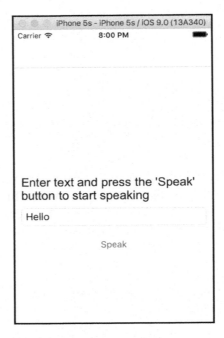

Well done! You have just completed your first iOS `Xamarin.Forms` application.

For some extra exercises, try changing the properties of volume and speech on the `SpeechUtterance` object for iOS.

Android text-to-speech implementation

Now let's implement the IoC container and text to speech for Android. Start by creating a folder for the both the Android Modules and Services, add in two files to it, `TextToSpeechDroid.cs` and `DroidModule.cs`.

Let's start with the text to speech service; for `TextToSpeechDroid.cs`. And add the following:

```
public class TextToSpeechDroid :  Java.Lang.Object, ITextToSpeech,
Android.Speech.Tts.TextToSpeech.IOnInitListener
    {
        private Android.Speech.Tts.TextToSpeech _speaker;

        private string _toSpeak;

        public void Speak (string msg)
        {
            var ctx = Forms.Context;
            _toSpeak = msg;

            if (_speaker == null)
            {
                _speaker = new Android.Speech.Tts.TextToSpeech (ctx, this);
            }
            else
            {
                var p = new Dictionary<string,string> ();
                speaker.Speak (_toSpeak, QueueMode.Flush, p);
            }
        }

        #region TextToSpeech.IOnInitListener implementation

        public void OnInit (OperationResult status)
        {
            if (status.Equals (OperationResult.Success))
            {
                var p = new Dictionary<string,string> ();
                _speaker.Speak (_toSpeak, QueueMode.Flush, p);
            }
        }

        #endregion
    }
```

This `IOnInitListener` interface requires the `OnInit` function to be implemented. The `OnInit` function is called to signal the completion of the `TextToSpeech` engine initialization. We then implement the interface's function `Speak` to speak the text passed in. At the start of the function, we check to see that a new `TextToSpeech` object has been initialized; if we have then speak the message.

Setting up IoC with Android

Now for the IoC implementation. It works exactly the same as iOS; let's add the Android module:

```
public class DroidModule : IModule
{
    public void Register(ContainerBuilder builer)
    {
        builer.RegisterType<TextToSpeechDroid> ().As<ITextToSpeech>
().SingleInstance ();
    }
}
```

Easy, right?

Now we have to set up the IoC container in our `MainActivity.cs` class; simply copy the iOS function in the `AppDelegate` file called `initIoC` and paste this into the `MainActivity` class, replace the instantiation of the `iOSModule` with your `DroidModule`, then simply add the function call after the initialization of `Xamarin.Forms`:

```
protected override void OnCreate (Bundle bundle)
{
    base.OnCreate (bundle);

    global::Xamarin.Forms.Forms.Init (this, bundle);

    InitIoC ();

    LoadApplication (new App ());
}

private void InitIoC()
{
    IoC.CreateContainer ();
    IoC.RegisterModule (new DroidModule());
    IoC.RegisterModule (new PCLModule());
    IoC.StartContainer ();
}
```

 You may have issues trying to get the speech to work on Android. One thing you may need to set up first is within **Settings** | **Controls** | **Text-to-Speech** options. Here is where you will have to install voice data if the default has not already been installed. If you run the app and no speech occurs, you will have to configure the voice data.

That's all for Android, now try running the app and hear some speech.

WinPhone text-to-speech implementation

Now we go back to Windows Phone for the last implementation. See how tricky it can be when you have to switch between multiple platforms. Imagine if we had to change languages and re-write IoC containers; the amount of work would be much greater. Not only that, there would be no point in using IoC, because we cannot share any code.

So firstly, don't forget to import the nuget package for **Autofac**:

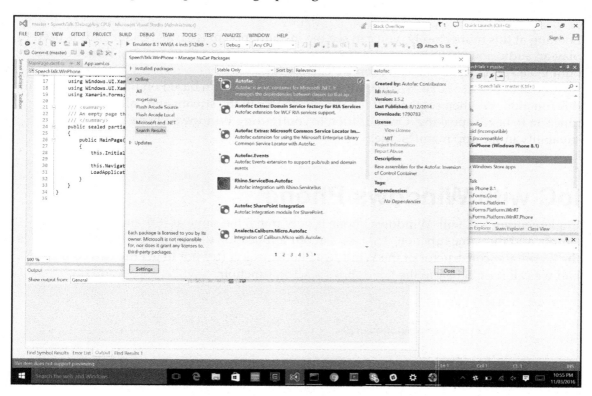

Now that we have access to the **Autofac** framework, let's continue implementing the text to speech service. Start with adding a new folder called **Services**, then add the `TextToSpeechWinPhone.cs` file and implement it:

```
public class TextToSpeechWinPhone : ITextToSpeech
    {
```

```
public async void Speak(string text)
{
        MediaElement mediaElement = new MediaElement ();

        var synth = new Windows.Media.SpeechSynthesis.
SpeechSynthesizer ();

        SpeechSynthesisStream stream = await
synth.SynthesizeTextToStreamAsync(text);

        mediaElement.SetSource(stream, stream.ContentType);
        mediaElement.Play();
    }
}
```

Looking at this more closely, you can see the instantiation of MediaElement; this is used to play an audio source. Our source in this case is SpeechSynthesisStream; this stream is built via a speech synthesizer. When we call the function SynthesizeTextToStreamAsync, it will be an audio stream based on the text inserted into this function. We then set the MediaElement source to the stream and call the Play function to begin speaking. One addition to configuring Windows Phone is checking the capability in the app manifest file.

IoC with Windows Phone

Implementing IoC with Windows Phone is very much the same as iOS and Android. We simply add the same function, InitIoC, at our application's starting point; in this case, it is the MainPage constructor of the Windows Phone project (try not to get the two confused), and we call it right before the LoadApplication function:

```
public MainPage()
    {
        InitializeComponent();

        InitIoC();

        NavigationCacheMode = NavigationCacheMode.Required;
        LoadApplication(new SpeechTalk.App());
    }

    private void InitIoC()
    {
        IoC.CreateContainer();
        IoC.RegisterModule(new WinPhoneModule ());
```

```
IoC.RegisterModule(new PCLModule ());
IoC.StartContainer();
}
```

Simple! Now we can run the Windows application.

Platform independent styling

Hold on! What has happened with the `MainPage`—no button, no text?

What is happening here is we have not specified colors for these elements, so the default color of the text has come up as white. Open up `MainPage.xaml` and change the text colors accordingly:

```
<Label x:Name="DesciptionLabel" Text="{Binding DescriptionMessage}"
TextColor="Black" Font="Arial, 20" Grid.Row="0" Grid.Column="0"/>

<Button x:Name="SpeakButton" Text="{Binding SpeakTitle}" TextColor="Blue"
Command="{Binding SpeakCommand}" Grid.Row="2" Grid.Column="0"/>
```

It might be a good idea to color the background of the `Entry` object as well, so we can see the text definition:

```
<Entry x:Name="SpeakEntry" Placeholder="{Binding SpeakEntryPlaceholder}"
BackgroundColor="Silver" Text="{Binding SpeakText, Mode=TwoWay}"
Grid.Row="1" Grid.Column="0"/>
```

Now run it again and see the text, button, and entry background display.

But wait! What if we don't want these colors to change for iOS and Android, or we want to set these colors differently based on the platform?

Here is another trick to try: in the `MainPage.xaml` sheet, we are going to change the background color of the entry based upon whether it is iOS, Android, or Windows Phone:

```
<Entry x:Name="SpeakEntry" Placeholder="{Binding SpeakEntryPlaceholder}"
Text="{Binding SpeakText, Mode=TwoWay}" Grid.Row="1" Grid.Column="0">
        <Entry.BackgroundColor>
            <OnPlatform x:TypeArguments="Color"
                Android="White"
                WinPhone="Silver"
                iOS="White">
            </OnPlatform>
        </Entry.BackgroundColor>
    </Entry>
```

We start by specifying the property tag we are changing, and then a tag for `OnPlatform` in which we specify the argument type, which is `Color`. Let's take it a step further and change the text colors for the `Button` and `Label` as well:

```
<Label x:Name="DesciptionLabel" Text="{Binding DescriptionMessage}"
Font="Arial, 20" Grid.Row="0" Grid.Column="0">
        <Label.TextColor>
            <OnPlatform x:TypeArguments="Color"
                Android="Black"
                WinPhone="Black"
                iOS="Black">
            </OnPlatform>
        </Label.TextColor>
    </Label>

    <Button x:Name="SpeakButton" Text="{Binding SpeakTitle}"
Command="{Binding SpeakCommand}" Grid.Row="2" Grid.Column="0">
        <Button.TextColor>
            <OnPlatform x:TypeArguments="Color"
                Android="Navy"
                WinPhone="Blue"
                iOS="Navy">
            </OnPlatform>
        </Button.TextColor>
    </Button>
```

This is a nice little variation between styles for the first page. As you build more complex XAML sheets, you may find some areas where you will have to change pixel items, change color, and perform other styling to give it that extra edge.

Let's call it a day and end this project here; it's now time to build our GPS locator.

Summary

In this chapter, we learned how to create a text to speech service using `Xamarin.Forms`. We have learned about native speech service libraries for each platform. In the next chapter, we will learn how to handle background location update events and using latitude and longitude to calculate positions. You will also learn how to implement location services on each platform by using `Xamarin.Forms` and `Xamarin.Forms.Maps`.

3
Building a GPS Locator Application

In this chapter, we will delve deeper into code sharing. We will build a `Xamarin.Forms` application that integrates native GPS location services and Google Maps APIs. We will cover more content on IoC containers, the `Xamarin.Forms.Maps` library, and techniques for c-sharp `async` and background tasks.

Expected knowledge:

- Web services
- JSON
- Google Maps
- Google Geocoding APIs (it helps to have a Google Developer account)

In this chapter, you will learn the following:

- Core location and GPS
- Navigation with `Xamarin.Forms`
- Google Maps integration
- Integrating Google Maps with `Xamarin.Forms.Maps`
- Reactive extensions
- Core location with iOS and the `CLLocationManager` Library
- Android and the `LocationManager`
- Creating our Windows project
- Core location services with Windows Phone
- The Application class

- Web services and data contracts
- Integrating with a Google APIs
- Creating the Geocoding web service controller
- `Newtonsoft.Json` and Microsoft HTTP client libraries
- `ModernHttpClient` and client message handlers
- Feeding JSON data into the `IObservable` framework more reactive extensions
- Resource (RESX) files
- Using the Geocoding web server controller
- `OnNavigatedTo` and `OnShow`
- Pythagoras equirectangular projection

Core location and GPS

All mobile phone platforms have access to core location services. These services are background tasks that run in the background and update the latitude and longitude values at certain intervals indefinitely until the service is stopped. 99% of smart phones come with a built-in GPS tracker, allowing you to integrate these latitude and longitude values with your application.

Project setup

Let's jump straight into project setup and create a new `Xamarin.Forms` application. We are going to start by setting up an IoC container with **Autofac**, exactly the same as the previous project, import **Autofac** into all three projects (PCL, Android, and iOS). We can reuse a lot of the PCL code from the IoC container implementation in the previous project.

> The more apps you build, the more problems you solve; why reinvent the wheel over and over? Eventually, when you have built multiple applications, future apps will be built mostly from piecing parts of different projects together.

Copy in the `IoC`, `Pages`, and `ViewModels` folders, and let's start building our `MainPage`:

```xml
<?xml version="1.0" encoding="UTF-8"?>
<ContentPage xmlns="http://xamarin.com/schemas/2014/forms"
    xmlns:x="http://schemas.microsoft.com/winfx/2009/xaml"
    x:Class="Locator.Pages.MainPage"
    BackgroundColor="White"
    Title="Welcome">
```

```
<ContentPage.Content>

<Grid x:Name="Grid" RowSpacing="10" Padding="10, 10, 10, 10"
VerticalOptions="Center">
    <Grid.RowDefinitions>
        <RowDefinition Height="*"/>
        <RowDefinition Height="Auto"/>
        <RowDefinition Height="Auto"/>
        <RowDefinition Height="Auto"/>
    </Grid.RowDefinitions>

    <Grid.ColumnDefinitions>
        <ColumnDefinition Width="*"/>
    </Grid.ColumnDefinitions>

    <Image x:Name="Image" Source="map.png" HeightRequest="120"
WidthRequest="120"
            Grid.Row="0" Grid.Column="0"/>

    <Label x:Name="DesciptionLabel" Text="{Binding DescriptionMessage}"
HorizontalOptions="Center" Font="Arial, 20" Grid.Row="1" Grid.Column="0">
        <Label.TextColor>
            <OnPlatform x:TypeArguments="Color"
                Android="Black"
                WinPhone="Black"
                iOS="Black">
            </OnPlatform>
        </Label.TextColor>
    </Label>

    <Button x:Name="LocationButton" Text="{Binding LocationTitle}"
Command="{Binding LocationCommand}" BackgroundColor="Silver" Grid.Row="2"
Grid.Column="0">
        <Button.TextColor>
            <OnPlatform x:TypeArguments="Color"
                Android="Navy"
                WinPhone="Blue"
                iOS="Black">
            </OnPlatform>
        </Button.TextColor>
    </Button>

    <Button x:Name="ExitButton" Text="{Binding ExitTitle}"
Command="{Binding ExitCommand}" BackgroundColor="Silver" Grid.Row="3"
Grid.Column="0">
        <Button.TextColor>
            <OnPlatform x:TypeArguments="Color"
                Android="Navy"
```

```
                    WinPhone="Blue"
                    iOS="Black">
                </OnPlatform>
            </Button.TextColor>
        </Button>
    </Grid>

    </ContentPage.Content>

</ContentPage>
```

This is very much the same as the previous `MainPage`, but this time we are adding two `Buttons`, a `Label`, and an `Image`.

 Before reading any further, have a look at the properties bounded to each element. See if you can build the properties for the view model.

Navigation with Xamarin.Forms

Before we start building any view models we are going to build our navigation system. `Xamarin.Forms` comes complete with navigation control for all platforms, so you won't have to worry about it. But as we always like to do things the hard way, we are going to show you a technique to separate our cross-platform structure a little more, in order to keep things more modular. Using one PCL project to contain both view models and views is great, but what if we could separate our views from view models into two PCL projects?

Why would we do this?

One small issue we have with the current PCL is that it relies completely on `Xamarin.Forms`. Only our XAML sheets and user interfaces rely on `Xamarin.Forms`; our view models do not. Then let's move the view models from the `Xamarin.Forms` PCL into an even lower-level PCL project that only relies on c-sharp libraries.

This is a good technique to keep the PCL projects completely separated. Developing a modular system is advantageous when it comes to code sharing. For example, we are building a new app that requires a login screen, a list view screen, and other similar screens most apps include. As we already have the view models that handle all the web services, JSON processing, and property bindings, do we really need to change much? Now that we have a low-level project that simply has the view models, let's just extract the ones we need, design our user interfaces for the view models, and bind them together. Not only can we reuse these view models for other apps, but if we wanted to develop an entirely separated application (for example, a WPF application), we can just compare the required screens, take the related view models, create new user interfaces, and bind them together. Keeping everything completely separated allows for complete plug-and-play capability, which will dramatically decrease the development time required to build similar applications.

Let's approach this pattern by creating a new PCL project and copying in the view models; call it **Locator.Portable**:

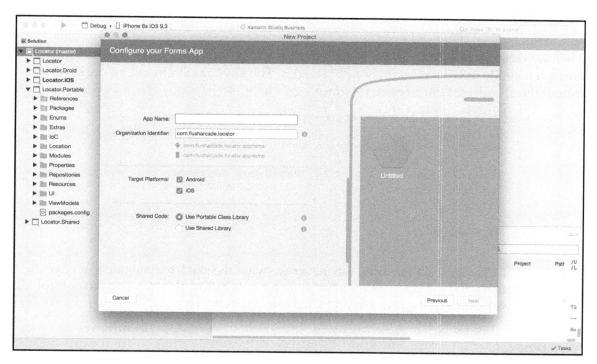

We also want to copy over the `IoC` folder as well.

Building the navigation control

Our first step is to create a folder called enum, add the PageNames.cs file, and copy in the following:

```
public enum PageNames
{
    MainPage,

    MapPage
}
```

Now let's add a new folder called UI and create a new file called INavigationService.cs:

```
public interface INavigationService
{
    Task Navigate(PageNames pageName);
}
```

Then we create a new folder in the Xamarin.Forms PCL (Locator) project called UI, and create a new file called NavigationService.cs. The NavigationService class will inherit the INavigationService interface:

```
public class NavigationService : INavigationService
{
    #region INavigationService implementation

    public async Task Navigate (PageNames pageName)
    {
    }

    #endregion
}
```

Simple, right? Navigate will be used whenever we want the stack to navigate to a page. In making an abstracted interface, as we have done for navigation, this allows us to control navigation way down in the lower-level PCL. Now, fill in the rest:

```
public async Task Navigate (PageNames pageName, IDictionary<string,
object> navigationParameters)
{
    var page = GetPage (pageName);

    if (page != null)
    {
        var navigablePage = page as INavigableXamarinFormsPage;
```

```
        if (navigablePage != null)
        {
            await IoC.Resolve<NavigationPage> ().PushAsync (page);
            navigablePage.OnNavigatedTo (navigationParameters);
        }
    }
}

private Page GetPage(PageNames page)
{
    switch(page)
    {
        case PageNames.MainPage:
            return IoC.Resolve<MainPage> ();
        case PageNames.MapPage:
            return IoC.Resolve<MapPage> ();
        default:
            return null;
    }
}
```

Firstly, look more closely at the private function `GetPage`; this will be called every time the `Navigate` function is called to retrieve the correct `ContentPage` object (which is registered in the `IoC` container) based upon the `PageName` enum passed to it, and if we have found the correct page, push it onto the navigation stack.

Finally, let's build our new `XamFormsModule` for registering the pages and navigation service:

```
public void Register(ContainerBuilder builer)
    {
        builer.RegisterType<MainPage> ().SingleInstance();
        builer.RegisterType<MapPage> ().SingleInstance();

        builer.Register (x => new
NavigationPage(x.Resolve<MainPage>())).AsSelf().SingleInstance();

        builer.RegisterType<NavigationService>
().As<INavigationService>().SingleInstance();
    }
```

We are registering one navigation page throughout the entire life of the application, and we set the starting page to the one main page item we registered before.

Now open up the `App.cs` file and update it accordingly:

```
public App ()
    {
        MainPage = IoC.Resolve<NavigationPage> ();
    }
```

Making sense now?

IoC is a very powerful pattern for cross-platform applications.

View model navigation

Now let's get back to our `MainPageViewModel` and update and modify the previous chapter's `MainPageViewModel` with the properties required for the data-bindings on `MainPage.xaml` shown previously. Firstly, let's implement the `private` properties:

```
public class MainPageViewModel : ViewModelBase
    {
                #region Private Properties
        private readonly IMethods _methods;

        private string _descriptionMessage = "Find your location";

        private string _locationTitle = "Find Location";

        private string _exitTitle = "Exit";

        private ICommand _locationCommand;

        private ICommand _exitCommand;

        #endregion

    }
```

Now for the `Public` properties:

```
#region Public Properties

        public string DescriptionMessage
        {
            get
            {
                return _descriptionMessage;
            }
```

```csharp
        set
        {
            if (value.Equals(_descriptionMessage))
            {
                return;
            }

            _descriptionMessage = value;
            OnPropertyChanged("DescriptionMessage");
        }
    }

    public string LocationTitle
    {
        get
        {
            return _locationTitle;
        }

        set
        {
            if (value.Equals(_locationTitle))
            {
                return;
            }

            _locationTitle = value;
            OnPropertyChanged("LocationTitle");
        }
    }

    public string ExitTitle
    {
        get
        {
            return _exitTitle;
        }

        set
        {
            if (value.Equals(_exitTitle))
            {
                return;
            }

            _exitTitle = value;
            OnPropertyChanged("ExitTitle");
        }
```

```
        }

        public ICommand LocationCommand
        {
            get
            {
                return _locationCommand;
            }

            set
            {
                if (value.Equals(_locationCommand))
                {
                    return;
                }

                _locationCommand = value;
                OnPropertyChanged("LocationCommand");
            }
        }

        public ICommand ExitCommand
        {
            get
            {
                return _exitCommand;
            }

            set
            {
                if (value.Equals(_exitCommand))
                {
                    return;
                }

                _exitCommand = value;
                OnPropertyChanged("ExitCommand");
            }
        }

        #endregion
```

Are we starting to see the same pattern here?

Now add the constructor, which is going to use the navigation service interface that we abstracted earlier through the IoC container:

```
        #region Constructors
```

```
        public MainPageViewModel (INavigationService navigation) : base
(navigation)
        {

        }

    #endregion
```

Now it's time to show you another trick using the IoC container. In our constructor, we need to be able to create a new `Command` object from the `Xamarin.Forms` library. We are lucky here, because since commands from `Xamarin.Forms` inherit the `ICommand` interface from `System.Windows.Input`, we are able to register this object in the IoC container. Open up `XamFormsModule.cs` and update the `Register` function to include the following:

```
builer.RegisterType<Xamarin.Forms.Command>
().As<ICommand>().InstancePerDependency();
```

 Take note that we are registering this type as an `InstancePerDependency` because we want an independent instance every time we create a command in the view model constructors.

Now let's create a new command through the constructor of `MainPageViewModel`; update the constructor like this:

```
    #region Constructors

        public MainPageViewModel (INavigationService navigation,
Func<Action, ICommand> commandFactory) : base (navigation)
        {
            _locationCommand = commandFactory (() =>
Navigation.Navigate(PageNames.MapPage));
        }

    #endregion
```

In the constructor, we are pulling a `Func` out of the `IoC` container, which takes an Action and returns an `ICommand` object, because we have registered this interface to a `Xamarin.FormsCommand` object, we will be left with a new `Command` with the action passed in the constructor as follows:

```
    locationCommand = commandFactory (() =>
Navigation.Navigate(PageNames.MapPage));
```

This is exactly the same as doing this if we were using the `Xamarin.Forms` library:

```
locationCommand = new Command (() =>
Navigation.Navigate(PageNames.MapPage));
```

Now we have a new `Command` set with and `Action` to push a new `MapPage` onto the stack when the button is pressed:

```
public class PortableModule : IModule
{
    public void Register(ContainerBuilder builer)
    {
        builer.RegisterType<MainPageViewModel> ().SingleInstance();
    }
}
```

Now to register our new view model with the `IoC` container. Create a new folder called `Modules` for the portable `IoC` module. Create a new file called `PortableModule.cs` and paste in the preceding code into it.

Integrating Google Maps using Xamarin.Forms.Maps

Our next step is to implement the `MapPage`; this page will show a panel that will display Google Maps. Underneath this panel, we will also display the location information (latitude, longitude, address, and so on) retrieved from our native platform core location services. To access these native services, we need to import `Xamarin.Forms.Maps`:

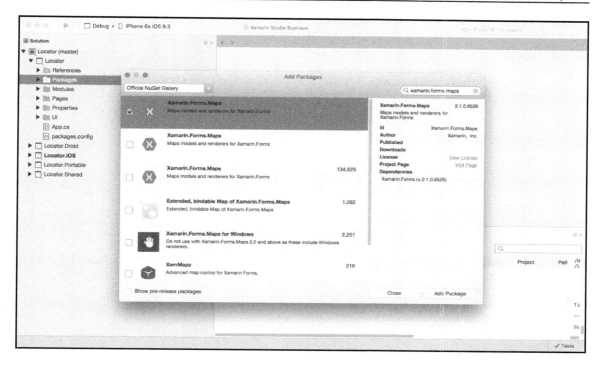

Now that we have imported the `Xamarin.Forms.Maps` library, we can access the native Google Maps services. We can now create the `Map` user interface element via `MapPage.xaml`:

```xml
<?xml version="1.0" encoding="UTF-8"?>
<ContentPage xmlns="http://xamarin.com/schemas/2014/forms"
    xmlns:x="http://schemas.microsoft.com/winfx/2009/xaml"
        xmlns:maps="clr-
namespace:Xamarin.Forms.Maps;assembly=Xamarin.Forms.Maps"
    x:Class="Locator.Pages.MapPage"
    BackgroundColor="White"
    Title="Map">

    <ContentPage.Content>

        <Grid x:Name="Grid" RowSpacing="10" Padding="10, 10, 10, 10">
            <Grid.RowDefinitions>
                <RowDefinition Height="*"/>
                <RowDefinition Height="80"/>
                <RowDefinition Height="60"/>
                <RowDefinition Height="60"/>
            </Grid.RowDefinitions>
```

```
            <Grid.ColumnDefinitions>
                <ColumnDefinition Width="*"/>
            </Grid.ColumnDefinitions>

            <maps:Map x:Name="MapView" IsShowingUser="true" Grid.Row="0"
Grid.Column="0"/>

            <Label x:Name="AddressLabel" Text="{Binding Address}"
TextColor="Black" Grid.Row="1" Grid.Column="0"/>

            <Button x:Name="GeolocationButton" Text="{Binding
GeolocationButtonTitle}"
                Command="{Binding GeolocationCommand}" Grid.Row="2"
Grid.Column="0"/>

            <Button x:Name="NearestAddressButton" Text="Find Nearest
Address"
                Command="{Binding NearestAddressCommand}" Grid.Row="3"
Grid.Column="0"/>
        </Grid>

    </ContentPage.Content>

</ContentPage>
```

See at the top how we imported the `Xamarin.Forms.Maps` library?

We have created four rows in the `Grid`, one for the `Map` (this will cover most of the screen), one for a label that will display the address, and two buttons for starting/stopping location updates and finding the closest location out of a list of addresses.

So where does the address come from?

We now need to implement the core location service; this is a background service that will send position information based upon your location. The information returned is very detailed; we can depict exact longitude and latitude values, as well as addresses.

 Core location services can drain device battery life, so when using core location, we must manage the usage and turn it on and off when required. As this is a background service, when the app is placed in the background, the location service will still be running.

To begin our core location implementation, we are going to create an abstracted geolocation interface called **IGeolocator**, but first we are going to add another library for processing our location updates.

Reactive Extensions

If you haven't heard of the RX framework before, you are about to enter a never-ending rabbit hole of asynchrony. RX gives developers the ability to use LINQ-style query operations for processing objects in observable sequences. It allows for full control over event-based operations between different elements of an application.

In our project, we are going to use a **Subject** for handling location events received on the native side. In cross-platform development, because we work in both PCL and native-level projects, it involves passing data and events up and down the project structure.

We could use the `event` framework, which is standard in c-sharp, but instead we are going to use a `Subject` to push events into an observable sequence, while we subscribe to the subject at a lower level to receive and handle these events.

Let's start by importing the **Reactive Extensions** interface in our native and PCL projects:

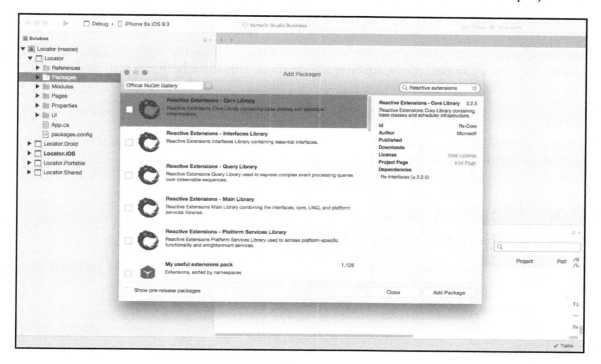

Now let's create our `IGeolocator` class:

```
public interface IGeolocator
{
    Subject<IPosition> Positions { get; set; }

    void Start();

    void Stop();
}
```

Notice the interface `IPosition`? We must also create a new interface, which is going to store all the location information:

```
public interface IPosition
{
    double Latitude {get; set;}

    double Longitude {get; set;}
}
```

The interface is designed to return these variables to be used for the `Xamarin.Forms` geolocator, so we can pull down address information. This information is returned by `CLLocationManager` with every position update.

Why do we need to create an interface for the position information?

As this information comes from different native services, we want to create our own object to contain the information we need in the lower-level projects.

Core location with iOS and the CLLocationManager library

`CLLocationManager` is used for the delivery of location and heading events; we must use this object in our Geolocator implementation, so let's begin:

```
public class GeolocatorIOS : IGeolocator
{
    public Subject<IPosition> Positions { get; set; }
}
```

From our interface, we must include the `Subject`. Now let's instantiate `CLLocationManager`. First, we must import the `CoreLocation` library:

```
using CoreLocation;
```

Now we instantiate `CLLocationManager` in the constructor when this is created through the IoC container. According to iOS standards, since changes to iOS 9 and iOS 8, we must implement a few separate calls to allow the location manager to begin sending location events:

```
public GeolocatorIOS()
        {
                Positions = new Subject<IPosition> ();
                locationManager = new CLLocationManager();
                locationManager.PausesLocationUpdatesAutomatically = false;

                // iOS 8 has additional permissions requirements
                if (UIDevice.CurrentDevice.CheckSystemVersion (8, 0))
                {
                    locationManager.RequestWhenInUseAuthorization ();
                }

                if (UIDevice.CurrentDevice.CheckSystemVersion (9, 0))
                {
                    locationManager.AllowsBackgroundLocationUpdates = true;
                }
        }
```

This is nothing major; in iOS 8 we must request the authorization before using the location manager. For iOS 9, we can also set some conditional settings. For our example, we have used this:

```
AllowsBackgroundLocationUpdates = true
```

This allows the location manager to keep sending events, even when the app is in the background. We can also do this:

```
if (UIDevice.CurrentDevice.CheckSystemVersion (8, 0))
        {
                locationManager.RequestWhenInUseAuthorization ();
        }
```

This will only allow events from `CLLocationManager` when the app is in the foreground. There are multiple settings that can be changed, between controlling location events in the foreground and background when using location services. We want to know whether our app is going to keep updates running in the background/foreground. Most of the time, we want location updates when the app is in the foreground to reduce battery consumption, but there are scenarios where updates should continue in the background.

Now for the rest of the class; let's begin handling the location events:

```
          private void handleLocationsUpdated (object sender,
    CLLocationsUpdatedEventArgs e)
        {
            var location = e.Locations.LastOrDefault ();
            if (location != null)
            {
                Console.WriteLine ("Location updated, position: " +
    location.Coordinate.Latitude + "-" + location.Coordinate.Longitude);

                // fire our custom Location Updated event
                Positions.OnNext (new Position ()
                {
                    Latitude = location.Coordinate.Latitude,
                    Longitude = location.Coordinate.Longitude,
                });
            }
        }
```

The previous function is called every time we receive a location update from `CLLocationManager`. From the event argument `CLLocationsUpdatedEventArgs`, we pull out a list of locations; as sometimes the `CLLocationManager` receives multiple updates at one time, we always want to take the very last location. Then once we create a new `Position`, assign the latitude and longitude values, and by calling the `OnNext` function, we push a new event into the observable sequence.

Our next step is to add some small additions to the `info.plist` file.

Let's add the following keys:

```
    <key>NSLocationAlwaysUsageDescription</key>
    <string>Can we use your location</string>
    key>NSLocationWhenInUseUsageDescription</key>
    <string>We are using your location</string>
```

 The preceding code is from the source of the `info.plist` file.

The `NSLocationAlwaysUsageDescription` and `NSLocationWhenInUseUsageDescription` keys will be displayed to the user in the alert that requests location data access. We must also add the background modes for the location in which we can set the iOS project properties:

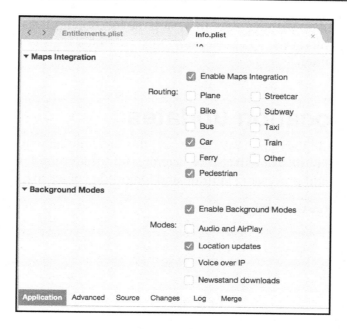

Now we must implement the Start and Stop functions:

```
public void Start()
{
    if (CLLocationManager.LocationServicesEnabled)
    {
        locationManager.DesiredAccuracy = 1;
        locationManager.LocationsUpdated += handleLocationsUpdated;
        locationManager.StartUpdatingLocation();
    }
}

public void Stop()
{
    locationManager.LocationsUpdated -= handleLocationsUpdated;
    locationManager.StopUpdatingLocation();
}
```

The Start function will check whether location services have been enabled, assign the LocationsUpdated event, and start the location updates:

```
public void Register(ContainerBuilder builer)
    {
builer.RegisterType<GeolocatorIOS>().As<IGeolocator>().SingleInstance();
    }
```

The `Stop` function will do nothing more than stop the location updates and remove the event handler. That's all for the iOS geolocator. Next, we must register this interface through the IoC container.

Handling location updates

Our next step is to build the `MapPageViewModel`; this view model will contain the `IGeolocator` we just built. We will also be listening for location updates from the observable sequence and processing latitude and longitude values to gather address details.

Let's begin with the constructor:

```
public MapPageViewModel (INavigationService navigation, IGeolocator
geolocator, Func<Action, ICommand> commandFactory,
        IGeocodingWebServiceController geocodingWebServiceController) :
base (navigation)
        {
            _geolocator = geolocator;
            _geocodingWebServiceController = geocodingWebServiceController;

            _nearestAddressCommand = commandFactory(() =>
FindNearestSite());
            _geolocationCommand = commandFactory(() =>
            {
                if (_geolocationUpdating)
                {
                    geolocator.Stop();
                }
                else
                {
                    geolocator.Start();
                }

                GeolocationButtonTitle = _geolocationUpdating ? "Start" :
"Stop";
                _geolocationUpdating = !_geolocationUpdating;
            });

            _positions = new List<IPosition> ();

            LocationUpdates = new Subject<IPosition> ();
            ClosestUpdates = new Subject<IPosition> ();
        }
```

Our constructor will retrieve the navigation service and the geolocator. Notice how we assign the `geolocator` class:

```
_geolocator = geolocator;
```

The constructor will also be responsible for creating the commands for the two buttons on our map page. Any view models that require objects from the IoC container are usually assigned as read-only properties because they will never change. We want the property name to be the exact same as the item in the constructor argument:

```
private readonly IGeolocator _geolocator;
```

Now let's create our private properties:

```
#region Private Properties
private IDisposable _subscriptions;

private readonly IGeolocator _geolocator;

private string _address;

#endregion
```

We have a new object, the `IDisposable` interface, which is used to take control of unmanaged resources, meaning we can release objects that have no control over memory disposal. In our case, we are going to be setting up a subscription to the events received via the observable sequence (`Subject`).

Let's look at this technique more closely:

```
public void OnAppear()
{
    _subscriptions = _geolocator.Positions.Subscribe (x =>
        {
            _currentPosition = x;
            LocationUpdates.OnNext(x);
        });
}


public void OnDisppear()
{
    geolocator.Stop ();

    if (subscriptions != null)
    {
```

```
                    subscriptions.Dispose ();
        }
    }
```

We are going to use these functions to be called when the `MapPage` appears and disappears. The `OnAppear` function will create a subscription to the `Subject`, so whenever a new position is pushed onto the observable sequence, we will receive an item on the other side where we subscribed. In this case, we will be calling the `OnNext` function on a different subject, meaning we are passing the item of the observable sequence into another observable sequence.

What a pointless function. We will show you why soon.

We are also assigning the subscription to our `IDisposable`. A subscription is an unmanaged resource, meaning that without the use of an `IDisposable`, we can't control the release of the subscription.

Why do we need to worry about disposing of the subscription?

Sometimes our observable streams may be propagating events to a user interface on the main UI thread. If we change pages, and the previous page's view model is still receiving events to update the previous page's interface, this means the events will be changing the user interface on a different thread from the main UI thread, which will break the application. This is just one example, but cleaning up subscriptions when we aren't using them is a good practice to control unwanted application processing.

Now for the `public` properties:

```
#region Public Properties

        public string Address
        {
            get
            {
                return address;
            }

            set
            {
                if (value.Equals(address))
                {
                    return;
                }

                address = value;
                OnPropertyChanged("Address");
```

```
        }
    }

    #endregion
```

All we need is a string that will be bound to `MapPageLabel` under the map item. It will be used to display the address of the current location. Now we must create a label on `MapPage`:

```
<Label x:Name="AddressLabel" Text="{Binding Address}" Grid.Row="1"
Grid.Column="0"/>
```

Our next step is to make use of the latitude and longitude values that we receive from `CLLocationManager`. We are going to use the `Geocoder` class to get address information from our positions. A `Geocoder` class is used to convert positions (latitudes and longitudes) into address information. We could actually do this conversion on the native side, but the idea of this exercise is to show you what is available in `Xamarin.Forms` to share between the different platforms.

Now let's get back to answering the questions about passing events between two observable sequences.

Let's start building the `MapPage.xaml.cs` sheet:

```
private MapPageViewModel viewModel;

    private IDisposable locationUpdateSubscriptions;

    private IDisposable closestSubscriptions;

    private Geocoder geocoder;

    public MapPage ()
    {
        InitializeComponent ();
    }

    public MapPage (MapPageViewModel model)
    {
        viewModel = model;
        BindingContext = model;
        InitializeComponent ();

        Appearing += handleAppearing;
        Disappearing += handleDisappearing;

        geocoder = new Geocoder ();
```

```
        }
```

Here we create another two `IDisposables` for handling the events from the view-model. We will also be subscribing to and disposing on the page's appearing and disappearing events, so now add the `HandleAppearing` and `HandleDisappearing` functions:

```
        private void HandleDisappearing (object sender, EventArgs e)
        {
            viewModel.OnDisppear ();

            if (locationUpdateSubscriptions != null)
            {
                locationUpdateSubscriptions.Dispose ();
            }

            if (closestSubscriptions != null)
            {
                closestSubscriptions.Dispose ();
            }
        }

        private void HandleAppearing (object sender, EventArgs e)
        {
            viewModel.OnAppear ();

            locationUpdateSubscriptions =
    viewModel.LocationUpdates.Subscribe (LocationChanged);
        }
```

We also create a new `Geocoder`, so every time we receive an event from the observable sequence in the view model, we use this position to retrieve the address information from `Geocoder` via the following function:

```
    private void LocationChanged (IPosition position)
        {
            try
            {
                var formsPosition = new
    Xamarin.Forms.Maps.Position(position.Latitude, position.Longitude);

                geocoder.GetAddressesForPositionAsync(formsPosition)
                    .ContinueWith(_ =>
                    {
                        var mostRecent = _.Result.FirstOrDefault();
                        if (mostRecent != null)
                        {
                            viewModel.Address = mostRecent;
```

```
                }
            })
            .ConfigureAwait(false);
        }
        catch (Exception e)
        {
            System.Diagnostics.Debug.WriteLine ("MapPage: Error with
moving map region - " + e);
        }
    }
```

That is everything we need to retrieve our latitude and longitude positions, as well as update the current address. The last step of our iOS version is to update the position on the map; we want the map view to zoom in to our current position and place the blue marker on the map. Next, we add the following to the end of LocationChanged function:

```
MapView.MoveToRegion (MapSpan.FromCenterAndRadius (formsPosition,
Distance.FromMiles (0.3)));
```

The MoveToRegion function requires a MapSpan; a MapSpan is created from the latitude, longitude point and the radius from the position point. A circle will be drawn from the point to give the view radius to be shown on the map; in our case the radius is 0.3 miles around the latitude and longitude position.

The ContinueWith function is used to execute some extra work as soon as the task finishes. As soon as we have retrieved all the possible address names, we wake the first on the list and assign it to the Address property of the variable.

Our final step is to complete the rest of the project; we must first create an iOS module for registering the geolocator class:

```
public class IOSModule : IModule
{
    public void Register(ContainerBuilder builer)
    {
builer.RegisterType<GeolocatorIOS>().As<IGeolocator>().SingleInstance();
    }
}
```

Then finally we add the extras to the AppDelegate.cs file (exactly the same as the previous example iOS project):

```
[Register ("AppDelegate")]
    public partial class AppDelegate :
global::Xamarin.Forms.Platform.iOS.FormsApplicationDelegate
    {
        public override bool FinishedLaunching (UIApplication app,
```

```
NSDictionary options)
        {
                global::Xamarin.Forms.Forms.Init (this, bundle);
                global::Xamarin.FormsMaps.Init (this, bundle);

                initIoC ();

                LoadApplication (new App ());

                return base.FinishedLaunching (app, options);
        }

        private void initIoC()
        {
            IoC.CreateContainer ();
            IoC.RegisterModule (new IOSModule());
            IoC.RegisterModule (new XamFormsModule());
            IoC.RegisterModule (new PortableModule());
            IoC.StartContainer ();
        }
    }
```

Excellent! Let's run the project and click on the **Find Location** button. Watch the map update with the address shown in the preceding label.

Let's move on to the Android project and implement the same features.

Android and the LocationManager

The Android LocationManager works like the CLLocationManager, but we will use an observable sequence to handle location updates. When a location update is received, a new Position object is instantiated with the latitude and longitude values from the location update. Then the resulting Position is pushed on to the Geolocator's Subject.

First we create the Geolocator implementation. It must also inherit the ILocationListener interface:

```
public class GeolocatorDroid : IGeolocator, ILocationListener
    {
        private string provider = string.Empty;

        public Subject<IPosition> Positions { get; set; }

        #region ILocationListener implementation
```

```
public void OnLocationChanged (Location location)
{
    Positions.OnNext (new Position ()
        {
            Latitude = location.Latitude,
            Longitude = location.Longitude
        });
}

public void OnProviderDisabled (string provider)
{
    Console.WriteLine (provider + " disabled by user");
}

public void OnProviderEnabled (string provider)
{
    Console.WriteLine (provider + " disabled by user");
}

public void OnStatusChanged (string provider, Availability status,
Bundle extras)
{
    Console.WriteLine (provider + " disabled by user");
}

#endregion
}
```

You may have noticed the `#define` keywords. These are useful for separating different sections and for referencing locations in code sheets, making code more readable.

The only one we are concerned about is the `OnLocationChanged` function; whenever a location update is received by the location manager, the listener function will be called with the latitude and longitude values, and we will then use these values to push into the observable sequence for the `Geocoder` and `MapSpan`.

We also have to implement the extra requirements for the `ILocationListener` interface. Since this interface inherits the `IJavaObject` interface, we are required to implement the `Dispose` function and the `IntPtr` object.

To save time, we can have the class inherit the `Java.Lang.Object` class like this:

```
public class GeolocatorDroid : Object, IGeolocator, ILocationListener
```

Next, we add the constructor:

```
private LocationManager locationManager;

    public GeolocatorDroid()
    {
        Positions = new Subject<IPosition> ();
        locationManager =
(LocationManager)Application.Context.GetSystemService(Context.LocationServi
ce);
        provider = LocationManager.NetworkProvider;
    }
```

In the constructor, we pull out the required system service using the `GetSystemService` function for the location service. The line underneath simply retrieves the `NetworkProvider` of the `LocationManager`; we need to use this for starting the location updates. There are further configurations we can set for retrieving correct providers (mainly logging purposes), but in this example we aren't going to bother too much as we are only interested in retrieving location positions.

Now it's time to implement the other required functions of the `IGeolocator` interface:

```
public void Start()
    {
        if (locationManager.IsProviderEnabled(provider))
        {
            locationManager.RequestLocationUpdates (provider, 2000, 1,
this);
        }
        else
        {
            Console.WriteLine(provider + " is not available. Does the
device have location services enabled?");
        }
    }
    public void Stop()
    {
        locationManager.RemoveUpdates (this);
    }
```

The `Start` function will first check whether we have these services enabled, then by calling the `RequestLocationUpdates` function, we pass in the provider, the minimum time between locations updates, the minimum location distance between updates, and the pending intent to be called on each location update; in our case, this is the geolocator (the same class that started the location updates) as we have implemented the `ILocationListener` class.

The Stop function simply removes the updates from the Geolocator, which in turn will stop the location updates from the location manager. Our next step in implementing the Android Geolocator is to create the Android IoC module, and register this implementation in the IoC container:

```
public void Register(ContainerBuilder builer)
{
builer.RegisterType<GeolocatorDroid>().As<IGeolocator>().SingleInstance();
}
```

Our final step is to set up the MainActivity class, which is exactly the same as the previous project:

```
[Activity (Label = "Locator.Droid", Icon = "@drawable/icon", MainLauncher =
true, ConfigurationChanges = ConfigChanges.ScreenSize |
ConfigChanges.Orientation)]
    public class MainActivity :
global::Xamarin.Forms.Platform.Android.FormsApplicationActivity
    {
        protected override void OnCreate (Bundle bundle)
        {
            base.OnCreate (bundle);

            global::Xamarin.Forms.Forms.Init (this, bundle);
            global::Xamarin.FormsMaps.Init (this, bundle);

            LoadApplication (new App ());
        }

        private void initIoC()
        {
            IoC.CreateContainer ();
            IoC.RegisterModule (new DroidModule());
            IoC.RegisterModule (new XamFormsModule());
            IoC.RegisterModule (new PortableModule());
            IoC.StartContainer ();
        }
    }
```

Take note of how much code we are starting to reuse from previous projects. Why reinvent the wheel when we can save a lot of time by pulling from similar problems that have already been solved in other projects?

The last step in the Android project is to apply some Android permissions to allow your app to use location services. Open up the `Mainfest.xml` and add the following:

```
<application android:label="Locator">
    <meta-data android:name="com.google.android.maps.v2.API_KEY"
android:value="YOUR-API-KEY" />
    <meta-data android:name="com.google.android.gms.version"
android:value="@integer/google_play_services_version" />
    </application>

    <uses-permission
android:name="android.permission.WRITE_EXTERNAL_STORAGE" />
    <uses-permission android:name="android.permission.ACCESS_FINE_LOCATION"
/>
    <uses-permission
android:name="android.permission.ACCESS_COARSE_LOCATION" />
<uses-permission android:name="android.permission.ACCESS_NETWORK_STATE" />
```

Inside the `<application>` tag, we have to place `API_KEY`, which is generated from the Google APIs platform (we will be doing this later). We then have to add the `ACCESS_FINE_LOCATION`, `ACCESS_COARSE_LOCATION`, and `ACCESS_NETWORK_STATE` permissions for **LocationManager** to work. We can switch these permissions on through the **Application** window:

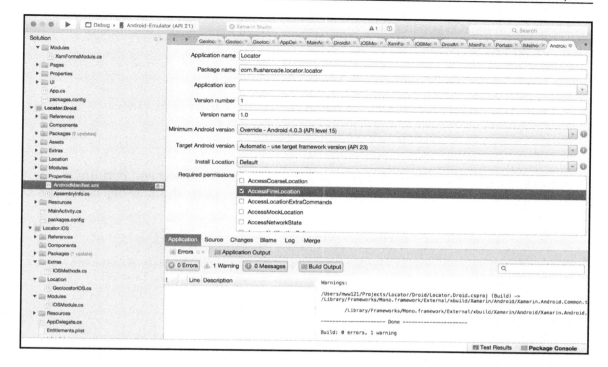

Creating an exit point

You may have noticed the extra button added on the starting page for exiting the application. We will have to go ahead and create an abstracted object for exiting the application. Start by creating a new folder called `Extras`, then create a new file for the `IMethods` interface:

```
public interface IMethods
{
    void Exit();
}
```

Before moving on with the tutorial, have a go at implementing the native side for each project on your own.

Let's begin with the iOS version:

```
public class IOSMethods
{
    public void Exit()
    {
        UIApplication.SharedApplication.PerformSelector(new
ObjCRuntime.Selector("terminateWithSuccess"), null, 0f);
    }
}
```

For the iOS version, we must dig into the SharedApplication object and perform a selector method terminateWithSuccess. We must then register this new object in our iOS module:

```
public void Register(ContainerBuilder builer)
    {
builer.RegisterType<GeolocatorIOS>().As<IGeolocator>().SingleInstance();
builer.RegisterType<IOSMethods>().As<IMethods>().SingleInstance();
    }
```

Now the Android implementation:

```
public class DroidMethods
{
    public void Exit()
    {
        Android.OS.Process.KillProcess(Android.OS.Process.MyPid());
    }
}
```

Using the Android operating system namespace, we use the static item Process to call the function KillProcess on the main process. Again, we also register this within the IoC container:

```
public void Register(ContainerBuilder builer)
    {
builer.RegisterType<GeolocatorDroid>().As<IGeolocator>().SingleInstance();
builer.RegisterType<DroidMethods>().As<IMethods>().SingleInstance();
    }
```

Finally, we use the IMethods interface in our MainPageViewModel to call the exit function:

```
public MainPageViewModel (INavigationService navigation, Func<Action,
ICommand> commandFactory,
        IMethods methods) : base (navigation)
    {
        exitCommand = commandFactory (() => methods.Exit());
```

```
        locationCommand = commandFactory (() =>
  Navigation.Navigate(PageNames.MapPage));
        }
```

Looking at this more closely, we are using the command factory to initialize the exit command to a new `Xamarin.Forms Command`, and when this command is executed, it will call the `Exit` method from the `IMethods` interface.

Our last step is to create an API key using the Google APIs for our Android version.

Creating an API key for Android

In order for us to create an API key, we will have to access the Google API portal. Android requires this extra step when configuring Google Maps:

You will need a Google Developer account to complete this section.

1. Visit the following link to create a new project in the API portal: `https://consol e.developers.google.com/iam-admin/projects`.

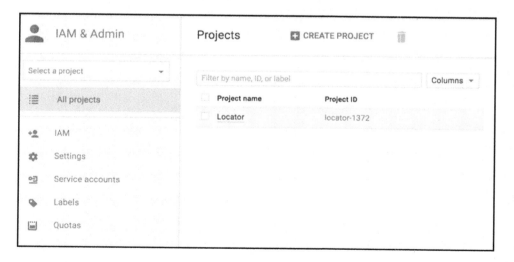

2. Select **Create Project** from the top menu and call the project `Locator`:

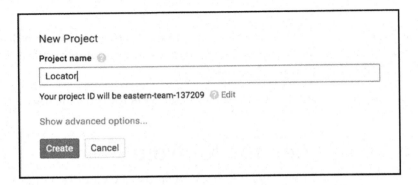

For more information on setting up an API key, visit this link: `https://de`
`velopers.google.com/maps/documentation/javascript/get-api-key#`
`get-an-api-key`.

3. Once we have our new project, visit the API Manager and select the **Google Maps Android API**:

4. Select the **Enable** button, then click **Credentials** from the left-hand menu. We want to create a new **API key** from the drop-down list:

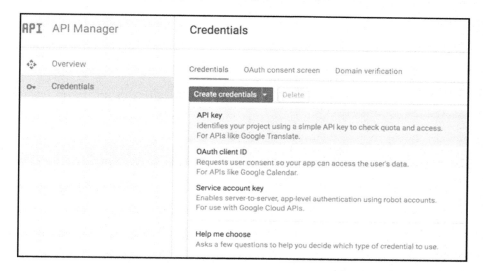

5. Make sure we select an **Android key**:

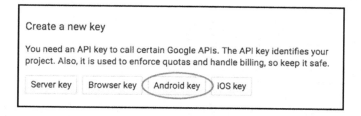

6. We are going to leave the name as `Android key 1`. Now click the **Create** button:

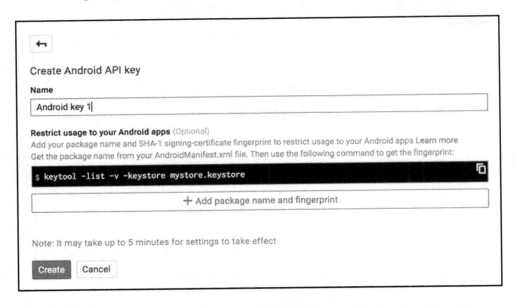

7. Finally, let's select our Android key and place it in the `AndroidManifest.xml` file where it states `YOUR-API-KEY`:

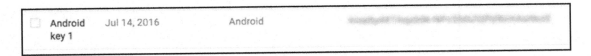

Congratulations, we have now integrated the iOS and Android location services with Google Maps.

Now let's move on to the Windows Phone version.

Creating our Windows project

Moving on to Visual Studio once again, let start by creating a new c-shape universal Windows project and calling it `Locator.WinRT`:

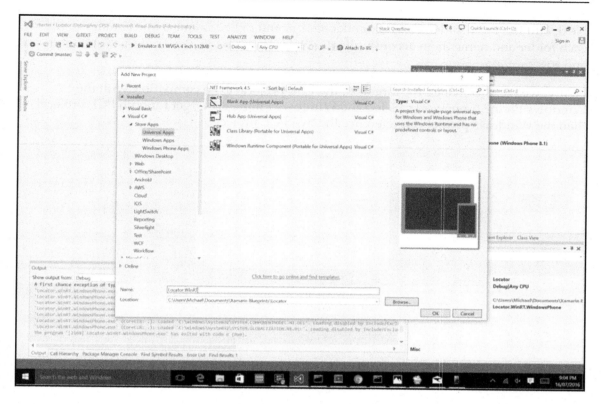

We can remove the Windows store and shared projects. Before you remove the shared projects, move the `app.xaml` files into the Windows Phone project.

The `Map` object from `Xamarin.Forms.Maps` is not usable in Windows Phone 8.1. We have to use the universal platform instead.

For our Windows Phone version, we need the following:

- A Windows Phone module for registering the geolocator and methods interfaces
- To implement the geolocator interface
- To implement the methods interface

Have a think about that for a second…
That's all we have to do to replicate the application for Windows Phone?
Think how much extra work would be involved if we were to rebuild this app from scratch entirely on the Windows platform.

Next, add the three folders, `Modules`, `Location`, and `Extras`, and create a new `.cs` file for each folder and name them accordingly: `WinPhoneModule.cs`, `GeolocatorWinPhone.cs`, and `WinPhoneMethods.cs`.

Firstly, we have to change the targets of the PCL projects to be compatible with the Windows Phone frameworks. Select the **Windows Phone 8.1** target for both PCL projects, then the Windows project can reference the two PCL projects:

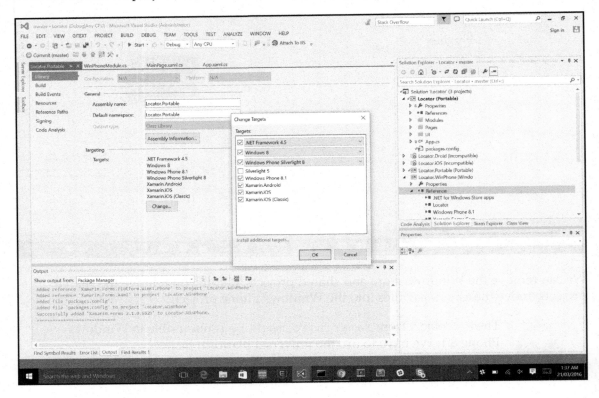

We must also import the `Xamarin.Forms`, `Xamarin.Forms.Maps`, and `Autofacnuget` packages.

Core Location Services with Windows Phone

Now for the exciting part. Let's integrate the core location services. First, we must turn on certain permissions. Open up the `package.appmanifest` file, select the **Capabilities** tab, and select the **Location** checkbox:

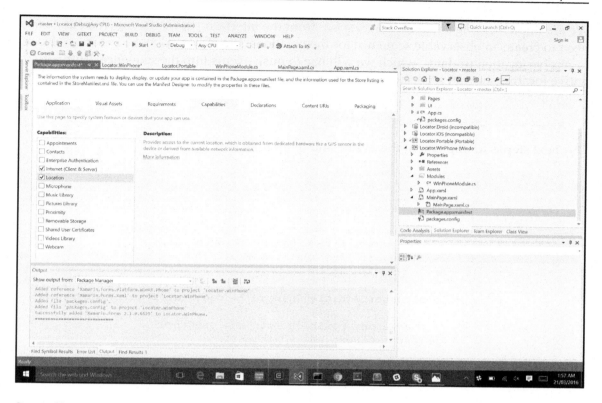

Secondly, open the `GeolocatorWinPhone.cs` file, and let's start building the Windows Phone locator class.

Let's start by creating the constructor:

```
public class GeolocatorWinPhone : IGeolocator
    {
        public Subject<IPosition> Positions { get; set; }

        Geolocator _geolocator;

        public GeolocatorWinPhone()
        {
            Positions = new Subject<IPosition>();

            geolocator = new Geolocator();
            _geolocator.DesiredAccuracyInMeters = 50;
        }
    }
```

We are implementing a native `Geolocator` from the interface `IGeolocator`, meaning we need to create an observable sequence for the positions. We also need a `Geolocator` object to receive location updates, which we will use to push events into the sequence. With all native locators, we can set accuracy for location points, which is what we are doing with the following line:

```
geolocator.DesiredAccuracyInMeters = 50;
```

Our next step is to implement the `Start` and `Stop` functions:

```csharp
public async void Start()
{
    try
    {
        var geoposition = await _geolocator.GetGeopositionAsync(
            maximumAge: TimeSpan.FromMinutes(5),
            timeout: TimeSpan.FromSeconds(10)
        );

        _geolocator.PositionChanged += geolocatorPositionChanged;

        // push a new position into the sequence
        Positions.OnNext(new Position()
            {
                Latitude = geoposition.Coordinate.Latitude,
                Longitude = geoposition.Coordinate.Longitude
            });
    }
    catch (Exception ex)
    {
        Console.WriteLine("Error retrieving geoposition - " + ex);
    }


}
```

The `Start` function uses `Geolocator` to retrieve the positions with the asynchronous function `GetGeopositionAsync`. The function will take the maximum age of a location, meaning once the time period is passed, the location will update again. The request for this location will cancel when the timeout value is reached during a location update. We also listen on the event handler `PositionChanged` via the following function:

```csharp
private void GeolocatorPositionChanged(Geolocator sender,
PositionChangedEventArgs args)
{
    // push a new position into the sequence
    Positions.OnNext(new Position ()
        {
```

```
                  Latitude = args.Position.Coordinate.Latitude,
                  Longitude =
args.Position.geoposition.Coordinate.Longitude
                    });
        }
```

We actually have two places, which will push a new geoposition's latitude and longitude into the observable sequence.

Now we add the Stop function:

```
public void Stop()
{
    // remove event handler
    _geolocator.PositionChanged -= GeolocatorPositionChanged;
}
```

All this does is remove the event handler function that we assigned in the Start function.

 You should be noticing the development patterns with this project, how we implement abstracted interfaces, generate modules, register types, and so on. The processes are all the same, no matter what platform.

That's all for the Geolocator class; we can now get on to the WinPhoneModule:

```
public class WinPhoneModule : IModule
{
    public void Register(ContainerBuilder builer)
    {
builer.RegisterType<GeolocatorWinPhone>().As<IGeolocator>().SingleInstance(
);
            builer.RegisterType<WinPhoneMethods>().As<
IMethods>().SingleInstance();
    }
}
```

Now let's get to the WinPhoneMethods class. We only need to implement the one function, Exit.

The Application class

The static class Application plays a similar role to the iOS UIApplication class. We simply reference the current application, and terminate:

```
public class WinPhoneMethods : IMethods
{
    public void Exit()
    {
        Application.Current.Terminate();
    }
}
```

Now we simply build the remaining elements with the MainPage.xaml page:

```
<forms:WindowsPhonePage
    x:Class="Locator.WinPhone.MainPage"
    xmlns="http://schemas.microsoft.com/winfx/2006/xaml/presentation"
    xmlns:x="http://schemas.microsoft.com/winfx/2006/xaml"
    xmlns:local="using:Locator.WinPhone"
    xmlns:d="http://schemas.microsoft.com/expression/blend/2008"
    xmlns:mc="http://schemas.openxmlformats.org/markup-compatibility/2006"
    xmlns:forms="using:Xamarin.Forms.Platform.WinRT"
    mc:Ignorable="d"
    Background="{ThemeResource ApplicationPageBackgroundThemeBrush}">
</forms:WindowsPhonePage>
```

And we do it for the MainPage.xaml.cs file:

```
public MainPage()
{
    InitializeComponent();

    InitIoC();

    NavigationCacheMode = NavigationCacheMode.Required;
    LoadApplication(new Locator.App());
}

private void InitIoC()
{
    IoC.CreateContainer();
        IoC.RegisterModule(new WinPhoneModule());
        IoC.RegisterModule(new SharedModule(true));
        IoC.RegisterModule(new XamFormsModule());
        IoC.RegisterModule(new PortableModule());
        IoC.StartContainer();
```

```
        }
```

Exactly the same as the previous chapter, we are starting the `IoC` container, adding our modules, and loading the `Xamarin.Forms.App` object. The only difference is the `SharedModule`, as we pass in true so the `NativeMessageHandler` is used.

Finally, we have one more issue to address. Since `Xamarin.Forms` 1.5, only Windows Phone Silverlight is supported for using Google Maps. We have to add an additional library to use maps in Windows Phone 8.1.

Personal thanks to *Peter Foot* for addressing this issue.

Luckily, an open source library is available to address this issue. We must install the nuget package `InTheHand.Forms.Maps`.

This library is only available up to `Xamarin.Forms` 2.1.0.6529, meaning this entire example must stick to this version of `Xamarin.Forms`.

Then, inside `App.xaml.cs`, we need to initialize `Xamarin.Forms` and `Xamarin.Forms.Maps`. The `Xamarin.Forms.Maps` framework is initialized through the library `InTheHand.Forms.Maps` like this:

```
if (rootFrame == null)
        {
                rootFrame = new Frame();

                rootFrame.CacheSize = 1;

                if (e.PreviousExecutionState ==
ApplicationExecutionState.Terminated)
                {
                }

                Xamarin.Forms.Forms.Init(e);
                InTheHand.FormsMaps.Init("YOUR-API-KEY");

                Window.Current.Content = rootFrame;
        }
```

Just like that, we now have the application on Windows Phone. Now that we have core location services running with Google Maps, let's take things one step further with the Google API platforms.

Web services and data contracts

We are now going to look at creating a web service controller to access web services provided by Google. These are useful implementations for downloading JSON data, deserializing it, and feeding this data in observable sequences for processing. With a web service controller, we get to use more of the `IObservable` interface. These sequences will be used to take in deserialized JSON objects from a web source, and feed these into our view models.

Our web service controller will be kept inside the **Locator.Portable** project. Remember, we can share this work across the different platforms as all use some form of HTTP client to connect to a web URL.

What about data contracts?

Your data contract is a JSON object that is used to absorb the elements of the deserialized objects, so whenever we pull down raw JSON data, your contract will be the deserialized object or objects.

So the next question is, what data are we pulling to our application?

We are going to use the Google `Geocoder` API to turn address information into latitude and longitude positions. We are going to pull down a list of addresses, calculate their latitude and longitude positions, calculate the closest address to our current position, and place a pin on the map.

Our first step is to create a new folder called `WebServices` in `Locator.Portable`. Inside this folder, we want to create another folder called `GeocodingWebServiceController`, and another folder inside this called `Contracts`. Let's first implement our contracts. A nice quick easy way to implement your JSON objects is to use an online application like this one: `http://json2csharp.com/`.

When we are pulling down JSON data, it takes time to look through the text and find all the properties required for your JSON object. This provides a nice way is to call the web service URL, retrieve some sample JSON data, and paste this JSON data into the box here:

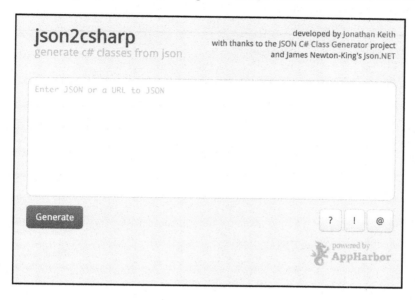

 Personal thanks to **Jonathan Keith** for saving us time.

This application creates c-sharp JSON objects based on the JSON data you entered. Now let's get our sample JSON data to paste in the box, but before we can do this we have to access the **Google API**.

Creating another API key for geocoding

Log back in to the Google Developer console, and our first step is to enable to the Geocoding API from the API manager:

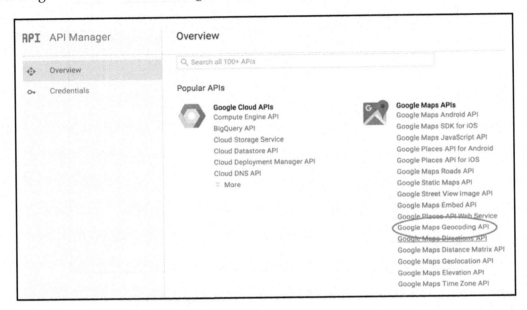

We then select the project `Locator` we created earlier, and this time we are going to create a browser key to access the Geocoding API via HTTP requests:

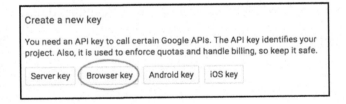

Call the key `Geocoding Key` and click **Create**. We are now going to use this key for every HTTP request passed to the Geocoding API:

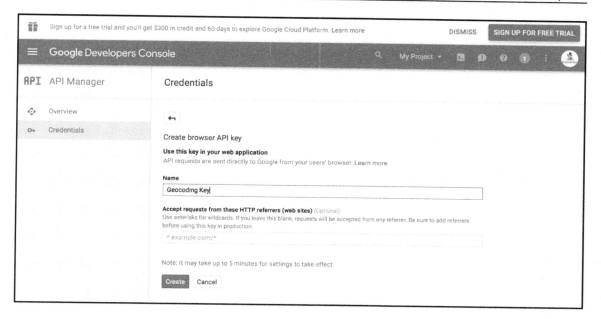

Creating GeocodingWebServiceController

Our first step creating `GeocodingWebServiceController` is to hit the web URL using your API key to pull down some sample JSON data; here is a test link:
`https://maps.googleapis.com/maps/api/geocode/json?address=1600+Amphithe` `atre+Parkway,+Mountain+View,+CA&key=YOUR_API_KEY`.

Where it says `YOUR_API_KEY`, replace this text with your newly created API key, and then paste this link into the browser. You should get JSON results like this:

```
{
    "results" : [
        {
            "address_components" : [
                {
                    "long_name" : "1600",
                    "short_name" : "1600",
                    "types" : [ "street_number" ]
                },
                {
                    "long_name" : "Amphitheatre Parkway",
                    "short_name" : "Amphitheatre Pkwy",
                    "types" : [ "route" ]
                },
```

```json
{
    "long_name" : "Mountain View",
    "short_name" : "Mountain View",
    "types" : [ "locality", "political" ]
},
{
    "long_name" : "Santa Clara County",
    "short_name" : "Santa Clara County",
    "types" : [ "administrative_area_level_2", "political" ]
},
```

We are going to copy and paste the entire resulting JSON into **Json2Sharp** to create our c-sharp objects:

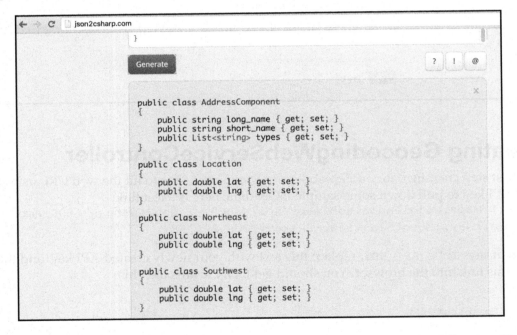

There are quite a few JSON objects, so in the `Contracts` folder, create the following files:

- AddressComponentContract.cs
- GeocodingContract.cs
- GeocodingResultContract.cs
- GeometryContract.cs
- LocationContract.cs
- NortheastContract.cs

- SouthwestContract.cs
- ViewportContract.cs

Let's begin with `AddressComponentContract.cs`:

```
public sealed class AddressComponentContract
    {
        #region Public Properties

        public string long_name { get; set; }

        public string short_name { get; set; }

        public List<string> types { get; set; }

        #endregion
    }
```

Make sure we keep all these contracts in the namespace
`Locator.Portable.GeocodingWebServiceController.Contracts`.

 Namespaces should be named according to the folder hierarchy.

Now for the `GeocodingContract`:

```
public sealed class GeocodingContract
{
    #region Public Properties

    public List<GeocodingResultContract> results { get; set; }

    public string status { get; set; }

    #endregion
}
```

The rest of the files are exactly the same; we simply copy the c-sharp objects created by
Json2Sharp. Now it's time to complete the others:

```
public sealed class GeocodingResultContract
{
    #region Public Properties

    public List<AddressComponentContract> address_components { get;
```

```
set; }

        public string formatted_address { get; set; }

        public GeometryContract geometry { get; set; }

        public string place_id { get; set; }

        public List<string> types { get; set; }

        #endregion
    }
```

Make sure you double-check the property names are exactly the same as the JSON properties, otherwise the values inside the JSON string will not be deserialized correctly.

We are not going to paste in every contract, as this should be enough direction for you to build the others.

Now that we have our geocoding contracts, let's create the interface for the GeocodingWebServiceController:

```
public interface IGeocodingWebServiceController
    {
        #region Methods and Operators

        IObservable<GeocodingContract> GetGeocodeFromAddressAsync (string
    address, string city, string state);

        #endregion
    }
```

This is only a small interface; we only have one function, GetGeocodeFromAddressAsync. The function requires three arguments to build the parameters in the web URL.

Now let's implement this interface.

A good practice with object-oriented and abstract coding is to declare interfaces before implementing the class which coincides; it will help you build the class quicker.

Newtonsoft.Json and Microsoft HTTP client libraries

As we are going to be deserializing JSON, we will need to import a JSON framework library. Newtonsoft is one of the most commonly used frameworks, so let's import this library into our **Locator.Portable** project:

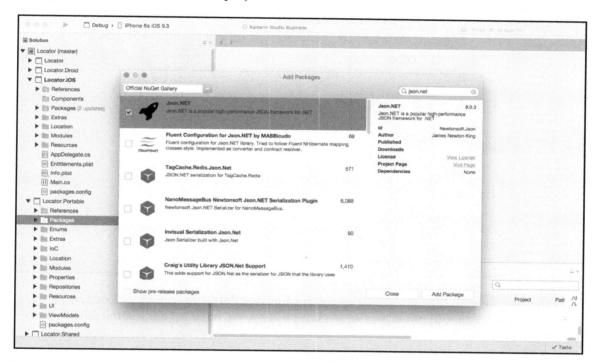

We will also need to import the HTTP client libraries for our web service controller to access online web services:

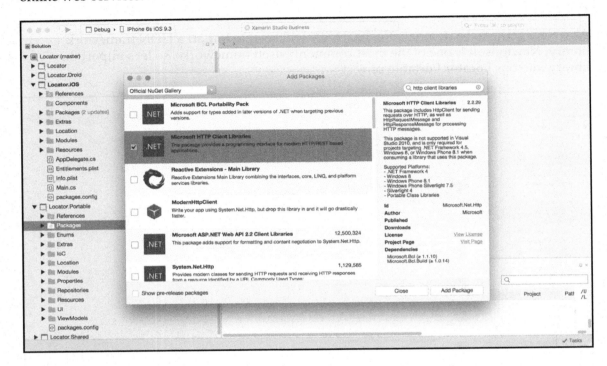

Now that we have all the extra libraries for our **Locator.Portable** project, before we implement the `IGeocodingWebServiceController`, we have to make some additions to the project structure:

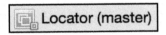

Right-click on the **Locator** and create a new shared project called **Locator.Shared**:

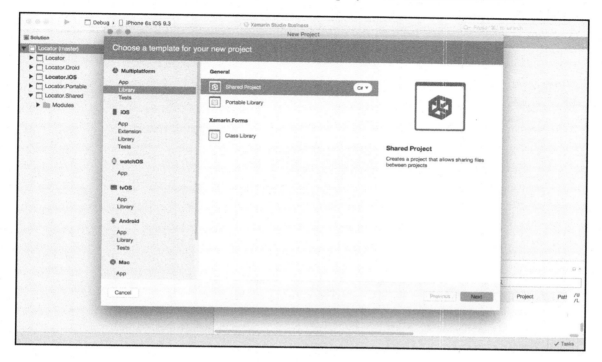

ModernHttpClient and client message handlers

In this project, we will be creating a shared module to register a `HttpClientHandler` class in the IoC container. `HttpClientHandler` is a message handler class that receives a HTTP request and returns a HTTP response. Message handlers are used on both the client and server side for handling/delegating requests between different end points.

In our example, we are interested in the client side, as we are calling the server; our client handler will be used to handle our HTTP messages sent from the HTTP client.

Let's begin by adding the `ModernHttpClient` library to our **Locator** (we will refer to this project as the `Xamarin.Forms` project) and all native projects:

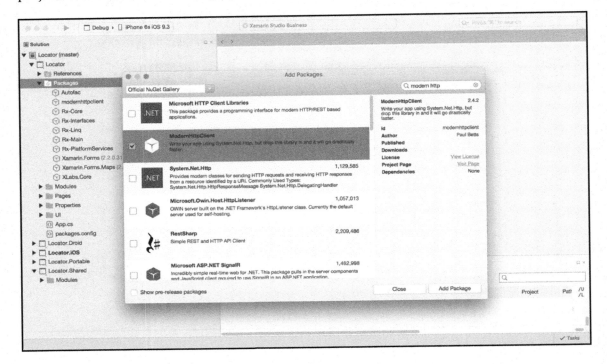

We also want to add the Microsoft Client Libraries package to all native projects.

In our shared project, remember we can't import libraries; these projects are only used to share code sheets. In this project, we want to create a folder called `Modules`. In the `Modules` folder, create a new file called `SharedModule.cs` and implement the following:

```
public sealed class SharedModule : IModule
    {
        #region Fields

        private bool isWindows;

        #endregion

        #region Constructors and Destructors

        public SharedModule(bool isWindows)
        {
            isWindows = isWindows;
```

```
        }

        #endregion

        #region Public Methods and Operators

        public void Register(ContainerBuilder builder)
        {
            HttpClientHandler clientHandler = isWindows ? new
HttpClientHandler() : new NativeMessageHandler();
            clientHandler.UseCookies = false;
            clientHandler.AutomaticDecompression =
DecompressionMethods.Deflate | DecompressionMethods.GZip;
            builder.Register(cb =>
clientHandler).As<HttpClientHandler>().SingleInstance();
        }
        #endregion
    }
```

One thing to notice is the minor change we have to make between the iOS and Android projects, and the Windows Phone project. Windows must use `NativeMessageHandler` for the `HttpClientHandler` in the IoC container. In iOS and Android, we can use a default `HttpClientHandler`.

We tell the client handler that we not going to be using cookies, and we allow for automatic decompression on the data being pulled through the client handler (**GZIP** is a common form of JSON data compression).

Now let's focus our attention on the constructor. We simply pass in a `bool` to determine whether we are using Windows to register the correct type of message handler for the current platform.

Now let's add this module to the registration in the `AppDelegate` and `MainActivity` file; it must be called before the `LoadApplication` function:

```
private void InitIoC()
    {
        IoC.CreateContainer ();
        IoC.RegisterModule (new IOSModule());
        IoC.RegisterModule (new SharedModule(false));
        IoC.RegisterModule (new XamFormsModule());
        IoC.RegisterModule (new PortableModule());
        IoC.StartContainer ();
    }
```

Excellent! We now have access to our HTTP client handler in the IoC container, so let's start building the `GeocodingWebServiceController` class:

```
public sealed class GeocodingWebServiceController :
IGeocodingWebServiceController
    {
        #region Fields

        /// <summary>
        /// The client handler.
        /// </summary>
        private readonly HttpClientHandler clientHandler;

        #endregion


#region Constructors and Destructors

        public GeocodingWebServiceController (HttpClientHandler
clientHandler)
        {
            clientHandler = clientHandler;
        }

        #endregion


    }
```

Feeding JSON data into the IObservable framework

As we are going to be registering this web service controller in the IoC container, we can pull out the client handler we just created and registered in the `SharedModule` class. Now we must implement the function we defined in the interface:

```
#region Public Methods

        public IObservable<GeocodingContract>
GetGeocodeFromAddressAsync(string address, string city, string state)
        {
            var authClient = new HttpClient (_clientHandler);

            var message = new HttpRequestMessage (HttpMethod.Get, new
Uri(string.Format(ApiConfig.GoogleMapsUrl, address, city, state)));
```

```
        return Observable.FromAsync(() => authClient.SendAsync(message,
new CancellationToken(false)))
            .SelectMany(async response =>
                {
                    if (response.StatusCode != HttpStatusCode.OK)
                    {
                        throw new Exception("Respone error");
                    }

                    return await response.Content.ReadAsStringAsync();
                })
            .Select(json =>
JsonConvert.DeserializeObject<GeocodingContract>(json));
        }


        #endregion
```

It may look a bit daunting at first, but let's break it down. Our web service controller is going to pull down data, deserialize the data into our main JSON object `GeocodingContract`, and create contracts in an observable sequence.

When we instantiate a new `HttpClient`, we must pass in our registered client handler to delegate the request messages being sent from the HTTP client. We then create a new `Http.Get` message; this will be sent from the `HttpClient` and delegated through the message handler (`HttpClientHandler`), which in turn will receive a JSON response.

This is where it gets tricky. Look at the `Observable.FromAsync` function; this method takes an asynchronous function, will run and await the function, and will return data as an observable sequence. The asynchronous function must return an `IObservable`.

The function we are passing is the `SendAsync` function of the `HttpClient`; we then use the RX function `SelectMany` to take all the response objects. If each response object incurs a HTTP status code `200` (`OK`), we return the response content as a string. Notice the `async` keyword in front of the expression; we have to use an asynchronous function to await the `ReadAsAsync` function and return the response content as a JSON string.

Finally, we use the RX function `Select` to take each response string and return the deserialized `GeocodingContract`. This contract will be fed into the observable sequence and returned to the original caller `Observable.FromAsync`, which in turn will be the data returned from the function.

More Reactive Extensions

Before we move on, let's talk more about the RX functions we just used. The `Select` function is used for iterating over any `List`, `Enumerable`, or `IObservable`, and taking the value of each item to create a new observable sequence.

Say we have a list of objects with a string property `Name`, and we do the following:

```
var newObservable = list.Select (x => x);
```

We are simply returning the same sequence of items, but then we do something like this:

```
var newObservable = list.Select (x => x.Name);
```

Our new sequence would be a stream of just the `Name` property for each object. These functions are very useful for filtering streams and lists.

Resource (RESX) files

Notice in our `GetGeocodeFromAddressAsync` function we are referencing a static class, `ApiConfig`:

```
ApiConfig.GoogleMapsUrl
```

This is a technique for containing your application's resources, such as strings, URLs, constant variables, settings properties, and so on. It is also used for languages in which we have different constant variable values, based on language settings. This is normally how you would make your app multilingual.

Let's create a new folder called `Resources` inside the **Locator.Portable** project:

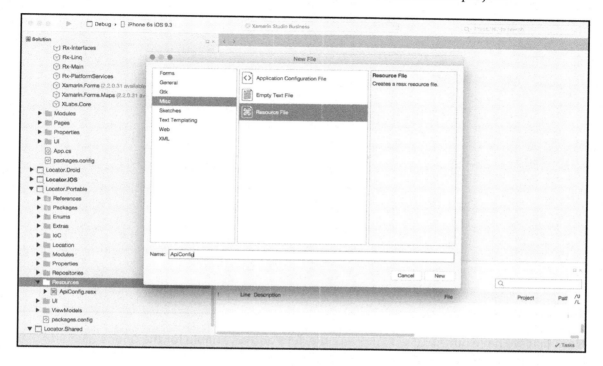

In the `ApiConfig.Designer.cs` file, we must have the namespace set according to the folder hierarchy. In this example, it is **Locator.Portable | Resources**.

Locator.Portable is the name assigned to our assembly. We must know the assembly name to reference where the folders will be stored when the app is built. To find out the name of your assembly, visit the properties page, shown in the next screenshot.

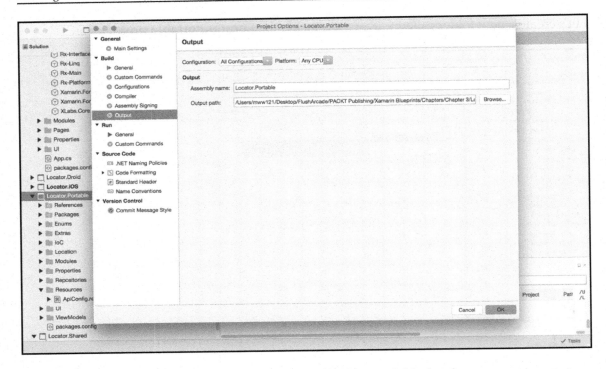

Now that we have our `ApiConfig.resx` file, let's add a variable for the `GoogleMapsUrl` property; paste the following in the `ApiConfig.resx` file:

```
<!-- url -->
<data name="GoogleMapsUrl" xml:space="preserve">
<value>https://maps.googleapis.com/maps/api/geocode/json?address={0},+{1},+
{2}&amp;key={YOUR-BROSWER-API-KEY}</value>
</data>
```

 When you save this file, you will notice the `ApiConfig.Designer.resx` file is automatically generated, meaning the namespace may change to incorrect folder paths. Sometimes we have to manually change the folder path every time this file regenerates.

Using GeocodingWebServiceController

Now that we have set up our web service controller, let's integrate it with our `MapPageViewModel`. Our first step is to register the web service controller inside the IoC container; open up `PortableModule.cs` and add the following to the `Register` function:

```
builer.RegisterType<GeocodingWebServiceController>
().As<IGeocodingWebServiceController>().SingleInstance();
```

Now we update the constructor inside `MapPageViewModel` to use `GeocodingWebServiceController` from the IoC container:

```
        #region Constructors

        public MapPageViewModel (INavigationService navigation, IGeolocator
geolocator,
                IGeocodingWebServiceController geocodingWebServiceController) :
base (navigation)
        {
            _geolocator = geolocator;
            _geocodingWebServiceController= geocodingWebServiceController;

            LocationUpdates = new Subject<IPosition> ();
        }

        #endregion
```

Our next step is to add an array of static addresses as a dictionary:

```
        #region Constants

        private IDictionary<int, string[]> addresses = new Dictionary<int,
string[]>()
        {
            {0, new string[] { "120 Rosamond Rd", "Melbourne", "Victoria"
}},
            {1, new string[] { "367 George Street", "Sydney", "New South
Wales" }},
            {2, new string[] { "790 Hay St", "Perth", "Western Australi"
}},
            {3, new string[] { "77-90 Rundle Mall", "Adelaide", "South
Australia" }},
            {4, new string[] { "233 Queen Street", "Brisbane", "Queensland"
}},
        };

        #endregion
```

We are going to use the geocoder API to determine latitude and longitude positions of all these address locations, and from your current location, determine which one is closer.

OnNavigatedTo and OnShow

Before we go any further with the Geocoding API, we need to make some additions to the navigation setup. Let's begin by implementing the `OnNavigatedTo` function for all content pages. Create a new file called `INavigableXamFormsPage.cs` and paste in the following:

```
internal interface INavigableXamarinFormsPage
{
    void OnNavigatedTo(IDictionary<string, object>
navigationParameters);
}
```

 Notice the `internal` keyword; this is because this class will never leave the `Xamarin.Forms` project.

Now we want every page to inherit this interface and create the `OnNavigatedTo` function:

```
public partial class MainPage : ContentPage, INavigableXamarinFormsPage
{
    public void OnNavigatedTo(IDictionary<string, object>
navigationParameters)
    {
    }
}

public partial class MapPage : ContentPage, INavigableXamarinFormsPage
{
    public void OnNavigatedTo(IDictionary<string, object>
navigationParameters)
    {
    }
}
```

Now we want to call the `OnNavigatedTo` function every time a page is navigated to. First, let's update our interface for the `NavigationService`:

```
public interface INavigationService
{
    Task Navigate (PageNames pageName, IDictionary<string, object>
navigationParameters);
}
```

Now open up the `NavigationService` class and update the `Navigate` function:

```
#region INavigationService implementation
```

```
    public async Task Navigate (PageNames pageName, IDictionary<string,
object> navigationParameters)
    {
        var page = getPage (pageName);

        if (page != null)
        {
            var navigablePage = page as INavigableXamarinFormsPage;

            if (navigablePage != null)
            {
                await IoC.Resolve<NavigationPage> ().PushAsync (page);
                navigablePage.OnNavigatedTo ();
            }
        }
    }

    #endregion
```

After the page is pushed, we then call the OnNavigatedTo function.

Now we want to do a similar thing with page view models. In your ViewModelBase class, add the following:

```
    public void OnShow(IDictionary<string, object> parameters)
    {
        LoadAsync(parameters).ToObservable().Subscribe(
            result =>
            {
                // we can add things to do after we load the view model
            },
            ex =>
            {
                // we can handle any areas from the load async function
            });
    }

    protected virtual async Task LoadAsync(IDictionary<string, object>
parameters)
    {
    }
```

The OnShow function will take in the navigation parameters from the coinciding page's OnNavigatedTo function.

Notice that the RX approach with handling asynchronous functions when the LoadAsync has finished?

We have options to handle results and errors from the `LoadAsync` function. You may have also noticed the short expressions used with arrows. This type of syntax is known as lambda expressions, a very common c-sharp syntax for abbreviating functions, arguments, and delegates. Our `LoadAsync` is also virtual, which means any page view model that implements this interface can override this function.

Now let's make some extra additions to the `Xamarin.Forms` project (`Locator`). Create a new file in the `UI` folder and call it `XamarinNavigationExtensions.cs`. Now for the implementation:

```
public static class XamarinNavigationExtensions
    {
        #region Public Methods and Operators

        // for ContentPage
        public static void Show(this ContentPage page, IDictionary<string,
object> parameters)
        {
            var target = page.BindingContext as ViewModelBase;
            if (target != null)
            {
                target.OnShow(parameters);
            }
        }

        #endregion

    }
```

Looking at this more closely, we are actually making extension functions for all `ContentPage` types. The `OnShow` function for a `ContentPage` will extract the binding context as a `ViewModelBase` and call the `OnShow` function of the view model, which in turn will call `LoadAsync`. Finally, we make the changes to `MapPage.xaml.cs` and `MainPage.xaml.cs`:

```
        public void OnNavigatedTo(IDictionary<string, object>
    navigationParameters)
        {
            this.Show (navigationParameters);
        }
```

Well done! What we just implemented is a Windows Phone principle. We know that when the `OnNavigatedTo` function is called, our layout for the `XAML` sheet is already sized accordingly. The advantage of having this is we can now retrieve x, y, height, and width figures from the page inside this function.

Pythagoras equirectangular projection

Now back to the Geocoding API. We are going to implement the math behind calculating the closest address to a latitude and longitude (current position).

For our first step, we need to add some properties for `MapPageViewModel`:

```
#region Private Properties
private IList<IPosition> _positions;

private Position _currentPosition;

private string _closestAddress;

private int _geocodesComplete = 0;

#endregion
```

Now for the extra `public` property, which will hold the string address of the closest position:

```
public string ClosestAddress
        {
            get
            {
                return _closestAddress;
            }

            set
            {
                if (value.Equals(_closestAddress))
                {
                    return;
                }

                _closestAddress = value;
                OnPropertyChanged("ClosestAddress");
            }
        }
```

Now we have to add another `Subject` sequence for when the closet position changes:

```
#region Subjects

public Subject<IPosition> ClosestUpdates { get; set; }

#endregion
```

This must be initialized in the constructor:

```
ClosestUpdates = new Subject<IPosition> ();
```

Now for the fun part.

How are we going to calculate the closest position?

Let's start with the first private function, which will get the positions from the address:

```
        public async Task GetGeocodeFromAddress(string address, string
city, string state)
        {
            var geoContract = await
_geocodingWebServiceController.GetGeocodeFromAddressAsync(address, city,
state);

            if (geoContract != null && geoContract.results != null &&
geoContract.results.Count > 0)
            {
                var result = geoContract.results.FirstOrDefault();

                if (result != null && result.geometry != null &&
result.geometry.location != null)
                {
                    _geocodesComplete++;

                    _positions.Add(new Position()
                    {
                        Latitude = result.geometry.location.lat,
                        Longitude = result.geometry.location.lng,
                        Address = string.Format("{0}, {1}, {2}",
address, city, state)
                    });

                    // once all geocodes are found, find the closest
                    if ((_geocodesComplete == _positions.Count) &&
_currentPosition != null)
                    {
                        FindNearestSite();
                    }
                }
            }
        }
```

In this function, we finally get to use our `GeocodingWebServiceController`.

See how we pass in the variables that will make up the web service URL?

For each address, we must ping this API call to get the latitude and longitudes required to calculate the closest position. Then we do a bunch of checks on the values in the data contracts to make sure they aren't null, until we get the `GeometryContract` values; we will then use these to create a new position and add it to the list.

Now let's make a small change to the `Position` class and interface:

```
public class Position : IPosition
{
    public string Address {get; set;}
}

public interface IPosition
{
    double Latitude {get; set;}

    double Longitude {get; set;}

    public string Address {get; set;}
}
```

Add the `Address` property so we can record the address string for the closest property. We need to record this in the position because as we fire off so many requests to the API, they will not necessarily finish in order so we can't expect to use index referencing to obtain the position index in the list, to be the coinciding address in the array.

Now let's add the mathematical functions for calculating distances using the `PythagorasEquirectangular` projection. It uses angular projection to calculate the distance between two coordinates on a map plane. We also need a `DegreesToRadians` conversion for the `PythagorasEquirectangular` function:

```
private double DegreesToRadians(double deg)
    {
        return deg * Math.PI / 180;
    }



        private double PythagorasEquirectangular
    (double lat1, double lon1, double lat2, double lon2)
        {
            lat1 = DegreesToRadians(lat1);
            lat2 = DegreesToRadians(lat2);
```

```
lon1 = DegreesToRadians(lon1);
lon2 = DegreesToRadians(lon2);

// within a 10km radius
var radius = 10;
var x = (lon2 - lon1) * Math.Cos((lat1 + lat2) / 2);
var y = (lat2 - lat1);
var distance = Math.Sqrt(x * x + y * y) * radius;

return distance;
}
```

If the distance falls outside the radius value, it will not be used.

Try playing around with this setting to see the results you get.

Now for the `FindNearestSite` function:

```
private void FindNearestSite()
{
    if (_geolocationUpdating)
    {
        _geolocationUpdating = false;
        _geolocator.Stop();
        GeolocationButtonTitle = "Start";
    }

    double mindif = 99999;
    IPosition closest = null;
    var closestIndex = 0;
    var index = 0;

    if (_currentPosition != null)
    {
        foreach (var position in _positions)
        {
            var difference =
PythagorasEquirectangular(_currentPosition.Latitude,
_currentPosition.Longitude,
                position.Latitude, position.Longitude);

            if (difference < mindif)
            {
                closest = position;
                closestIndex = index;
```

```
                        mindif = difference;
                    }

                index++;
            }

        if (closest != null)
        {
            var array = _addresses[closestIndex];
            Address = string.Format("{0}, {1}, {2}", array[0],
array[1], array[2]);
            ClosestUpdates.OnNext(closest);
        }
    }
}
```

We will call this when all the geocodes for the address have been obtained and added to the positions list. We then go through all the positions and compare each to our current position, determine which coordinate difference is the smallest, and use this as our closest position. Then we push a new position onto the `ClosestUpdates` observable sequence, which we will subscribe to on the `MapPage`.

Our last step on the `MapPageViewModel` is to override the `LoadAsync` function:

```
        protected override async Task LoadAsync (IDictionary<string,
object> parameters)
        {
            var index = 0;

            for (int i = 0; i < 5; i++)
            {
                var array = _addresses [index];
                index++;

                GetGeocodeFromAddress(array[0], array[1],
array[2]).ConfigureAwait(false);
            }
        }
```

This is where everything will kick off; when the page loads, it will iterate through every address and download the geocode, then once we count the entire count of the address list, we find the nearest positions and push onto the `ClosestUpdates` sequence. We also want to run the `GetGeocodeFromAddress` function in parallel for each address; this is why we have `ConfigureAwait` set to false.

Now let's make changes to the `MapPage`. We are going to use two `IDisposables` now for the `MapPage`, one for each subject in the view model:

```
private IDisposable _locationUpdateSubscriptions;

private IDisposable _closestSubscriptions;
```

Now we update the `OnAppear` and `OnDisappear` functions to handle the subscribing to and disposing of the `Subjects`:

```
private void HandleDisappearing (object sender, EventArgs e)
    {
        _viewModel.OnDisppear ();

        if (_locationUpdateSubscriptions != null)
        {
            _locationUpdateSubscriptions.Dispose ();
        }

        if (_closestSubscriptions != null)
        {
            _closestSubscriptions.Dispose ();
        }
    }

    private void HandleAppearing (object sender, EventArgs e)
    {
        _viewModel.OnAppear ();

        _locationUpdateSubscriptions =
_viewModel.LocationUpdates.Subscribe (LocationChanged);
        _closestSubscriptions = _viewModel.ClosestUpdates.Subscribe
(ClosestChanged);
    }
```

And our final touch is to add the function that is called every time for the `ClosetUpdates` observable sequence:

```
private void ClosestChanged (IPosition position)
    {
        try
        {
            var pin = new Pin()
            {
                Type = PinType.Place,
                Position = new Xamarin.Forms.Maps.Position
(position.Latitude, position.Longitude),
                Label = "Closest Location",
```

```
                    Address = position.Address
            };

            MapView.Pins.Add(pin);

            MapView.MoveToRegion(MapSpan.FromCenterAndRadius(new
    Xamarin.Forms.Maps.Position(position.Latitude, position.Longitude)

    Distance.FromMiles(0.3)));
                }
            catch (Exception e)
            {
                System.Diagnostics.Debug.WriteLine ("MapPage: Error with
    moving pin - " + e);
                }
            }
        }
```

We are creating a pin to place on the map. This pin will also show the address information when we click on the pin. We then move to the region on the map to show this pin, using the `MoveToRegion` function.

That is everything; we have now integrated with Google Maps and Geocoding.

Summary

In this chapter, we discussed development with `Xamarin.Forms` and `Xamarin.Forms.Maps`. We learned how to implement location services on each platform, handling backgrounding location update events and using latitudes and longitudes to calculate positions. Have a play around with the application on all three platforms, and watch how the location updates and nearest positions update the regions on the map. In the next chapter, we will jump back into native development, and build an application that will control a sound file like an audio player.

4

Building an Audio Player Application

In this chapter, we move back to native Xamarin. We will integrate native audio functions for processing a sound file using the `AVFramework` in iOS with the `AVAudioSessions`, `AVAudioSettings`, and `AVAudioRecorder` objects. In Android you will use the `MediaPlayer` object from the `Android.Media` library.

Expected knowledge:

- Some knowledge of either iOS `AVAudioSessions`, `AVAudioSettings`, and `AVAudioRecorder`, or the Android `MediaPlayer` and `MediaRecorder` classes
- NSLayoutConstraints

In this chapter, you will learn the following:

- Project setup
- Inversion of control with MVVMCross
- View models with Xamarin native
- Creating the bindings
- NSLayoutContraints
- MVVMCross setup inside the Portable Class Library
- Setting up MVVMCross with iOS

- Setting up MVVMCross with Android
- The `SoundHandler` interface
- Implementing the iOS `SoundHandler` using the `AVAudioPlayer` framework
- The Mvx IoC container
- The audio player
- A cleaner code approach to `NSLayout`
- Creating `AudioPlayerPageViewModel`
- Implementing the Android `SoundHandler` using the `MediaPlayer` framework
- XML and Mvx bindings

Solution setup

Now that we are back to Xamarin native, it's time to get your mind out of XAML and back into native iOS and Android. We aren't going to spend much time on user interface design, but more on audio processing using the native frameworks.

 If you are testing this application on your computer, the microphone will still work as it will be using your laptop's microphone.

As we have looked into cross-platform applications and code sharing, we are going to apply some of these principles to native development and setup an MVVM architecture. Let's begin by setting up three different projects, an iOS, Android, and PCL project:

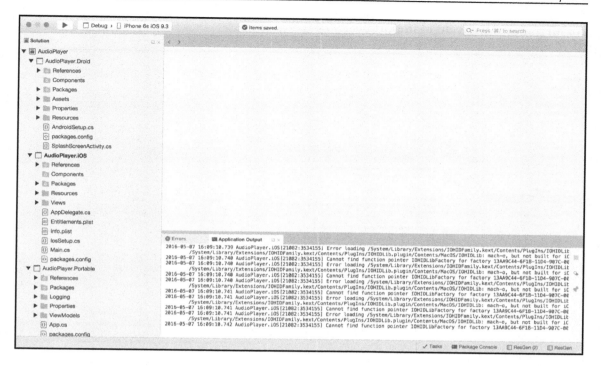

Inversion of control with MVVMCross

In the last two chapters, we looked at the IoC container and bootstrapping fundamentals; now it's time to use a different library for this principle with Xamarin native.

For all projects, we want to import the `MVVMCross` library:

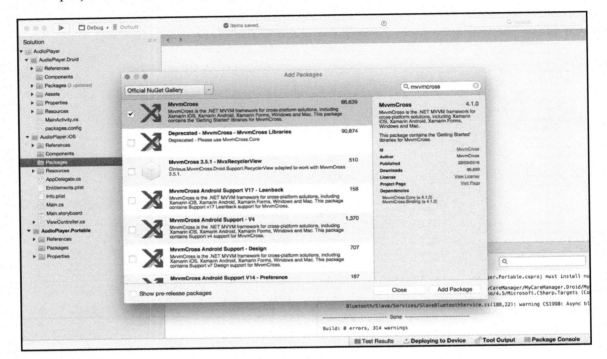

MVVMCross is available for `Xamarin.Forms`, `Xamarin.iOS`, `Xamarin.Android`, `Xamarin.Mac`, and Windows, so take your pick.

MVVMCross is set up quite differently to `AutoFac`, but the principles are the same.

View-models with Xamarin native

After we add the libraries, let's start with the `AudioPlayer.Portable` project. Create a new folder called `ViewModels`, and add a new file called `MainPageViewModel.cs`. Let's start implementing our first view-model with MVVMCross:

```
namespace AudioPlayer.Portable.ViewModels
{
    using MvvmCross.Core.ViewModels;
```

```
public class MainPageViewModel : MvxViewModel
{
    public MainPageViewModel()
    {
    }
}
}
```

When we built our `Xamarin.Forms` view-models, we created our own base view-model for handling property changes; using this library we can cut a few corners with base properties. `MvxViewModel` has a similar implementation with handling property changes; for our `MainPage`, we are going to develop the same first page as the last chapter, so let's start with the private properties:

```
public class MainPageViewModel : MvxViewModel
{
    #region Private Properties

    private string _descriptionMessage = "Welcome to the Music Room";

    private string _audioPlayerTitle = "Audio Player";

    private string _exitTitle = "Exit";

    private MvxCommand _audioPlayerCommand;

    private MvxCommand _exitCommand;

    #endregion
}
```

Notice how we are using a different `Command` type, called `MvxCommand`? It works very much the same as the `Xamarin.Forms.Command`. Let's add the public properties and see how we handle property changes:

```
#region Public Properties

public string DescriptionMessage
{
    get
    {
        return _descriptionMessage;
    }
    set
    {
        if (value.Equals(_descriptionMessage))
        {
```

```
                  _descriptionMessage = value;
                  RaisePropertyChanged (() => DescriptionMessage);
              }
          }
      }

      public MvxCommand AudioPlayerCommand
      {
          get
          {
              return _audioPlayerCommand;
          }

          set
          {
              if (value.Equals(_audioPlayerCommand))
              {
                  _audioPlayerCommand = value;
                  RaisePropertyChanged (() => AudioPlayerCommand);
              }
          }
      }

      #endregion
```

Easy, right?

It is exactly the same as the set function. We are checking whether the value has changed; if it has, then we set the private property and call RaisePropertyChanged. The only difference is we are passing an action into the function with the public property.

Now we can start building the user interface for the MainPage. This time, we are going to develop the iOS interface entirely off a .cs sheet. Add a new .cs file and call it MainPage.cs:

```
[MvxViewFor(typeof(MainPageViewModel))]
    public partial class MainPage : MvxViewController
    {
        public MainPage ()
        {
        }
    }
```

Creating the bindings

Our first step is to build the user interface. We are going to add two UIButtons, UILabel, and UIImageView to the view controller:

```
public override void ViewDidLoad ()
        {
            base.ViewDidLoad ();

        var mainView = new UIView ()
        {
            TranslatesAutoresizingMaskIntoConstraints = false,
            BackgroundColor = UIColor.White
        };

        var imageView = new UIImageView()
        {
            TranslatesAutoresizingMaskIntoConstraints = false,
            ContentMode = UIViewContentMode.ScaleAspectFit,
            Image = new UIImage("audio.png")
        };

        var descriptionLabel = new UILabel ()
        {
            TranslatesAutoresizingMaskIntoConstraints = false,
            TextAlignment = UITextAlignment.Center
        };
        var audioPlayerButton = new UIButton (UIButtonType.RoundedRect)
        {
            TranslatesAutoresizingMaskIntoConstraints = false
        };

        var exitButton = new UIButton (UIButtonType.RoundedRect)
        {
            TranslatesAutoresizingMaskIntoConstraints = false
        };

        View.Add (mainView);

        // add buttons to the main view
        mainView.Add (imageView);
        mainView.Add (descriptionLabel);
        mainView.Add (audioPlayerButton);
        mainView.Add (exitButton);

    }
```

Now let's create the bindings for the user interface elements. Add the following to the bottom of the ViewDidLoad function:

```
var set = this.CreateBindingSet<MainPage, MainPageViewModel> ();
        set.Bind(this).For("Title").To(vm => vm.Title);
        set.Bind(descriptionLabel).To(vm => vm.DescriptionMessage);
        set.Bind(audioPlayerButton).For("Title").To(vm =>
vm.AudioPlayerTitle);
        set.Bind(audioPlayerButton).To(vm => vm.AudioPlayerCommand);
        set.Bind(exitButton).For("Title").To(vm => vm.ExitTitle);
        set.Bind(exitButton).To(vm => vm.ExitCommand);
        set.Apply ();
```

When we create a binding context (BindingSet), we will set up all the bindings through the binding set. The first binding is with the description label. The object we are binding too must be a string (DescriptionMessage is our string object from the view-model).

Further on, we can specify the particular properties of a UI element using the For function, and in the parameter we specify the name of the property. In our case, we are specifying the Title property of UIButton, then calling the To function to bind our specified string object. We have also done this with UIViewController.

Finally, the last bindings we are using are MvxCommands from our view-model. We don't need to specify the property name for this; all we do is call the To function and specify the command in the view-model.

 In the UIImageView we created, we used an image called audio.png. You can put in any image you like, provided the name matches the one being loaded inside the UIImage. All resources for this example can be found via the GitHub link: https://github.com/flusharcade/chapter4 -audioplayer.

NSLayoutContraints

Let's have a closer look at where we are initializing our UI elements. The TranslatesAutoresizingMaskIntoConstraints property is used to determine whether we are going to use NSLayoutConstraints to build our user interface. When we set it to false, it means we have to implement the layout constraints for this element.

Now we want to build the user interface using layout constraints. Let's add the following after the elements are added to mainView:

```
View.AddConstraints (NSLayoutConstraint.FromVisualFormat("V:|[mainView]|",
NSLayoutFormatOptions.DirectionLeftToRight, null, new
NSDictionary("mainView", mainView)));
          View.AddConstraints
(NSLayoutConstraint.FromVisualFormat("H:|[mainView]|",
NSLayoutFormatOptions.AlignAllTop, null, new NSDictionary ("mainView",
mainView)));

          mainView.AddConstraints
(NSLayoutConstraint.FromVisualFormat("V:|-80-[welcomeLabel]-
[audioPlayerButton]-[exitButton]",
NSLayoutFormatOptions.DirectionLeftToRight, null, new
NSDictionary("welcomeLabel", welcomeLabel, "audioPlayerButton",
audioPlayerButton, "exitButton", exitButton)));
          mainView.AddConstraints
(NSLayoutConstraint.FromVisualFormat("H:|-5-[welcomeLabel]-5-|",
NSLayoutFormatOptions.AlignAllTop, null, new NSDictionary ("welcomeLabel",
welcomeLabel)));
          mainView.AddConstraints
(NSLayoutConstraint.FromVisualFormat("H:|-5-[audioPlayerButton]-5-|",
NSLayoutFormatOptions.AlignAllTop, null, new NSDictionary
("audioPlayerButton", audioPlayerButton)));
          mainView.AddConstraints
(NSLayoutConstraint.FromVisualFormat("H:|-5-[exitButton]-5-|",
NSLayoutFormatOptions.AlignAllTop, null, new NSDictionary ("exitButton",
exitButton)));
```

In the first two lines, we are adding constraints for the UIView. As the view contains only one UIView, we create two constraints for the vertical and horizontal properties of the mainView object. The vertical property is set to the following:

```
"V:|[mainView]|"
```

This means mainView will be stretched to the entire height of the containing view, and the same applies for the horizontal property:

```
"H:|[mainView]|"
```

The width of the mainView object will be stretched to the entire width of the containing view. These two text lines are known as VisualFormat.NSLayoutContraints, and they use text input as a visual representation, describing how views present in their parent views.

Looking at the other properties we pass into the `AddConstraints` function, we pass in `NSLayoutFormatOption` used for the view to abide by (that is, aligned left/top), then the metrics and `NSDictionary`, which will contain the UI elements involved in the constraint. You will notice some other constraints, such as these:

```
"H:|-5-[audioPlayerButton]-5-|"
```

These constraints include padding around the UI element:

```
"H:|-[audioPlayerButton]-|"
```

We can even simply place a dash character around the UI element, which will place a default padding of 8.

MVVMCross setup inside the PCL

Further into the MVVMCross framework, let's begin by building the `MvxApplication` class.

 This is not the same as the application class inside a `Xamarin.Forms` application.

```
public class App : MvxApplication
    {
        public override void Initialize()
        {
            CreatableTypes()
                .EndingWith("Service")
                .AsInterfaces()
                .RegisterAsLazySingleton();
        }
    }
```

Pay attention to the `CreatableTypes` function being called; the function uses reflection to find all classes in the core assembly that are `Creatable`, meaning they have a public constructor and they are not abstract. Then, following this function, only register the class interfaces with their names ending in `Service` as lazy singletons.

The lazy singleton ensures that if a class implements `IOne` and `ITwo`, then the same instance will be returned when resolving both `IOne` and `ITwo`.

There is one more part to add to the `Application` class. We must register the starting point, so add the following line under the `RegisterAsLazySingleton` function:

```
RegisterAppStart<MainPageViewModel>();
```

Setting up MVVMCross with iOS

Now we move over to the iOS project. For each platform, we must implement a `Setup` class that will be used to instantiate the `MvxApplication` class. Add a new class called `IosSetup` and implement the following:

```
public class IosSetup : MvxIosSetup
    {
        public IosSetup(MvxApplicationDelegate applicationDelegate,
    UIWindow window) : base(applicationDelegate, window)
        {
        }

        protected override IMvxApplication CreateApp()
        {
            return new App();
        }

        protected override IMvxTrace CreateDebugTrace()
        {
            return new DebugTrace();
        }
    }
```

Firstly, we must include a constructor that takes in an `MvxApplicationDelegate` and `UIWindow`; these will be passed into the base on instantiation. We also have two functions that are overriden as part of the `MvxIosSetup` object.

Start with the `CreateApp` function. All we are doing here is instantiating the `MvxApplication` class that we implemented previously. We will break this down into more detail when we implement the `AppDelegate` class.

Building an Audio Player Application

We must also override the `CreateDebugTrace` functions, which will instantiate a new `DebugTrace` object. Firstly, let's create a new folder called `Logging` inside our PCL project, add a new file called `DebugTrace.cs`, and implement the following:

```
public class DebugTrace : IMvxTrace
    {
        public void Trace(MvxTraceLevel level, string tag, Func<string>
message)
        {
            Debug.WriteLine(tag + ":" + level + ":" + message());
        }

        public void Trace(MvxTraceLevel level, string tag, string message)
        {
            Debug.WriteLine(tag + ":" + level + ":" + message);
        }

        public void Trace(MvxTraceLevel level, string tag, string message,
params object[] args)
        {
            try
            {
                Debug.WriteLine(string.Format(tag + ":" + level + ":" +
message, args));
            }
            catch (FormatException)
            {
                Trace(MvxTraceLevel.Error, tag, "Exception during trace of
{0} {1}", level, message);
            }
        }
    }
```

As part of the `IMvxTrace` interface, we must implement all these functions. The functions are not complicated; we are simply catching errors and outputting text to the console when these functions are called. All the functions called via the `DebugTrace` object are routed via a singleton object. We will be sharing this object between the two platform projects.

Great! Now that we have completed all our MVVMCross requirements for iOS, let's piece it all together via the `AppDelegate` class:

```
public override bool FinishedLaunching (UIApplication application,
NSDictionary launchOptions)
        {
            _window = new UIWindow (UIScreen.MainScreen.Bounds);

            var setup = new IosSetup (this, window);
```

[158]

```
        setup.Initialize();

        var startup = Mvx.Resolve<IMvxAppStart>();
        startup.Start();

        _window.MakeKeyAndVisible ();

        return true;
    }
```

What exactly are we doing in the `FinishedLaunching` function?

Firstly, we instantiate our `UIWindow` to the size of the main screen bounds. Then we instantiate the `IosSetup` class by passing in the new `UIWindow` object, and call the `Initialize` function we implemented in our `MvxApplication` in the PCL. Then, we use the Mvx IoC container to resolve the `IMvxAppStart` interface and call `Start` to begin the application at our `MainPageViewModel`.

Excellent! We have now set up MVVMCross with our iOS project; let's go ahead and do the same for the Android project.

Setting up MVVMCross with Android

As we already completed the `PCL` setup for `MVVMCross`, we only need to create the setup object, which will inherit the `MvxAndroidSetup` class.

Create a new file called `AndroidSetup.cs` and implement the following:

```
public class AndroidSetup : MvxAndroidSetup
    {
        public AndroidSetup(Context context) :base(context)
        {
        }

        protected override IMvxApplication CreateApp()
        {
            return new App();
        }

        protected override IMvxTrace CreateDebugTrace()
        {
            return new DebugTrace();
        }
    }
```

This is very much the same as the iOS setup, but in the constructor we must pass in the Android context.

Now for the final setup on Android. We don't normally have an application to override. Instead, MVVMCross by default provides a splash screen. Delete the `MainActivity` class that is automatically created, and replace it with a new activity called `SplashScreenActivity`:

```
[Activity(Label = "AudioPlayer.Droid"
    , MainLauncher = true
    , Icon = "@drawable/icon"
    , Theme = "@style/Theme.Splash"
    , NoHistory = true
    , ScreenOrientation = ScreenOrientation.Portrait)]
    public class SplashScreenActivity : MvxSplashScreenActivity
    {
        public SplashScreenActivity(): base(Resource.Layout.SplashScreen)
        {
        }
    }
```

We don't need to add anything into our constructor, but we must add the `MainLauncher = true` flag to the attribute to ensure this is the first thing created when the platform starts. We must also create the new XML view for the splash screen activity. For this example, we are going to create a simple screen with a `TextView`:

Try creating a splash screen that will display an image to give the application branding.

```
<?xml version="1.0" encoding="utf-8"?>
<LinearLayout xmlns:android="http://schemas.android.com/apk/res/android"
    android:orientation="vertical"
    android:layout_width="fill_parent"
    android:layout_height="fill_parent">
    <TextView
    android:layout_width="fill_parent"
    android:layout_height="wrap_content"
    android:text="Loading...."/>
</LinearLayout>
```

That's everything; lets test run both platforms and we should now have the following screen:

The SoundHandler interface

One issue with playing audio across multiple platforms is we can't share much code when processing audio. We must create an interface and register implementations through an IoC container.

Our next step is to create the `ISoundHandler` interface. In the `AudioPlayer.Portable` project, add in a new folder called `Sound`. In this folder, add a new file called `ISoundHandler.cs` and implement the following:

```
public interface ISoundHandler
    {
        bool IsPlaying { get; set; }

        void Load();

        void PlayPause();

        void Stop();

        double Duration();

        void SetPosition(double value);
```

```
            double CurrentPosition();

            void Forward();

            void Rewind();
      }
```

Our interface will describe all the functions we will be using to process our audio streams via the AudioPlayerPage interface.

Now let's go ahead and start with the iOS implementation.

Implementing the iOS SoundHandler using the AVAudioPlayer framework

The AVAudioPlayer class is the framework we will be using to play and control our audio streams in iOS, so let's begin by adding a new folder called Sound to the iOS project. We then want to create a new file called SoundHandler.cs that will inherit the ISoundHandler interface:

```
      public class SoundHandler : ISoundHandler
          {
          }
```

Now let's create a private AVAudioPlayer object and add our public IsPlaying, which will hold the playing status of the audio player:

```
      private AVAudioPlayer _audioPlayer;

      public bool IsPlaying { get; set; }
```

Then we add in the functions of the interface. In each function, we will be using the audio player object to do all our audio processing:

```
      public void Load()
          {
                  _audioPlayer = AVAudioPlayer.FromUrl(NSUrl.FromFilename("Moby -
      The Only Thing.mp3"));
          }

      public void PlayPause()
          {
                  if (_audioPlayer != null)
                  {
```

```
        if (IsPlaying)
        {
            _audioPlayer.Stop();
        }
        else
        {
            _audioPlayer.Play();
        }

        IsPlaying = !IsPlaying;
    }
}
```

The first function will load the file from the `Resources` folder. In this example, we are going to be loading in a Moby song (personally one of my favorites).

> You can add in any audio file, provided the name matches the filename being loaded via the `NSURL` object. If you want to use the same file as this one, visit the GitHub link stated previously.

The second function will control starting and stopping the audio. If we click the play button first, it will play and set the status of `IsPlaying` to `true`. Then if we click the play button again, it will stop the audio and set the `IsPlaying` to `false`.

Now for the rest of the implementation:

```
public void Stop()
    {
        if (_audioPlayer != null)
        {
            _audioPlayer.Stop();
        }
    }

    public double Duration()
    {
        if (_audioPlayer != null)
        {
            return _audioPlayer.Duration;
        }

        return 0;
    }

    public void SetPosition(double value)
    {
```

```
    if (_audioPlayer != null)
    {
        _audioPlayer.CurrentTime = value;
    }
}

public double CurrentPosition()
{
    if (_audioPlayer != null)
    {
        return _audioPlayer.CurrentTime;
    }

    return 0;
}

public void Forward()
{
    if (_audioPlayer != null)
    {
        IsPlaying = false;

        _audioPlayer.Stop();
        _audioPlayer.CurrentTime = audioPlayer.Duration;
    }
}

public void Rewind()
{
    if (_audioPlayer != null)
    {
        IsPlaying = false;

        _audioPlayer.Stop();
        _audioPlayer.CurrentTime = 0;
    }
}
```

All of this is straightforward: our Stop function will stop the audio. Our Rewind function will stop the audio and set the current time to 0 (meaning the beginning of the audio stream). Our Forward function will stop the audio and move the current time to the end of the stream. The last two functions will set the current position of the audio stream to the double value passed in. This will be used with our progress slider; when the slider position changes, the value will be passed into this function to update the position of the audio stream. Finally, the last function will retrieve the current time value so we can update our user interface with this detail.

Great! Now that we have our sound handler implemented for iOS, we want to register this through the IoC container.

The Mvx IoC container

MVVMCross comes with its very own IoC container. It works exactly like our previous example with Autofac, but we are not going to be using modules. Let's begin by registering our sound handler implementation; open our `AppDelegate.cs` file and create a new private function called `setupIoC`:

```
private void SetupIoC()
{
    Mvx.RegisterType<ISoundHandler, SoundHandler>();
}
```

We must also register our view-models so we can retrieve registered interfaces within our view-model's constructor. Let's add a new folder called `IoC` inside our `AudioPlayer.Portable` project. Add a new file called `PortableMvxIoCRegistrations.cs` and implement the following:

```
public static class PortableMvxIoCRegistrations
{
    public static void InitIoC()
    {
        Mvx.IocConstruct<MainPageViewModel>();
        Mvx.IocConstruct<AudioPlayerPageViewModel>();
    }
}
```

Now we must call the static function `InitIoC` from the `AppDelegate` function `SetupIoC`:

```
private void SetupIoC()
{
    Mvx.RegisterType<ISoundHandler, SoundHandler>();
    PortableMvxIoCRegistrations.InitIoC();
}
```

Now that we have everything we require registered inside the IoC container, let's begin building the `AudioPlayerPage`.

The audio player

Our next step in this project is to build the user interface for controlling the audio. Add a new file called `AudioPlayerPage.cs` inside the `Views` folder; don't forget to add the attribute above the class declaration to register the view-model for the MVVMCross framework:

```
[MvxViewFor(typeof(AudioPlayerPageViewModel))]
public class AudioPlayerPage : MvxViewController
{
    private UIButton playButton;

        private UISlider _progressSlider;

        private bool _playing;

        private AudioPlayerPageViewModel _model;
}
```

We have declared some local scope variables that need to be used across multiple functions; you will see how these will be used later.

Now let's create the UI elements via the `ViewDidLoad` function:

```
public override void ViewDidLoad()
        {
        base.ViewDidLoad();

        var mainView = new UIView()
        {
            TranslatesAutoresizingMaskIntoConstraints = false,
            BackgroundColor = UIColor.White
        };

        var buttonView = new UIView()
        {
            TranslatesAutoresizingMaskIntoConstraints = false,
            BackgroundColor = UIColor.Clear
        };

        var imageView = new UIImageView()
        {
            TranslatesAutoresizingMaskIntoConstraints = false,
            ContentMode = UIViewContentMode.ScaleAspectFit,
            Image = new UIImage("moby.png")
```

```
    };

    var descriptionLabel = new UILabel()
    {
        TranslatesAutoresizingMaskIntoConstraints = false,
        TextAlignment = UITextAlignment.Center
    };

    var startLabel = new UILabel()
    {
        TranslatesAutoresizingMaskIntoConstraints = false,
        TextAlignment = UITextAlignment.Left,
    };

    var endLabel = new UILabel()
    {
        TranslatesAutoresizingMaskIntoConstraints = false,
        TextAlignment = UITextAlignment.Right,
    };

    _progressSlider = new UISlider()
    {
        TranslatesAutoresizingMaskIntoConstraints = false,
        MinValue = 0
    };

    _playButton = new UIButton(UIButtonType.Custom)
    {
        TranslatesAutoresizingMaskIntoConstraints = false,
    };
    var rewindButton = new UIButton(UIButtonType.Custom)
    {
        TranslatesAutoresizingMaskIntoConstraints = false,
    };
    var fastForwardButton = new UIButton(UIButtonType.Custom)
    {
        TranslatesAutoresizingMaskIntoConstraints = false,
    };
}
```

We have labels for displaying the current track name, the start time, and the end time. We also have our buttons for controlling the audio stream (play, pause, rewind, and forward). Finally, we have our progress slider for animating the current time of the audio; we are also going to be using this to change the position of the audio.

We now want to add the button events for controlling some UI changes on the button images; add the event handler assignation under the declaration of the play button:

```
_playButton.TouchUpInside += HandlePlayButton;
            _playButton.SetImage(UIImage.FromFile("play.png"),
UIControlState.Normal);
```

 The TouchUpInside event will fire every time we click the button.

Then create the function for the event handler:

```
private void HandlePlayButton(object sender, EventArgs e)
{
    _playing = !_playing;
    _playButton.SetImage(UIImage.FromFile(playing ? "pause.png" :
"play.png"), UIControlState.Normal);
}
```

Every time we click the play button, it will move the image back and forth between the play and pause icon. Now let's add the rewind and forward button handlers; add the following lines under each UI element declaration:

```
rewindButton.TouchUpInside += HandleRewindForwardButton;
            rewindButton.SetImage(UIImage.FromFile("rewind.png"),
UIControlState.Normal);
fastForwardButton.TouchUpInside += HandleRewindForwardButton;
fastForwardButton.SetImage(UIImage.FromFile("fast_forward.png"),
UIControlState.Normal);
```

Now we add the event handler function:

```
private void HandleRewindForwardButton(object sender, EventArgs e)
{
    _playing = false;
    _playButton.SetImage(UIImage.FromFile("play.png"),
UIControlState.Normal);
}
```

This is similar to the play button handler, but this time we always set the playing status to false, and set the play button image to the play icon.

For all audio images, please visit the GitHub link given previously.

A cleaner code approach to NSLayout

On our previous screen, we built a very simple user interface using `NSLayoutContraints`.

Would you agree that the code looked quite clunky?

With our `AudioPlayerPage`, we are going to use a cleaner approach to coding the `NSLayoutConstraints`. Firstly, create a new folder called `Extras`, and add a new file called `DictionaryViews.cs`:

This class is going to inherit the `IEnumerable` interface in order to create an `NSDictionary`; part of this interface is we must specify the `GetEnumerator` function. It will pull this from the `NSDictionary`; we also have our `Add` function, which simply adds a new `UIView` to the dictionary. Then we have the static implicit operator which will return the object as an `NSDictionary` (this is used so we can directly pass the object as an `NSDictionary` to the `FromVisualLayout` function):

```
public class DictionaryViews : IEnumerable
    {
        private readonly NSMutableDictionary _nsDictionary;

        public DictionaryViews()
        {
            _nsDictionary = new NSMutableDictionary();
        }

        public void Add(string name, UIView view)
        {
            _nsDictionary.Add(new NSString(name), view);
        }

        public static implicit operator NSDictionary(DictionaryViews us)
        {
            return us.ToNSDictionary();
        }

        public NSDictionary ToNSDictionary()
        {
            return _nsDictionary;
        }

        public IEnumerator GetEnumerator()
        {
            return ((IEnumerable)_nsDictionary).GetEnumerator();
        }
    }
```

Now let's go ahead and create one of these inside our `AudioPlayerPage`; paste the following under the declaration of the fast forward button:

```
var views = new DictionaryViews()
    {
        {"mainView", mainView},
        {"buttonView", buttonView},
        {"imageView", imageView},
        {"descriptionLabel", descriptionLabel},
        {"startLabel", startLabel},
```

```
            {"endLabel", endLabel},
            {"progressSlider", progressSlider},
            {"playButton", playButton},
            {"rewindButton", rewindButton},
            {"fastForwardButton", fastForwardButton}
    };
```

Great! We now have a new `IEnumerable/NSDictionary` with all the required views to be used through the entire interface. We can directly pass this object into the `NSLayoutConstraint` function `FromVisualFormat` so we don't need to repeat the declaration of new dictionaries when we create each `NSLayoutContraint`. Now add all the UI elements to the correct parent views:

```
View.Add(mainView);

    mainView.Add(imageView);
    mainView.Add(descriptionLabel);
    mainView.Add(buttonView);
    mainView.Add(startLabel);
    mainView.Add(endLabel);
    mainView.Add(progressSlider);

    buttonView.Add(playButton);
    buttonView.Add(rewindButton);
    buttonView.Add(fastForwardButton);
```

Then let's build all the `NSLayoutConstraints`; our first is the `UIViewController's`UIView:

```
View.AddConstraints(
        NSLayoutConstraint.FromVisualFormat("V:|[mainView]|",
NSLayoutFormatOptions.DirectionLeftToRight, null, views)
    .Concat(NSLayoutConstraint.FromVisualFormat("H:|[mainView]|",
NSLayoutFormatOptions.AlignAllTop, null, views))
        .ToArray());
```

We have our new approach, using the `System.Linq` function `Concat` to combine all the `NSLayoutContraints` required for the view. We only have to call the `AddConstraints` function once, and pass in one array of all the required constraints for that parent view.

Let's add our constraint for `mainView` and `buttonView`:

```
mainView.AddConstraints(
        NSLayoutConstraint.FromVisualFormat("V:|-100-
    [imageView(200)]-[descriptionLabel(30)]-[buttonView(50)]-[startLabel(30)]-
    [progressSlider]", NSLayoutFormatOptions.DirectionLeftToRight, null, views)
        .Concat(NSLayoutConstraint.FromVisualFormat("V:|-100-
```

```
[imageView(200)]-[descriptionLabel(30)]-[buttonView(50)]-[endLabel(30)]-
[progressSlider]", NSLayoutFormatOptions.DirectionLeftToRight, null,
views))
            .Concat(NSLayoutConstraint.FromVisualFormat("H:|-20-
[progressSlider]-20-|", NSLayoutFormatOptions.AlignAllTop, null, views))
            .Concat(NSLayoutConstraint.FromVisualFormat("H:|-25-
[startLabel(70)]", NSLayoutFormatOptions.AlignAllTop, null, views))
    .Concat(NSLayoutConstraint.FromVisualFormat("H:[endLabel(70)]-25-|",
NSLayoutFormatOptions.AlignAllTop, null, views))
            .Concat(NSLayoutConstraint.FromVisualFormat("H:|-5-
[descriptionLabel]-5-|", NSLayoutFormatOptions.AlignAllTop, null, views))
            .Concat(NSLayoutConstraint.FromVisualFormat("H:|-5-
[imageView]-5-|", NSLayoutFormatOptions.AlignAllTop, null, views))
            .Concat(new[] { NSLayoutConstraint.Create(buttonView,
NSLayoutAttribute.CenterX, NSLayoutRelation.Equal, mainView,
NSLayoutAttribute.CenterX, 1, 0) })
            .ToArray());

        buttonView.AddConstraints(
            NSLayoutConstraint.FromVisualFormat("V:|-5-
[rewindButton]-5-|", NSLayoutFormatOptions.AlignAllTop, null, views)
            .Concat(NSLayoutConstraint.FromVisualFormat("V:|-5-
[playButton]-5-|", NSLayoutFormatOptions.AlignAllTop, null, views))
            .Concat(NSLayoutConstraint.FromVisualFormat("V:|-5-
[fastForwardButton]-5-|", NSLayoutFormatOptions.AlignAllTop, null, views))
            .Concat(NSLayoutConstraint.FromVisualFormat("H:|-20-
[rewindButton]-[playButton(100)]-[fastForwardButton]-20-|",
NSLayoutFormatOptions.AlignAllTop, null, views))
            .ToArray());
```

This is exactly the same approach, but it looks much nicer and it reduces the number of times we call `AddConstraints`. The view only needs to add all the constraints once, and lay out the elements once, so it is much more efficient.

Our final step in building the user interface is to set up the MVVMCross bindings; we use the same approach as the `MainPage`. Let's create a new binding set between the `AudioPlayerPage` and the `AudioPlayerPageViewModel`:

```
        var set = CreateBindingSet<AudioPlayerPage,
AudioPlayerPageViewModel>();
        set.Apply();
```

Before we get into creating our bindings, let's first build our `AudioPlayerPageViewModel` for the `AudioPlayer.Portable` project.

Creating AudioPlayerPageViewModel

Our `AudioPlayerPageViewModel` must include our `ISoundHandler` interface. We are going to be controlling the audio from this view-model, so our buttons can initiate the required events on the sound handler. Let's begin by making a new file inside the `ViewModels` folder called `AudioPlayerPageViewModel.cs`, and implementing the private properties to begin with:

```
public class AudioPlayerPageViewModel : MvxViewModel
    {
        #region Private Properties

        private readonly ISoundHandler _soundHandler;

        private string _title = "Audio Player";

        private string _descriptionMessage = "Moby - The Only Thing";

        private MvxCommand _playPauseCommand;

        private MvxCommand _forwardCommand;

        private MvxCommand _rewindCommand;

        private float _audioPosition;

        private double _currentTime;

        private double _endTime;

        private bool _updating;

        #endregion
```

Then we must add the `public` properties.

 We are only going to show two of the `public` properties as examples, as the code is repetitive.

```
public MvxCommand PlayPauseCommand
    {
        get
        {
            return _playPauseCommand;
```

```
            }

        set
        {
            if (!value.Equals(_playPauseCommand))
            {
                _playPauseCommand = value;
                RaisePropertyChanged (() => PlayPauseCommand);
            }
        }
    }

    public MvxCommand RewindCommand
    {
        get
        {
            return _rewindCommand;
        }

        set
        {
            if (!value.Equals(_rewindCommand))
            {
                _rewindCommand = value;
                RaisePropertyChanged(() => RewindCommand);
            }
        }
    }
```

We also need to add these two public variables, which are going to take both the
CurrentTime and EndTime double values and create a formatted string from a TimeSpan
value.

Notice how we are also calling RaisePropertyChanged on the string inside the double
setter? Every time we get a new current time value, the formatted string needs to update as
well:

```
public string CurrentTimeStr
        {
            get
            {
                return
TimeSpan.FromSeconds(CurrentTime).ToString("mm\\:ss");
            }
        }

        public double CurrentTime
```

```
    {
        get
        {
            return _currentTime;
        }

        set
        {
            if (!value.Equals(_currentTime))
            {
                _currentTime = value;
                RaisePropertyChanged(() => CurrentTime);
                // everytime we change the current time, the time span
values must also update
                RaisePropertyChanged(() => CurrentTimeStr);
            }
        }
    }

    public string EndTimeStr
    {
        get
        {
            return TimeSpan.FromSeconds(EndTime).ToString("mm\\:ss");
        }
    }


    public double EndTime
    {
        get
        {
            return _endTime;
        }

        set
        {
            if (!value.Equals(_endTime))
            {
                _endTime = value;
                RaisePropertyChanged(() => EndTime);
                RaisePropertyChanged(() => EndTimeStr);
            }
        }
    }
```

Now for our constructor function:

```
#region Constructors

        public AudioPlayerPageViewModel (ISoundHandler soundHandler)
        {
            _soundHandler = soundHandler;

            // load sound file
            _soundHandler.Load();

            EndTime = _soundHandler.Duration();
        }

        #endregion
```

Here we are pulling out the `ISoundHandler` implementation from the IoC container, as we will be registering this view-model inside the IoC container.

Our next step is to add two new functions to the view-model, `Load` and `Dispose`. These two functions will be called when the `AudioPlayerPage` is shown, and when it disappears. They will also be used when the audio stream is started and stopped.

Let's first add the `Load` function:

```
public void Load()
        {
            // make sure we only start the loop once
            if (!_updating)
            {
                _updating = true;

                // we are going to post a regular update to the UI with the
current time
                var context = SynchronizationContext.Current;

                Task.Run(async () =>
                {
                    while (_updating)
                    {
                        await Task.Delay(1000);

                        context.Post(unused =>
                        {
                            var current = _soundHandler.CurrentPosition();
;
```

```
                              if (current > 0)
                              {
                                  CurrentTime = current;
                              }
                      }, null);
                  }
              });
          }
      }
```

The `Load` function will be called when the page is shown, and when the audio stream starts. The function uses the `Task` framework to run a repeating loop in the background, so every second we will retrieve the current time of the audio stream from the `ISoundHandler` interface. We propagate the updates to the current time label on the `AudioPlayerPage` interface.

Notice how we are using the `SynchronisationContext.Current` variable?

This is used for threading purposes so we make sure that we set our `CurrentTime` variable on the main UI thread. Since this loop is running on a separate thread, if we made changes to this variable on a separate thread, it will break the application because you are trying to make UI changes off the main UI thread.

Now for the `Dispose` function; this will be called every time the `AudioPlayerPage` disappears and when the audio stream is stopped (we don't need to make updates to the UI when the audio stream is not playing). This ensures we stop the background loop when the page is not visible:

```
public void Dispose()
    {
        _updating = false;
        _soundHandler.Stop();
    }
```

The private variable _updating is used to control the status of whether the background loop is running, so we make sure that only one background loop is running at any one time.

Now let's initiate the audio commands:

```
_playPauseCommand = new MvxCommand(() =>
    {
        // start/stop UI updates if the audio is not playing
        if (soundHandler.IsPlaying)
        {
            Dispose();
```

```
    }
    else
    {
        Load();
    }

    _soundHandler.PlayPause();
});

_rewindCommand = new MvxCommand(() =>
{
    // set current time to the beginning
    CurrentTime = 0;
    _soundHandler.Rewind();
    Dispose();
});

_forwardCommand = new MvxCommand(() =>
{
    // set current time to the end
    CurrentTime = _soundHandler.Duration();
    _soundHandler.Forward();
    Dispose();
});
```

Looking more closely at these commands, using `PlayPauseCommand` we will call `Load` or `Dispose` based on the playing status of the audio stream, and it will also call `PlayPause` on the `ISoundHandler` interface, which controls the audio stream. The `rewindCommand` property will set the current time to 0, set the current time on the audio stream to 0, and stop the background loop. The `forwardCommand` property will set the current time to the end duration of the audio stream (which it will retrieve from the `ISoundHandler` interface), set the current time on the audio stream to the end duration, and stop the background loop.

Finally, we have to create a `public` function to set the current time of the audio stream. This will be used by our progress slider every time the value changes, this function will be called:

```
public void UpdateAudioPosition(double value)
{
    _soundHandler.SetPosition(value);
}
```

Now revert back to the `AudioPlayerPage` and add the final additions.

Since we declared a local variable before for the view-model that is bound to the view, we want to pull this out of the data context of the `UIView`:

```
_model = (AudioPlayerPageViewModel)DataContext;
```

Our local variable has the bounded view-model. We need to call some public methods on the view-model from our view. We must add in our event handler for the `ValueChanged` event on the progress slider. Add the following under the declaration of the progress slider:

```
progressSlider.ValueChanged += ProgressSliderValueChanged;
```

Then create the event handler function:

```
private void ProgressSliderValueChanged(object sender, EventArgs e)
{
    _model.UpdateAudioPosition(_progressSlider.Value);
}
```

And add the calls to the `Load` function when the page appears:

```
public override void ViewDidAppear(bool animated)
{
    _model.Load();

    base.ViewDidAppear(animated);
}
```

Override `ViewDidDisappear` to call the `Dispose` function:

```
public override void ViewDidDisappear(bool animated)
{
    _model.Dispose();

    base.ViewDidDisappear(animated);
}
```

And create the following bindings in the binding set:

```
set.Bind(this).For("Title").To(vm => vm.Title);
        set.Bind(descriptionLabel).To(vm => vm.DescriptionMessage);
        set.Bind(currentLabel).To(vm => vm.CurrentTime);
        set.Bind(endLabel).To(vm => vm.EndTime);
        set.Bind(progressSlider).For(v => v.Value).To(vm =>
vm.CurrentTime);
        set.Bind(progressSlider).For(v => v.MaxValue).To(vm =>
vm.EndTime);
```

```
set.Bind(playButton).To(vm => vm.PlayPauseCommand);
set.Bind(rewindButton).To(vm => vm.RewindCommand);
set.Bind(fastForwardButton).To(vm => vm.ForwardCommand);
```

We have our labels bound to the description, which are hard coded. This is why we must make changes to the CurrentTime variable on the main UI thread, because it affects what is displayed on the currentLabel. We also have our MvxCommand bindings on our audio buttons. Finally, we have our bindings on the Value property of the progress slider to match the CurrentTime variable, and the MaxValue to match the end time of the audio stream, so it matches the percentage playing time of the audio stream.

Excellent! Try running the application and playing around with the play/pause and progress slider functionality.

Let's move on to building the equivalent for the Android version.

Implementing the Android SoundHandler using the MediaPlayer framework

To implement the same functionality for the sound handler interface in Android, we will be using the the MediaPlayer framework.

Let's create a new folder in the Android project called Sound, and create a new file called SoundHandler.cs:

```
public class SoundHandler : ISoundHandler
{
        private MediaPlayer _mediaPlayer;

        public bool IsPlaying { get; set; }
}
```

The same as the iOS version, let's add the Load and PlayPause functions:

```
public void Load()
    {
        try
        {
            _mediaPlayer = new MediaPlayer();
            _mediaPlayer.SetAudioStreamType(Stream.Music);

            AssetFileDescriptor descriptor =
Android.App.Application.Context.Assets.OpenFd("Moby - The Only Thing.mp3");
            _mediaPlayer.SetDataSource(descriptor.FileDescriptor,
descriptor.StartOffset, descriptor.Length);

            _mediaPlayer.Prepare();
            _mediaPlayer.SetVolume(1f, 1f);
        }
        catch (Exception e)
        {
            Debug.WriteLine(e);
        }
    }

    public void PlayPause()
    {
        if (_mediaPlayer != null)
        {
            if (IsPlaying)
            {
                _mediaPlayer.Pause();
            }
            else
            {
                _mediaPlayer.Start();
            }

            IsPlaying = !IsPlaying;
        }
    }
```

We have some exception handling in the `Load` function just in case for any reason the file doesn't load; it will stop our app from crashing. When you place the `.mp3` inside the Android project, it must be placed in the `Assets` folder, and make sure the file build action is set to `AndroidAsset`:

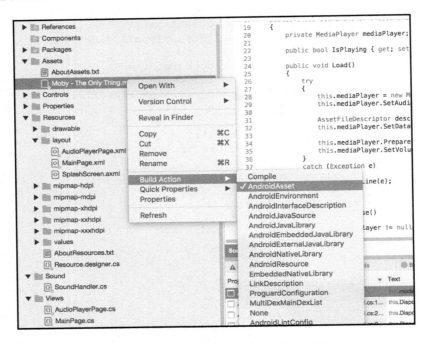

Inside our `load` function, after we initialize the `MediaPlayer` object, we set the stream type to `Stream.Music`, and then we use `AssestFileDescriptor` to retrieve the `.mp3` file. The `MediaPlayer`'s source is then set to the `.mp3` file from `AssetFileDescriptor`. We then call `Prepare` and set the volume to full (1.0f).

Our `PlayPause` function is very simple; we simply check whether the audio is playing to determine whether we pause or start the audio stream.

Now for the other functions:

```
public void Stop()
        {
            if (_mediaPlayer != null)
            {
                _mediaPlayer.Stop();
                _mediaPlayer.Reset();
            }
```

```
    }

public double Duration()
{
    if (_mediaPlayer != null)
    {
        return _mediaPlayer.Duration / 1000;
    }

    return 0;
}

public void SetPosition(double value)
{
    if (_mediaPlayer != null)
    {
        _mediaPlayer.SeekTo((int)value * 1000);
    }
}

public double CurrentPosition()
{
    if (_mediaPlayer != null)
    {
        return _mediaPlayer.CurrentPosition / 1000;
    }

    return 0;
}

public void Forward()
{
    if (_mediaPlayer != null)
    {
        IsPlaying = false;

        _mediaPlayer.Pause();
        _mediaPlayer.SeekTo(_mediaPlayer.Duration);
    }
}

public void Rewind()
{
    if (_mediaPlayer != null)
    {
        IsPlaying = false;

        _mediaPlayer.Pause();
```

```
            _mediaPlayer.SeekTo(0);
        }
    }
```

The `Stop` function requires the `Reset` function to be called on the `MediaPlayer` after we call `Stop`. The `Duration` and `CurrentPosition` functions require the value to be divided by 1,000, as the values from `MediaPlayer` are in milliseconds. This is the same when we call `SeekTo` on `MediaPlayer`; because we are passing in a value in seconds, it has to be multiplied by 1,000 to give the answer in milliseconds. Then on to the `Rewind` and `Forward` functions; we must `Pause` the audio stream first then call the `SeekTo` method to set the stream position.

Excellent! We now have our Android implementation for the `ISoundHandler` interface, so let's get on to building the Android user interface.

XML and Mvx bindings

Our Android user interface will start at `MainPage`, so we need to add a new file called `MainPage.xml`, and a new `MvxActivity` called `MainPage.cs`. Firstly, add in a new folder called `Views`; this is where we will be storing our `MvxActivities`. Let's add a new file called `MainPage.cs` to the `Views` folder, and create a new file in the **Resources | Layout** folder called `Main.xml`. Our `Main.xml` is going to start with a `LinearLayout` and contain four elements: `ImageView`, `TextView`, and two `Buttons`:

```xml
<?xml version="1.0" encoding="utf-8"?>
<LinearLayout xmlns:android="http://schemas.android.com/apk/res/android"
    xmlns:local="http://schemas.android.com/apk/res-auto"
    android:orientation="vertical"
    android:layout_width="fill_parent"
    android:layout_height="fill_parent"
    android:gravity="center">
<ImageView
    android:id="@+id/AudioImage"
    android:layout_width="200dp"
    android:layout_height="200dp"
    android:src="@drawable/audio" />
<TextView
    android:id="@+id/DescriptionText"
    android:textSize="32sp"
    android:layout_marginBottom="5dp"
    android:layout_marginTop="5dp"
    android:layout_width="wrap_content"
    android:layout_height="wrap_content"
```

```
        local:MvxBind="Text DescriptionMessage" />
    <Button
        android:id="@+id/AudioPlayerButton"
        android:layout_width="200dp"
        android:layout_height="wrap_content"
        local:MvxBind="Text AudioPlayerTitle; Click AudioPlayerCommand" />
    <Button
        android:id="@+id/ExitButton"
        android:layout_width="200dp"
        android:layout_height="wrap_content"
        local:MvxBind="Text ExitTitle; Click ExitCommand" />
</LinearLayout>
```

Let's look more closely at the `local:Mvxbind` properties on the `Buttons` and `TextView`. This is where we will set up our bindings to the view-model. We must also add this line:

```
xmlns:local="http://schemas.android.com/apk/res-auto"
```

Does this look familiar?

It is the same as our XAML sheets in `Xamarin.Forms`; we must import this namespace so we can use the binding properties on our UI elements.

 Don't forget to copy all the images into the `drawable` folder before you try building the project.

MvxActivities

`MvxActivities` are an extended object from a regular Android `Activity`; the app knows we are using the MVVMCross binding system.

Let's implement `MainPageMvxActivity`:

```
[Activity(Label = "Audio Player")]
    public class MainPage : MvxActivity
    {
        protected override void OnCreate(Bundle bundle)
        {
            base.OnCreate(bundle);

            SetupIoC();

            SetContentView(Resource.Layout.MainPage);
```

```
    }

    private void SetupIoC()
    {
        Mvx.RegisterType<ISoundHandler, SoundHandler>();
        PortableMvxIoCRegistrations.InitIoC();
    }
}
```

We will need to set up our IoC registrations in the IoC container when this activity is created. Then we simply set the content view to the XML sheet we created previously. Let's test out the Android application and click run; you should now have a MainPage screen like this:

Now we move on to the fun part: let's add a new .xml and MvxActivity for the AudioPlayerPage. Before we begin implementing the user interfaces for this page, we will need to create a custom SeekBar, because we want to register a new type of event for the "UP" motion event. Create a new folder called Controls and add a new file called CustomSeekBar.cs, then implement the following:

```
public class CustomSeekBar : SeekBar
    {
        public event EventHandler ValueChanged;

        protected CustomSeekBar(IntPtr javaReference, JniHandleOwnership
transfer)
            : base(javaReference, transfer)
        {
        }

        public CustomSeekBar(Context context)
            : base(context)
        {

        }

        public CustomSeekBar(Context context, IAttributeSet attrs)
            : base(context, attrs)
        {
        }

        public CustomSeekBar(Context context, IAttributeSet attrs, int
defStyle)
            : base(context, attrs, defStyle)
        {
        }

        public override bool OnTouchEvent(MotionEvent evt)
        {
            if (!Enabled)
                return false;

            switch (evt.Action)
            {
                // only fire value change events when the touch is released
                case MotionEventActions.Up:
                    {
                        if (ValueChanged != null)
                        {
                            ValueChanged(this, EventArgs.Empty);
                        }
                    }
```

```
                }
                break;
        }

        // we also want to fire all base motion events
        base.OnTouchEvent(evt);

        return true;
    }
}
```

We need to do this custom event because we are binding the progress of the audio stream to the SeekBar. Since we want to control the audio position, we need to make sure that only this event fires when we finish moving the seek bar.

Why can't we just use the ProgressChanged event, isn't that the same thing?

If we were to register the view-model function UpdateAudioPosition to the ProgressChanged event, every time the background loop updates the current time property, the SeekBar will call this event and try to set the audio position every second we update the SeekBar.

Now let's build the XML for the AudioPlayerPage:

```
<?xml version="1.0" encoding="utf-8"?>
<LinearLayout xmlns:android="http://schemas.android.com/apk/res/android"
    xmlns:local="http://schemas.android.com/apk/res-auto"
    android:orientation="vertical"
    android:layout_width="fill_parent"
    android:layout_height="fill_parent"
    android:gravity="center">
    <ImageView
        android:id="@+id/AudioImage"
        android:layout_marginTop="20dp"
        android:layout_marginBottom="80dp"
        android:layout_width="200dp"
        android:layout_height="200dp"
        android:src="@drawable/moby" />
    <LinearLayout
        android:layout_width="wrap_content"
        android:layout_height="wrap_content"
        android:orientation="horizontal"
        android:gravity="center">
        <ImageButton
            android:id="@+id/RewindButton"
            android:layout_width="50dp"
            android:layout_height="50dp"
```

```
          android:src="@drawable/rewind"
          local:MvxBind="Click RewindCommand" />
      <ImageButton
          android:id="@+id/PlayButton"
          android:layout_marginLeft="20dp"
          android:layout_marginRight="20dp"
          android:layout_width="50dp"
          android:layout_height="50dp"
          android:src="@drawable/play"
          local:MvxBind="Click PlayPauseCommand" />
      <ImageButton
          android:id="@+id/ForwardButton"
          android:layout_width="50dp"
          android:layout_height="50dp"
          android:src="@drawable/fast_forward"
          local:MvxBind="Click ForwardCommand" />
  </LinearLayout>
  <LinearLayout
      android:layout_width="fill_parent"
      android:layout_height="wrap_content"
      android:orientation="horizontal"
      android:gravity="center">
      <TextView
          android:id="@+id/CurrentTimeText"
          android:textSize="32sp"
          android:layout_marginBottom="5dp"
          android:layout_marginTop="5dp"
          android:layout_marginLeft="20dp"
          android:layout_width="wrap_content"
          android:layout_height="wrap_content"
          android:layout_weight="1"
          android:gravity="left"
          local:MvxBind="Text CurrentTimeStr" />
      <TextView
          android:id="@+id/EndTimeText"
          android:textSize="32sp"
          android:layout_marginBottom="5dp"
          android:layout_marginTop="5dp"
          android:layout_marginRight="20dp"
          android:layout_width="wrap_content"
          android:layout_height="wrap_content"
          android:layout_weight="1"
          android:gravity="right"
          local:MvxBind="Text EndTimeStr" />
  </LinearLayout>
  <AudioPlayer.Droid.Controls.CustomSeekBar
      android:layout_width="fill_parent"
      android:layout_height="wrap_content"
```

```
                android:layout_gravity="center_vertical"
                android:layout_marginLeft="20dp"
                android:layout_marginRight="20dp"
                android:id="@+id/seekBar"
                local:MvxBind="Progress CurrentTime; Max EndTime" />
    </LinearLayout>
```

It is a fairly large .xml sheet. Starting from the top, we have LinearLayout, which contains ImageView at the very top where we will display the album art. We then have two LinearLayouts, which contain horizontal orientation for the three ImageButtons and the TextViews. These are stacked one under the other.

Finally, we have our custom SeekBar at the very bottom under the TextView items. You will notice the layout_weight property used on the TextView items, so both have the same width. We then use gravity to float each label to either side of the SeekBar.

Fantastic! Now let's add the MvxActivity for the AudioPlayerPage to the Views folder, and implement the following:

```
[Activity(NoHistory = true)]
    public class AudioPlayerPage : MvxActivity
    {
        private bool _playing;

        private ImageButton _playButton;

        private CustomSeekBar _seekBar;

        private AudioPlayerPageViewModel _model;

        protected override void OnCreate(Bundle bundle)
        {
            base.OnCreate(bundle);

            SetContentView(Resource.Layout.AudioPlayerPage);

            _seekBar = FindViewById<CustomSeekBar>(Resource.Id.seekBar);
            _seekBar.ValueChanged += handleValueChanged;

            _playButton =
FindViewById<ImageButton>(Resource.Id.PlayButton);
            _playButton.SetColorFilter(Color.White);
            _playButton.Click += handlePlayClick;

            var rewindButton =
FindViewById<ImageButton>(Resource.Id.RewindButton);
            rewindButton.SetColorFilter(Color.White);
```

```
        rewindButton.Click += handleRewindForwardClick;

        var forwardButton =
 FindViewById<ImageButton>(Resource.Id.ForwardButton);
        forwardButton.SetColorFilter(Color.White);
        forwardButton.Click += handleRewindForwardClick;

        _model = (AudioPlayerPageViewModel)ViewModel;
    }
}
```

It all looks very similar to the iOS page. We assign the same types of event for each audio button. Now add the event functions:

```
private void HandleValueChanged(object sender, System.EventArgs e)
    {
        _model.UpdateAudioPosition(_seekBar.Progress);
    }

    private void HandlePlayClick(object sender, System.EventArgs e)
    {
        _playing = !_playing;
        _playButton.SetImageResource(playing ? Resource.Drawable.pause
 : Resource.Drawable.play);
    }

    private void handleRewindForwardClick(object sender,
System.EventArgs e)
    {
        _playing = false;
        _playButton.SetImageResource(Resource.Drawable.play);
    }

    protected override void OnDestroy()
    {
        _model.Dispose();

        base.OnDestroy();
    }
```

You will notice the NoHistory flag set to true on this Activity, so every time we load the Activity, it loads a new Activity, and does not load any previously created AudioPlayerPage. We also override the OnDestroy function so it will call the Dispose method on our view-model.

There is an equivalent to the following iOS line:

```
_model = (AudioPlayerPageViewModel)DataContext;
```

This is much more straightforward in Android:

```
_model = (AudioPlayerPageViewModel)ViewModel;
```

And voila! We now have our Android version.

Try running the project and relax to one of Moby's greatest hits.

Summary

In this chapter, we implemented audio on iOS and Android using `Xamarin.iOS` and `Xamarin.Android`. We learned how to load audio, stream audio, and process audio via start, stop, play, pause, rewind, and fast forward commands. We also built an MVVM architecture for native using MVVM Cross. In the next chapter, we will build an application for absorbing a web service using `Xamarin.Forms`. We will set up a `ListView` and create an `ObservableCollection` for displaying JSON objects.

Building a Stocklist Application

5

In this chapter, we step back into `Xamarin.Forms` and look at detailing our XAML interfaces using CustomRenderers, Styles, and ControlTemplates. We will also look at the use of animations and a basic introduction to compound animations. Then, we are going to build a simple web service providing our mobile application with a JSON feed.

Expected knowledge:

- JSON serialization/deserialization
- Some understanding of API controllers
- Visual Studio
- Some understanding of Linq queries
- Some understanding of Observables and IObservables
- Some knowledge of IIS

In this chapter, you will learn the following:

- Understanding the backend
- Creating an ASP.Net Web API 2 project
- Building an API controller
- Setting up mobile projects
- Building core mobile projects
- Improving app performance
- Creating a global `App.xaml`
- Theming with `ControlTemplates`
- Updating the `MainPageViewModel`
- Creating Stocklist web service controller
- `ListViews` and `ObservableCollections`

- Value converters
- Styles
- Further optimization with XAML
- Creating `StockItemDetailsPage`
- Custom renderers
- Adding styles for custom elements
- Creating the `StockItemDetailsPageViewModel`
- Setting up native platform projects
- Hosting the Web API project locally

Understanding the backend

As mobile developers, we are client side developers. We build user interfaces and absorb JSON data from web services. One advantage of developing in both server and client is the ability to tailor the back end to meet the needs of the mobile application. This can result in enhancing performance with data transactions on a web API. Building fast and reliable mobile applications can be difficult if we have to build off an old, slow-running back end. If users experience slow and unstable applications, they will normally never return to use it again.

In this example, we will build a simple web service that our mobile application will use. Let's begin by opening up Visual Studio.

Creating an ASP.Net Web API 2 project

We are going to start with creating a new project in Microsoft Visual Studio. Go to **File** | **New Project** and select a new Visual C# ASP.Net project:

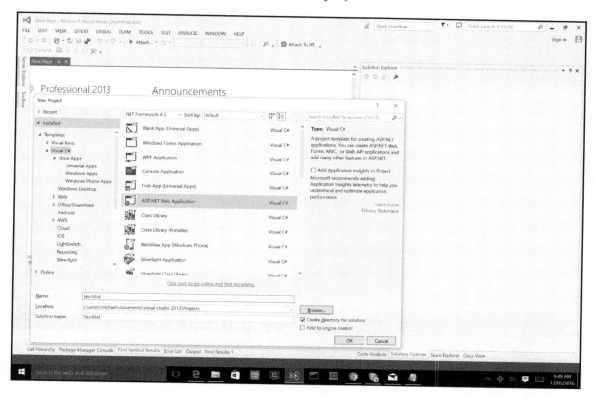

We want to then select the **Empty** template and click the **Web API** checkbox.

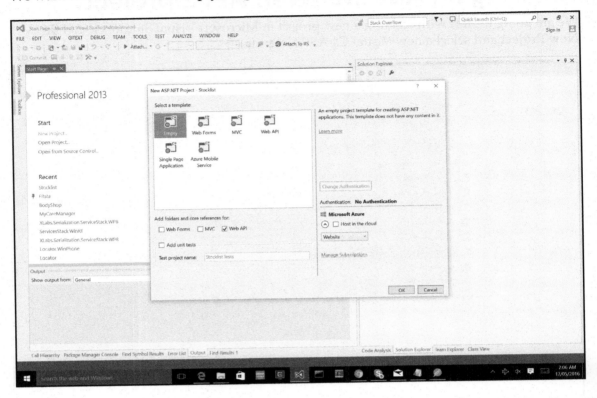

We can actually test the project right away and click **Run**, it will automatically deploy the site and run the application in your default browser. We now have our base **ASP.NET** application template, let's look more closely at the project structure. In the Solution Explorer, starting with the `Models` folder, this is where we create all our data objects that represent the data in the application, which are the objects that will be serialized to JSON and sent over HTTP requests. Then, in the `Controllers` folder, this is where we have our API controllers, which are objects that handle HTTP requests. These are the main two areas we are going to be focusing on.

Let's start with creating a data model for a single stock item. Add a new file to the `Models` folder called `StockItem.cs`:

```
public class StockItem
    {
        public int Id { get; set; }
        public string Name { get; set; }
        public string Category { get; set; }
        public decimal Price { get; set; }
    }
```

This object will be serialized into JSON and passed through our API controllers for the mobile application to retrieve. Normally, in every `MVC` / `ASP.NET` application, we have a data source layer and a Web API layer. In our data source layer, this is where the database sits, we store data here where our business logic layer will perform reads and writes. Our API layer will normally use the business logic layer to access the data and send over the network, a visual representation can be seen as follows:

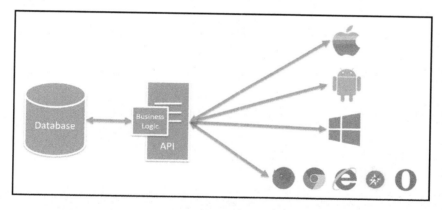

Building an API controller

Web API controllers are used to handle web requests. 99% of the time, mobile applications will always use an API layer in which it will call web requests to retrieve data, perform login, and so on. For our example, we are going to add a new empty WEBAPI 2 controller.

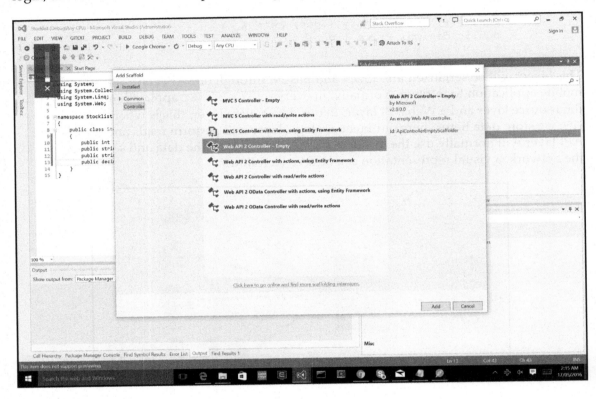

Implement the following:

```
public class StockItemsController : ApiController
    {
        List<StockItem> StockItems = new List<StockItem>()                    {
            new StockItem { Id = 1, Name = "Tomato Soup", Category =
"Groceries", Price = 1 },
            new StockItem { Id = 2, Name = "Yo-yo", Category = "Toys",
Price = 3.75M },
            new StockItem { Id = 3, Name = "Hammer", Category = "Hardware",
Price = 16.99M }
        };
```

```
public IEnumerable<StockItem> GetAllStockItems()
{
    return StockItems;
}

public StockItem GetStockItem(int id)
{
    var stockItem = StockItems.FirstOrDefault((p) => p.Id == id);
    if (stockItem == null)
    {
        return null;
    }

    return StockItem;
}
}
```

Looking more closely at the code above, the API has two functions, one for returning all stock items, and another for returning a particular stock item. If we want to access this API controller via HTTP requests, the URLs will be:

- Get all stock items

  `api/GetAllStockItems`

- Get a particular stock item by ID

  `api/GetStockItem`

Does this format look familiar?

We will use these two calls inside our mobile application to retrieve data we have sitting on the backend.

 In order to have this API live we have two options: we can either deploy the site online (that is, using Azure or Amazon), or we can host it locally (using localhost).

Let's test the API layer and run the project. When the browser opens, paste the following URL into the browser: `localhost:{PORT}/api/GetAllStockItems`.

The port number will be automatically assigned when the project is run so make sure you paste the correct port number specific to your project.

You should see an XML displayer with the results from the items in the API controller.

Setting up the mobile projects

Moving back to the client side, we now need to start building our mobile applications. Let's start with creating a blank `Xamarin.Forms` application:

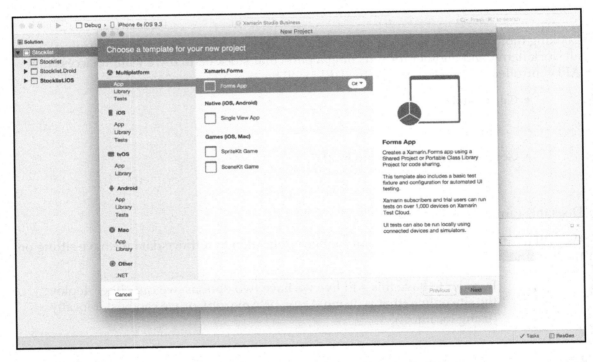

Call the application `Stocklist`, and let's start with the iOS application.

Building core mobile projects

Let's add two new PCL projects, call them `Stocklist.XamForms` and `Stocklist.Portable`.

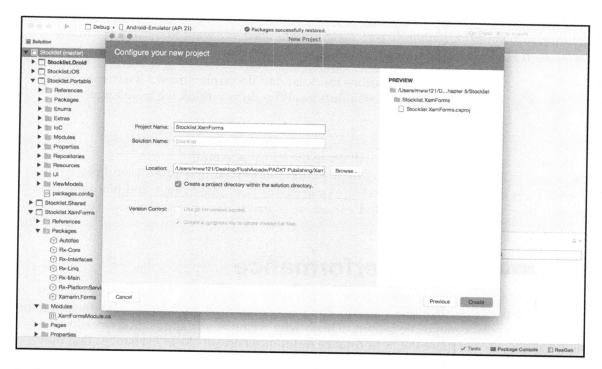

In the **Stocklist.Portable** project we want to add the following nuget packages:

- Microsoft HTTP client libraries
- Autofac
- Newtonsoft.Json
- Reactive extensions (main library)

In the `Stocklist.XamForms` project we want to add the following nuget packages:

- Microsoft HTTP client libraries
- Autofac
- Xamarin.Forms
- Reactive extensions (main library)

Just copy the exact names of the libraries to bring up the libraries you require via the Package Manager tool.

Now that we have our projects ready to go we can begin coding. From our previous solution in `Chapter 3`, *Building a GPS Locator Application*, we want to reuse some major parts, such as the `IoC` container, modules, and cross-platform navigation.

Keeping mobile solutions modular and decoupled makes it easier to share code between different solutions. Why do you think we have nuget packages?

Like our `Locator` application, we will reuse the `MainPage` and `MainPageViewModel` objects. Copy these items over to your new projects and place the XAML page into a new folder called `Pages` in `Stocklist.XamForms`, and place the view-model object into a new folder called `ViewModels` inside `Stocklist.Portable`.

Improving app performance

Let's look at a few ways we can improve application performance. Mobile phones do not have desktop processors, users typically run your application an older devices, meaning the performance power maybe be lacking. This is why we must test applications on older and newer devices to compare the performance difference and any API/OS changes that may effect behavior.

Running applications on simulators can give different results when running on devices. Make sure you always test on physical devices before releasing.

Let's take a look at the `MainPage.xaml` page from the `Locator` project. Here we will make small tweaks in the XAML layout to slightly improve the performance. The changes are very minor and will only improve performance by a millisecond here and there, but when you combine 100s of these small improvements, the end result will make a difference.

We can see a **Grid** with three elements inside, now why did we pick a Grid? Grids are good for views which we use to control any overlaying, or covering entire section/pages in which it is placed. Our first question is do we need to cover the entire screen for the landing page? No we don't, so we can replace the Grid with a `StackLayout`.

One rule to apply, don't use a Grid when a `StackLayout` will do, and don't use multiple StackLayouts when a Grid will do.

One `StackLayout` will render faster than a single Grid when we don't need to cover the screen or do any overlaying. Let's replace the containing Grid with a `StackLayout`:

```
<StackLayout x:Name="StackLayout" Spacing="10" Orientation="Vertical"
Padding="10, 10, 10, 10" VerticalOptions="Center">
        <Label x:Name="DesciptionLabel" Text="{Binding DescriptionMessage}"
HorizontalOptions="Center" Font="Arial, 20">
            <Label.TextColor>
                <OnPlatform x:TypeArguments="Color"
                    Android="Black"
                    WinPhone="Black"
                    iOS="Black">
                </OnPlatform>
            </Label.TextColor>
        </Label>

        <Button x:Name="StocklistButton" Text="{Binding LocationTitle}"
Command="{Binding LocationCommand}" BackgroundColor="Silver">
            <Button.TextColor>
                <OnPlatform x:TypeArguments="Color"
                    Android="Navy"
                    WinPhone="Blue"
                    iOS="Black">
                </OnPlatform>
            </Button.TextColor>
        </Button>

        <Button x:Name="ExitButton" Text="{Binding ExitTitle}"
Command="{Binding ExitCommand}" BackgroundColor="Silver">
            <Button.TextColor>
                <OnPlatform x:TypeArguments="Color"
                    Android="Navy"
                    WinPhone="Blue"
                    iOS="Black">
                </OnPlatform>
            </Button.TextColor>
        </Button>
    </StackLayout>
```

Don't stop now, let's add some more. Turn attention to the `DescriptionLabel`, creating bindings for static text values that never change is wasteful. Instead, we will use `Spans` because they are a tad faster to render. First, create a new `.resx` file called `LabelResources.resx`, add a new variable called `DescriptionMessage`, and set the value to the string `Welcome to the Grocery Store`:

```xml
<?xml version="1.0" encoding="utf-8"?>
<root>
    <resheader name="resmimetype">
        <value>text/microsoft-resx</value>
    </resheader>
    <resheader name="version">
        <value>2.0</value>
    </resheader>
    <resheader name="reader">
        <value>System.Resources.ResXResourceReader, System.Windows.Forms,
Version=4.0.0.0, Culture=neutral, PublicKeyToken=b77a5c561934e089</value>
    </resheader>
    <resheader name="writer">
        <value>System.Resources.ResXResourceWriter, System.Windows.Forms,
Version=4.0.0.0, Culture=neutral, PublicKeyToken=b77a5c561934e089</value>
    </resheader>

    <data name="DecriptionMessage" xml:space="preserve">
        <value>Welcome to the Grocery Store</value>
    </data>
</root>
```

 Ignore everything above the first `data` tag; this will be automatically generated when the file is created.

Now, let's import the `namespace` prefix in our `MainPage`:

```
xmlns:resx="clr-
namespace:Stocklist.Portable.Resources;assembly=Stocklist.Portable"
```

Add the preceding line to the starting tag of the page:

```xml
<ContentPage xmlns="http://xamarin.com/schemas/2014/forms"
    xmlns:x="http://schemas.microsoft.com/winfx/2009/xaml"
    xmlns:resx="clr-
namespace:Stocklist.Portable.Resources;assembly=Stocklist.Portable"
    x:Class="Stocklist.XamForms.Pages.MainPage"
    BackgroundColor="White">
```

Now let's rebuild the label item:

```
<Label x:Name="DesciptionLabel" HorizontalOptions="Center" >
        <Label.FormattedText>
            <FormattedString>
                <Span Text="{x:Static
resx:LabelResources.DecriptionMessage}"
                    FontFamily="Arial"
                    FontSize="24">
                    <Span.ForegroundColor>
                        <OnPlatform x:TypeArguments="Color"
                            Android="Black"
                            WinPhone="Black"
                            iOS="Black">
                        </OnPlatform>
                    </Span.ForegroundColor>
                </Span>
            </FormattedString>
        </Label.FormattedText>
    </Label>
```

Looking at this more closely, we have a Span that is enclosed by a FormattedString tag, and the FormattedString tag is enclosed in the Label.FormattedText property. The Span is taking a static reference from our new LabelResources, and we have also moved the OnPlatform changes into the Span object (exactly the same as the label, but instead of the TextColor property, we are using the Foreground property).

These are two tiny enhancements for one label, you probably won't notice much of a difference in performance. If we had a page with a lot of static labels, it would make a small difference in loading speeds. Rendering labels is expensive.

We can also apply these performance improvements to both button titles. Let's remove the bindings for the Text property on both buttons and replace them with the static values. Open up the LabelResources file and add the static values as follows:

```
<data name="ExitTitle" xml:space="preserve">
        <value>Exit</value>
    </data>
    <data name="StocklistTitle" xml:space="preserve">
        <value>Stock list</value>
    </data>
```

Then we apply it to the properties of the buttons:

```
Text="{x:Static resx:LabelResources.StocklistTitle}"
Text="{x:Static resx:LabelResources.ExitTitle}"
```

To finish off the landing page, let's add an image above the buttons:

```
<Image x:Name="Image" Source="stocklist.png" IsOpaque="true"
HeightRequest="120" WidthRequest="120"/>
```

All image files can be retrieved from the GitHub link: `https://github.co`
`m/flusharcade/chapter5-stocklist`.

The property `IsOpaque` is flagged to true on this image because the image is opaque.
Setting this property to `true` allows another small performance enhancement. Transparent
images are expensive to render.

Our last addition to the page is to set the title of the page to another static value from our
`LabelResources`. Add a new value called `WelcomeTitle`:

```
<data name="WelcomeTitle" xml:space="preserve">
    <value>Welcome</value>
</data>
```

Now let's add it to the starting flag for `MainPage`:

```
Title="{x:Static resx:LabelResources.WelcomeTitle}"
```

Our finished implementation will look as follows:

```
<StackLayout x:Name="StackLayout" Spacing="10" Orientation="Vertical"
Padding="10, 10, 10, 10" VerticalOptions="Center"
HorizontalOptions="Center" >
        <Image x:Name="Image" Source="stocklist.png" IsOpaque="true"
HeightRequest="120" WidthRequest="120"/>
        <Label x:Name="DesciptionLabel" >
            <Label.FormattedText>
                <FormattedString>
                    <Span Text="{x:Static
resx:LabelResources.DecriptionMessage}"
                        FontFamily="Arial"
                        FontSize="24">
                    <Span.ForegroundColor>
                        <OnPlatform x:TypeArguments="Color"
                            Android="Black"
                            WinPhone="Black"
                            iOS="Black">
                        </OnPlatform>
                    </Span.ForegroundColor>
                    </Span>
```

```
            </FormattedString>
        </Label.FormattedText>
    </Label>

    <Button x:Name="StocklistButton" Text="{x:Static
resx:LabelResources.StocklistTitle}" Command="{Binding StocklistCommand}"
BackgroundColor="Silver">
        <Button.TextColor>
            <OnPlatform x:TypeArguments="Color"
                Android="Navy"
                WinPhone="Blue"
                iOS="Black">
            </OnPlatform>
        </Button.TextColor>
    </Button>

    <Button x:Name="ExitButton" Text="{x:Static
resx:LabelResources.ExitTitle}" Command="{Binding ExitCommand}"
BackgroundColor="Silver">
        <Button.TextColor>
            <OnPlatform x:TypeArguments="Color"
                Android="Navy"
                WinPhone="Blue"
                iOS="Black">
            </OnPlatform>
        </Button.TextColor>
    </Button>
</StackLayout>
```

Let's review the small changes we made to this one ContentPage:

- Don't use a StackLayout when a Grid will do
- Don't use multiple StackLayouts, use a Grid
- Replace bindings with static values where possible
- Set the IsOpaque flag to true when the image is opaque
- Use FormattedText and Span on labels with static label values

The more enhancements we can apply, the faster your application will run. We will look at more enhancements in later projects.

Creating a global App.xaml

In all Xamarin.Forms projects we must create an Application file that inherits the Application class. We are going to extend this Application file and create a global resource dictionary. If you came from WPF you will recognize the use of a global resource dictionary that we can reference in all XAML sheets. This global resource dictionary is kept in the App.xaml file. It will have references to different converters, styles, and data templates. Rather than declaring static resource dictionaries at the top of every ContentPage or ContentView, we want to create only one dictionary that every XAML interface can access. This means we only create one dictionary at startup throughout the entire life of the application, rather than creating multiple dictionaries on views when they are displayed.

Let's create a new ContentPage, call it App.xaml, and place it in the Stocklist.XamForms project. We can now remove the App.cs file that already exists in this project. Inside the App.xaml file, implement the following:

```
<Application
    xmlns="http://xamarin.com/schemas/2014/forms"
    xmlns:x="http://schemas.microsoft.com/winfx/2009/xaml"
    x:Class="Stocklist.XamForms.App">
    <Application.Resources>
        <ResourceDictionary>
        </ResourceDictionary>
    </Application.Resources>
</Application>
```

We declare an Application object using XAML, and in the resources section of the application we create the global dictionary. We also need to open the App.xaml.cs file and initialize the component (exactly the same as the initialization of the ContentPage and ContentView), the resource dictionary, and the MainPage object in the Application:

```
public partial class App : Application
    {
        public App()
        {
            this.InitializeComponent();

// The Application ResourceDictionary is available in Xamarin.Forms 1.3 and later
        if (Application.Current.Resources == null)
        {
            Application.Current.Resources = new ResourceDictionary();
        }
```

```
            this.MainPage = IoC.Resolve<NavigationPage>();
        }

        protected override void OnStart()
        {
            // Handle when your app starts
        }

        protected override void OnSleep()
        {
            // Handle when your app sleeps
        }

        protected override void OnResume()
        {
            // Handle when your app resumes
        }
    }
```

Didn't we forget to do something prior to resolving `NavigationPage`?

We must add our `XamForms` module to the `IoC` container. First, let's reuse the navigation setup from the `Locator` project. Create a new folder called `UI` and copy the following files from the `Xamarin.Forms` project in the `Locator` application:

- `INavigableXamarinFormsPage.cs`
- `NavigationService.cs`
- `XamarinNavigationExtensions.cs`

We will need to change the namespace in each file from `Locator.UI` to `Stocklist.XamForms.UI`, and make changes to the `PageNames` enum in the `GetPage` function:

```
private Page GetPage(PageNames page)
    {
        switch(page)
        {
            case PageNames.MainPage:
                return IoC.Resolve<MainPage> ();
            case PageNames.StocklistPage:
                return IoC.Resolve<Func<StocklistPage>>()();
            default:
                return null;
        }
    }
```

Great! We now have the navigation service ready, let's register this with the `XamFormsModule`. Create a new folder in the `Stocklist.XamForms` project, add a new file for `XamFormsModule`, implementing the following:

```
public class XamFormsModule : IModule
    {
        public void Register(ContainerBuilder builer)
        {
            builer.RegisterType<MainPage>().SingleInstance();
            builer.RegisterType<StocklistPage>().SingleInstance();

            builer.RegisterType<Xamarin.Forms.Command>
().As<ICommand>().SingleInstance();

            builer.Register (x => new
NavigationPage(x.Resolve<MainPage>())).AsSelf().SingleInstance();

            builer.RegisterType<NavigationService>
().As<INavigationService>().SingleInstance();
        }
    }
```

Now that our `XamFormsModule` is registered, we can resolve the `NavigationPage` and `NavigationService`.

Let's start building the items that will be contained in the global resource dictionary.

Theming with ControlTemplates

`ControlTemplates` allow separation of logical view hierarchy from visual hierarchy. Similar to a `DataTemplate`, a `ControlTemplate` will produce the visual hierarchy for your controller page. One advantage of `ControlTemplates`, is the concept of theming. Many software applications provide settings to change user interface styles (Visual Studio and Xamarin Studio offer a dark and light theme). We are going to implement two themes for the `MainPage` and provide a `Button` to switch between the two.

Let's start with opening the `App.xaml` page, and adding the first `ControlTemplate` for the black theme:

```
<ControlTemplate x:Key="MainBlackTemplate">
            <StackLayout x:Name="StackLayout" Spacing="10"
    Orientation="Vertical" Padding="10, 10, 10, 10" BackgroundColor="Black"
            VerticalOptions="Center" HorizontalOptions="Center" >
            <Image x:Name="Image" Source="stocklist.png" HeightRequest="120"
```

```
WidthRequest="120"/>
        <Label x:Name="DesciptionLabel">
          <Label.FormattedText>
            <FormattedString>
              <Span Text="{x:Static
resx:LabelResources.DecriptionMessage}"
                FontFamily="Arial"
                FontSize="24"
                ForegroundColor="White"/>
            </FormattedString>
          </Label.FormattedText>
        </Label>

      <Button x:Name="StocklistButton"
          Text="{x:Static resx:LabelResources.StocklistTitle}"
          Command="{TemplateBinding StocklistCommand}"
          Style="{StaticResource HomeButtonStyle}"
          BackgroundColor="Gray"
          TextColor="White"/>

      <Button x:Name="ExitButton"
          Text="{x:Static resx:LabelResources.ExitTitle}"
          Command="{TemplateBinding ExitCommand}"
          Style="{StaticResource HomeButtonStyle}"
          BackgroundColor="Gray"
          TextColor="White"/>

      <ContentPresenter />
    </StackLayout>
      </ControlTemplate>
```

Here we simply copy the content of the `MainPage` apply minor color changes as the templates are changed.

Now let's add another `ControlTemplate` for the white theme:

```
<ControlTemplate x:Key="MainWhiteTemplate">
          <StackLayout x:Name="StackLayout" Spacing="10"
    Orientation="Vertical" Padding="10, 10, 10, 10" VerticalOptions="Center"
    HorizontalOptions="Center" >
        <Image x:Name="Image" Source="stocklist.png" HeightRequest="120"
    WidthRequest="120"/>
        <Label x:Name="DesciptionLabel" >
          <Label.FormattedText>
            <FormattedString>
              <Span Text="{x:Static
resx:LabelResources.DecriptionMessage}"
                FontFamily="Arial"
```

```
                    FontSize="24"
                    ForegroundColor="Black"/>
            </FormattedString>
        </Label.FormattedText>
        </Label>

    <Button x:Name="StocklistButton"
        Text="{x:Static resx:LabelResources.StocklistTitle}"
        Command="{TemplateBinding StocklistCommand}"
        Style="{StaticResource HomeButtonStyle}"/>

    <Button x:Name="ExitButton"
        Text="{x:Static resx:LabelResources.ExitTitle}"
        Command="{TemplateBinding ExitCommand}"
        Style="{StaticResource HomeButtonStyle}"/>

    <ContentPresenter />
    </StackLayout>
        </ControlTemplate>
```

Notice the use of the `ContentPresenter` object in each template?

This is used to position content that will be shared across multiple templates. Open up `MainPage.xaml` and replace the content with the following:

```
<?xml version="1.0" encoding="UTF-8"?>
<ContentPage xmlns="http://xamarin.com/schemas/2014/forms"
  xmlns:x="http://schemas.microsoft.com/winfx/2009/xaml"
  xmlns:resx="clr-
namespace:Stocklist.Portable.Resources;assembly=Stocklist.Portable"
  xmlns:vm="clr-
namespace:Stocklist.Portable.ViewModels;assembly=Stocklist.Portable"
  x:Class="Stocklist.XamForms.Pages.MainPage"
  ControlTemplate="{StaticResource MainBlackTemplate}"
  BackgroundColor="Black"
  Title="{x:Static resx:LabelResources.WelcomeTitle}"
  StocklistCommand="{Binding StocklistCommand}"
  ExitCommand="{Binding ExitCommand}">
  <ContentPage.Content>
    <Button Text="Change Theme" Clicked="ChangeThemeClicked" />
  </ContentPage.Content>
</ContentPage>
```

The content placed on the `MainPage` will be positioned where the `ContentPresenter` objects are situated in the `ControlTemplates`. The content is simply a button that will be shared across both `ControlTemplates`. We will start by setting the default `ControlTemplate` to the black theme.

Notice the two command bindings set up on the `ContentPage`?

As our `ControlTemplates` need to bind to the `Commands` in our `MainPageViewModel`, we have to add some extra work setting up these bindings. Open up the `MainPage.xaml.cs` and implement these custom bindings:

```
public static readonly BindableProperty StocklistCommandProperty =
BindableProperty.Create("StocklistCommand", typeof(ICommand),
typeof(MainPage), null);
        public static readonly BindableProperty ExitCommandProperty =
BindableProperty.Create("ExitCommand", typeof(ICommand), typeof(MainPage),
null);

        public ICommand StocklistCommand
        {
            get { return (ICommand)GetValue(StocklistCommandProperty); }
        }

        public ICommand ExitCommand
        {
            get { return (ICommand)GetValue(ExitCommandProperty); }
        }
```

These custom bindings will set up the link between each `ControlTemplate` and the view-model. Now each `Command` inside the `ControlTemplate` will respond to the `Command` implemented in the view-model.

Now let's finish off the **Change Theme** addition. First, let's add the two template definitions:

```
private bool _originalTemplate = true;
private ControlTemplate _blackTemplate;
private ControlTemplate _whiteTemplate;
```

The `originalTemplate` Boolean is used as a flag for switching to the opposite template with every
button click. Next, we must initiate `ControlTemplate` from our global resource dictionary:

```
public MainPage()
    {
        InitializeComponent();

        _blackTemplate =
(ControlTemplate)Application.Current.Resources["MainBlackTemplate"];
        _whiteTemplate =
(ControlTemplate)Application.Current.Resources["MainWhiteTemplate"];
    }
```

Finally, let's add the ChangeThemeClicked function for the button:

```
public void ChangeThemeClicked(object sender, EventArgs e)
    {
        _originalTemplate = !_originalTemplate;
        ControlTemplate = _originalTemplate ? _blackTemplate :
_whiteTemplate;
        BackgroundColor = _originalTemplate ? Color.Black : Color.White;
    }
```

Each time the button is pressed, it will check to see if we are on the default template (the black theme) and switch to the white template if we are on the black template. We will also switch the background color between black and white to match the current theme.

All done. Now let's move over to the MainPageViewModel to finish up the page's BindingContext.

Updating the MainPageViewModel

Now that we have rebuilt our MainPage, let's make some small changes to the MainPageViewModel. Since we replaced the label bindings with static values, we remove the following variables, DescriptionMessage, ExitTitle, and LocationTitle.

Now we should have the following private properties:

```
#region Private Properties
        private readonly IMethods _methods;

        private ICommand _stocklistCommand;

        private ICommand _exitCommand;

        #endregion
```

Now simply update `LocationCommand` to the following:

```
public ICommand StocklistCommand
    {
        get
        {
            return stocklistCommand;
        }

        set
        {
            if (value.Equals(stocklistCommand))
            {
                return;
            }

            _stocklistCommand = value;
            OnPropertyChanged("StocklistCommand");
        }
    }
```

We must also update our constructor:

```
#region Constructors

        public MainPageViewModel (INavigationService navigation,
Func<Action, ICommand> commandFactory,
            IMethods methods) : base (navigation)
        {
            this.exitCommand = commandFactory (() => methods.Exit());
            this.stocklistCommand = commandFactory (async () => await
this.Navigation.Navigate(PageNames.StocklistPage, null));
        }

        #endregion
```

Here we simply rename some variables to match our application. We must also copy over the `Enums` and `Extras` folder, and replace the `LocationPage` enum to `StocklistPage`.

Next, we need to add the `PortableModule`. Create a new folder called `Modules` and copy the `PortableModule` from `Location.Portable`. Change the `PortableModule` class to the following:

```
public class PortableModule : IModule
    {
        public void Register(ContainerBuilder builer)
        {
            builer.RegisterType<MainPageViewModel> ().SingleInstance();
```

```
              builer.RegisterType<StocklistPageViewModel>
    ().SingleInstance();
          }
      }
```

Finally, we need to add `INavigationService`. Create a new folder called `UI` and add `INavigationService` from `Location.Portable` into the new `UI` folder.

Building project templates can reduce time spent setting up projects and recreating similar modules.

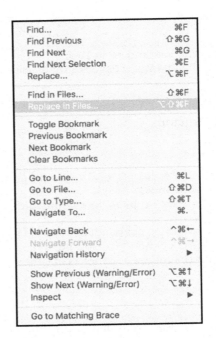

Before we move any further we must update the namespaces in the code sheets copied from the `Locator` project. The easiest way is by using **Search | Replace in Files…**. We want to replace the text `Location.Portable` with the text.

Be careful doing this; only apply a global replacement when the string is specific.

Creating the Stocklist web service controller

Let's build our client web service controller to access the API. Since we built the back end, we should be able to whip this up very quickly. Our first step is to create the object which will deserialize a `StockItem`. We refer to these as contracts. Add a new folder in your `Stocklist.Portable` project called `StocklistWebServiceController`, and add another folder in this called `Contracts`. Create a new file called `StockItemContract.cs` and implement the following:

```
public sealed class StockItemContract
    {
        #region Public Properties

        public int Id { get; set;}

        public string Name { get; set; }

        public string Category { get; set; }

        public decimal Price { get; set; }

        #endregion
    }
```

Now let's go ahead and build the `IStocklistWebServiceController` interface:

```
public interface IStocklistWebServiceController
    {
        #region Methods and Operators

        IObservable<StockItemContract> GetAllStockItems ();

        Task<StockItemContract> GetStockItemById(int id);

        #endregion
    }
```

The functions match the exact functions we have in the API controller. Before we implement this interface we have to create a new file called `Config.resx` in the `Resources` folder. For now, let's just add some empty values for each URL path because we don't know these until we either have the site running locally, or if we deploy it somewhere:

```
<data name="ApiAllItems" xml:space="preserve">
    <value></value>
</data>
<data name="GetStockItem" xml:space="preserve">
```

```
                <value></value>
        </data>
```

Now let's implement the `IStocklistWebServiceController` interface. Starting the constructor; we will have to retrieve the `HttpClientHandler` (we will register this in the `IoC` container later):

```
#region Constructors and Destructors

        public StocklistWebServiceController(HttpClientHandler
clientHandler)
        {
                _clientHandler = clientHandler;

        }

        #endregion
```

Now let's implement the first function to retrieve all the items. It will use a `HttpClient` to create an `Observable` from the asynchronous function `SendAsync` via an `HttpClient`. The `Observable` stream will be generated from the results returned from this function. We will then retrieve the response as a string (this will be JSON), and deserialize the string into multiple `StockItemContracts`, which then (using Linq) will be passed into the `Observable` stream and returned to the result of the function:

```
public IObservable<StockItemContract> GetAllStockItems ()
        {
                var authClient = new HttpClient (this.clientHandler);

                var message = new HttpRequestMessage (HttpMethod.Get, new Uri
(Config.ApiAllItems));

                return Observable.FromAsync(() => authClient.SendAsync
(message, new CancellationToken(false)))
                        .SelectMany(async response =>
                        {
                                if (response.StatusCode != HttpStatusCode.OK)
                                {
                                        throw new Exception("Respone error");
                                }

                                return await response.Content.ReadAsStringAsync();
                        })
                        .Select(json =>
                JsonConvert.DeserializeObject<StockItemContract>(json));
        }
```

And now for the `GetStockItem` function:

```
public IObservable<StockItemContract> GetStockItem (int id)
    {
            var authClient = new HttpClient (this.clientHandler);

            var message = new HttpRequestMessage (HttpMethod.Get, new
Uri (string.Format (Config.GetStockItem, id)));

            return await Observable.FromAsync(() =>
authClient.SendAsync (message, new CancellationToken (false)))
                .SelectMany (async response =>
                    {
                        if (response.StatusCode != HttpStatusCode.OK)
                        {
                            throw new Exception ("Respone error");
                        }

                        return await response.Content.ReadAsStringAsync ();
                    })
                .Select (json =>
JsonConvert.DeserializeObject<StockItemContract> (json));
        }
```

Great! We now have our `StockListWebServiceController`; we now need to register this object to the interface inside the IoC container. Open up the `PortableModule` class and add the following:

```
builer.RegisterType<StockListWebServiceController>
() .As<IStockListWebServiceController> () .SingleInstance();
```

ListViews and ObservableCollections

Now we move on to `StockListPage` and `StockListPageViewModel`; these will be used to display all the items we pull down from the API. On the frontend we will be using<span highlight=""> </span>`ListView`, they are the most common UI elements for displaying lists of data that are pulled down from any API. The beauty of `ListViews` is how they are presented via each platform. Placing a `ListView` in our XAML sheet via `Xamarin.Forms` on iOS will render a `UITableView`, on Android a native `ListView`, and in Windows a `FrameworkElement`. We can also create custom cell items and set up data bindings specific to each item, so with each contract that is deserialized, we want to have a separate view-model that will be used for representing the data on each cell.

Let's add a new file to the ViewModels folder in the Stocklist.Portable project called StockItemViewModel.cs and implement the constructor:

```
public class StockItemViewModel : ViewModelBase
    {
        #region Constructors

        public StockItemViewModel (INavigationService navigation) : base
(navigation)
        {
        }

        #endregion
    }
```

Now we want to add the private properties; they will be the same properties as in StockItemContract:

We can choose to only represent certain items in a custom view cell. Inside the view-model we only create properties that will be displayed on the view.

```
#region Private Properties

private int _id;

private string _name;

private string _category;

private decimal _price;

private bool _inProgress;

#endregion
```

Then we simply create the public properties for each private variable, following is one to get you started:

```
public int Id
        {
            get
            {
                return id;
            }
        }
```

```
        set
        {
            if (value.Equals(_id))
            {
                return;
            }

            _id = value;
            OnPropertyChanged("Id");
        }
    }
```

Here we are building a translation layer between the objects we deserialize and the objects we want to display. This is good for separating the logic contained in the view-models, as they have extra logic for processing the data to be displayed. We want our contracts to purely reflect the properties in the JSON object.

Next, we add a public method on the view-model called `Apply`. This will take a `StockItemContract` as a parameter and update the properties of the view-model. It will be called when we want to update the data to be displayed:

```
#region Public Methods

public void Apply(StockItemContract contract)
{
    Id = contract.Id;
    Name = contract.Name;
    Category = contract.Category;
    Price = contract.Price;
}

#endregion
```

Our next step is to implement the StocklistPageViewModel. This view-model will contain an `ObservableCollection`, which will be used to bind to the `ListView`. After we retrieve a list of contracts, we build another list of `StockItemViewModels`. Each item will apply the data from the contract and the new `StockItemViewModel` will be added to the `ObservableCollection`. We will apply the contract to update the data and then add the view-model to `ObservableCollection`.

Let's begin by adding a new file to the `ViewModels` folder called `StocklistPageViewModel.cs`, and start by creating a new view-model with its constructor:

```
#region Constructors

        public StocklistPageViewModel(INavigationService navigation,
    IStocklistWebServiceController stocklistWebServiceController,
            Func<StockItemViewModel> stockItemFactory) : base(navigation)
        {
            _stockItemFactory = stockItemFactory;

            _stocklistWebServiceController = stocklistWebServiceController;

            StockItems = new ObservableCollection<StockItemViewModel>();
        }

        #endregion
```

The navigation service is the same as the one used in the `Locator` project. We will register this later on in `Stocklist.XamForms` project. We use the `IStocklistWebServiceController` to fetch the `StockItems` from the API.

We then need to register our `StockItemViewModel` inside `PortableModule`:

```
public void Register(ContainerBuilder builer)
{
        . . .

builer.RegisterType<StockItemViewModel>().InstancePerDependency();

}
```

Notice how we are using the `InstancePerDependency` function instead of `SingleInstance`?
Since we are instantiating multiple items, if we used `SingleInstance`, the same data would be copied and changed across all `StockItemViewModels`.

Now let's add the `private` and `public` properties:

```
        #region Private Properties

        private readonly IStocklistWebServiceController
    _stocklistWebServiceController ;

        private readonly Func<StockItemViewModel> _stockItemFactory;
```

```
    #endregion

    #region Public Properties

    public ObservableCollection<StockItemViewModel> StockItems;

    #endregion
```

Now we have all the properties, we can build the list of items for the ObservableCollection. Next, we add the LoadAsync function, it is responsible for creating the list of StockItemViewModels:

```
#region Methods

    protected override async Task LoadAsync(IDictionary<string, object>
parameters)
    {
      try
      {
        InProgress = true;

        // reset the list everytime we load the page
        StockItems.Clear();

        var stockItems = await
_stocklistWebServiceController.GetAllStockItems();

        // for all contracts build stock item view model and add to the
observable collection
        foreach (var model in stockItems.Select(x =>
          {
            var model = _stockItemFactory();
            model.Apply(x);
            return model;
          }))
        {
          StockItems.Add(model);
        }

        InProgress = false;
      }
      catch (Exception e)
      {
        System.Diagnostics.Debug.WriteLine(e);
      }
    }

    #endregion
```

The `LoadAsync` function will be used to retrieve all contracts and build a list of `StockItemViewModels`. Every time we add a new `StockItemViewModel` to `ObservableCollection`, a `CollectionChanged` event will be fired to notify the `ListView` to update.

Have a look at how we are instantiating `StockItemViewModel` through `stockItemfactory`. It uses Func (`Func<StockItemViewModel>`) to generate a new view model every time we execute `Func`. This is why we need to call `InstancePerDependency`, so separate items are created. If we left the ending function on the registration as `SingleInstance`, even though we are calling `Func` on `StockItemViewModel`, it will only ever create one object.

Now let's build the user interface for the `StocklistPage`. It will contain the `ListView` for displaying the `StockItems` from the API:

```xml
<?xml version="1.0" encoding="UTF-8"?>
<ContentPage xmlns="http://xamarin.com/schemas/2014/forms"
    xmlns:x="http://schemas.microsoft.com/winfx/2009/xaml"
      xmlns:maps="clr-
namespace:Xamarin.Forms.Maps;assembly=Xamarin.Forms.Maps"
    x:Class="Stocklist.XamForms.Pages.StocklistPage">
    <ContentPage.Content>
        <Grid>
        <Grid.RowDefinitions>
          <RowDefinition Height="*"/>
        </Grid.RowDefinitions>

        <Grid.ColumnDefinitions>
          <ColumnDefinition Width="*"/>
        </Grid.ColumnDefinitions>

        <ActivityIndicator  x:Name="ActivityIndicator" IsRunning="{Binding
InProgress}" Grid.Row="0" Grid.Column="0"/>
        <ListView x:Name="StockItemsListView"
          IsVisible="{Binding InProgress, Converter={StaticResource
notConverter}}"
          CachingStrategy="RecycleElement"
          ItemsSource="{Binding StockItems}"
          ItemTemplate="{StaticResource ListItemTemplate}"
          SelectedItem="{Binding Selected, Mode=TwoWay}"
          RowHeight="100"
          Margin="10, 10, 10, 10"
          Grid.Row="0" Grid.Column="0"/>
      </Grid>
      </ContentPage.Content>
</ContentPage>
```

Why can't we use StackLayout?

Since we need one element overlaying another, we have to use Grid. The
`ActivityIndicator` is used to show the loading progress of our `LoadAync` function.
When this is loading, our `ListView` will be invisible and the loading indicator is displayed.

Value converters

In some cases, there are times when we need to data bind two properties of incompatible
types. A `Converter` is an object that converts the value from source to target and vice
versa. Each converter must implement the `IValueConverter` interface, which implements
two functions, `Convert` and `ConvetBack`. We are going to create a converter that will take
a `bool` as the source, and simply return the opposite value to the value in the source.

The `ConvertBack` method will only be used if the data binding is a `TwoWay` binding.

In the `Stocklist.XamForms` project, add a new folder called `Converters`, and inside this
folder create a new file called `NotConverter.cs`, implement the following:

```
public class NotConverter : IValueConverter
{
    public object Convert(object value, Type targetType, object
parameter, System.Globalization.CultureInfo culture)
    {
        var b = value as bool?;

        if (b != null)
        {
            return !b;
        }

        return value;
    }

    public object ConvertBack(object value, Type targetType, object
parameter, System.Globalization.CultureInfo culture)
    {
        throw new NotImplementedException();
    }
}
```

Even though the InProgress property doesn't use a two way binding, we still have to implement the ConvertBack function as part of the interface.

Now back to the StocklistPage.xaml. When the bool property in the view-model changes, the Convert function of the NotConverter will be called. When the IsProgress value changes, the converter will be called and will return the opposite value for the IsVisible state on the ListView. When the progress is running, the ListView is invisible, and when the progress is not running, the ListView is visible.

Now we are going to look at creating an App.xaml which will contain the DataTemplate used for each cell.

Adding a DataTemplate to the global resource dictionary

Now let's get back to the App.xaml file. Since we require a custom cell in our ListView on the StocklistPage, we are going to create a DataTemplate in the global resource dictionary. DataTemplate can be created in two ways, as an inline template or in a resource dictionary. There is no better method, it's more on personal preference. In our example, we are going to be creating ours in a resource dictionary.

Open up the App.xaml file and insert the DataTemplate in the resource dictionary like this:

```xml
<DataTemplate x:Key="ListItemTemplate">
    <ViewCell>
        <StackLayout Margin="20, 15, 20, 5">
            <Label x:Name="NameLabel" Text="{Binding Name}"/>
            <Label x:Name="CategoryLabel" Text="{Binding Category}"/>
            <Label x:Name="PriceLabel" Text="{Binding Price}"/>
        </StackLayout>
    </ViewCell>
</DataTemplate>
```

Now we want to set the `ItemTemplate` property on our `ListView` in the `StocklistPage`. Open up the `StocklistPage` and add the following to the `ListView` declaration:

```
<ListView x:Name="StockItemsListView" ItemsSource="{Binding
StockItems}" ItemTemplate="{StaticResource ListItemTemplate}"/>
```

If we wanted to use the inline template approach, we would do this:

```
<ListView x:Name="StockItemsListView" ItemsSource="{Binding StockItems">
        <ListView.ItemTemplate>
            <DataTemplate>
                <ViewCell>
        <StackLayout Margin="20, 15, 20, 5">
          <Label x:Name="NameLabel" Text="{Binding Name/>
          <Label x:Name="CategoryLabel" Text="{Binding Category}"/>
          <Label x:Name="PriceLabel" Text="{Binding Price}"/>
        </StackLayout>
                </ViewCell>
            </DataTemplate>
        </ListView.ItemTemplate>
    </ListView>
```

Styles

In our custom cell we have three labels without any styling or font assignation. We are going to spice up the look of each cell using `Style`. A `Style` groups a collection of property values into one object that can be applied to multiple visual element instances. The idea of this is to reduce repetitive markup so we can reuse similar styles across similar controls in our XAML. There are multiple ways to apply styling to a control in `Xamarin.Forms`. In this example, we will show you how to create a global style in the `App.xaml` file, and apply it to different controls in our application.

Our first global style will be for the title label in our custom cell. Let's open up the `App.xaml` file and insert the following into our resource dictionary:

```
<Style x:Key="TitleStyle" TargetType="Label">
        <Setter Property="TextColor" Value="Black" />
        <Setter Property="FontAttributes" Value="Bold" />
        <Setter Property="FontFamily" Value="Arial" />
    </Style>
```

In preceding markup, each style will contain a list of `Setter` properties. These refer to the `BindableProperties` on our control. Now that we have our `Style`, we can refer to this static resource inside our `DataTemplate`:

```
<Label x:Name="NameLabel" Text="{Binding Name}" Style="{StaticResource TitleStyle}"/>
```

Great! We have just created and set our first style on a `Label`. Let's add some more styles to `MainPageControlTemplates`. We are going to style the buttons as they both share the same styled properties. Add the following to the global resource dictionary:

```
<Style x:Key="HomeButtonStyle" TargetType="Button">
        <Setter Property="TextColor">
            <Setter.Value>
                <OnPlatform x:TypeArguments="Color"
                    Android="Navy"
                    WinPhone="Blue"
                    iOS="Black">
                </OnPlatform>
            </Setter.Value>
        </Setter>
        <Setter Property="BackgroundColor" Value="Silver" />
</Style>
```

Looking closer at the preceding style, we can even use the `<OnPlatform>` tags to change setter values based on the platform.

Now let's apply this `Style` to our `MainPage` buttons:

```
<Button x:Name="StocklistButton"
        Text="{x:Static resx:LabelResources.StocklistTitle}"
        Command="{Binding StocklistCommand}"
        Style="{StaticResource HomeButtonStyle}"/>

    <Button x:Name="ExitButton"
        Text="{x:Static resx:LabelResources.ExitTitle}"
        Command="{Binding ExitCommand}"
        Style="{StaticResource HomeButtonStyle}"/>
```

See how we are reducing the size of the markup?

This is one example of how we can apply `Styles`, we will see more techniques in further chapters.

Further optimization with XAML

Previously, we talked about some minor changes we can apply to our XAML to improve on the performance. Let's look at how we can apply some performance enhancements on a `ListView`. If you have worked with any native `ListView` or `UITableView`, one of the biggest problems is the memory usage when we have a lot of elements to load whilst we are scrolling (that is, loading an image into each bitmap for every cell).

How do we solve this issue?

We use techniques for caching cells and reusing cells. Since `Xamarin.Forms` 2.0, they have introduced some new features and enhancements around cell recycling mechanisms and caching strategies on `ListViews`. In order to set a caching strategy, we have two options:

- `RetainElement`: This is the default behavior. It will generate a cell for each item in the list, cell layout will run for each cell creation. We should only be using this method if the cell layout is frequently changing, or if a cell has a large number of bindings.
- `RecycleElement`: This takes advantage of native cell recycling mechanisms on iOS and Android. It will minimize the memory footprint and maximize the performance of a `ListView`. We should use this method if cells have a small to moderate amount of bindings, are similar in layout, and the cell view-model contains all the data.

 We should always be aiming to use the second element, try to design your cells around this setting.

We are going to use the second caching strategy on our `ListView`:

```
<ListView x:Name="StockItemsListView" CachingStrategy="RecycleElement"
ItemsSource="{Binding StockItems}" ItemTemplate="{StaticResource
ListItemTemplate}"/>
```

`RecycleElement` should be used as much as possible as we always want to tailor our apps to maximize performance wherever we can. Since we have a fairly simple cell design with a small amount of bindings and we keep all the data inside our view-model, we are able to use this setting.

Now let's have a look at another simple addition we can use to improve the loading speed of our XAML sheets. Turning on XAML compilation allows your XAML sheets to be compiled rather than interpreted, which can provide multiple benefits:

- Helps markup errors
- Reduces application size
- Removes load and instantiation time

It is highly recommended to have this setting on with all your Xamarin.Forms applications as it will increase the loading speed of your user interfaces (in particular with Android). We can add the compiled XAML by opening up the App.xaml.cs file and pasting the code below the preceding namespace:

```
[assembly:
Xamarin.Forms.Xaml.XamlCompilation(Xamarin.Forms.Xaml.XamlCompilationOption
s.Compile)]
```

If we add up all the performance additions we have applied to the project, we should see some improvement in the user interfaces as they present between different screens.

Creating StockItemDetailsPage

Now we move on to our last page of the application. We are going to add another page for displaying the details of a selected stock item from the previous StocklistPage. Firstly, we need to handle items selected from ListView, so open up StocklistPage.xaml and update the ListView element with the SelectedItem object bound to the Selected item in our view-model (we will add this after the XAML update). This will be set as a TwoWay binding because the data will change from both sides (from the view as we selected items, and the view-model as we will need the selected object data when we navigate to the stock details page):

```
<ListView x:Name="StockItemsListView"
        IsVisible="{Binding InProgress, Converter={StaticResource
notConverter}}"
        CachingStrategy="RecycleElement"
        ItemsSource="{Binding StockItems}"
        ItemTemplate="{StaticResource ListItemTemplate}"
        SelectedItem="{Binding Selected, Mode=TwoWay}"
        RowHeight="100"
        Margin="10, 10, 10, 10"
        Grid.Row="0" Grid.Column="0"/>
```

Now let's add to the `StocklistPageViewModel`; we need to add a `publicStockItemViewModel` property that will hold the data of our binding when an item is selected from the list. The ID property of the selected `StockItemViewModel` will be passed through the navigation parameters for our `StockItemDetailsPage`:

```
private StockItemViewModel _selected;
. . . .
public StockItemViewModel Selected
    {
      get
      {
        return _selected;
      }

      set
      {
        if (value.Equals(_selected))
        {
          return;
        }
        else
        {
          Navigation.Navigate(Enums.PageNames.StockItemDetailsPage, new
Dictionary<string, object>()
          {
            {"id", value.Id},
          }).ConfigureAwait(false);
        }

        _selected = value;
        OnPropertyChanged("Selected");
      }
    }
```

Now let's add the new `StocklistItemDetailsPage`. Create a new XAML `ContentPage` and add the following:

```
<ContentPage.Content>
    <StackLayout Margin="20, 20, 20, 5">
      <Label x:Name="TitleLabel" >
        <Label.FormattedText>
          <FormattedString>
            <Span Text="{x:Static
resx:LabelResources.StockItemDetailsTitle}"
              FontFamily="Arial"
              FontSize="24">
              <Span.ForegroundColor>
```

```
                    <OnPlatform x:TypeArguments="Color"
                        Android="Black"
                        WinPhone="Black"
                        iOS="Black">
                    </OnPlatform>
                </Span.ForegroundColor>
            </Span>
        </FormattedString>
      </Label.FormattedText>
      </Label>
      <Label x:Name="NameLabel" Text="{Binding Name}"
  Style="{StaticResource TitleStyle}"/>
        <controls:CustomLabel x:Name="CategoryLabel" Text="{Binding
  Category}" Style="{StaticResource CustomLabelStyle}"/>
            <controls:CustomLabel x:Name="PriceLabel" Text="{Binding
  Price}" Style="{StaticResource CustomLabelStyle}"/>

        <ActivityIndicator x:Name="ActivityIndicator" IsRunning="{Binding
  InProgress}"/>
      </StackLayout>
    </ContentPage.Content>
```

Looking more closely at the code, we have added four labels and `ActivityIndicator`, which are used to show the progress of our page loading the data. We have also included a custom control `CustomLabel`, we reference this item via the namespace as follows:

```
xmlns:controls="clr-
namespace:Stocklist.XamForms.Controls;assembly=Stocklist.XamForms"
```

Whatever name follows the `xmlns` keyword, this name must be called first to reference the item within the namespace we are trying to use, like this:

```
<controls:CustomLabel/>
```

Now we must create our `CustomLabel` object, which will be used for a `CustomRenderer` for Android, as we are going to set the font of this label to a custom `Typeface`, which we will include in both native projects. Create a new folder called `Controls` in the `Stocklist.XamForms` project, and create the following file, called `CustomLabel.cs`:

```
public class CustomLabel : Label
    {
        public static readonly BindableProperty AndroidFontStyleProperty =
    BindableProperty.Create<CustomLabel, string>(
            p => p.AndroidFontStyle, default(string));

        public string AndroidFontStyle
        {
```

```
        get
        {
            return (string)GetValue(AndroidFontStyleProperty);
        }
        set
        {
            SetValue(AndroidFontStyleProperty, value);
        }
    }
}
```

In our `CustomLabel`, we are adding a custom binding, which will be used specifically to set the font style for Android. When we set the font style on the native side, we have to set the custom font by the filename not the font name, whereas in iOS we reference the custom font by the font name and not the filename.

When we set up custom bindings, we must always include a `static` property, this is our `BindableProperty`, which is used to reference the item of the UI element that we are binding on. Then we must always include the actual property which is referenced in the XAML:

```
<controls:CustomLabel AndroidFontStyle="GraCoRg_" />
```

Custom renderers

You will find `Xamarin.Forms` covers most of the native controls via cross-platform elements such as XAML objects, but there are some UI elements which we must implement ourselves using `CustomRenderers`. `CustomRenderers` allows anyone to override the rendering process for specific controls placed in our XAML, and render native elements on the platform side. We must place a renderer specific to each platform, but for this example, we are only going to apply a custom renderer for the Android project as we want our custom labels to use custom fonts. iOS doesn't need a renderer to allow custom fonts; all we have to do is add the reference to our font file in the `info.plist` file. Open up the `info.plist` file in your iOS project and add a new entry called `Fonts provided by application` (for an array element we simply add the path of our font file `GraCoRg_.ttf`). Then add the font file into the `Resources` folder of the iOS project, make sure the build action of the font file is set to `BundleResource` (do this by right-clicking on the file):

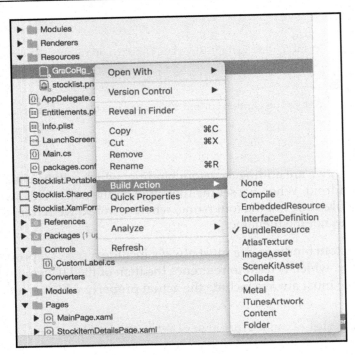

We also want to add this font file into the `Assets` folder of the Android project, and make sure we set the build action to `AndroidAsset`.

You can grab this font file from the GitHub link: `https://github.com/flusharcade/chapter5-stocklist`.

To implement the equivalent for Android, we must create a `CustomRenderer` for the `CustomLabel` item in our `Controls` folder. Open the Android project, create a new folder called `Renderers`, and add a new file called `CustomLabelRenderer`, and implement the following:

```
public class CustomLabelRenderer : LabelRenderer
    {
        protected override void OnElementChanged
(ElementChangedEventArgs<Label> e)
        {
            base.OnElementChanged (e);

            if (!string.IsNullOrEmpty((e.NewElement as
CustomLabel)?.AndroidFontStyle))
            {
                try
```

```
        {
            var font = default(Typeface);

            font =
Typeface.CreateFromAsset(Forms.Context.ApplicationContext.Assets,
(e.NewElement as CustomLabel)?.AndroidFontStyle + ".ttf");

            if (Control != null)
            {
                Control.Typeface = font;
                Control.TextSize = (float)e.NewElement.FontSize;
            }
        }
        catch (Exception ex)
        {
            Console.WriteLine(ex);
        }
    }
}
}
```

In just about all the renderers, we are exposed to the OnElementChanged function which is called when a Xamarin.Forms custom control is created in order to render the corresponding native control. In some circumstances, the OnElementChanged method can be called multiple times, so care must be taken when instantiating a new native control in order to prevent memory leaks, which can have a large performance impact. In our case, we are not rendering a new control, so we only need to check that the NewElement and Control objects are not null when the function is called. We must also cast the NewElement item to our custom item, as this is the object which contains the custom binding for the AndroidFontStyle property. The NewElement will always be the custom item, so we can always cast it.

We can also now access the native UI frameworks; in this case, we are using the Android Typeface framework to create a custom Typeface which will use our font file. Then this Typeface is set to the Typeface property of the Control element (this is the actual element which will be displayed), in this case, because it is a LabelRenderer, the Control element is an Android TextView.

 In other renderers, we can set this control element to specific native elements, which we will be doing in further chapters.

Finally, we have to add the following line to export and register the renderer:

```
[assembly:
Xamarin.Forms.ExportRenderer(typeof(Stocklist.XamForms.Controls.CustomLabel
), typeof(Stocklist.Droid.Renderers.CustomLabel.CustomLabelRenderer))]
```

Adding styles for custom elements

We still have one more addition to finalise the `StockItemDetailsPage`. We are going to add a style for the `CustomLabel`. Open up the `App.xaml` file and add the following style:

```
<Style x:Key="CustomLabelStyle" TargetType="controls:CustomLabel">
            <Setter Property="TextColor" Value="Black" />
        <Setter Property="FontFamily" Value="Gravur-Condensed" />
        <Setter Property="AndroidFontStyle" Value="GraCoRg_" />
            </Style>
```

We have included a `Setter` for the `AndroidFontStyle` property we created earlier. Don't forget we must also add the namespace reference for the `Controls`:

```
xmlns:controls="clr-
namespace:Stocklist.XamForms.Controls;assembly=Stocklist.XamForms"
```

That's everything for the user interface. Now let's move on to implementing the view-model for the `StockItemDetailsPage`.

Creating StockItemDetailsPageViewModel

Now we move on to the last view-model in our application. Add a new file called `StockItemDetailsPageViewModel` to our ViewModels folder in the `Stocklist.Portable` project.

Let's start by implementing the `private` properties:

```
#region Private Properties

        private readonly IStocklistWebServiceController
_stocklistWebServiceController;

        private int _id;

        private string _name;
```

```
private string _category;

private decimal _price;

private bool _inProgress;
#endregion
```

You should be able to add the `public` properties yourself. Here is the first to get you started:

```
public int Id
    {
        get
        {
            return _id;
        }

        set
        {
            if (value.Equals(_id))
            {
                return;
            }

            _id = value;
            OnPropertyChanged("Id");
        }
    }
```

Now we need to add the `LoadAsync` function, which will use `StocklistWebServiceController` to pull the data from our API for a specific `StockItem`. Notice the use of the `InProgress` property, this is used to track the loading progress; as we are downloading in the background we want to display this progress to the user interface via an `ActivityIndicator`:

```
#region Methods

    protected override async Task LoadAsync(IDictionary<string, object>
parameters)
    {
        InProgress = true;

        if (parameters.ContainsKey("id"))
        {
            Id = (int)parameters["id"];
        }
```

```
            var contract = await
_stocklistWebServiceController.GetStockItem(Id);

            if (contract != null)
            {
                this.Name = contract.Name;
                this.Category = contract.Category;
                this.Price = contract.Price;
            }

            InProgress = false;
        }

        #endregion
```

Then we add our constructor which will pull out the registered IoC objects and assign our `private` properties accordingly:

```
#region Constructors

        public StockItemDetailsPageViewModel(INavigationService navigation,
IStocklistWebServiceController stocklistWebServiceController,
            Func<Action, ICommand> commandFactory) : base(navigation)
        {
            _stocklistWebServiceController = stocklistWebServiceController;
        }

        #endregion
```

Finally, we need to register the view-model in the `CommonModule`:

```
builer.RegisterType<StockItemDetailsPageViewModel>().InstancePerDependency(
);
```

Add the extra enum for the `StockItemDetailsPage` to `PageEnums.cs`:

```
public enum PageNames
    {
        MainPage,

        StocklistPage,

        StockItemDetailsPage
    }
```

And add the extra switch case to `NavigationService`:

```
case PageNames.StockItemDetailsPage:
                    return IoC.Resolve<Func<StockItemDetailsPage>>()();
```

Setting up the native platform projects

Now we move on to the native platform layer and prepare the iOS, Android, and Windows Phone projects. We are going to start with iOS; let's start by adding the NuGet packages required for the project:

- Microsoft HTTP client libraries
- Modern HTTP client
- Autofac
- Reactive extensions (main library)

Once we've added these packages to the project, let's open the `AppDelegate` file and add the same `InitIoC` function we used in the `Locator` project:

```
private void InitIoC()
{
  IoC.CreateContainer();
  IoC.RegisterModule(new DroidModule());
  IoC.RegisterModule(new SharedModule(false));
  IoC.RegisterModule(new XamFormsModule());
  IoC.RegisterModule(new PortableModule());
  IoC.StartContainer();
}
```

Then call this method before we load the application:

```
public override bool FinishedLaunching(UIApplication app, NSDictionary
options)
        {
            global::Xamarin.Forms.Forms.Init();

            InitIoC();

            LoadApplication(new App());

            return base.FinishedLaunching(app, options);
        }
```

Before running the iOS application, let's also set up the Android project. We want to start by adding the same libraries as iOS, then opening `MainActivity.cs`, and adding the same function `InitIoC` as shown in the preceding example. Then, finally, we call the `InitIoC` function before we load the application:

```
protected override void OnCreate(Bundle bundle)
    {
        base.OnCreate(bundle);

        InitIoC();

        global::Xamarin.Forms.Forms.Init(this, bundle);

        LoadApplication(new App());
    }
```

Simple, right? See how much code we are simply copying from another project?

The more problems we solve in other projects, the quicker we can piece together apps that have similar functionality.

Hosting the Web API project locally

Before we can access the API layer from our mobile application, we have to set up hosting. For this example, we are going to walkthrough setup for hosting locally.

Hosting locally does not require much work, but it will require an instance of Windows and Mac OSX running together. You can achieve this by simply running parallels, or using a **Windows** and **Mac** computer.

Our first step is to open Visual Studio from our Windows instance and click the run button:

When the project starts, it will automatically open up your default web browser and show the application.

Since we don't have any visible web pages, we don't need to have the browser open. If the project is running, the web API will be running so we will be able to ping it over an HTTP request.

Now that we have the backend running, how do we access the API?

If you are running via two separate computers, we should be able to simply access the API through the IP address of the computer. In order to find out the IP address of the computer, open up a new command prompt window and type in `ipconfig`. This will display the IPv4 address that the computer has been assigned to on the current network.

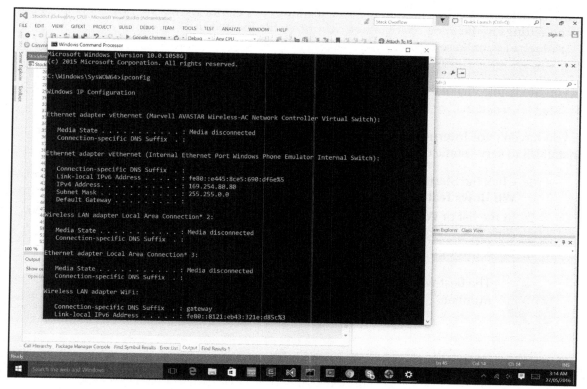

In order for the local set up to work, please make sure both the mobile device and the computer hosting the WEB API are both on the same **WIFI/LAN** connection.

To confirm we have this working, paste the following URL into a web browser on the Windows instance and see if we get results:

```
"localhost:{port}/api/StockItems"
```

 The port is automatically assigned when the project is run, so when the browser appears with the localhost URL, paste the URL extension `api/StockItems`.

Now we want to test this link on the Mac instance, but before we do, we have to change some settings in the `applicationhost.config` file located in `"C:\Users[YourName]\Documents\IISExpress\config\applicationhost.config"`.

If you are using Visual Studio 2015, it will be located in `/{project folder}/.vs/config/applicationhost.config`.

If you haven't got **Internet Information Services (IIS)** switched on, follow these steps, to install IIS to serve static content:

1. Click the Start button, click **Control Panel**, click **Programs**, and then click **Turn Windows features** on or off.
2. In the list of **Windows features**, select **Internet Information Services**, and then click **OK**.
3. Look through the file until you can file your application entry like this:

 The best way to find your particular entry is by searching for the `port` number.

```
<site name="Stocklist" id="43">
        <application path="/"
        applicationPool="Clr4IntegratedAppPool">
            <virtualDirectory path="/"
physicalPath="C:\Users\Michael\Documents\Stocklist\Stocklist" />
        </application>
        <bindings>
```

```
        <binding protocol="http" bindingInformation="*:
        {PORT}:localhost" />
    </bindings>
</site>
```

4. In the `<bindings>` section, we want to add another row:

```
<binding protocol="http" bindingInformation="*:{PORT}:{IPv4
Address}" />
```

5. Now we want to allow incoming connections on this `PORT` and `IPv4 Address` from other computers.

 If you're running Windows 7, most incoming connections are locked down, so you need to specifically allow incoming connections to your application.

6. First, start an administrative command prompt and run these commands, replacing `{IPv4}:{PORT}` with the `IPv4 Address` and `PORT` you are using:

```
> netsh http add urlacl url=http://{IPv4}:{PORT}/ user=everyone
```

7. This just tells `http.sys that it's OK to talk to this URL`. Next, run the following command:

```
> netsh advfirewall firewall add rule name="IISExpressWeb"
dir=in protocol=tcp localport={PORT} profile=private
remoteip=localsubnet action=allow
```

8. This adds a rule in the Windows Firewall, allowing incoming connections to the port for computers on your local subnet.

9. Now we should be able to access the running API from our Mac instance. This time, paste the URL with the IPv4 address instead of `localhost`: `{IPv4 address}:{port}/api/StockItems`.

10. If all was successful, we should have the following XML layout displayed like this:

11. Excellent! Now let's add these URL settings to our mobile application. Open up the `Config.resx` file in the `Resources` folder of the `Stocklist.Portable` project, and fill in these values:

```
<data name="ApiAllItems" xml:space="preserve">
    <value>http://{IPv4}:{PORT}/api/StockItems</value>
</data>
<data name="GetById" xml:space="preserve">
    <value>http://{IPv4}:{PORT}/api/GetItemById</value>
</data>
```

Now let's test our project on iOS and Android, and we should be able to see our `StocklistPage` fill with items from our API controller.

Summary

In this chapter, we have built an application for retrieving a web service using `Xamarin.Forms`. We set up a `ListView` and created an `ObservableCollection` for displaying JSON objects. We also learned how to set up a simple web service on the back end. In the next chapter, we will create an application for both iOS and Android using the native libraries. We will use Signal R on the client and server side, and set up a hub and proxy connections via a client.

6
Building a Chat Application

In this chapter, we will be moving back into Xamarin native. Our user interface will move away from an MVVM design and follow a new paradigm called **Model-View-Presenter (MVP)**. We will also step further into the backend and setup a SignalR hub and client to simulate a chat service, which data will be sent between the server and clients instantly as the messages become available. Another key topic of focus is project architecture, spending time on separating the project into modules, and creating a nicely tiered structure that will maximize code sharing across different platforms.

The following knowledge is expected:

- Some understanding of Xamarin native (iOS and Android)
- Visual Studio
- Some understanding of the OWIN specification
- Some understanding of OAuth

In this chapter, you will learn the following:

- The Model-View-Presenter (MVP) pattern
- Architecture
- SignalR
- Starting with Open Web Interface for .NET (OWIN)
- Creating an authorization server using OWIN OAuth 2.0
- `OAuthAuthorizationServerProvider`
- Authorization server providers
- `UseOAuthBearerAuthentication`
- Setting up the Authentication Repository
- Configuring the Web API

- Building the AccountController
- Configuring OAuth Authentication with our Web API
- Building the SignalR Hub
- Setting up mobile projects
- Creating the `SignalRClient`
- Building the Web API access layer
- Application State
- Setting up the navigation service
- Building the iOS navigation service
- Building the Android navigation service
- Building the iOS interface
- Handling Hub proxy callbacks
- Implementing the `LoginPresenter`
- Creating the connection between Presenter and View
- Building the `LoginActivity`
- Implementing the `ClientsListPresenter`
- Creating the `ClientListViewController`
- The `TaskCompletionSource` framework
- Creating the `ClientsListActivity`
- Overriding the Activity `OnBackPressed()`
- Building the `ListAdapter`
- Building the `ChatPresenter`
- Building the iOS `ChatView`
- Extending the `UIColor` framework
- Android `TableLayouts`
- Building the Android `ChatActivity`
- Running the server and clients

The Model-View-Presenter (MVP) pattern

In all our previous chapters we have focused our development patterns around the **Model-View-View-Model (MVVM)** approach. This time we are going to be setting up our project around the MVP design pattern. In MVP the presenter centralizes the user interface functionality between the model and the view, meaning all presentation logic is pushed to the presenter.

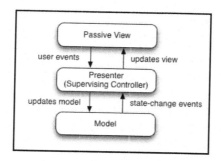

So why bother with this approach?

The advantage with this approach is we can apply unit testing to our presenters, meaning all UI logic is tested via the presenter. We also have the ability to keep our user interfaces in native, and share a great amount of the UI logic between the different platforms.

Architecture

When it comes to cross-platform applications, our goal is to share as much code as possible. We focus our attention on architecture, having a nice clean project structure that lends itself to a maximization of code sharing across platforms. So how do we solve this problem? Ask yourself:

- What are the different layers?
- How do we set up the folder structure?
- What parts go in which projects?

There are many different approaches to this problem; here are some of the most common architectural layers:

- **Data layer**: This stores the database
- **Data access layer**: This layer focuses on the objects and wrappers that apply operations on the data layer (Read, Write, Update)
- **Business layer (logic)**: This layer focuses on the different domains (domain-driven design), separating the different areas of logic into objects that handle operations for each domain
- **Service access layer**: The area that focuses operations on the web API, how we handle JSON, and data sent and received between the API Controllers
- **Application/platform layer**: Code which is not shared, specific to the native platform
- **Common layer**: A shared project, code which is shared to all native projects
- **User interface layer**: The layer which contains all the UI design (XAML sheets, UIViewControllers, AXML)

How do we determine which layers our project needs?

In this example it is quite simple; we don't have a database so we don't need the data layer or data access layer. Everything else we will require, so let's begin building our project from the ground up, starting with the lower layers first.

We are going to start building the project from the service access layer; it will include everything involved with SignalR, so our first step is to build the backend SignalR hub.

SignalR

SignalR is a library that provides real-time web functionality to applications using WebSocket transport (if HTML 5 is supported; older transport methods will be used if it is not supported). It has the ability for a server to push data to its clients in real-time as it becomes available; this means we do not have to repeatedly ask the server for data (such as refreshing/recalling the Web API).

In order to set up SignalR, we must first set up a SignalR **Hub** on the server side; our clients (mobile projects) will use access this **Hub** by creating a **HubConnection** and creating a **HubProxy** from which the server and client can call functions on either side.

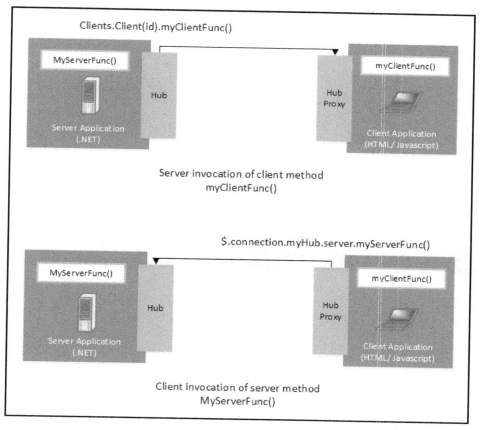

Now let's get into development; we will have the same hardware set up as the last chapter. We will set up a locally hosted backend via Visual Studio and build our mobile projects via Xamarin Studio on MacOSX. Open up Visual Studio, create a `newASP.NET` web application, and call it `Chat`.

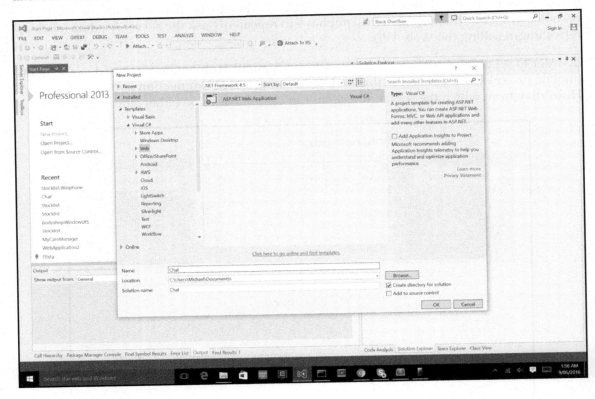

Then we must select a template; select the **Empty** template:

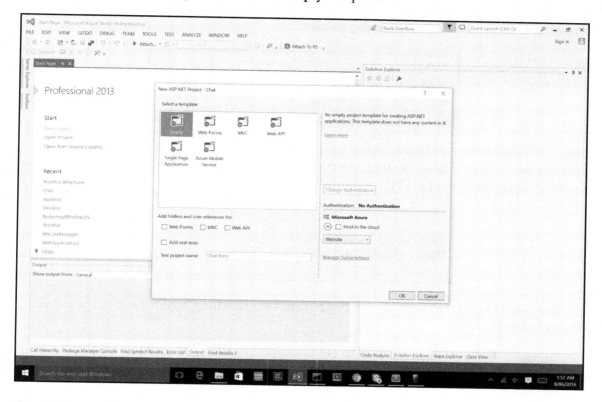

Great! We now have our empty project, let's start by adding the NuGet
package, **Microsoft.AspNet.SignalR**.

A readme file will appear with some basic directions on setting up the SignalR **Hub**. We also want to add Web API 2.2 features for OWIN as we will be adding a small Web API to the project to handle login, register, and account functionality. Let's add in the following libraries:

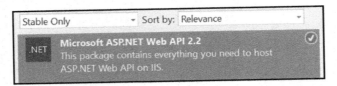

This will install Web API functionality so we can create API controllers and map routes through the `Startup` class. We then want to add the Web API 2.2 OWIN library to integrate the OWIN pipeline to our HTTP configuration:

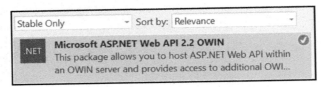

We also want to add the `OWIN.Security` libraries for handling account authorization using **Bearer tokens**.

Bearer tokens are used in HTTP request headers for authorizing access to OAuth 2.0 protected resources.

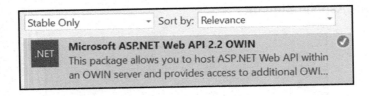

Finally, we have to add another package called
`Microsoft.AspNet.Identity.Framework`. This library will be used to handle storage of user accounts (usernames and passwords) using the `UserManager` framework.

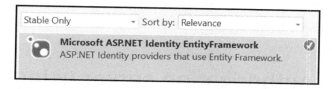

Now that we have all our packages added, let's start building the web application from the ground up.

Starting with Open Web Interface for .NET (OWIN)

OWIN is a standard interface between .NET servers and web applications. It provides a middleware for decoupling a web server from a web application. The biggest advantage of OWIN is that we are able to host the web application anywhere, and keep the server and application completely separated.

> For more information on OWIN, the best place to start is with the Katana Project. Katana is a collection of projects that support OWIN with various Microsoft components.

So what does OWIN have to do with our project?

If you notice the code above we see all references to OWIN namespaces, and we register in the assembly the `OwinStartup` object to our `Startup` class. We must have at least one `Startup` class registered in the `OwinStartup` attribute. The `Startup` class has one function called `Configuration`. All `Startup` classes must include this function, and it must accept `IAppBuilder`. Additional services, such as `IHostingEnvironment` and `ILoggerFactory` may also be specified, in which case these services will be injected by the server if they are available. The `Configuration` specifies how the application will respond to individual HTTP requests. Finally, in our `Configuration` method, we will be calling the `MapSignalR` (an extension to the `IAppBuilder` object). This will define the route for clients to use to connect to your **Hub/s.**

The route is set to the app builder pipeline at the URL `/signalr` by default: we can also customize this URL if required.

Our next step is to bring in some security.

Creating an authorization server using OWIN OAuth 2.0

The OAuth 2.0 framework enables a server to provide clients with limited access for HTTP services. Protected server resources can only be accessed via access tokens that expire after certain periods of time. Clients will shoot a HTTP request at a domain endpoint URL (normally `/token`), the server will send a response with token details (such as expiration, access token, time/date issued), and the access token will be used for a period of time with other HTTP request headers to authorize access to protected resources.

Access tokens are strings denoting specified scope, lifetime, and other access attributes.

So where do we begin to set up server authorization?

Our first step is to build the logic behind granting clients access from username and password credentials.

OAuthAuthorizationServerProvider

An `OAuthAuthorizationServerProvider` determines how we validate user credentials using `OAuthGrantResourceOwnerCredentialsContext`. Its job is to simply handle the authentication of users. This item provides the context in which we handle resource grants.

Let's add a new folder called `Providers`, and add a new file in this folder called `AuthorizationServerProvider.cs`. Implement the following:

```
public class AuthorizationServerProvider : OAuthAuthorizationServerProvider
    {
        public override async Task
ValidateClientAuthentication(OAuthValidateClientAuthenticationContext
context)
```

```
        {
            context.Validated();
        }
        public override async Task
    GrantResourceOwnerCredentials(OAuthGrantResourceOwnerCredentialsContext
    context)
        {
            context.OwinContext.Response.Headers.Add("Access-Control-Allow-
    Origin", new[] { "*" });
            string userName = null;
            using (AuthenticationRepository authenticationRepository = new
    AuthenticationRepository())
            {
                IdentityUser user = await
    authenticationRepository.FindUser(context.UserName, context.Password);
                if (user == null)
                {
                    context.SetError("invalid_grant", "Incorrect user name
    or password");
                    return;
                }
                userName = user.UserName;
            }
            var identity = new
    ClaimsIdentity(context.Options.AuthenticationType);
            identity.AddClaim(new Claim("Role", "User"));
            identity.AddClaim(new Claim("UserName", userName));
            context.Validated(identity);
        }
    }
```

Our implementation of the `OAuthAuthorizationServerProvider` will override the `ValidateClientAuthentication` function, which simply returns whether the `usercontext` has been validated. We then override the `GrantResourceOwnerCredentials()` function, which is called when a request to the token endpoint (`/token`) arrives with a `grant_type` of `password` (this key is set in the request header along with the username and password). The function will simply initialize a new `AuthenticationRepository` to access the `UserManager` framework and check if the user exists; if it doesn't we return, and the context will still be invalid. If the user exists, we create a new `ClaimsIdentity` object with two claims, one for the *role* and *username* principles of there source owner (the user who sent the HTTP request). Finally, we then place the `ClaimsIdentity` object into the `context.Validated()` function in order to issue the access token. This `ClaimsIdentity` object is now the ticket that contains the claims about the resource owner (the user) associated with the access token.

A ClaimsIdentity is an object that is a collection of Claim objects to represent an entity's identity. Each Claim object is simply a statement describing an identity's role, permission, or an other quality of an entity.

Use OAuthBearerAuthentication

Our next step is to add the logic behind handling bearer tokens (these are the access tokens granted by the authorization server provider). UseOAuthBearerAuthentication has the job of ensuring that only authenticated users can access your protected server resources (in our example the ChatHub). Add a new file called OAuthBearerTokenAuthenticationProvider.cs and implement the following:

```
public class OAuthBearerTokenAuthenticationProvider :
OAuthBearerAuthenticationProvider
    {
        public override Task RequestToken(OAuthRequestTokenContext context)
        {
            string cookieToken = null;
            string queryStringToken = null;
            string headerToken = null;
            try
            {
                cookieToken =
context.OwinContext.Request.Cookies["BearerToken"];
            }
            catch (NullReferenceException)
            {
                System.Diagnostics.Debug.WriteLine("The cookie does not
contain the bearer token");
            }
            try
            {
                queryStringToken =
context.OwinContext.Request.Query["BearerToken"].ToString();
            }
            catch (NullReferenceException)
            {
                System.Diagnostics.Debug.WriteLine("The query string does
not contain the bearer token");
            }
            try
            {
                headerToken =
context.OwinContext.Request.Headers["BearerToken"];
```

```
        }
        catch (NullReferenceException)
        {
            System.Diagnostics.Debug.WriteLine("The connection header
does not contain the bearer token");
        }
        if (!String.IsNullOrEmpty(cookieToken))
            context.Token = cookieToken;
        else if (!String.IsNullOrEmpty(queryStringToken))
            context.Token = queryStringToken;
        else if (!String.IsNullOrEmpty(headerToken))
            context.Token = headerToken;
        return Task.FromResult<object>(null);
    }
}
```

Let's look at this item more closely. We are overriding the `RequestToken()` function to access the `OAuthRequestTokenContext` from every HTTP request that hits the server. Inside the `OwinContext` object, we can access the HTTP request that just hit the server, check through the dictionary of headers for our `BearerToken`, and then extract this access token and assign it to the `OAuthRequestTokenContext.Token` property.

Setting up the AuthenticationRepository

Now we move on to the `AuthenticationRepository`. This is the object that will handle access and storage using the `UserManager` framework provided by the `Identity.EntityFramework` library. Add in a new folder called `Repositories`, then add a new file called `AuthenticationRepository.cs`, and implement the following:

> The `UserManager` class is a facade for providing identity management in any ASP.Net application

```
public class AuthenticationRepository : IDisposable
    {
        private AuthenticationContext authenticationContext;
        private UserManager<IdentityUser> userManager;
        public AuthenticationRepository()
        {
            authenticationContext = new AuthenticationContext();
            userManager = new UserManager<IdentityUser>(new
UserStore<IdentityUser>(authenticationContext));
        }
```

```
public async Task<IdentityResult> RegisterUser(UserModel userModel)
{
    IdentityUser newUser = new IdentityUser()
    {
        UserName = userModel.Username
    };
    var foundUser = await
userManager.FindByNameAsync(newUser.UserName);
    if (foundUser != null)
    {
        await userManager.RemovePasswordAsync(foundUser.Id);
        return await userManager.AddPasswordAsync(foundUser.Id,
userModel.Password);
    }
    else
    {
        return await userManager.CreateAsync(newUser,
userModel.Password);
    }
}
public async Task<IdentityUser> FindUser(string userName, string
password)
{
    return await userManager.FindAsync(userName, password);
}
public void Dispose()
{
    authenticationContext.Dispose();
    userManager.Dispose();
}
}
```

Our main concern here involves two functions, one for registering users if they don't exist, and one for finding users. The authorization server provider uses `FindUser` to determine whether a user exists to confirm authentication.

We also need to add another file called `AuthenticationContext.cs` and implement the following:

```
public class AuthenticationContext : IdentityDbContext<IdentityUser>
{
    public AuthenticationContext()
        : base("AuthenticationContext")
    {
    }
}
```

This is a very simple class which inherits the `IdentityDBContext` of type `IdentityUser`. This object is the access layer for retrieving data objects (`IdentityUser` objects) via the `EntityFramework`. The following diagram shows the layers of logic between your ASP.Net application and `EntityFramework`:

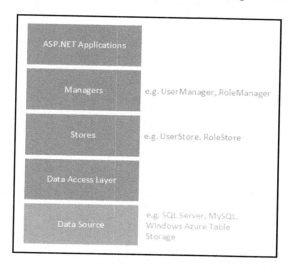

Fantastic! Hopefully those topic weren't too confusing. Now let's start building the Web API.

Configuring the Web API

Our next step is to configure the Web API. Let's add in a new folder called `App_Start`. Inside this folder add a new file called `WebApiConfig.cs` and implement the following:,

```
public static class WebApiConfig
    {
        public static void Register(HttpConfiguration config)
        {
            config.Routes.MapHttpRoute(
                name: "DefaultApi",
                routeTemplate: "api/{controller}/{action}/{id}",
                defaults: new { id = RouteParameter.Optional }
            );
        }
    }
```

Look more closely at the `routeTemplate`; notice the `{action}` addition? This means we have to include the `ActionName` attribute with each function in our `AccountController`. The `ActionName` attribute represents the URL extension, for example:

```
ActionName("Register") = http://{IP Address}:{Port}/Register
```

Now let's add another file called `Startup.cs` and implement the following:,

```
public class Startup
    {
        public void Configuration(IAppBuilder app)
        {
            HttpConfiguration config = new HttpConfiguration();
            WebApiConfig.Register(config);
            app.UseWebApi(config);
        }
    }
```

Now let's move on to building the `AccountController` to handle incoming HTTP requests for user login and registration.

Building the AccountController

Now that we have configured the Web API, let's build the first API controller. Add in a new folder called `Models`. Inside this folder, add a new file called `UserModel.cs`, and implement the following:

```
public class UserModel {
        [Required]
        public string Username { get; set; }
        [Required]
        public string Password { get; set; }
    }
```

The object will contain the username and password fields passed in through the HTTP request from the client. The `Register` attribute is used to make sure that this property is included with the HTTP request. We can then map this attribute to the API controller `ModelState.IsValid` check, so if any of the properties with this attribute are missing, the `IsValid` property will be `false`. Next, let's add in another folder called `Controllers`. Inside this folder add in a new file, `AccountController.cs`, and implement the following:

```
public class AccountController : ApiController
    {
        private AuthenticationRepository authenticationRepository;
```

```
    public AccountController()
    {
        authenticationRepository = new AuthenticationRepository();
    }

    [HttpPost]
    [AllowAnonymous]
    [ActionName("Register")]
    public async Task<IHttpActionResult> Register(UserModel userModel)
    {
        if (!ModelState.IsValid)
        {
            return BadRequest(ModelState);
        }

        var result = await
authenticationRepository.RegisterUser(userModel);
        return Ok();
    }
}
```

Our first step is the `Register` function, which is responsible for storing a new user into the `UserManager` through the `AccountRepository`.

Notice the if statement on `ModalState.IsValid`?

If either the `Username` or `Password` properties are missing from the HTTP request, it will return `false`.

Let's now add the `Login` function:

```
    [HttpPost]
        [AllowAnonymous]
        [ActionName("Login")]
        public async Task<bool> Login(UserModel userModel)
        {
            if (!ModelState.IsValid)
            {
                return false;
            }
            var result = await
            authenticationRepository.FindUser(userModel.Username,
            userModel.Password);
            return (result != null);
        }
```

This is exactly the same as `Register` but we are using the `FindUser` function to check if the user exists in the `UserManager`. Finally, to avoid any memory leakage, we need to make sure that the `AuthenticationRepostiory` is disposed when the API controller is disposed. Let's override the `Dispose` function like this:

```
protected override void Dispose(bool disposing)
{
    if (disposing)
        authenticationRepository.Dispose();

    base.Dispose(disposing);
}
```

Great! That's everything for the `AccountController`, now we must integrate the OAuth authentication and Web API together.

Configuring OAuth Authentication with our Web API

In order to integrate our OAuth module with the Web API we must add some extra configuration in `Startup.cs`. Add in a new function called `ConfigureOAuth` like this:

```
public class Startup
    {
        ...

public void ConfigureOAuth(IAppBuilder app)
        {
            OAuthAuthorizationServerOptions OAuthServerOptions = new
OAuthAuthorizationServerOptions()
            {
                AllowInsecureHttp = true,
                TokenEndpointPath = new PathString("/token"),
                AccessTokenExpireTimeSpan = TimeSpan.FromDays(1),
                Provider = new AuthorizationServerProvider()
            };
            app.UseOAuthAuthorizationServer(OAuthServerOptions);
            app.UseOAuthBearerAuthentication(new
OAuthBearerAuthenticationOptions()
            {
                Provider = new OAuthBearerTokenAuthenticationProvider()
            });
        }
```

. . .
}

Looking more closely, we start with instantiating a new
OAuthAuthorizationServerOptions object, we set the endpoint URL, expiration period
for an access token, and the provider is set to our AuthorizationServerProvider class
created in the preceding example. We then add this object into the IAppBuilder object
using the function UseOAuthAuthorizationServer. Finally, we create a new
OAuthBearerAuthenticationOptions object where the provider is set to our
OAuthBearerTokenAuthenticationProvider object created in the preceding example.

That's all for now; we now have OAuth authentication integrated with our Web API. Now
let's implement the final part of our server application.

Building the SignalR Hub

The ChatHub will be responsible for routing messages between clients using a
ConnectionId. Let's add in a new file called ChatHub and start with overriding the
OnConnected and OnDisconnected functions:

```
[Authorize]
    public class ChatHub : Hub
    {
        public static readonly ConcurrentDictionary<string, SigRUser> Users
            = new ConcurrentDictionary<string,
SigRUser>(StringComparer.InvariantCultureIgnoreCase);
    public override Task OnConnected()
        {
            var userName = (Context.User.Identity as
ClaimsIdentity).Claims.FirstOrDefault(claim => claim.Type ==
"UserName").Value;
            string connectionId = Context.ConnectionId;
            var user = Users.GetOrAdd(userName, _ => new SigRUser
            {
                Name = userName,
                ConnectionIds = new HashSet<string>()
            });
            lock (user.ConnectionIds)
            {
                user.ConnectionIds.Add(connectionId);
                NotifyOtherConnectedUsers(userName);
            }
            return base.OnConnected();
        }
```

```
        public override Task OnDisconnected(bool stopCalled)
        {
            var userName = (Context.User.Identity as
    ClaimsIdentity).Claims.FirstOrDefault(claim => claim.Type ==
    "UserName").Value;
            string connectionId = Context.ConnectionId;
            SigRUser user;
            Users.TryGetValue(userName, out user);
            if (user != null)
            {
                lock (user.ConnectionIds)
                {
                    SigRUser removedUser;
                    Users.TryRemove(userName, out removedUser);
                    NotifyOtherConnectedUsers(userName);
                }
            }
            return base.OnDisconnected(stopCalled);
        }
    }
```

HashSetUsers is static because we are going to use this later on in our
AccountController.

Notice the Authorize attribute?

This is how we created a protected server resource; only clients with granted access tokens
can connect to the ChatHub.

Now let's turn our attention to the OnConnected function. When a client connects to
the ChatHub, the username is retrieved from the HubCallerContext property, which is
actually a ClaimsIdentity object. When we login through the AccountController,
inside the AuthorizationServerProvider we store the identity object inside the context
when the function GrantResourceOwnerCredentials is called. We also store a Claim
object of type username inside the identity, which we can now retrieve from the user's
identity in the HubCallerContext. This is how we integrate OAuth with SignalR.

Now that we have the username, we are going to try and retrieve a `SigRUser` object from the `ConcurrentDictionary`; if the username doesn't exist we create a new `SignRUser` and add it to the `HashSet`. We then lock the `ConnectionIdsConcurrentDictionary` making it thread safe as multiple threads (different user connections) can make changes on this property. Inside the lock statement we add the new `ConnectionId` and notify all other usernames connected to the `ChatHub` using the function `NotifyOtherConnectedUsers`. Let's now add this function to the `ChatHub`:

```
public void NotifyOtherConnectedUsers(string userName)
    {
        var connectionIds = Users.Where(x => !x.Key.Contains(userName))
        .SelectMany(x => x.Value.ConnectionIds)
        .Distinct();
        foreach (var cid in connectionIds)
        {
            Clients.Client(cid).displayMessage("clients",
JsonConvert.SerializeObject(Users.Select(x => x.Key)));
        }
    }
```

This function will call `displayMessage`, sending a serialized JSON object of the `ConcurrentDictionary Users` to all other connected clients (we will see why later).

Now let's turn our attention to the `OnDisconnected` function. This function will simply check there is a `SigRUser` with the username equal to the one retrieved from the `HubCallerContext` object. If this user exists, we try and remove it from the `ConcurrentDictionary` and call the `NotifyOtherConnectedUsers` again sending the updated dictionary of clients to the remaining connected clients.

> We call this function every time a user connects or disconnects to the hub, so in our mobile application we can update a list of connected clients in real time without refreshing the page.

Now that we can handle an updated list of connected clients, our last step is to add the function which will send a message between two clients. The `Send` function will be called through the client's hub proxy with two parameters (message and username):

```
public void Send(string message, string to)
    {
        SigRUser receiver;
        if (Users.TryGetValue(to, out receiver))
        {
            var userName = (Context.User.Identity as
ClaimsIdentity).Claims.FirstOrDefault(claim => claim.Type ==
```

```
"UserName").Value;
                SigRUser sender;
                Users.TryGetValue(userName, out sender);

                lock (receiver.ConnectionIds)
                {
                    foreach (var cid in receiver.ConnectionIds)
                    {
                        Clients.Client(cid).displayMessage("chat",
message);
                    }
                }
            }
        }
    }
```

That's all for our backend. We have now created our first addition to the server's service access layer.

> The server service access layer will sit in a different service access layer to the mobile projects. With server and client code, each side of the system will have its own architecture and layers.

Now let's move onto the client side and start building our mobile applications.

Setting up mobile projects

Now we move back to the mobile side; in our mobile projects we are going to be setting up SignalR clients on both Android and iOS natively. We will also be creating a presenter layer to share the UI logic between both native platforms. Open up Xamarin Studio and create a new shared project called `Chat.Common`; inside this project add two empty folders called `Model` and `Presenter`.

We then want to create a **single view iOS application**, a **general Android application** and a shared project called `Chat.ServiceAccess`. Our project structure will look like this:

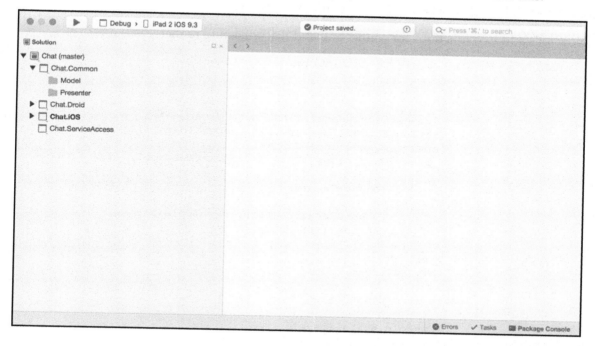

Creating the SignalRClient

We are going to start implementing a new class called `SignalRClient`. This will sit in the service access layer, the shared project called `Chat.ServiceAccess`. Create a new file called `SignalRClient.cs`, and implement the following:

```
public class SignalRClient
    {
        private readonly HubConnection _connection;
        private readonly IHubProxy _proxy;
        public event EventHandler<Tuple<string, string>> OnDataReceived;
        public SignalRClient()
        {
            _connection = new HubConnection("http://{IP
Address}:{Port}/");
            _proxy = _connection.CreateHubProxy("ChatHub");
        }
    }
```

Now let's look more closely. We have two `readonly` properties in which we only initialize once when the object is created, the hub connection which is set to the server URL, and the `HubProxy` which is created off the connection to the server.

Now let's add two functions for connecting and disconnecting to the `ChatHub`:

```
public async Task<bool> Connect(string accessToken)
{
    try
    {
        _connection.Headers.Add("Authorization",
        string.Format("Bearer {0}", accessToken));
        await _connection.Start();
        _proxy.On<string, string>("displayMessage", (id, data) =>
        {
            if (OnDataReceived != null)
            {
                OnDataReceived(this, new Tuple<string,
                string>(id, data));
            }
        });
        return true;
    }
    catch (Exception e)
    {
        Console.WriteLine(e);
    }
    return false;
}
public void Disconnect()
{
    _connection.Stop();
    _connection.Dispose();
}
```

The `Connect` function requires an access token which we add to the `Headers` dictionary of the `HubConnection` object.

The access token is used as a Bearer token to authorize access to the `ChatHub`.

The function On called from the proxy takes in two parameters, the name of the function on the server we are listening for, and the action that will be performed every time this function is called on the Hub's connected clients. In this example, our proxy will fire this action whenever two strings are received from the server. The first string is an ID for the data passed in the second string (this could be a JSON list of connected clients or it could be a simple chat message). This data will then be passed a Tuple<string, string> object to the EventHandler.

> We can call On for multiple functions, and fire different actions for as many different functions being called on the Hub.

The Disconnect function simply closes the connection and disposes the HubConnection object. Finally, we add another function for invoking the Send function via the ChatHub object on the server:

```
public async Task SendMessageToClient(string user, string message)
{
    await _proxy.Invoke("Send", new object[]
    {
        message,
        user
    });
}
```

When we invoke server functions, we use an array of objects, in order to match the parameters required on the server function.

Since the `SignalRClient` will sit in a shared project, the same code will be used for each different platform, but the libraries referenced from the `using` statements will come from each platform project. Now let's have both the iOS and Android projects reference this shared project. We also want to add the `Microsoft.AspNet.SignalR.Client` NuGet package for all the platform projects (iOS and Android).

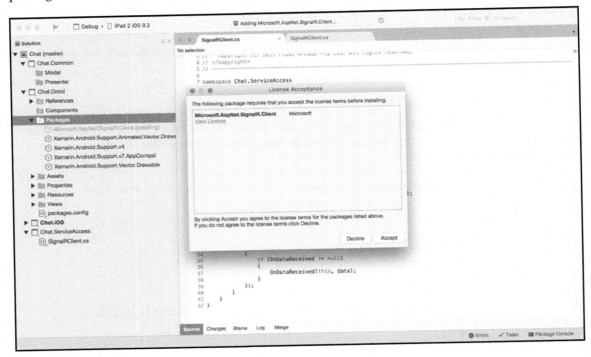

If you are trying to add the NuGet package for SignalR version 2.2.0 with Xamarin.iOS 1.0, the package will fail to add. If so, visit the following link and add the correct `.dll` files from the `lib` folder to each platform project's references: `https://components.xamarin.com/auth?redirect_to=%2fdownload%2fsignalr`.

To add the references correctly, right-click the folder **References** for each project, click the **.Net assembly** tab, and click the **Browse** button to add the `.dll` files (`Microsoft.AspNet.SignalR.Client`, `System.Net.Http.Extensions`, and `System.Net.Http.Primitives`).

For each platform project, we also need to add the `Json.Net` package from NuGet, then right-click on the **References,** click the **All** tab, and select **System.Net** and **System.Net.Http**.

Now that we have **SignalR** configured, let's move on to building the `WebApiAccess` layer.

Building the WebApiAccess layer

Our `WebApiAccess` object will be mapped to the `AccountController` on the server. Let's add in a new file called `WebApiAccess.cs`, and implement the `LoginAsync` function:

```
public class WebApiAccess
    {
        private string _baseAddress = "http://{IP Address}:{Port}/";
        public async Task<bool> LoginAsync(string name, string password,
        CancellationToken? cancellationToken = null)
        {
            var httpMessage = new HttpRequestMessage(HttpMethod.Post,
            new Uri(_baseAddress + "api/Account/Login"))
            {
```

```
                    Content = new StringContent(string.Format
                        ("Username={0}&Password={1}", name, password),
Encoding.UTF8,
                        "application/x-www-form-urlencoded"),
                };
                var client = new HttpClient();
                var response = await client.SendAsync(httpMessage,
                cancellationToken ?? new CancellationToken(false));
                switch (response.StatusCode)
                {
                    case HttpStatusCode.NotFound:
                        throw new Exception(string.Empty);
                }
                var responseContent = await
response.Content.ReadAsStringAsync();
                var loginSuccess = false;
                bool.TryParse(responseContent, out loginSuccess);
                return loginSuccess;
            }
        }
```

The _baseAddress property will be the same as the SignalRHubConnection address; this is our server link. In our LoginAsync function, we start with creating a new HttpRequestMessage set as a HttpMethod.Post. We also set the content to a new StringContent object, which takes the username and password. This message is used in a new HttpClient to send to the server, and the response received is read as a string and parsed in to a new bool object to determine the success of the login.

Let's go ahead and implement the rest of the access layer:

```
public async Task<bool> RegisterAsync(string name, string password,
CancellationToken? cancellationToken = null)
            {
                var httpMessage = new HttpRequestMessage(HttpMethod.Post,
                new Uri(_baseAddress + "api/Account/Register"))
                {
                    Content = new StringContent(string.Format
                        ("Username={0}&Password={1}", name, password),
Encoding.UTF8,
                        "application/x-www-form-urlencoded"),
                };
                var client = new HttpClient();
                var response = await client.SendAsync(httpMessage,
                cancellationToken ?? new CancellationToken(false));
                return response.StatusCode == HttpStatusCode.OK;
            }
```

The `Register` function is very much the same, but we only check that the response status code is a `200` (`OK`) response; if so, then we have registered successfully.

```
public async Task<TokenContract> GetTokenAsync(string name, string
password, CancellationToken? cancellationToken = null)
        {
            var httpMessage = new HttpRequestMessage(HttpMethod.Post,
            new Uri(_baseAddress + "token"))
            {
                Content = new StringContent(string.Format
                ("Username={0}&Password={1}&grant_type=password", name,
                password), Encoding.UTF8, "application/x-www-form-
urlencoded"),
            };
            var client = new HttpClient();
            var response = await client.SendAsync(httpMessage,
            cancellationToken ?? new CancellationToken(false));
            switch (response.StatusCode)
            {
                case HttpStatusCode.NotFound:
                    throw new Exception(string.Empty);
            }
            var tokenJson = await response.Content.ReadAsStringAsync();
            return
    JsonConvert.DeserializeObject<TokenContract>(tokenJson);
        }
```

The `GetTokenAsync` function is responsible for retrieving the access token from the OAuth endpoint (`/token`). The JSON response will be of the type `TokenContract`; let's go ahead and add this object into the `Chat.ServiceAccess` project. Create a new folder called `Contracts` inside the `Web` folder, add in a new file called `TokenContract.cs`, and implement the following:

```
public class TokenContract
    {
        [JsonProperty("access_token")]
        public string AccessToken { get; set; }
        [JsonProperty("token_type")]
        public string TokenType { get; set; }
        [JsonProperty("expires_in")]
        public int ExpiresIn { get; set; }
        [JsonProperty("userName")]
        public string Username { get; set; }
        [JsonProperty(".issued")]
        public string IssuedAt { get; set; }
        [JsonProperty(".expires")]
        public string ExpiresAt { get; set; }
```

```
}
```

Notice the `JsonProperty` attribute?

We can map properties from the JSON objects into other named variables for the class.

Now for the final Web API function, `GetAllConnectedUsersAsync`. This function will be called when a user logs in for the first time. We need to have both an API call and a real-time update with the **SignalRClient** to keep track of the current connected clients because when a new user logs in, the server will call `displayMessage` on all other clients. Even if we were to call `displayMessage` on `Clients.All` (this is a reference to all the connected clients on any **SignalR Hub**), the newly connected client won't appear in the Clients list as there is a minor delay with the connection.

> This minor delay is something we cannot control; only sometimes would the newly connected client receives the updated list through the `HubProxy` event. So, to make things more reliable, we add this update through the API access layer.

Let's add the final Web API function for `GetAllConnectedUsersAsync`. This function will deserialized an IEnumerable of strings which represents the list of connected clients from the **ChatHub**:

```
public async Task<IEnumerable<string>>
  GetAllConnectedUsersAsync(CancellationToken? cancellationToken = null)
      {
            var httpMessage = new HttpRequestMessage(HttpMethod.Get,
            new Uri(_baseAddress + "api/Account/GetAllConnectedUsers"));
            var client = new HttpClient();
            var response = await client.SendAsync(httpMessage,
            cancellationToken ?? new CancellationToken(false));
            switch (response.StatusCode)
            {
                case HttpStatusCode.NotFound:
                    throw new Exception(string.Empty);
            }
            var responseContent = await
response.Content.ReadAsStringAsync();
            return JsonConvert.DeserializeObject<IEnumerable<string>>
(responseContent);
        }
```

Great! We now have our Web API access layer. Our next step is to start building the application state and navigation service required for each presenter.

Application state

In MVP, every presenter must include the current application state. When we cross between different screens, the persistent state of application data is kept alive throughout the entire life of the application (this includes search results, downloaded JSON objects, and so on.

In some most MVP applications, the application state will include a service for saving and loading this persistent data between different sessions. For an extra learning activity, try implementing a new service called IApplicationStateService. This will be responsible for saving and loading the ApplicationState object locally to your device.

Excellent! Now let's add another file called ApplicationState.cs, and implement the following:

```
public class ApplicationState
    {
        #region Public Properties
        public string AccessToken { get; set; }
        public string Username { get; set; }
        #endregion
    }
```

Nothing much to it, right?

We only ever want one instance of this object throughout the entire life of the application, so we will build upon the persistent data to be kept alive between each screen.

Setting up the navigation service

Implementing a navigation service in MVP is very different from our Xamarin.Forms navigation service. Our navigation service will not be used in an IoC container this time; instead, we will be instantiating one of these objects at the start of our application in the AppDelegate and MainActivity classes. Since we are working in native, we will also be implementing a separate navigation service for each platform that will share the same interface.

Let's start with creating the shared interface. Add a new file to the Chat.Common folder **Presenter** | **Services**, call it INavigationService.cs, and implement the following:

```
public interface INavigationService { void PushPresenter(BasePresenter
presenter); }
```

Building the iOS navigation service

Let's start with the iOS navigation service. Add in a new folder called `Services` to the `Chat.iOS` project, create a new file called `NavigationService.cs`, and implement the following:

```
public class NavigationService : INavigationService
    {
        #region Private Properties
        private UINavigationController _navigationController;
        #endregion
        #region Constructors
        public NavigationService(UINavigationController
navigationController)
        {
            _navigationController = navigationController;
        }
        #endregion
        #region INavigationService implementation
        public void PushPresenter(BasePresenter presenter)
        {
            if (presenter is LoginPresenter)
            {
                var viewController = new LoginViewController
                (presenter as LoginPresenter);
                _navigationController.PushViewController(viewController,
true);
            }
        }
        public void PopPresenter(bool animated)
        {
            _navigationController.PopViewController(animated);
        }
        #endregion
    }
```

When we instantiate this object we always want to pass in the `UINavigationController` that is assigned to our `RootViewController` of the `UIWindow` object created in our `AppDelegate`. We also have to implement the `Push` function, which takes a `BasePresenter` object (any presenter), and we perform a type check to determine which presenter is being passed, and pushing the related `UIViewController`, onto the navigation stack. We must always pass the presenter to the new `UIViewController`, so we can register the new view to the current presenter.

Building the Android navigation service

Before we move onto the Android navigation service, we have to add an extra class to hold persistent state on the current activity, current presenter, and current context. Add in a new file called `Application.cs` and implement the following:

```
[Application]
    public class ChatApplication : Application
    {
        #region Public Properties
        public object Presenter
        {
            get;
            set;
        }
        public Activity CurrentActivity
        {
            get;
            set;
        }
        #endregion
        #region Constructors
        public ChatApplication()
            : base()
        {
        }
        public ChatApplication(IntPtr javaReference,
        JniHandleOwnership transfer)
            : base(javaReference, transfer)
        {
        }
        #endregion
        #region Public Methods
        public static ChatApplication GetApplication(Context context)
        {
            return (ChatApplication)context.ApplicationContext;
        }
        #endregion
    }
```

This class will extend off the Android application, so when we reference the Android application class in other parts of our application, we have reference to the extra persistent objects.

Now let's implement the Android navigation service. Add in a new folder to the Android project called `Services`, add a new file called `NavigationService.cs`, and implement the following:

```
public class NavigationService : INavigationService
{
    private ChatApplication _application;
    public NavigationService(ChatApplication application)
    {
        _application = application;
    }
    public void PushPresenter(BasePresenter presenter)
    {
        var oldPresenter = _application.Presenter as BasePresenter;
        if (presenter != oldPresenter)
        {
            _application.Presenter = presenter;
            Intent intent = null;
            if (presenter is LoginPresenter)
            {
                intent = new Intent(_application.CurrentActivity,
                typeof(LoginActivity));
            }
            if (intent != null)
            {
                _application.CurrentActivity.StartActivity(intent);
            }
        }
    }
    public void PopPresenter(bool animated)
    {
        _application.CurrentActivity.Finish();
    }
}
```

In the constructor, we pass in the `Application` object and keep this stored as a private variable inside the navigation service. The `Push` function requires the `Application` everytime we push a new `Activity` onto the stack, because we require the current activity reference to start the new intent from the current activity held inside the `Application` object.

Now that we have our navigation service and application state, let's start building our user interface for iOS.

Building the iOS interface

Since we don't really know how the user interface is going to look for each screen, we can't define the logic in our presenters. So let's loosely talk about how the user interface is going to look.

> We should normally have screen mock-ups at this point before we move to the UI layer of a project.

We have three screens in our application, one of which is going to be list which displays all the connected clients live on the **ChatHub** on our server. A user will be able to select this user from the list; when a user selects another client from the list, this client should receive a message asking for permission to start a chat conversation. When a user accepts, this will move to another screen which will show a typical chat conversation, much the same as with any other SMS application (speech bubbles on either side). The following diagram is a quick mock-up of the three screens and workflow. All we see is the first screen showing a login screen, then another showing a list with the connected clients, and the last screen showing a conversation between two connected clients.

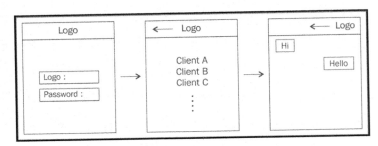

Excellent! Now that we have an idea as to how our screens are going to look, let's talk about the logic behind the first screen that we can share. We have a screen with two entry boxes for a username and password. The screen will be able to perform logins and registrations on our Web API, so we will require a button for each. If we are successful with login, this will push the list page on to the navigation stack.

Let's consider a cross-platform approach; what can we share here?

- Web API layer
- **EventHandlers** to handle the click events for a login and register
- Navigation service to handle push/pop onto our navigation stack

We have a rough idea of the logic behind our first screen; let's build our first **Presenter**. Create two new files called `BasePresenter.cs` and `IView.cs`. We will start with the `IView` class:

```
public interface IView
    {
     void SetMessage(string message);
     bool IsInProgress
       {
         get;
         set;
       }
    }
```

We want all screens to have an `IsInProgress` variable, if any screen is loading or processing, we can display loading activity to the user. The `SetMessage` function is used to display any errors to the user through an alert dialog.

Now for the `BasePresenter`, this is an abstract class which will be used for all presenters. All presenters require the `ApplicationState`, `INavigationService`, and the `SignalRClient`. Throughout our entire application, each screen requires events from the `SignalRClient` to function, so we can bring it into the `BasePresenter` object. We have created two `EventHandlers`; these are fired based upon the data received via the **hub proxy** on the `SignalRClient`. If we receive a list of **Clients**, we will fire the `ConnectedClientsUpdated` event. If we receive a `string`, we will fire the `ChatReceived` event, so we can actually control all `SignalR` data via the `BasePresenter` class, and channel specific data types to specific events for our views to register. We also have the `WebApiAccess` object for accessing the Web API and a string for holding the access token when we login successfully:

```
public abstract class BasePresenter
      {
          #region Private Properties
          private IDictionary<string, Action<string>> _signalREvents;
          #endregion
          #region Protected Properties
          protected INavigationService _navigationService;
          protected ApplicationState _state;
          protected SignalRClient _signalRClient;
          protected WebApiAccess _webApiAccess;
          protected string _accessToken;
          #endregion

          #region Events
          public event EventHandler<ConnectedClientsUpdatedEventArgs>
```

```
        ConnectedClientsUpdated;
        public event EventHandler<ChatEventArgs> ChatReceived;
        #endregion
    }
```

Handling Hub proxy callbacks

Let's turn our attention to the `SignalRClient`; we created an `EventHandler`, which fires every time data is received from the **Hub**. The `BasePresenter` will be responsible for handling the data received from this `EventHandler`:

```
        #region Constructors
        public BasePresenter()
        {
            _webApiAccess = new WebApiAccess();
            _signalREvents = new Dictionary<string, Action<string>>()
            {
                {"clients", (data) =>
                    {
                        var list =
JsonConvert.DeserializeObject<IEnumerable<string>>(data);
                        if (ConnectedClientsUpdated != null)
                        {
                            ConnectedClientsUpdated(this, new
ConnectedClientsUpdatedEventArgs(list.Select(x => new Client
                            {
                                Username = x,
                            }))));
                        }
                    }
                },
                {"chat", (data) =>
                    {
                        if (ChatReceived != null)
                        {
                            ChatReceived(this, new ChatEventArgs(data));
                        }
                    }
                },
            };
        }
        #endregion
        #region Protected Methods
        protected void HandleSignalRDataReceived(object sender,
Tuple<string, string> e)
        {
```

```
        _signalREvents[e.Item1](e.Item2);
    }
    #endregion
```

The private dictionary `_signalREvents` is used instead of a switch statement.

With each `Tuple` received from the SignalRClient's `OnDataReceived` event, the first string will be the key matching the indexed `Action<string>` in the dictionary. The other string of the `Tuple` is the data string (either a serialized JSON of `HashSet<string>`, or a string which represents a chat message), which is passed as the input parameter for our `Action<string>`, then, out of this input parameter, we will create the correct arguments used for the specified event.

We could take things a step further and abstract a `view` object into the `BasePresenter`, as every presenter requires a `view`, but because each view logic is independent, it is very hard to centralize this logic in one area. The need for this will come if multiple views have similar behaviors. Then we can look at abstracting these areas into the `BasePresenter`.

But wait! You may have noticed that we have two types of arguments being passed into each `EventHandler`. Add a new file to the `Events` folder in the `Chat.Common` project called `ConnectedClientsUpdatedEventArgs.cs`, and implement the following:

```
public class ConnectedClientsUpdatedEventArgs : EventArgs
    {
        public IList<Client> ConnectedClients { private set; get;

    }
        public ConnectedClientsUpdatedEventArgs(IEnumerable<Client>
connectedClients)
        {
            ConnectedClients = new List<Client>();
            foreach (var client in connectedClients)
            {
                ConnectedClients.Add(client);
            }
        }
    }
```

We also need another file called `ChatEventArgs.cs`. Add this to the `Events` folder and implement the following:

```
public class ChatEventArgs : EventArgs
```

```
    {
        public string Message { private set; get;
    }
        public ChatEventArgs(string message)
        {
            Message = message;
        }
    }
```

This object is the wrapper for every message received for a chat message. Now we have everything ready to implement our first presenter object.

Implementing the LoginPresenter

Create a new file called LoginPresenter.cs, add it to the Presenter folder in the Chat.Common project, and implement the following:

```
public class LoginPresenter : BasePresenter
    {
        #region Private Properties
        private ILoginView _view;
        #endregion
        #region IClientsListView
        public interface ILoginView : IView
        {
            event EventHandler<Tuple<string, string>> Login;
            event EventHandler<Tuple<string, string>> Register;
        }
        #endregion
        #region Constructors
        public LoginPresenter(ApplicationState state, INavigationService
navigationService)
        {
            _navigationService = navigationService;
            _state = state;
            _webApiAccess = new WebApiAccess();
        }
        #endregion


#region Public Methods
        public void SetView(ILoginView view)
        {
            _view = view;
            _view.Login -= HandleLogin;
            _view.Login += HandleLogin;
```

```
                _view.Register  -= HandleRegister;
                _view.Register  += HandleRegister;
            }
        #endregion
    }
```

Our `LoginPresenter` contains a new `ILoginView` interface with two new event handlers for the two buttons that will appear on the login screen. We also include a new `WebApiAccess` object as we will need to perform logins and registrations on the Web API. We also need another function called `SetView`, this will take the user interface object and register any `EventHandlers` specified by the `ILoginView` interface. Let's now add the function for handling logins:

```
        #region Private Methods
        private async void HandleLogin(object sender, Tuple<string,
   string> user)
        {
            if (!_view.IsInProgress)
            {
                _state.Username = user.Item1;
                _view.IsInProgress = true;
                if (user.Item2.Length >= 6)
                {
                    var loggedIn = await
_webApiAccess.LoginAsync(user.Item1, user.Item2, CancellationToken.None);
                    if (loggedIn)
                    {
                        var tokenContract = await
_webApiAccess.GetTokenAsync(user.Item1, user.Item2,
CancellationToken.None);
                        if
(!string.IsNullOrEmpty(tokenContract.AccessToken))
                        {
                            var presenter = new
ClientsListPresenter(_state, _navigationService,
tokenContract.AccessToken);
                            _navigationService.PushPresenter(presenter);
                        }
                        else
                        {
                            _view.SetErrorMessage("Failed to register
user.");
                        }
                    }
                    else
                    {
                        _view.SetErrorMessage("Invalid username or
```

```
         password.");
                                    }
                            }
                            else
                            {
                                _view.SetErrorMessage("Password must be at least 6
         characters.");
                            }
                            _view.IsInProgress = false;
                    }
            }
```

The `HandleLogin` function will check first if the screen is currently progressing from another login; we want to make sure that only one login or registration can occur at any one time. Firstly, we call the `LoginAsync` and check that the user exists in the `UserManager`, then we call the `GetTokenAsync` function to retrieve the access token which will be used in our `HubConnection`. If both are successful, we push on the `ClientsListViewController` using the `NavigationService`. If either fails, we use the `SetErrorMessage` function for displaying an error.

We control the navigation stack by the presenter type passed into the `PushPresenter`/`PopPresenter` functions.

Now let's add the function for handling registrations:

```
private async void HandleRegister(object sender, Tuple<string, string>
user)
            {
                    // make sure only once can we be registering at any one time
                    if (!_view.IsInProgress)
                    {
                        _state.Username = user.Item1;
                        _view.IsInProgress = true;
                        if (user.Item2.Length >= 6)
                        {
                                var registerSuccess = await
_webApiAccess.RegisterAsync(user.Item1, user.Item2,
CancellationToken.None);
                                if (registerSuccess)
                                {
                                    _view.SetErrorMessage("User successfully
registered.");
                                }
                        }
```

```
            else
            {
                _view.SetErrorMessage("Password must be at least 6
characters.");
            }
            _view.IsInProgress = false;
        }
    }
    #endregion
```

Very much the same as the `LoginAsync`, but we call the `RegisterAsync` and simply wait for the call to finish and check we have the HTTP status code of `200` `(OK)`.

Creating the connection between Presenter and View

Now we move on to the user interface design and demonstrate how we set up the link between our presenters. Developing the user interface is no different to developing natively for iOS and Android; the only difference with MVP is that we initialize a view with its related presenter in the constructor.

Let's start by adding a new folder to the `Chat.iOS` project called `Views`, add in a new file called `LoginViewController.cs`, and implement the following:

```
public class LoginViewController : UIViewController,
LoginPresenter.ILoginView
    {
        #region Private Properties
        private bool _isInProgress = false;
        private LoginPresenter _presenter;
        private UITextField _loginTextField;
        private UITextField _passwordTextField;
        private UIActivityIndicatorView _activityIndicatorView;
        #endregion
        #region Constructors
        public LoginViewController(LoginPresenter presenter)
        {
            _presenter = presenter;
        }
        #endregion
    }
```

We start off simply with the private properties and the constructor, where we are passing a new `LoginPresenter` object that we create from the `AppDelegate` as the starting presenter. The two text fields are used for the username and password entries. We have these as a local variable as we will need to access one instance of each from multiple functions. We also have a `UIActivityIndicatorView` for displaying the progress when we login and register.

Let's go ahead and add the `ViewDidLoad` function. We will implement this in a few parts. First we are going to set the view of the presenter and initialize all the UI elements and add them into the `View`:

```
#region Public Methods
        public override void ViewDidLoad()
        {
            base.ViewDidLoad();
            View.BackgroundColor = UIColor.White;
            _presenter.SetView(this);
            var width = View.Bounds.Width;
            var height = View.Bounds.Height;
            Title = "Welcome";
            var titleLabel = new UILabel()
            {
                TranslatesAutoresizingMaskIntoConstraints = false,
                Text = "Chat",
                Font = UIFont.FromName("Helvetica-Bold", 22),
                TextAlignment = UITextAlignment.Center
            };
            _activityIndicatorView = new UIActivityIndicatorView()
            {
                TranslatesAutoresizingMaskIntoConstraints = false,
                Color = UIColor.Black
            };
            var descriptionLabel = new UILabel()
            {
                TranslatesAutoresizingMaskIntoConstraints = false,
                Text = "Enter your login name to join the chat room.",
                Font = UIFont.FromName("Helvetica", 18),
                TextAlignment = UITextAlignment.Center
            };
            _loginTextField = new UITextField()
            {
                TranslatesAutoresizingMaskIntoConstraints = false,
                Placeholder = "Username",
                Font = UIFont.FromName("Helvetica", 18),
                BackgroundColor = UIColor.Clear.FromHex("#DFE4E6"),
                TextAlignment = UITextAlignment.Center
            };
```

```
        _passwordTextField = new UITextField()
        {
            TranslatesAutoresizingMaskIntoConstraints = false,
            Placeholder = "Password",
            Font = UIFont.FromName("Helvetica", 18),
            BackgroundColor = UIColor.Clear.FromHex("#DFE4E6"),
            TextAlignment = UITextAlignment.Center
        };
        var buttonView = new UIView()
        {
            TranslatesAutoresizingMaskIntoConstraints = false
        };
        var loginButton = new UIButton(UIButtonType.RoundedRect)
        {
            TranslatesAutoresizingMaskIntoConstraints = false
        };
        loginButton.SetTitle("Login", UIControlState.Normal);
        loginButton.TouchUpInside += (sender, e) =>
            Login(this, new Tuple<string,
string>(_loginTextField.Text, _passwordTextField.Text));
        var registerButton = new UIButton(UIButtonType.RoundedRect)
        {
            TranslatesAutoresizingMaskIntoConstraints = false
        };
        registerButton.SetTitle("Register", UIControlState.Normal);
        registerButton.TouchUpInside += (sender, e) =>
            Register(this, new Tuple<string,
string>(_loginTextField?.Text, _passwordTextField?.Text));
        Add(titleLabel);
        Add(descriptionLabel);
        Add(_activityIndicatorView);
        Add(_loginTextField);
        Add(_passwordTextField);
        Add(buttonView);
        buttonView.Add(loginButton);
        buttonView.Add(registerButton);
    }
    #endregion
```

This is a large block of code, but we are creating quite a few UI elements. All have the `TranslatesAutoresizingMaskIntoConstraints` set to `false` ready for **NSLayout**. Have a look at how we integrate the `ILoginView` implementation with the Login and `RegisterEventHandlers` as they are wired to the `TouchUpInside` event of each button.

Now let's start building the NSLayoutConstraints. Add the following to the bottom of the ViewDidLoad function:

TIP

We are using the DictionaryViews object that we used in previous chapters. Create a new folder called Extras and add this object into the Extras folder.

```
var views = new DictionaryViews()
            {
                {"titleLabel", titleLabel},
                {"descriptionLabel", descriptionLabel},
                {"loginTextField", _loginTextField},
                {"passwordTextField", _passwordTextField},
                {"loginButton", loginButton},
                {"registerButton", registerButton},
                {"activityIndicatorView", _activityIndicatorView},
                {"buttonView", buttonView}
            };
            buttonView.AddConstraints(
                NSLayoutConstraint.FromVisualFormat("V:|-[registerButton]-
|", NSLayoutFormatOptions.DirectionLeftToRight, null, views)
                .Concat(NSLayoutConstraint.FromVisualFormat("V:|-
[loginButton]-|", NSLayoutFormatOptions.DirectionLeftToRight, null, views))
                .Concat(NSLayoutConstraint.FromVisualFormat("H:|-
[registerButton]-30-[loginButton]-|",
NSLayoutFormatOptions.DirectionLeftToRight, null, views))
                .ToArray());
            View.AddConstraints(
                NSLayoutConstraint.FromVisualFormat("V:|-100-
[titleLabel(50)]-[descriptionLabel(30)]-10-[loginTextField(30)]-10-
[passwordTextField(30)]-10-[buttonView]",
NSLayoutFormatOptions.DirectionLeftToRight, null, views)
                .Concat(NSLayoutConstraint.FromVisualFormat("V:|-100-
[activityIndicatorView(50)]-[descriptionLabel(30)]-10-
[loginTextField(30)]-10-[passwordTextField(30)]-10-[buttonView]",
NSLayoutFormatOptions.DirectionLeftToRight, null, views))
                .Concat(NSLayoutConstraint.FromVisualFormat("H:|-10-
[titleLabel]-10-|", NSLayoutFormatOptions.AlignAllTop, null, views))
.Concat(NSLayoutConstraint.FromVisualFormat("H:[activityIndicatorView(30)]-
10-|", NSLayoutFormatOptions.AlignAllTop, null, views))
                .Concat(NSLayoutConstraint.FromVisualFormat("H:|-10-
[descriptionLabel]-10-|", NSLayoutFormatOptions.AlignAllTop, null, views))
                .Concat(NSLayoutConstraint.FromVisualFormat("H:|-30-
[loginTextField]-30-|", NSLayoutFormatOptions.AlignAllTop, null, views))
                .Concat(NSLayoutConstraint.FromVisualFormat("H:|-30-
[passwordTextField]-30-|", NSLayoutFormatOptions.AlignAllTop, null, views))
```

```
                    .Concat(new[] { NSLayoutConstraint.Create(buttonView,
NSLayoutAttribute.CenterX, NSLayoutRelation.Equal, View,
NSLayoutAttribute.CenterX, 1, 1)
  })
                    .ToArray());
```

The constraints will position the `buttonView` to the center of the screen horizontally; each buttons inside will be positioned horizontally next to each other. The rest of the layout is very self-explanatory. We are simply stacking the remaining element vertically down the page. The `UIActivityIndicatorView` will be positioned to the top right of the screen next to the `TitleLabel`. The rest of the layout will make more sense when we try running the application.

Finally, we add the remaining interface implementations; we require both Login and `Register` for the `ILoginView` interface. We also require `IsInProgress` bool and the `SetErrorMessage` function; this will create a new `UIAlertView` showing the error message. We also override the get and set of `IsInProgress` to control the start and stop animation of the `UIActivityIndicatorView`:

```
#region ILoginView implementation
public event EventHandler<Tuple<string, string>> Login;
public event EventHandler<Tuple<string, string>> Register;
#endregion
#region IView implementation

public void SetErrorMessage(string message)
{
    var alert = new UIAlertView()
    {
        Title = "Chat",
        Message = message
    };
    alert.AddButton("OK");
    alert.Show();
}
public bool IsInProgress
  {
     get
    {
        return _isInProgress;
    }
    set
    {
        if (value == _isInProgress)
        {
            return;
```

```
            }
            // we control the activity view when we set 'IsInProgress'
            if (value)
            {
                _activityIndicatorView.StartAnimating();
            }
            else
            {
                _activityIndicatorView.StopAnimating();
            }
            _isInProgress = value;
        }
    }
    #endregion
```

The link between our first view and presenter is not as clean as an MVVM **BindingContext** with Xamarin.Forms, but the advantage is having no middle layer of rendering between the native user interface and the data to be displayed.

Building the LoginActivity

Let's move back into the Chat.Droid project; before we create our Activity we need to create the layout using a new XML sheet. Add a new file called LoginView.xml into the **Resources | layout** and implement the following:

```xml
<?xml version="1.0" encoding="utf-8"?>
<LinearLayout xmlns:android="http://schemas.android.com/apk/res/android"
    android:id="@+id/tableLayout"
    android:layout_width="fill_parent"
    android:layout_height="fill_parent"
    android:orientation="vertical"
    android:gravity="center"
    android:background="#FFFFFF">
    <TextView
        android:id="@+id/titleTextView"
        android:text="Chat"
        android:fontFamily="helvetica"
        android:textStyle="bold"
        android:textSize="22dp"
        android:textColor="#000000"
        android:paddingBottom="20dp"
        android:layout_width="wrap_content"
        android:layout_height="wrap_content" />
    <TextView
```

```
                android:id="@+id/descriptionTextView"
                android:text="Enter your login name to join the chat room."
                android:fontFamily="helvetica"
                android:textColor="#000000"
                android:paddingBottom="20dp"
                android:layout_centerInParent="true"
                android:layout_width="wrap_content"
                android:layout_height="wrap_content" />
        <EditText
                android:id="@+id/usernameField"
                android:textColor="#000000"
                android:layout_width="fill_parent"
                android:layout_height="50dp"
                android:paddingBottom="20dp"
                android:hint="Enter Username" />
        <EditText
                android:id="@+id/passwordField"
                android:textColor="#000000"
                android:layout_width="fill_parent"
                android:layout_height="50dp"
                android:hint="Enter Password" />
        <LinearLayout
                android:id="@+id/tableLayout"
                android:gravity="center"
                android:layout_width="fill_parent"
                android:layout_height="150dp"
                android:orientation="horizontal"
                android:background="#FFFFFF">
            <Button
                    android:id="@+id/registerButton"
                    android:text="Register"
                    android:textColor="#417BB5"
                    android:background="@android:color/transparent"
                    android:layout_height="50dp"
                    android:layout_width="100dp" />
            <Button
                    android:id="@+id/loginButton"
                    android:text="Login"
                    android:textColor="#417BB5"
                    android:background="@android:color/transparent"
                    android:paddingLeft="20dp"
                    android:layout_height="50dp"
                    android:layout_width="100dp" />
        </LinearLayout>
</LinearLayout>
```

The XMLlayout will stack the page vertically, with the two buttons placed side-by-side.

A quick way of checking your layouts in Xamarin.Studio is to click the **Designer** window:

Now let's create a new folder called Views, add in a new file called LoginActivity.cs, and implement the first section:

```
[Activity(MainLauncher = true, Label = "Chat", ScreenOrientation =
ScreenOrientation.Portrait)]
    public class LoginActivity : Activity, LoginPresenter.ILoginView
    {
        #region Private Properties
        private bool _isInProgress = false;
        private bool _dialogShown = false;
        private LoginPresenter _presenter;
        private EditText _loginField;
        private EditText _passwordField;
        private ProgressDialog progressDialog;
        #endregion
        #region Protected Methods
        protected override void OnCreate(Bundle bundle)
        {
            base.OnCreate(bundle);
```

```
SetContentView(Resource.Layout.LoginView);
progressDialog = new ProgressDialog(this);
progressDialog.SetMessage("Loading...");
progressDialog.SetCancelable(false);
_loginField =
FindViewById<EditText>(Resource.Id.usernameField);
_passwordField =
FindViewById<EditText>(Resource.Id.passwordField);
var registerButton =
FindViewById<Button>(Resource.Id.registerButton);
registerButton.Touch += (sender, e) =>
    Register(this, new Tuple<string, string>(_loginField.Text,
_passwordField.Text));
var loginButton =
FindViewById<Button>(Resource.Id.loginButton);
loginButton.Touch += (sender, e) =>
    Login(this, new Tuple<string, string>(_loginField.Text,
_passwordField.Text));
var app = ChatApplication.GetApplication(this);
var state = new ApplicationState();
_presenter = new LoginPresenter(state, new
NavigationService(app));
_presenter.SetView(this);
app.CurrentActivity = this;
        }
    #endregion
```

Since we already have the UI logic in our presenter, building the interface for
LoginActivity is much easier as the answers all lie in the presenter. This is the advantage
of code-sharing using the MVP pattern.

In our OnCreate() function, we will start with setting the ContentView to the XMLlayout
we created previously. We will then register the button Touch events to the ILoginView
interface, very much like the iOS version with the TouchUpInside events. We then retrieve
the application from the GetApplication function. We also create an instance of the
ApplicationState, and create a new LoginPresenter.

We must also add the requirements of the ILoginView and IView interfaces. The
SetErrorMessage will use the AlertDialog.Builder framework to create the same
popup as the iOS version. We only set one button for this dialog which will simply close the
dialog when we press **OK**:.

```
#region ILoginView implementation
public event EventHandler<Tuple<string, string>> Login;
public event EventHandler<Tuple<string, string>> Register;
#endregion
```

```
#region IView implementation
public void SetErrorMessage(string message)
{
    if (!_dialogShown)
    {
        _dialogShown = true;
        AlertDialog.Builder builder = new
AlertDialog.Builder(this);
        builder
            .SetTitle("Chat")
            .SetMessage(message)
            .SetNeutralButton("Ok", (sender, e) => { _dialogShown
= false ;})
            .Show();
    }
}
public bool IsInProgress
{
    get
    {
        return _isInProgress;
    }
    set
    {
        if (value == _isInProgress)
        {
            return;
        }
        // we control the activity view when we set 'IsInProgress'
        if (value)
        {
            progressDialog.Show();
        }
        else
        {
            progressDialog.Dismiss();
        }
        _isInProgress = value;
    }
}
#endregion
}
```

See how the structure is the exact same as iOS?

We just have to match the UI elements for each platform independently. Our final part to the activity is the `OnResume` function. This function will reset the `CurrentActivity` in the `Application`:

 It is important that every time an activity is resumed we reset the `CurrentActivity`, otherwise the navigation service will not push/pop on the correct `Activity`.

```
protected override void OnResume()
        {
            base.OnResume();
            var app = ChatApplication.GetApplication(this);
            app.CurrentActivity = this;
            if (_presenter != null)
            {
                _presenter.SetView(this);
            }
        }
        #endregion
```

Excellent! Now we have created the first screen, presenter, and linked it up with the navigation service. Let's hop back into the `Chat.iOS` project and build the next screen of our application.

Implementing the ClientsListPresenter

Create a new file called `ClientsListPresenter.cs`, add it to the `Presenter` folder in the `Chat.Common` project, and implement the following:

```
public class ClientsListPresenter : BasePresenter
    {
        #region Private Properties
        private IClientsListView _view;
        #endregion
        #region IClientsListView
        public interface IClientsListView : IView
        {
            event EventHandler<ClientSelectedEventArgs> ClientSelected;
            void NotifyConnectedClientsUpdated(IEnumerable<Client>
clients);
        }
        #endregion
```

```
            #region Constructors
            public ClientsListPresenter(ApplicationState state,
INavigationService navigationService,
                                    string accessToken)
        {
            _navigationService = navigationService;
            _state = state;
            _state.AccessToken = accessToken;
            InitSignalR(accessToken).ConfigureAwait(false);
        }
        #endregion
    }
```

We have declared a new **IClientsListView** interface specific to the current **UIViewController** (this must be done for every screen). It simply extends off the **IView** interface, and we add an extra event handler for selected items in our **UITableView**. We then have our constructor which we must pass in an **ApplicationState**,**NavigationService**, and an access token. We also initialize the **SignalRClient**: the `ConfigureAwait` function is set to false because we don't want to wait for this task to finish.

We now need to add another function called `SetView`.This will take the action user interface object and register any `EventHandlers` specified by the **IClientsListView** interface. We also make another call to the Web API to retrieve the current clients connected to the **ChatHub**. We also specify that we don't want to wait on this task via the `ConfigureAwait`function.

In each `SetView` that will be responding to real-time data updates from the **SignalRClient,** we have to reregister to the OnDataReceived`EventHandler` so the correct presenter function `HandleSignalRDataReceived` is called:

```
    #region Public Methods public void SetView(IClientsListView view)
        {
            _view = view;
            _signalRClient.OnDataReceived -= HandleSignalRDataReceived;
            _signalRClient.OnDataReceived += HandleSignalRDataReceived;
            _view.ClientSelected -= HandleClientSelected;
            _view.ClientSelected += HandleClientSelected;
            ConnectedClientsUpdated -= HandleConnectedClientsUpdated;
            ConnectedClientsUpdated += HandleConnectedClientsUpdated;
            GetAllConnectedClients().ConfigureAwait(false);
        }
    #endregion
```

A presenter can also have the opposite to the `SetView` function called `ReleaseView`. It will be responsible for disposing EventHandlers when screens disappear. This ensures we don't have events on any previous pages doing work when they are not visible. Add the following under the `SetView` function:

```
public void ReleaseView()
    {
        _signalRClient.OnDataReceived -= HandleSignalRDataReceived;
    }
```

Now let's add the `Signout` function. This will be called when a user wants to disconnect from the **ChatHub** (when the user leaves the **ClientsListViewController**):

```
public void Signout()
    {
        _signalRClient.Disconnect();
        _navigationService.PopPresenter(true);
    }
```

Let's add two more functions: `HandleClientSelected` will use the **INavigationService** to push the next screen on to the stack, and the other function, `HandleConnectedClientsUpdated` will call the native implementation in the user interface object. We will also filter the list of clients using Linq to include all other clients but the current user:

```
#region Private Methods
        private void HandleClientSelected(object sender,
ClientSelectedEventArgs e)
        {
            var presenter = new ChatPresenter(_state, _navigationService,
e.Client, _signalRClient);
            _navigationService.PushPresenter(presenter);
        }
        private void HandleConnectedClientsUpdated(object sender,
        ConnectedClientsUpdatedEventArgs e)
        {
            _view.NotifyConnectedClientsUpdated(e.ConnectedClients
                                    .Where(x =>
!x.Username.ToLower()
.Contains(_state.Username.ToLower()))));
        }
        #endregion
```

Since we know that we require a **UITableView** on the **ClientsListView** screen, we need to create a **TableSource** object that will show all our clients that are connected to the **ChatHub**. We also need a model object to hold the data to be displayed for each **Client**.

Firstly, create a new folder in the **Chat.Common** project called **Model**, add in a new file called `Client.cs` and implement the following:

```
public class Client { public string Username; }
```

For each cell, we are only going to display one text label showing the username of the connected client. Now let's add in a new file called `ClientsTableSource.cs` and start with the following:

```
public class ClientsTableSource : UITableViewSource
{
        #region Public Properties

        public event EventHandler<Client> ItemSelected;

        #endregion

        #region Private Properties

        private List<Client> _clients;

        string CellIdentifier = "ClientCell";

        #endregion

        #region Constructors

        public ClientsTableSource ()
        {
            _clients = new List<Client> ();
        }

        #endregion
}
```

We require a private `List` for holding the latest clients connected, we have our `CellIdentifier` label set as `ClientCell`, and we have an `EventHandler` for selected cell events that will occur from the `UITableView`.

Every time one of these events are fired from the `TableSource`, we will be firing the event handler in our `ClientsListPresenter` presenter. Now let's implement the rest of the overrides required by the `UITableViewSource` class:

```
#region Methods
        public void UpdateClients (IEnumerable<Client> clients)
        {
            foreach (var client in clients)
            {
                _clients.Add (client);
            }
        }
        public override nint NumberOfSections (UITableView tableView)
        {
            return 1;
        }
        public override nint RowsInSection (UITableView tableview, nint
    section)
        {
            return _clients.Count;
        }
        public override void RowSelected (UITableView tableView,
    NSIndexPath indexPath)
        {
            if (ItemSelected != null)
            {
                ItemSelected (this, _clients[indexPath.Row]);
            }
            tableView.DeselectRow (indexPath, true);
        }
        public override nfloat GetHeightForRow (UITableView tableView,
    NSIndexPath indexPath)
        {
            return 80;
        }
        public override UITableViewCell GetCell (UITableView tableView,
    NSIndexPath indexPath)
        {
            UITableViewCell cell =
    tableView.DequeueReusableCell(CellIdentifier);
            var client = _clients[indexPath.Row];
            if (cell == null)
            {
                cell = new UITableViewCell(UITableViewCellStyle.Default,
    CellIdentifier);
            }
            cell.TextLabel.Text = client.Ip;
            return cell;
```

```
            }
    #endregion
```

Our `GetCell` function will use the default `UITableViewCellStyle`, and the text will be set to the username of the `Client` object. Our `RowSelected` function will fire our custom `EventHandlerItemSelected`. We will register a delegate on this `EventHandler` for firing
our related presenter `Event`. Finally, our `UpdateClients` will be called whenever we receive a
proxy event when the client count changes.

Creating ClientListViewController

Now we will move on to the user interface design and demonstrate how we set up the link between our presenters. Developing the user interface is no different to developing natively for iOS and Android; the only difference with MVP is that we initialize a view with its related presenter in the constructor.

Let's start by adding a new folder to the `Chat.iOS` project called `Views`, add in a new file called `ClientsListViewController.cs`, and implement the following:

```
public class ClientsListViewController : UIViewController,
ClientsListPresenter.IClientsListView
    {
        #region Private Properties
        private UITableView _tableView;
        private ClientsTableSource _source;
        private ClientsListPresenter _presenter;
        private UIActivityIndicatorView _activityIndicatorView;
        #endregion
        #region Constructors
        public ClientsListViewController(ClientsListPresenter presenter)
        {
            _presenter = presenter;
            _source = new ClientsTableSource();
            _source.ItemSelected += (sender, e) =>
            {
                if (ClientSelected != null)
                {
                    ClientSelected(this, new ClientSelectedEventArgs(e));
                }
            };
        }
        #endregion
```

```
        }
```

Notice how we pass the presenter in the constructor of the `UIViewController`?

We will be doing this with every view that is added to the navigation service.

Inside the constructor, we are also registering the `itemSelected` event to fire the interface event for our presenter. Let's add in the following:

```
#region Public Methods
        public override void ViewDidLoad()
        {
                base.ViewDidLoad();
                // Perform any additional set up after loading the view,
typically from a nib.
                UIBarButtonItem backButton = new UIBarButtonItem("< Back",
UIBarButtonItemStyle.Bordered, HandleSignout);
                NavigationItem.SetLeftBarButtonItem(backButton, false);
                View.BackgroundColor = UIColor.White;
                _presenter.SetView(this);
                var width = View.Bounds.Width;
                var height = View.Bounds.Height;
                Title = "Clients";
                var titleLabel = new UILabel()
                {
                    TranslatesAutoresizingMaskIntoConstraints = false,
                    Text = "Connected Clients",
                    Font = UIFont.FromName("Helvetica-Bold", 22),
                    TextAlignment = UITextAlignment.Center
                };
                var descriptionLabel = new UILabel()
                {
                    TranslatesAutoresizingMaskIntoConstraints = false,
                    Text = "Select a client you would like to chat with",
                    Font = UIFont.FromName("Helvetica", 18),
                    TextAlignment = UITextAlignment.Center
                };
                _tableView = new UITableView(new CGRect(0, 0, width, height))
                {
                    TranslatesAutoresizingMaskIntoConstraints = false
                };
                _tableView.AutoresizingMask = UIViewAutoresizing.All;
                _tableView.Source = _source;
                Add(titleLabel);
                Add(descriptionLabel);
                Add(_tableView);
```

```
            var views = new DictionaryViews()
            {
                {"titleLabel", titleLabel},
                {"descriptionLabel", descriptionLabel},
                {"tableView", _tableView},
            };
            View.AddConstraints(
                NSLayoutConstraint.FromVisualFormat("V:|-100-
[titleLabel(30)]-[descriptionLabel(30)]-[tableView]|",
NSLayoutFormatOptions.DirectionLeftToRight, null, views)
    .Concat(NSLayoutConstraint.FromVisualFormat("H:|[tableView]|",
NSLayoutFormatOptions.AlignAllTop, null, views))
                .Concat(NSLayoutConstraint.FromVisualFormat("H:|-10-
[titleLabel]-10-|", NSLayoutFormatOptions.AlignAllTop, null, views))
                .Concat(NSLayoutConstraint.FromVisualFormat("H:|-10-
[descriptionLabel]-10-|", NSLayoutFormatOptions.AlignAllTop, null, views))
    .ToArray());
            }


        #endregion
```

In the `ViewDidLoad` function, we will always be calling the `SetView` on a presenter class, and passing the view itself to the presenter. We are also going to add another little trick on this screen to override the `navbar` back button. We must create a `UIBArButtonItem`, which will be set as the left button of the navigation bar. When we instantiate this item, the `HandleSignout` function will be called when this button is pressed. Let's add this to the `UIViewController`:

```
public async void HandleSignout(object sender, EventArgs e)
        {
            bool accepted = await ShowAlert("Chat", "Would you like to
signout?");
            if (accepted)
            {
                _presenter.Signout();
            }
        }
```

The function will show an alert and wait for a response to be provided by the user. In this case, it will be "Yes" or "No". We are going to add another function `ShowAlert()`, which will use the `TaskCompletionSource` framework to allow us to await a response from a `UIAlertView`.

The TaskCompletionSource framework

The `ShowAlert` function will instantiate a new instance of a `TaskCompletionSource` of type `bool`. We then invoke the action on the main thread using the `UIApplication.SharedApplication`, and then return the `Task` object of the `TaskCompletionSource`. This means we can wait for the task to be returned When we create the `UIAlertView`, we set the `Clicked` event of the dialog to call the `SetResult` function of the `TaskCompletionSource`, so the `Task` will not finish until this click event has occurred:

```
public Task<bool> ShowAlert(string title, string message)
{
    var tcs = new TaskCompletionSource<bool>();
    UIApplication.SharedApplication.InvokeOnMainThread(new
Action(() =>
    {
        UIAlertView alert = new UIAlertView(title, message, null,
NSBundle.MainBundle.LocalizedString("Cancel", "Cancel"),
NSBundle.MainBundle.LocalizedString("OK", "OK"));
        alert.Clicked += (sender, buttonArgs) =>
  tcs.SetResult(buttonArgs.ButtonIndex != alert.CancelButtonIndex);
        alert.Show();
    }));
    return tcs.Task;
}
```

Now that we have overriden the back button, when a user tries to click back on the clients list screen to return to the login, the `UIAlertView` will appear, asking if the user wants to signout (meaning the user will disconnect from the `ChatHub`). If the user presses **Yes**, we will call the `Signout` function on the `ClientsListPresenter`.

Now let's get back to the `ViewDidLoad` function and add in the `NSLayoutConstraints` to build the screen:

```
View.AddConstraints(NSLayoutConstraint.FromVisualFormat("V:|-100-
[titleLabel(30)]-[descriptionLabel(30)]-[tableView]|",
NSLayoutFormatOptions.DirectionLeftToRight, null, views)
.Concat(NSLayoutConstraint.FromVisualFormat("H:|[tableView]|",
NSLayoutFormatOptions.AlignAllTop, null, views))
        .Concat(NSLayoutConstraint.FromVisualFormat("H:|-10-
[titleLabel]-10-|", NSLayoutFormatOptions.AlignAllTop, null, views))
        .Concat(NSLayoutConstraint.FromVisualFormat("H:|-10-
[descriptionLabel]-10-|", NSLayoutFormatOptions.AlignAllTop, null, views))
        .ToArray());
```

We have all the elements stacked vertically, taking up the entire width of the screen with padding.

Finally, we also want to add the `ViewDidUnload` function, so we can remove the `OnDataReceived` event on the `SignalRClient`:

```
public override void ViewDidUnload()
        {
            base.ViewDidUnload();
            _presenter.ReleaseView();
        }
```

Creating the ClientsListActivity

Let's move back again to the `Chat.Droid` project. Create a new folder called `Views`, add in a new file called `ClientsListView.cs`, and implement the following:

```
[Activity(Label = "Chat Room", Icon = "@drawable/icon", ScreenOrientation =
ScreenOrientation.Portrait)]
    public class ClientsListActivity : ListActivity,
ClientsListPresenter.IClientsListView
    {
        #region Private Properties
        private ClientsListPresenter _presenter;
        private ClientsListAdapter _adapter;
        private bool _dialogShown = false;
        #endregion
        #region Protected Methods
        protected override void OnCreate(Bundle bundle)
        {
            base.OnCreate(bundle);
            ListView.SetBackgroundColor(Color.White);
             var app = ChatApplication.GetApplication(this);
            app.CurrentActivity = this;
            _presenter = app.Presenter as ClientsListPresenter;
            _presenter.SetView(this);
            _adapter = new ClientsListAdapter(this);
            ListAdapter = _adapter;
        }
        protected override void OnResume()
        {
            base.OnResume();
            var app = ChatApplication.GetApplication(this);
            app.CurrentActivity = this;
            if (_presenter != null)
```

```
            {
                _presenter.SetView(this);
            }
        }
    }

    #endregion
    }
```

For the first section of the `ClientsListActivity`, let's look at the `OnCreate` override. We will start with the `ChatApplication` instance and set the current `Activity` to the `ClientsListView` activity. We then instantiate a new `ClientsListPresenter`, add in the state, and add a new `NavigationService`. We will also set the view object of the presenter to the `ClientsListView`. Finally, we simply instantiate a new `ClientsListAdapter` and set it to the `ListAdapter` of the `Activity`, as we are inheriting a `ListActivity`. We are going to have a different layout to iOS and only show the `ListView` on this screen so we can demonstrate the `ListActivity`; therefore, we don't need an `XML` sheet for the layout of this `Activity`.

The `OnResume` function is the same as the `LoginActivity`; we have to maintain the current `Activity` shown to the user. We also want to override the `OnPause` function to call `ReleaseView` on the `ClientsListPresenter` so we remove the `EventHandler` on the `OnDataReceived` property of the `SignalRClient`. This ensures we don't call `HandleSignalRDataReceived` whilst the screen is not visible.

```
    protected override void OnPause()
        {
            base.OnPause();
            if (_presenter != null)
            {
                _presenter.ReleaseView();
            }
        }
```

Now let's add the `IClientsListView` and `IView` implementation. The `NotifyConnectedClientsUpdated` will call the `UpdateClients` function on the `ListAdapter`, and we must propogate the `NotifyDataSetChanged` on the main thread as we are making data changes to the `ListView`:

```
    #region IClientsListView implementation
        public event EventHandler<ClientSelectedEventArgs> ClientSelected;
        public void NotifyConnectedClientsUpdated(IEnumerable<Client>
    clients)
        {
            if (_adapter != null)
            {
```

```
                    _adapter.UpdateClients(clients);
                    // perform action on UI thread
                    Application.SynchronizationContext.Post(state =>
                        {
                            _adapter.NotifyDataSetChanged();
                        }, null);
                }
            }
            #endregion
            #region IView implementation
            public void SetErrorMessage(string message)
            {
                if (!_dialogShown)
                {
                    _dialogShown = true;
                    AlertDialog.Builder builder = new
    AlertDialog.Builder(this);
                    builder
                        .SetTitle("Chat")
                        .SetMessage(message)
                        .SetNeutralButton("Ok", (sender, e) => { _dialogShown
    = false; })
                        .Show();
                }            }
            public bool IsInProgress { get; set;
    }

            #endregion
```

The SetErrorMessage() will initiate a dialog similar to iOS, using the
AlertDialog.Builder framework. In this case, we only need to set the original button
since we only need one button on the dialog.

Overriding the OnBackPressed activity

With our iOS implementation we integrated an override to the navigation back button, so
when a user leaves the ClientListViewController, we ask the user if they would like to
signout from the ChatHub. We are going to do the same here but on the Android platform.
We will be building the alert from the AlertDialog.Builder framework:

```
    public override void OnBackPressed()
            {
                //Put up the Yes/No message box
                AlertDialog.Builder builder = new AlertDialog.Builder(this);
                builder
                    .SetTitle("Chat")
```

```
            .SetMessage("Would you like to signout?")
            .SetNegativeButton("No", (sender, e) => { })
            .SetPositiveButton("Yes", (sender, e) =>
                {
                        _presenter.Signout();
                })
            .Show();
        }
```

We start with instantiating a new builder object which must take the `Activity` context as the only parameter. We then set the title and message of the dialog, and two buttons for the `"Yes"` and `"No"` selections. Only when the user selects `"Yes"` does an action occur by calling the same `Signout` as with iOS.

Our last piece of this `Activity` is to override the `OnListItemClick`. When an item in the list is selected, we want to fire the `ClientSelected` event specified by the interface, so we can tie this event logic into the `ClientsListPresenter`:

```
        protected override void OnListItemClick(ListView l,
    Android.Views.View v, int position, long id)
        {
            var item = _adapter[position];
            if (ClientSelected != null)
            {
                ClientSelected(this, new ClientSelectedEventArgs(item));
            }
        }
    #endregion
```

Building the ListAdapter

Before we build our `ListAdapter`, we need to create another AXML sheet for the **CustomCell**, add another file to the **Resources | layout** folder called `CustomCell.xml`, and implement the following:

```
<?xml version="1.0" encoding="utf-8"?> <LinearLayout
xmlns:android="http://schemas.android.com/apk/res/android"
    android:orientation="horizontal"
    android:layout_width="match_parent"
    android:layout_height="match_parent"
    android:weightSum="4">
    <TextView
        android:id="@+id/username"
        android:layout_width="wrap_content"
```

```
            android:layout_height="wrap_content"
            android:layout_weight="1" />
    </LinearLayout>
```

This is another simple layout which has one `TextView` wrapped in a `LinearLayout`. The `TextView` will display the `ConnectionId` for each `Client`.

Now let's get back to the `ListAdapter`. Inside the `Views` folder, add another file called `ClientsListAdapter.cs` and implement the following:

```
public class ClientsListAdapter : BaseAdapter<Client>
    {
        private List<Client> _clients;
        private Activity _context;
        public ClientsListAdapter(Activity context) : base()
        {
            _context = context;
            _clients = new List<Client>();
        }
    }
```

Firstly, we are just creating a new class which inherits the `BaseAdapter` class which is typecasted to the `Client` object. We also have a private `List` which is going to store the clients retrieved from the `SignalRClient`, and finally we have the current **Activity Context**. Now let's add in the required override functions from the `BaseAdapter`:

```
public override Client this[int position]
    {
        get
        {
            return _clients[position];
        }
    }
public override Java.Lang.Object GetItem (int position)
    {
        return null;
    }

public override long GetItemId(int position)
    {
        return position;
    }
public override int Count
    {
        get
        {
            return _clients.Count;
```

```
                }
            }

        public override View GetView(int position, View convertView,
    ViewGroup parent)
            {
            View view = convertView; // re-use an existing view, if one is
    available
                if (view == null)
                {
                    // otherwise create a new one
                    view =
    _context.LayoutInflater.Inflate(Resource.Layout.CustomCell, null);
                }
                // set labels
                var connectionIdTextView = view.FindViewById<TextView>
    (Resource.Id.username);
                connectionIdTextView.Text = _clients[position].Username;
                return view;
            }
```

The first override is to implement an index reference to the _clientslist. All the override functions are the same as we implemented in Chapter 1, *Building a Gallery Application*. Let's turn our attention to the GetView function; we are simply creating a new CustomCell layout using the LayoutInflater framework (this will take any AXML file and create a new instance of the view).

Then, now that we have our new view, we will set the Text property of the TextView object in the CustomCell view to the Username in our Client object.

Finally, our last step is to add a another function called UpdateClients (as specified in our presenter). This will simply take a new IEnumerable of **Clients**, and the List will be updated accordingly:

```
    public void UpdateClients(IEnumerable<Client> clients)
            {
                foreach (var client in clients)
                {
                    _clients.Add(client);
                }
            }
```

With complete direction from the presenter class, look how fast we developed the android interface.

Before we can test the connection to the server **Hub**, we have to make changes to the application.config and `http.sys` using `netsh` in the command prompt. Follow the section *Hosting the Web API project locally* in `Chapter 5`, *Building a Stocklist Application*.

You can try testing the first page. Startup the server **Hub** and watch the list update whenever we connect or disconnect a new client. A good test on this example is to use multiple running instances of the application on different devices.

Building the ChatPresenter

Now we move on to the next screen; this will be our chat window in which we will be passing messages between different clients connected to the server **Hub**. Our first step is to build the ChatPresenter:

```
public class ChatPresenter : BasePresenter
    {
        #region Private Properties
        private Client _client;
        private IChatView _view;
        #endregion
        #region IChatView
        public interface IChatView : IView
        {
            void NotifyChatMessageReceived(string message);
        }
        #endregion
    }
```

We are going to start by inheriting the BasePresenter class. It will include two private properties, one for the Client selected from the previous ClientListView screen and another for the IChatView interface. The IChatView interface inherits the IView interface and it will include one function for handling messages received from the receiving Client.

Let's implement the following:

```
#region Constructors
        public ChatPresenter(ApplicationState state, INavigationService
navigationService, Client client)
        {
            _navigationService = navigationService;
            _state = state;
            _client = client;
```

```
    }
    #endregion
    #region Public Methods
    public void SetView(IChatView view)
    {
        _view = view;
        ChatReceived -= HandleChatReceived;
        ChatReceived += HandleChatReceived;
    }
    public async Task SendChat(string message)
    {
        await _signalRClient.SendMessageToClient(_client.ConnectedId,
message);
    }

    #endregion
    #region Private Methods
    private void HandleChatReceived(object sender, ChatEventArgs e)
    {
        _view.NotifyChatMessageReceived(e.Message);
    }
    #endregion
```

It is the same set up as the `ClientsListPresenter`; our `SetView` function will take the native view object and register the events. We also have another function, `SendChat` which will invoke the `SendChat` function on the **Hub**. Don't forget the `ReleaseView` function; this will be exactly the same as the `ClientsListPresenter`:

```
public void ReleaseView()
    {
        _signalRClient.OnDataReceived -= HandleSignalRDataReceived;
    }
```

Now that we have built all our presenter objects, we need to make a small update to the navigation service implementations to allow navigation for the other screens. Open the Android `NavigationService.cs`, and in the `PushPresenter` function update the `if` statement to the following:

```
if (presenter is LoginPresenter)
            {
                intent = new Intent(_application.CurrentActivity,
    typeof(LoginActivity));
            }
            else if (presenter is ClientsListPresenter)
            {
                intent = new Intent(_application.CurrentActivity,
    typeof(ClientsListActivity));
```

```
                }
                else if (presenter is ChatPresenter)
                {
                        intent = new Intent (_application.CurrentActivity,
        typeof(ChatActivity));
                }
```

For the iOS `NavigationService.cs`, update the if statement to the following:

```
if (presenter is LoginPresenter)
                {
                        var viewController = new LoginViewController(presenter as
        LoginPresenter);
                        _navigationController.PushViewController(viewController,
        true);
                }
                else if (presenter is ClientsListPresenter)
                {
                        var viewController = new
        ClientsListViewController(presenter as ClientsListPresenter);
                        _navigationController.PushViewController(viewController,
        true);
                }
                else if (presenter is ChatPresenter)
                {
                        var viewController = new ChatViewController(presenter as
        ChatPresenter);
                        _navigationController.PushViewController(viewController,
        true);
                }
```

Building the iOS ChatView

Add a new file called `ChatViewController` into the `Views` project of the `Chat.iOS` project and implement the following:

```
public class ChatViewController : UIViewController, ChatPresenter.IChatView
{
        #region Private Properties
        private ChatPresenter _presenter;
        private UITextField _chatField;
        private UIScrollView _scrollView;
        private int _currentTop = 20;
        private nfloat _width;
        #endregion
```

```
#region Constructors
public ChatViewController(ChatPresenter presenter)
{
    _presenter = presenter;
}
#endregion
```

```
}
```

We have multiple `Private` properties, one for the presenter, a local `UITextField`. We need this UI object to be local, as we need to extract the `Text` value to send through the `SignalRClient`, and we also need the `UIScrollView` to be local so we can change the content size and add in `ChatView` objects. The integers are use to record the current top (y-axis + height) of the all chat messages which will display on the screen. Finally, the remaining `nfloat` is used for recording the height and width of the screen.

 We will see all these variables used further on through the class functions.

Let's now add the `ViewDidLoad` function to build the user interface:

```
#region Public Methods
        public override void ViewDidLoad()
        {
            base.ViewDidLoad();
            Title = "Chat Room";
            _presenter.SetView(this);
            View.BackgroundColor = UIColor.White;
            _width = View.Bounds.Width;
            var _sendButton = new UIButton(UIButtonType.RoundedRect)
            {
                TranslatesAutoresizingMaskIntoConstraints = false
            };
            _sendButton.SetTitle("Send", UIControlState.Normal);
            _sendButton.TouchUpInside += HandleSendButton;
            _chatField = new UITextField()
            {
                TranslatesAutoresizingMaskIntoConstraints = false,
                BackgroundColor = UIColor.Clear.FromHex("#DFE4E6"),
                Placeholder = "Enter message"
            };
            _scrollView = new UIScrollView()
            {
                TranslatesAutoresizingMaskIntoConstraints = false,
            };
```

```
                Add(_chatField);
                Add(_sendButton);
                Add(_scrollView);
                var views = new DictionaryViews()
                {
                    {"sendButton", _sendButton},
                    {"chatField", _chatField},
                    {"scrollView", _scrollView},
                };
                this.View.AddConstraints(
                    NSLayoutConstraint.FromVisualFormat("V:|-68-
        [chatField(60)]", NSLayoutFormatOptions.DirectionLeftToRight, null, views)
                    .Concat(NSLayoutConstraint.FromVisualFormat("V:|-62-
        [sendButton(60)]-20-[scrollView]|",
        NSLayoutFormatOptions.DirectionLeftToRight, null, views))
                    .Concat(NSLayoutConstraint.FromVisualFormat("H:|-5-
        [chatField]-[sendButton(60)]-5-|", NSLayoutFormatOptions.AlignAllTop, null,
        views))
        .Concat(NSLayoutConstraint.FromVisualFormat("H:|[scrollView]|",
        NSLayoutFormatOptions.AlignAllTop, null, views))
                        .ToArray());
            }
            #endregion
```

The chat screen will contain a `UITextField`, a `UIButton`, and a `UIScrollView`. The button is for notifying the current `Text` value of the `UITextField` to be sent to the server **Hub**, and our `UIScrollView` will contain all the messages published from each client.

We also want to add the `ViewDidUnload()` function, so we can remove the `OnDataReceived` event on the `SignalRClient`:

```
public override void ViewDidUnload()
        {
            base.ViewDidUnload();
            _presenter.ReleaseView();
        }
```

Let's then add the `IView` implementation:

```
#region IView implementation
        public void SetMessage(string message)
        {
            var alert = new UIAlertView()
            {
                Title = "Chat",
                Message = message
            };
            alert.AddButton("OK");
```

```
                alert.Show();
        }
        public bool IsInProgress { get; set; } #endregion
```

The `IView` implementation is the same as with the `ClientsListViewController`.

Let's create a new file called `ChatBoxView.cs` and add it to the `Views` folder. We will create a new one of these for every chat message:

```
public class ChatBoxView : UIView
    {
        private UILabel messageLabel;
        public ChatBoxView(string message)
        {
            Layer.CornerRadius = 10;
            messageLabel = new UILabel()
            {
                TranslatesAutoresizingMaskIntoConstraints = false,
                Text = message
            };
            Add(messageLabel);
            var views = new DictionaryViews()
            {
                {"messageLabel", messageLabel},
            };
AddConstraints(NSLayoutConstraint.FromVisualFormat("V:|[messageLabel]|",
NSLayoutFormatOptions.AlignAllTop, null, views)
                .Concat(NSLayoutConstraint.FromVisualFormat("H:|-5-
[messageLabel]-5-|", NSLayoutFormatOptions.AlignAllTop, null, views))
                .ToArray());
        }
    }
```

This is a very simple object that contains one `UILabel` for the chat message. We also set the height and width of this label to the height and width of the `UIView` using `NSAutoLayout`. We also round the corners of the `Layer` to 5.

If you have ever used the **SMS** application on any iOS device, you will see we have two colors, distinguishing between you and the person you are talking to. We are going to do the same with our application but instead of using standard colors from the `UIColor` interface, we are going to use custom hex colors.

Extending the UIColor framework

In this section we are going to apply a common technique for extending on standard iOS classes. In the `UIColor` class, there is no function for applying hex strings to determine a color, so let's add this on top. Create a new folder called `Extensions`, add in a new file called `UIColorExtensions.cs`, and implement the following:

```
public static class UIColorExtensions
    {
        public static UIColor FromHex(this UIColor color, string hexValue,
float alpha = 1.0f)
        {
            var colorString = hexValue.Replace("#", "");
            if (alpha > 1.0f)
            {
                alpha = 1.0f;
            }
            else if (alpha < 0.0f)
            {
                alpha = 0.0f;
            }
            float red, green, blue;
            switch (colorString.Length)
            {
                case 3: // #RGB
                    {
                        red = Convert.ToInt32(string.Format("{0}{0}",
                        colorString.Substring(0, 1)), 16) / 255f;
                        green = Convert.ToInt32(string.Format("{0}{0}",
                        colorString.Substring(1, 1)), 16) / 255f;
                        blue = Convert.ToInt32(string.Format("{0}{0}",
                        colorString.Substring(2, 1)), 16) / 255f;
                        return UIColor.FromRGBA(red, green, blue, alpha);
                    }
                case 6: // #RRGGBB
                    {
                        red = Convert.ToInt32(colorString.Substring(0, 2),
16) / 255f;
                        green = Convert.ToInt32(colorString.Substring(2,
2), 16) / 255f;
                        blue = Convert.ToInt32(colorString.Substring(4,
2), 16) / 255f;
                        return UIColor.FromRGBA(red, green, blue, alpha);
                    }
                default:
                    throw new
ArgumentOutOfRangeException(string.Format("Invalid color value {0} is
```

```
invalid. It should be a hex value of the form #RBG, #RRGGBB", hexValue));
                }
        }
    }
```

When we extend a class with extra functions, the first input parameter must always start with the `this` keyword; this represents the current object calling the function. The next two parameters are a string representing the hex value and an alpha percentage (between 0 and 1) for transparency.

Firstly, we remove the # character from the hex string. We then double-check if the alpha character is below 0, if so, set the alpha to 0, and vice versa with the alpha if it is greater than 1. Then our switch statement will select a case based on the hex string length (either an RGB or RRGGBB value). Then we simply extract the red, green, and blue string values and return a new `UIColor` from the red, green, and blue values.

Now we can apply a hex color string to the `UIColor` framework like this:

```
UIColor.Clear.FromHex("#FFFFFF");
```

Since MonoTouch 5.4, we have to apply the `FromHex` extension to a `Color.Clear`. Previously we were able to use a parameterless constructor like this: `new UIColor().FromHex("FFFFFF")`.

Now that we have our `UIColor` additions, let's use these for our chatbox `BackgroundColor` property. We are going to add in a new function to the `ChatView`, which will create a new `ChatBox` and set the color according to whether it was sent or received. We will also do the same with the x-axis position and set the `ChatBox` to the left if sent and to the right if received:

```
public void CreateChatBox(bool received, string message)
{
    _scrollView.ContentSize = new CGSize(_width, _currentTop);
    _scrollView.AddSubview(new ChatBoxView(message)
    {
        Frame = new CGRect(received ? _width - 120 : 20,
_currentTop, 100, 60),
        BackgroundColor = UIColor.Clear.FromHex(received ?
"#4CD964" : "#5AC8FA")
    });
    _currentTop += 80;
}
```

We first update the `ContentSize` property of the `UIScrollView`; this represents the dimensions of the scroll area. The `currentTop` variable is used to record the last ChatBox's y-axis value so we know the height of the UIScrollView's content, and so we know the next y-axis position for the next `ChatBox`. Then we add the new `ChatBox` object, pass in the new message, and assign the message to the `Title` of the `UILabel`. We also use our new extension function to set the `BackgroundColor` property of the `ChatBox`.

Now, where do we call this function?

We have two areas, whenever the `Send` button is pressed, or when a message is received. Let's add the `TouchUpInside` callback on the `_sendButton`:

```
#region Private Properties private void HandleSendButton(object sender,
EventArgs e)
        {
                _presenter.SendChat(_chatField.Text).ConfigureAwait(false);
                CreateChatBox(false, _chatField.Text);
        }
    #endregion
```

The `HandleSendButton` will also call the presenter function, `SendChat`, and send the message to the server **Hub**. We also need to add the `IChatView` implementation. The `NotifyChatMessageReceived` function will also use `CreateChatBox`, but this time we will set the `received` flag to `true`. This must also be invoked on the main thread as sometimes the event might fire this function on another thread:

```
#region IChatView implementation
        public void NotifyChatMessageReceived(string message)
        {
            InvokeOnMainThread(() => CreateChatBox(true, message));
        }
        #endregion
```

Fantastic!

Now that we have finished the iOS `ChatView`, try testing. Connect two iOS clients to the **Hub**, select the other client from either client, try entering messages into the `UITextField`, press Send, and watch the magic happen.

That's enough of iOS development, let's move back over to Android and complete the `ChatView`.

Android TableLayouts

Let's move back to the Android implementation. This part is easy, we have already mapped the UI logic to the `ChatPresenter` so let's get straight into building the interface. For our `ChatView.xml` file, we are going to introduce a `TableLayout`. TableLayouts are similar to **Grids** in `Xamarin.Forms`; we simply split an area into rows and columns. We are able to set UI objects to specific rows and columns as well as span specific UI objects across multiple rows and columns.

Let's add a new file called `ChatView.xml` to the **Resources | layout** folder and implement the following:

```xml
<?xml version="1.0" encoding="utf-8"?>
<TableLayout xmlns:android="http://schemas.android.com/apk/res/android"
    android:id="@+id/tableLayout"
    android:layout_width="fill_parent"
    android:layout_height="fill_parent"
    android:background="#FFFFFF">
    <TableRow
        android:id="@+id/tableRow1"
        android:layout_width="fill_parent"
        android:layout_height="100dp"
        android:padding="5dip">
        <EditText
            android:id="@+id/chatField"
            android:hint="Enter message"
            android:textColor="#000000"
            android:layout_weight="2"
            android:layout_column="1" />
        <Button
            android:id="@+id/sendButton"
            android:text="Send"
            android:textColor="#417BB5"
            android:background="@android:color/transparent"
            android:focusableInTouchMode="false"
            android:layout_weight="1"
            android:layout_column="3" />
    </TableRow>
    <TableRow
        android:id="@+id/tableRow2"
        android:layout_width="fill_parent"
        android:layout_weight="1"
        android:padding="5dip">
        <ScrollView
            android:id="@+id/scrollView"
            android:layout_width="match_parent"
```

```
                    android:layout_height="match_parent"
                    android:fillViewport="true"
                    android:layout_weight="2"
                    android:layout_span="4">
                    <LinearLayout
                        android:id="@+id/scrollViewInnerLayout"
                        android:layout_width="match_parent"
                        android:layout_height="wrap_content"
                        android:orientation="vertical" />
            </ScrollView>
        </TableRow>
    </TableLayout>
```

Each row is declared using the `<TableRow>` tag; our first row contains an `EditText` item for the messages, and a button to call the `SendChat` function on the `SignalRClient`.

Building the Android ChatActivity

Let's move back to the Android implementation. This part is easy, we have already mapped the UI logic to the `ChatPresenter`, so let's get straight into building the interface. Add a new file to the `Views` folder in the `Chat.Droid` project, call it `ChatActivity.cs`, and implement the first part:

```
[Activity(Label = "Chat", ScreenOrientation = ScreenOrientation.Portrait)]
    public class ChatView : ListActivity, ChatPresenter.IChatView
    {
        #region Private Properties
        private ChatPresenter _presenter;
        private LinearLayout _scrollViewInnerLayout;
        private EditText _editText;
        private long _lastSendClick = 0;
        private int _width;
        private float _currentTop;
        private bool _dialogShown = false;
    #endregion
        #region Protected Methods
        protected override void OnCreate(Bundle bundle)
        {
            base.OnCreate(bundle);
            SetContentView(Resource.Layout.ChatView);
            var metrics = Resources.DisplayMetrics;
            _width = (int)(( metrics.WidthPixels) /
            Resources.DisplayMetrics.Density);
            _scrollViewInnerLayout = FindViewById<LinearLayout>
            (Resource.Id.scrollViewInnerLayout);
```

```
_editText = FindViewById<EditText>(Resource.Id.chatField);
var sendButton = FindViewById<Button>(Resource.Id.sendButton);
sendButton.Touch += HandleSendButton;
var app = ChatApplication.GetApplication(this);
app.CurrentActivity = this;
_presenter = app.Presenter as ChatPresenter;
_presenter.SetView(this);
app.CurrentActivity = this;
}
#endregion

}
```

In the `OnCreate` function, we are setting the content view to the `ChatView` layout. We then retrieve the width of the screen as we need to be able position the x-axis of the chat box to the left or right of the screen, based on whether it was sent/received. We then assign the SendButton's `Touch` event to call the `HandleSendButton` function. Finally, we retrieve the `ChatApplication` object and cast the presenter to a `ChatPresenter`, call the `SetView` function, and pass the `ChatActivity`. Then we set the `CurrentActivity` of the `ChatApplication` object to the `ChatActivity`. Let's also add an override on the `OnPause` so we can call `ReleaseView` on the `ChatPresenter` to remove the `OnDataReceived` event from the `SignalRClient`. This is the equivalent to the `ViewDidUnload` override on a `UIViewController`:

```
protected override void OnPause()
{
    base.OnPause();
    if (_presenter != null)
    {
        _presenter.ReleaseView();
    }
}
```

Now we have to add the `IChatView` implementation; `CreateChatBox` must be propagated to the main thread as this event will sometimes call this function on a different thread:

```
#region IChatView implementation
    public void NotifyChatMessageReceived(string message)
    {
        // perform action on UI thread
        Application.SynchronizationContext.Post(state =>
        {
            CreateChatBox(true, message);
        }, null);
    }
#endregion
```

Now we have to add the `IView` implementation, which we can simply copy from the previous activity:

```
#region IView implementation
        public void SetErrorMessage(string message)
        {
            if (!_dialogShown)
            {
                _dialogShown = true;
                AlertDialog.Builder builder = new
AlertDialog.Builder(this);
                builder
                    .SetTitle("Chat")
                    .SetMessage(message)
                    .SetNeutralButton("Ok", (sender, e) => { _dialogShown
= false; })
                    .Show();
            }
        }
        public bool IsInProgress { get; set; }
        #endregion
```

Before we add the remaining functions, we are going to add another layout for the `ChatBoxView` in Android. Add a new file called `ChatBoxView.xml`, add it to the **Resources | layout** folder, and implement the following:

```
<?xml version="1.0" encoding="utf-8"?>
<LinearLayout
xmlns:android="http://schemas.android.com/apk/res/android"
    android:orientation="horizontal"
    android:layout_width="match_parent"
    android:layout_height="match_parent"
    android:weightSum="4">
    <TextView
        android:id="@+id/messageTextView"
        android:layout_width="wrap_content"
        android:layout_height="wrap_content"
        android:layout_weight="1" />
</LinearLayout>
```

This is a very simple view which contains a `LinearLayout` that contains one `TextView` to display the chat message.

Finally, we add the remaining `HandleSendButton` and `CreateChatBox` functions; they are the same functions as iOS, but use Android objects:

```
#region Private Methods
        private void HandleSendButton(object sender, View.TouchEventArgs
  e)
        {
            // multiple-clicking prevention using a threshold of 1000 ms
            if (SystemClock.ElapsedRealtime() - _lastSendClick < 1000)
            {
                return;
            }
            _lastSendClick = SystemClock.ElapsedRealtime();
            _presenter.SendChat(_editText.Text).ConfigureAwait(false);
            CreateChatBox(false, _editText.Text);
        }
#endregion
#region Public Methods
        public void CreateChatBox(bool received, string message)
        {
            var view = LayoutInflater.Inflate(Resource.Layout.ChatBoxView,
  null);
            view.SetX(received ? _width : 0);
            view.SetY(_currentTop);
            var messageTextView = view.FindViewById<TextView>
            (Resource.Id.messageTextView);
            messageTextView.Text = message;
            var color = Color.ParseColor(received ? "#4CD964" :
  "#5AC8FA");
            messageTextView.SetBackgroundColor(color);
            _scrollViewInnerLayout.AddView(view);
            _currentTop += 60;
        }
#endregion
```

The `HandleSendButton` function will do the exact same: call the presenter function, `SendChat`, create a new chatbox, and add it to the `ScrollView`. The `CreateChatBox` function will use the context's `LayoutInflator` and create a new `ChatBoxView`. We will then set the x, y, width and height properties, retrieve the `TextView` property of the view, and set the `Text` property to the message. We then call `SetBackgroundColor` on the view and change the background color according to whether it has been sent or received. Finally, we add the new view to the `ScrollView` and record the current y-axis value.

Running the server and clients

Before we can test everything together, please revisit the section in Chapter 5, *Building a Stocklist Application*, called **Hosting a Web API project locally**. This must be done before we can connect to the server side from our mobile clients. Once we have the server application running, build and run the mobile application from either platform and register a user first before we login. The Register button will place the new account in the UserManager, allowing us to perform a **Login** with those account details as they now exist in the UserManager. Once we login, we can't do anymore unless we have another mobile client that can run the app and login. It is best to test this application with two mobile devices running the mobile application. Once both have logged in and the clients list screen has been loaded, each user will be connected to the user, and both users can now click on each other to navigate to the chat window and begin sending messages to each other.

To further understand everything going on, try adding debug breakpoints to server functions, and test these server functions by clicking between the different screens of the mobile application. This will give a better overview as to what is happening between server and client on each screen.

Summary

In this chapter, we created an application for iOS and Android using the native libraries. We integrated SignalR on the client and server side by building a hub and proxy connections via a client. In the next chapter, we will see how to store files locally with Xamarin.Forms using dependency services. You will learn about shared projects and their differences to PCL projects. We will also run through SQLite, setting it up with Android, iOS, and WinPhone and share the same code using different platform-specific libraries.

7
Building a File Storage Application

In this chapter, we will walk through advanced development with `Xamarin.Forms`. We take a look at the use of Behaviors on UI elements. Then we will build a custom layout using the `Layout <View>` framework. We will also build our first SQLite database for storing text files. The following topics will be covered in this chapter:

Expected knowledge:

- Basic Xamarin.Forms
- XAML
- MVVM
- SQL
- C# threading

In this chapter, you will learn the following:

- Project structure setup
- Building a data access layer using SQLite
- Building the ISQLiteStorage interface
- Additional threading techniques
- Creating the AsyncSemaphore
- Creating the AsyncLock
- Implementing native setup requirements for SQLite
- Implementing the IoC container and modules
- Implementing cross-platform logging

- Implementing the SQLiteStorage class
- Introduction to C# 6.0 syntax
- Handling alerts in view-models
- Building the IMethods interface
- Building the ExtendedContentPage
- Building a CarouselView using custom layouts
- Adding scroll control to the CarouselView
- Building a CustomRenderer for native gestures
- Building the user interface
- Using a SynchronizationContext
- Building the EditFilePage
- Challenge
- Building the Windows Phone version

Project structure setup

Let's begin by creating a new Xamarin.Forms project. Select **File** | **New** | **Solution** and create a new **Forms App**, as shown in the following screenshot:

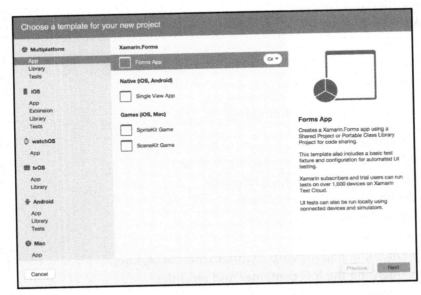

Call the project `FileStorage`. Once the project is created, create another portable class library called `FileStorage.Portable`, as shown in the following screenshot:

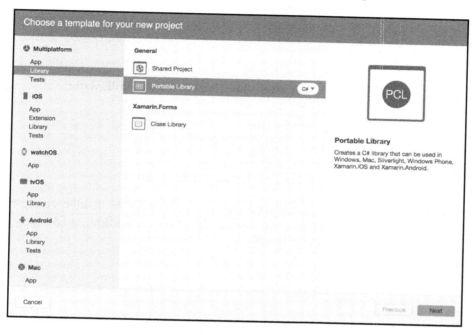

We are going to start at the lower level and work upwards to native projects.

Building a data access layer using SQLite

In the previous chapter, we focused on project architecture and we discussed the concepts one layer for data access this is where our database layer sits. Our data access layer is where we will be storing local text files.

SQLite is the most commonly used database framework for mobiles. It is an in-process library that implements a self-contained, serverless, zero-configuration, transactional SQL database engine, and is free to use.

There are other frameworks that Xamarin supports such as ADO.NET and Realm, but it has been proven that SQLite is the most efficient database layer.

The first step in the setup process is to add the following SQLite NuGet packages in our `FileStorage.Portable` project:

- `SQLite.Net.Async-PCL`
- `SQLite.Net.Core-PCL`
- `SQLite.Net-PCL`

Once you add these in your packages, they should look like the following:

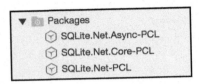

The next step is to add a new folder called `DataAccess`. Inside this folder, create two subfolders called `Storable` and `Storage`. Inside the `Storable` folder, add a new file called `IStorable.cs` and implement the following:

```
public interface IStorable
    {
        string Key { get; set; }
    }
```

This will be the interface for every object type stored in the database. In the preceding example, we are only going to have one storable, and each storable must have a string property called `Key`. This property will be used as the primary key for each database table.

Create another file in the `Storable` folder called `FileStorable.cs` and implement the following:

```
public class FileStorable : IStorable
    {
        #region Public Properties
        [PrimaryKey] public string Key { get; set; }
        public string Contents { get; set; }
        #endregion
    }
```

The `FileStorable` object will be used as the data model for the file storable table in the database. In SQLite, during the setup of the database, tables are created from objects using the following:

```
CreateTable<FileStorable>(CancellationToken.None);
```

The `FileStorable` object we pass as the type to the `CreateTable` function is used to map columns in the table.

Building the ISQLiteStorage interface

Now we must set up another class, which will be used to control the queries performed on the database. Add a new file called `ISQLiteStorage.cs` into the `Storage` folder and implement the following:

```
public interface ISQLiteStorage
    {
        void CreateSQLiteAsyncConnection();
        Task CreateTable<T>(CancellationToken token) where T : class,
IStorable, new();
        Task InsertObject<T>(T item, CancellationToken token) where T :
class, IStorable, new();
        Task<IList<T>> GetTable<T>(CancellationToken token) where T :
class, IStorable, new();
        Task<T> GetObject<T>(string key, CancellationToken token) where T
: class, IStorable, new();
        Task ClearTable<T>(CancellationToken token) where T : class,
IStorable, new();
        Task DeleteObjectByKey<T>(string key, CancellationToken token)
where T : class, IStorable, new();
        void CloseConnection();
    }
```

The preceding interface defines all the functions that will be executed on the database. The advantage of using SQLite is that it performs all processing asynchronously, so every function that executes an SQL query returns a task. If you look closely at the `InsertObject` and `DeleteObjectByKey` functions, these require a type, meaning that we can execute queries to specific tables using types.

Adding additional threading techniques

This is where we will add some finesse with a common threading approach known as **asynchronous locking**. Since there will only be one instance of the **SQLiteStorage** object, this means we have the possibility of a race condition as multiple threads can make changes to the same database connection at the same time.

 Race conditions are a common threading issue where multiple threads try to perform operations at the same time on shared data.

How do we solve this problem?

Locking is the most common C# approach for restricting shared resources between multiple threads. In order to avoid this situation, we create an object for locking as follows:

```
private Object lockObject = new Object();
```

Then, to restrict code blocks to one thread at any one time, we do the following:

```
lock (thisLock)
    {
        ...
    }
```

This is the perfect approach when our code is synchronous. The problem we have is our SQLite implementation is asynchronous, and the restriction with basic locking is we cannot execute asynchronous code inside a lock statement. This is where we have to implement the async-lock pattern.

Creating the AsyncSemaphore

Let's add a new folder called `Threading` to the `FileStorage.Portable` project. Inside this folder, we are going to add a new file called `AsyncSemaphore.cs` and implement the first part as follows:

```
public class AsyncSemaphore
    {
        private readonly static Task s_completed = Task.FromResult(true);
        private readonly Queue<TaskCompletionSource<bool>> m_waiters = new
Queue<TaskCompletionSource<bool>>();
```

```
        private int m_currentCount;
        public AsyncSemaphore(int initialCount)
        {
            if (initialCount < 0) throw new
ArgumentOutOfRangeException("initialCount");
            m_currentCount = initialCount;
        }
        public Task WaitAsync()
        {
            lock (m_waiters)
            {
                if (m_currentCount > 0)
                {
                    --m_currentCount;
                    return s_completed;
                }
                else
                {
                    var waiter = new TaskCompletionSource<bool>();
                    m_waiters.Enqueue(waiter); return waiter.Task;
                }
            }
        }
    }
}
```

 A SemaphoreSlim object is used to limit the number of threads that can access a resource.

The AsyncSemaphore keeps a count (the m_count property), which is the number of open *slots* it has available to satisfy waiters.

The Task returned from the WaitAsync function (the static s_completed property) will enter the completed state when the AsyncSemaphore has given it an available slot. That same Task will enter the Canceled state if the CancellationToken is signaled before the wait is satisfied; in that case, the AsyncSemaphore does not lose a slot.

 A waiter is simply a TaskCompletionSource of type bool. It contains a Task, which is the operation to be performed by a single thread.

Creating the AsyncLock

Now that we have built the `AsyncSemaphore` class, we will use this object inside the `AsyncLock` object. Let's add a new file called `AsyncLock.cs` into the `Threading` folder and implement the following:

```
public class AsyncLock
{
    private readonly AsyncSemaphore m_semaphore;
    private readonly Task<Releaser> m_releaser;
    public AsyncLock()
    {
        m_semaphore = new AsyncSemaphore(1);
        m_releaser = Task.FromResult(new Releaser(this));
    }
    public Task<Releaser> LockAsync()
    {
        var wait = m_semaphore.WaitAsync();
        return wait.IsCompleted ?
        m_releaser :
        wait.ContinueWith((_, state) =>
        new Releaser((AsyncLock)state),
            this, CancellationToken.None,
            TaskContinuationOptions.ExecuteSynchronously,
    TaskScheduler.Default);
    }
    public struct Releaser : IDisposable
    {
        private readonly AsyncLock m_toRelease;
        internal Releaser(AsyncLock toRelease) { m_toRelease =
    toRelease; }
        public void Dispose()
        {
            if (m_toRelease != null)
                m_toRelease.m_semaphore.Release();
        }
    }
}
```

The `AsyncLock` class uses the `AsyncSemaphore` to ensure that only one thread at any one time has access to the bounded code block after the `LockAsync` function. The lock can be acquired asynchronously by calling `LockAsync`, and it is released by disposing the result of that task. The `AsyncLock` takes an optional `CancellationToken`, which can be used to cancel the acquiring of the lock.

The `Task` returned from the `LockAsync` function will enter the `Completed` state when it has acquired the `AsyncLock`. That same `Task` will enter the Canceled state if the `CancellationToken` is signaled before the wait is satisfied; in that case, the `AsyncLock` is not taken by that task.

Now let's get back to implementing the `SQLiteStorage` class; this is where we are going to implement the async-lock pattern.

Implementing native setup requirements for SQLite

Our next step is to add the final setup requirements. Each device platform has a specific framework that it must use when setting up the connection to the local database. This means we are going to add another dependency-injected interface to set these native side requirements.

Add a new file called `ISqliteSetup.cs` to the `Storage` folder and implement the following:

```
public interface ISQLiteSetup
    {
        string DatabasePath { get; set; }
        ISQLitePlatform Platform { get; set; }
    }
```

Before we implement this class in the platform projects, we need to add the following SQLite NuGet packages for all platform projects:

- `SQLite.Net.Async-PCL`
- `SQLite.Net.Core-PCL`
- `SQLite.Net-PCL`

Now let's turn our attention to the iOS project. Add a new folder called `DataAccess`, add in a new file called `SQLiteSetup.cs`, and implement the following:

```
public class SQLiteSetup : ISQLiteSetup
    {
        public string DatabasePath { get; set; }
        public ISQLitePlatform Platform { get; set; }
        public SQLiteSetup(ISQLitePlatform platform)
        {
            DatabasePath =
```

```
Path.Combine(Environment.GetFolderPath(Environment.SpecialFolder.Personal),
"filestorage.db3");;
                Platform = platform;
    }
}
```

The main property that we need to focus on is `ISQLitePlatform`. This comes from the `SQLite.Net.Interop` library. We will be registering this item inside an IoC container as we will need this instance down in the portable project when we create a connection to the database.

Before we go any further, we need to set up the IoC container with Autofac.

Implementing the IoC container and modules

Just like our last projects, we are going to set up another IoC container using Autofac. Let's first add the Autofac nuget packages to all projects in the solution. We can then copy the `IoC` folder from the `Stocklist.Portable` project in Chapter 5, *Building a Stocklist Application*. Make sure you include both the `IoC.cs` and `IModule.cs` files.

Now let's hop over to the native projects, add the `Modules` folder in the iOS and Android projects, and implement `IOSModule.cs` and `DroidModule.cs`:

```
public class IOSModule : IModule
    {
        #region Public Methods
        public void Register(ContainerBuilder builder)
        {
builder.RegisterType<SQLiteSetup>().As<ISQLiteSetup>().SingleInstance();
builder.RegisterType<SQLitePlatformIOS>().As<ISQLitePlatform>().SingleInsta
nce();
        }
        #endregion
    }
```

and the DroidModule,

```
public class DroidModule : IModule
    {
        #region Public Methods
        public void Register(ContainerBuilder builder)
        {
builder.RegisterType<SQLiteSetup>().As<ISQLiteSetup>().SingleInstance();
builder.RegisterType<SQLitePlatformAndroid>().As<ISQLitePlatform>().SingleI
nstance();
```

```
            }
      #endregion
}
```

 Notice how quick we are piecing things together?
When you have the right direction in building cross-platform applications,
the complexity of multiple platform support should not be an issue.

Inside both of the aforementioned modules we are registering the SQLiteSetup and
SQLitePlatformIOS/Droid objects so the SQLiteStorage implementation can use these
items inside the FileStorage.Portable project.

Before we get back to finishing off the SQLiteStorage implementation, we are going to set
up a useful logging approach that can be used in all cross-platform applications.

Implementing cross-platform logging

Now that we have our IoC container, we are going to use dependency injection for logging.
Adding customized logging features in cross-platform applications is very useful for
tracking operations between all of the different projects. The first step is to add a new folder
called Logging, add a new file called ILogger.cs, and implement the following:

```
public interface ILogger
    {
        #region Methods
        void WriteLine(string message);
        void WriteLineTime(string message, params object[] args);
        #endregion
    }
```

For this example, our logger is going to use the standard Debug console from
System.Diagnostics with iOS, but in Android we are going to use the extensive logging
functionality provided by Android.

Now let's add the `Logging` folder in both iOS and Android and implement the following:

```
public class LoggeriOS : ILogger
    {
        #region Public Methods
        public void WriteLine(string text)
        {
            Debug.WriteLine(text);
        }
        public void WriteLineTime(string text, params object[] args)
        {
            Debug.WriteLine(DateTime.Now.Ticks + " " + String.Format(text,
args));
        }
        #endregion
    }
```

Nothing too flash with iOS logging, but we have an extra output line for logging statements with current time.

Now, for the Android implementation, we are going to use native logging from the `Android.Util` library:

```
public class LoggerDroid : ILogger
    {
        #region Public Methods
        public void WriteLine(string text)
        {
            Log.WriteLine(LogPriority.Info, text, null);
        }
        public void WriteLineTime(string text, params object[] args)
        {
            Log.WriteLine(LogPriority.Info, DateTime.Now.Ticks + " " +
            String.Format(text, args), null);
        }
        #endregion
    }
```

In the `Log` object from the `Android.Util` library, we have the option to specify priorities (`info`, `debug`, `error`). The more we can dig into the specifics of what we want the application to spit out, the better we can track exactly what is happening under the hood.

Excellent! Now let's get back to building the `SQLiteStorage` implementation.

Implementing the SQLiteStorage class

Now back to the `FileStorage.Portable` project. Let's add another file into the `Storage` folder called `SQLiteStorage.cs` and implement the `private` variables:

```
public class SQLiteStorage : ISQLiteStorage
    {
        #region Private Properties
        private readonly AsyncLock asyncLock = new AsyncLock();
        private readonly object lockObject = new object();
        private SQLiteConnectionWithLock _conn;
        private SQLiteAsyncConnection _dbAsyncConn;
        private readonly ISQLitePlatform _sqlitePlatform;
        private string _dbPath;
        private readonly ILogger _log;
        private readonly string _tag;
        #endregion
    }
```

We have a private `AsyncLock` object as we will be doing synchronous and asynchronous locking implementations. We then have two SQLite objects for creating the connection to our local database. The `_dbPath` variable is used to hold the local database path; this will be used for setting up the connection. We also have our dependency service interface `ILogger` and another string for tagging the current object. Tagging is useful with logging as it tells the logger what class is logging.

Introduction to C# 6.0 syntax

Now let's add in the constructor as follows:

```
public SQLiteStorage(ISQLiteSetup sqliteSetup, ILogger log)
    {
        _dbPath = sqliteSetup?.DatabasePath;
        _sqlitePlatform = sqliteSetup?.Platform;
        _log = log; _tag = $"{GetType()} ";
    }
```

Here we can see some C# 6.0 syntax. Using the question mark (?) after the constructor parameter `sqliteSetup` means that, if the object is not null, we can access the property. This avoids having to create an `if` statement such as the following:

```
If (sqliteSetup != null)
    _dbPath = sqliteSetup?.DatabasePath;
```

There is also some more C# 6.0 syntax with the following:

```
_tag = $"{GetType()} ";
```

The dollar sign ($) character is used for interpolated strings. Interpolated string expressions create a string by replacing the contained expressions with the ToString representations of the expressions' results.

Look more closely at the items we are assigning. We are using the SQLiteSetup object to set the database path and SQLite platform properties.

Let's add our first two methods:

```
public void CreateSQLiteAsyncConnection()
    {
        var connectionFactory = new Func<SQLiteConnectionWithLock>(() =>
        {
            if (_conn == null)
            {
                _conn = new SQLiteConnectionWithLock(_sqlitePlatform, new
SQLiteConnectionString(_dbPath, true));
            }
            return _conn;
        });
        _dbAsyncConn = new SQLiteAsyncConnection(connectionFactory);
    }
        public async Task CreateTable<T>(CancellationToken token) where T :
class, IStorable, new()
        {
            using (var releaser = await asyncLock.LockAsync())
            {
                await _dbAsyncConn.CreateTableAsync<T>(token);
            }
        }
```

The CreateSQLiteAsyncConnection function creates a new Func of type SQLiteConnectionWithLock, we use this Func to instantiate a new SQLiteAsyncConnection. The Func checks if we have already created a connection to the database. If we haven't yet established this connection, it will create a new instance of the SQLiteConnectionWithLock object and pass in the database path and platform we retrieved from the SQLSetup object.

In the CreateTable function, we will take our first look at the async-lock pattern. The great thing about the AsyncLock object is that we can contain the await inside a using statement. When one thread is creating a table on the one instance of the SQLiteAsyncConnection, another thread will have to wait at the using line until the previous thread has finished creating the table.

Our next function is `GetTable`. This will use the async-lock pattern again to make sure that only one thread is querying the database at any one time. This function will perform a standard SQL query for selecting all the items of a table:

```
SELECT * FROM {TableName};
```

The table will be determined by the type `T` passed, and the result received from the database will be all the table's items as an `IEnumerable` of type `T`:

```
public async Task<IList<T>> GetTable<T>(CancellationToken token) where T :
class, IStorable, new()
    {
        var items = default(IList<T>);
        using (var releaser = await asyncLock.LockAsync())
        {
            try
            {
                items = await
_dbAsyncConn.QueryAsync<T>(string.Format("SELECT * FROM {0};",
typeof(T).Name));
            }
            catch (Exception error)
            {
                var location = string.Format("GetTable<T>() Failed to
'SELECT *' from table {0}.", typeof(T).Name);
                _log.WriteLineTime(_tag + "\n" + location + "\n" +
"ErrorMessage: \n" + error.Message + "\n" + "Stacktrace: \n " +
error.StackTrace);
            }
        }
        return items;
    }
```

Notice how we are catching any exception that may occur in this query?

We are building a location string to pinpoint the exact location in our application where the exception is coming from. Then we use our `ILogger` implementation to route the custom-built exception string to the specific native output console.

Next we have the `InsertObject` function. This will be responsible for adding a new item to the correct table in the database. We will also make use of the async-lock pattern to lock the connection from being accessed while an insertion is taking place:

```
public async Task InsertObject<T>(T item, CancellationToken token) where T
 : class, IStorable, new()
```

```
        {
                using (var releaser = await asyncLock.LockAsync())
                {
                    try
                    {
                        var insertOrReplaceQuery =
item.CreateInsertOrReplaceQuery();
                        await _dbAsyncConn.QueryAsync<T>(insertOrReplaceQuery);
                    }
                    catch (Exception error)
                    {
                        var location = string.Format("InsertObject<T>() Failed to
insert
                        or replace object with key {0}.", item.Key);
                        _log.WriteLineTime(_tag + "\n" + location + "\n" +
"ErrorMessage:
                        \n" + error.Message + "\n" + "Stacktrace: \n " +
                        error.StackTrace);
                    }
                }
        }
```

Notice the `CreateInsertOrReplaceQuery` function?

We are going to add an extension class to the `IStorable` interface. Add a new file called `StorableExtensions.cs` to the location **DataAccess | Storable** in the `FileStorage.Portable` project and implement the following:

```
    public static class StorableExtensions
        {
            #region Public Methods
            public static string CreateInsertOrReplaceQuery(this IStorable
    storable)
                {
                    var properties = storable.GetType().GetRuntimeProperties();
                    var tableName = storable.GetType().Name;
                    string propertiesString = "";
                    string propertyValuesString = "";
                    var index = 0;
                    foreach (var property in properties)
                    {
                        propertiesString += (index == (properties.Count() - 1)) ?
                        property.Name : property.Name + ", ";
                        var value = property.GetValue(storable);
                        var valueString = value == null ? "null" : value is bool ?
        "'"
                        + ((bool)value ? 1 : 0) + "'" : "'" + value + "'";
                        // if data is serialized if (property.Name.Equals("Data") &&
```

```
        !valueString.Equals("null"))
        {
            valueString = valueString.Replace("""", """");
        }
        propertyValuesString += valueString +
        ((index == (properties.Count() - 1)) ? string.Empty : ", ");
        index++;
    }
        return string.Format("INSERT OR REPLACE INTO {0}({1})
        VALUES ({2});", tableName, propetiesString,
propertyValuesString);
    }
      #endregion
  }
```

The preceding function is clever enough to build an insert and replace query out of any item that inherits the `IStorable` interface. It uses the `System.Reflection` library to retrieve all properties of an `IStorable` object using the `GetRuntimeProperties` function. We then iterate through all properties and build a query according to the following syntax:

```
INSERT OR REPLACE INTO names (prop1, prop2, ...) VALUES (val1, val2,
...)
```

 If we didn't have the `PrimaryKey` attribute set on the `Key` property in the `FileStorable` class, the update would not work and a new item would be added every time.

Now for the `DeleteObjectByKey` function. This will be used to delete an item from a table using the `Key` property from the `IStorable` interface:

```
public async Task DeleteObjectByKey<T>(string key, CancellationToken token)
where T : class, IStorable, new()
    {
        using (var releaser = await asyncLock.LockAsync())
        {
            try
            {
                await _dbAsyncConn.QueryAsync<T>(string.Format("DELETE FROM
{0} WHERE Key='{1}';", typeof(T).Name, key));
            }
            catch (Exception error)
            {
                var location = string.Format("DeleteObjectByKey<T>()
Failed to
                delete object from key {0}.", key);
                _log.WriteLineTime(_tag + "\n" + location + "\n" +
```

```
                    "ErrorMessage: \n" + error.Message + "\n" + "Stacktrace:
\n " +
                    error.StackTrace);
            }
        }
    }
```

Fantastic! SQLite has been set up and integrated with the async-lock pattern to make it thread-safe. Our final step is to add the `PortableModule` for the IoC container and register the `SqliteStorage` class.

Inside the `FireStorable.Portable` project, create a new folder called `Modules`, add in a new file called `PortableModule.cs`, and implement the following:

```
public class PortableModule : IModule
    {
        #region Public Methods
        public void Register(ContainerBuilder builder)
        {
builder.RegisterType<SQLiteStorage>().As<ISQLiteStorage>().SingleInstance()
;
        }
        #endregion
    }
```

Now we can start with the user interface layer and begin building some custom UI objects.

Handling alerts in view-models

Handling alerts via view-models is important as we handle many errors via `try/catch` statements. To respond to these errors, we want to display an alert dialog showing the error message to the user. There are two ways we are going to do this:

- Using an `EventHandler` for pushing events to the current page so that we can call the `DisplayAlert` function with different messages
- Using an interface for dependency injection where we will implement native alerts

Our first step is to add the `ViewModelBase` class; this is where alerts will be fired from.

Create a new folder in the `FileStorage.Portable` project called `ViewModels`, add a new file called `ViewModelBase.cs`, and implement the following:

```
public class ViewModelBase : INotifyPropertyChanged
```

```
        {
            #region Public Events
              public event PropertyChangedEventHandler PropertyChanged;
              public event EventHandler<string> Alert;
            #endregion
            #region Private Properties
              private IMethods _methods;
            #endregion
            #region Public Properties
              public INavigationService Navigation;
            #endregion
            #region Constructors
              public ViewModelBase(INavigationService navigation, IMethods
    methods)
                {
                    Navigation = navigation;
                    _methods = methods;
                }
            #endregion
        }
```

We are using the same `ViewModelBase` implementation we used in Chapter 5, *Building a Stocklist Application*, except we are adding an extra `IMethods` interface in the constructor (we will implement this later), which is used to show native alerts.

Next, add the protected methods `OnPropertyChanged` and `LoadAsync` as follows:

```
#region Protected Methods
protected virtual void OnPropertyChanged([CallerMemberName] string
propertyName = null)
  {
      PropertyChangedEventHandler handler = PropertyChanged;
      if (handler != null)
        {
            handler(this, new PropertyChangedEventArgs(propertyName));
        }
  }
  protected virtual async Task LoadAsync(IDictionary<string, object>
parameters)
  {
  }
#endregion
```

And the public methods as follows:

```
#region Public Methods
public Task<string> ShowEntryAlert(string message)
  {
```

```
        var tcs = new TaskCompletionSource<string>();
        _methods.DisplayEntryAlert(tcs, message);
        return tcs.Task;
    }
  public void NotifyAlert(string message)
    {
        if (Alert != null)
        {
          Alert(this, message);
        }
    }
  public void OnShow(IDictionary<string, object> parameters)
    {
        LoadAsync(parameters).ToObservable().Subscribe( result =>
          {
            // we can add things to do after we load the view model }, ex =>
            {
              // we can handle any areas from the load async function });
          }
    #endregion
```

Even though we are working in the portable project, this is still part of the presentation layer when it comes to architecture.

The `NotifyAlert` function is used to display alerts via the `Xamarin.Forms` function `DisplayAlert` on a `ContentPage`. The `ShowEntryAlert` function is used to display alerts via the `IMethod` interface.

Notice the use of the TaskCompletionSource?

This means we can await the `ShowEntryAlert` function. When the user responds to the alert, the `Task` will enter the completed state. This ensures that the code is executed only once a response is received.

Building the IMethods interface

Let's start by creating a new folder in the `FileStorage.Portable` project, adding a new file called `IMethods.cs`, and implementing the following:

```
public interface IMethods
  {
    #region Methods
```

```
    void Exit();
    void DisplayEntryAlert(TaskCompletionSource<string> tcs, string
message);
    #endregion
  }
```

For all native projects, add a new folder called Extras. Let's start with the iOS project. add a new file called IOSMethods.cs, and implement the following:

```
public class IOSMethods : IMethods
  {
    #region Public Methods
    public void Exit()
    {
        UIApplication.SharedApplication.PerformSelector(new
ObjCRuntime.Selector("terminateWithSuccess"), null, 0f);
    }
    public void DisplayEntryAlert(TaskCompletionSource<string> tcs, string
message)
    {
      UIAlertView alert = new UIAlertView(); alert.Title = "Title";
      alert.AddButton("OK");
      alert.AddButton("Cancel");
      alert.Message = message;
      alert.AlertViewStyle = UIAlertViewStyle.PlainTextInput;
      alert.Clicked += (object s, UIButtonEventArgs ev) =>
        {
          if (ev.ButtonIndex == 0)
            {
              tcs.SetResult(alert.GetTextField(0).Text);
            }
          else
            {
              tcs.SetResult(null);
            }
        };
      alert.Show();
    }
    #endregion
  }
```

We should recognize the Exit function from previous chapters. The DisplayEntryAlert function creates a PlainTextInputUIAlertView. This alert will ask for text input via a textbox and we can retrieve this text value using the GetTextField function. The alert will also display a Yes and No button, so when the user enters text and presses Yes, a new file will be created with the text input set as the filename.

Now let's replicate the same procedure for Android. Add a new file called `DroidMethods.cs` and implement the following:

```
public class DroidMethods : IMethods
    {
      #region Public Methods
      public void Exit()
        {
          Android.OS.Process.KillProcess(Android.OS.Process.MyPid());
        }
      public void DisplayEntryAlert(TaskCompletionSource<string> tcs, string
message)
        {
          var context = Forms.Context;
          LayoutInflater factory = LayoutInflater.From(context);
          var view = factory.Inflate(Resource.Layout.EntryAlertView, null);
          var editText = view.FindViewById<EditText>(Resource.Id.textEntry);
          new AlertDialog.Builder(context)
            .SetTitle("Chat")
            .SetMessage(message)
            .SetPositiveButton("Ok", (sender, e) =>
              {
                tcs.SetResult(editText.Text);
              })
            .SetNegativeButton("Cancel", (sender, e) =>
              {
                tcs.SetResult(null);
              })
            .SetView(view)
            .Show();
        }
      #endregion
    }
```

This time for Android, we are using the `AlertDialog.Builder` framework. We use the `Forms.Context` property to retrieve the current context, which we use to create a new `AlertDialog.Builder`. We have to use the `SetView` function in this framework to assign a custom view for text input. This custom view is created using a new XML layout.

Add a new file called `EntryAlertView.xml` to the **Resources | layout** folder and implement the following:

```
<?xml version="1.0" encoding="utf-8"?>
<EditText xmlns:android="http://schemas.android.com/apk/res/android"
    android:id="@+id/textEntry" android:layout_height="wrap_content"
    android:layout_width="250px" android:layout_centerHorizontal="true"
    android:singleLine="true" />
```

All we have is an `EditText` object to retrieve the filename from the user in the alert dialog. Using `FindViewById` in the `DroidMethods` class, we can reference this `EditText` item to retrieve the text value entered by the user.

That's everything. Our next step is a customized `ContentPage` to handle the `Alert` events from each view-model.

Building the ExtendedContentPage

Add a new folder called `UI` inside the `FileStorage` project, add in a new file called `ExtendedContentPage.cs`, and implement the following:

```
public class ExtendedContentPage : ContentPage
  {
    #region Private Properties
      private ViewModelBase _model;
    #endregion
    #region Constructors
      public ExtendedContentPage(ViewModelBase model)
      {
        _model = model;
        _model.Alert -= HandleAlert;
        _model.Alert += HandleAlert;
      }
    #endregion
    #region Private Methods
      private async void HandleAlert(object sender, string message)
      {
        await DisplayAlert("FileStorage", message, "OK");
      }
    #endregion
  }
```

The `_model` property is used to reference the view-model of each page as every view-model inherits the `ViewModelBase` class. When the page is created, we register the `HandleAlert` function to the view-model `Alert` event. Every time this function is called, it will call the `DisplayAlert` function from `Xamarin.Forms`.

Why are we implementing two different techniques for showing alerts?

The cross-platform feature for displaying alerts does not allow us to use the text input addition that we built natively.

Great! We now have a nice solution for multiple types of alert in out cross-platform projects. Our next step is to implement our first custom layout known as a CarouselView.

Xamarin.Forms has its own CarouselView, but it has been removed until the UI object is more stable.

Building a CarouselView using custom layouts

Xamarin.Forms is a very young layout system, meaning that the number of layouts is quite limited. There are times when we will need to implement our own custom layouts to give us control over exactly where and how our views and controls appear on screen. The requirement will come from situations where you need to improve performance on screens that display a lot of views and controls, and sometimes the standard layouts are not good enough. We want to implement our custom layouts to carry out the absolute minimum amount of work required to produce the required layout.

All layouts derive from the Xamarin.Forms.Layout class, which provides the required mechanisms for adding and removing children internally as well as some key utilities for writing a layout.

Let's start by adding a new folder called Controls in the FireStorable project. Add a new file called CarouselLayout.cs and implement the first part as follows:

```
public class CarouselLayout : Layout<View>
    {
      #region Private Properties
        private IDisposable dataChangesSubscription;
        public double LayoutWidth;
      #endregion
    }
```

All layouts must inherit the `Layout` framework. `Xamarin.Forms.Layout<T>` provides a publicly exposed `IList<T>` Children that end users can access. We want all children of this collection to be of type `View`.

We have two `private` properties, one for the layout width and an `IDisposable` for handling data change subscriptions.

Let's add in some more properties:

```
#region Public Properties
public Object this[int index]
   {
      get
      {
        return index < ItemsSource.Count() ? ItemsSource.ToList()[index] :
null;
      }
   }
public DataTemplate ItemTemplate { get; set; }
public IEnumerable<Object> ItemsSource { get; set; }
#endregion
```

We have an indexing reference that will return an array element from the `ItemsSource` `IEnumerable`, and the `ItemTemplate` property, which is used to render a view layout for every child in `ItemsSource`. We have to use the `Linq` function `ToList` to allow us to access an `IEnumerable` via an index value.

Now we are going to add some overrides to the `Layout` framework. Every custom layout must override the `LayoutChildren` method. This is responsible for positioning children on screen:

```
protected override void LayoutChildren(double x, double y, double width,
double height)
   {
     var layout = ComputeLayout(width, height);
     var i = 0;
     foreach (var region in layout)
       {
         var child = Children[i];
         i++;
         LayoutChildIntoBoundingRegion(child, region);
       }
   }
```

The preceding function will call another method, `ComputeLayout`, which will return an `IEnumerable` of **Rectangles** (also known as **regions**). We then iterate through the `IEnumerable` and call `LayoutChildIntoBoundingRegion` for each region. This method will handle positioning the element relative to the bounding region.

Our layout must also implement the `OnMeasure` function. This is required to make sure the new layout is sized correctly when placed inside other layouts. During layout cycles, this method may be called many times depending on the layout above it and how many layout exceptions are required to resolve the current layout hierarchy. Add the following below the `LayoutChildren` function:

```
protected override SizeRequest OnMeasure(double widthConstraint, double
heightConstraint)
{
    List<Row> layout = ComputeNiaveLayout(widthConstraint,
heightConstraint);
    var last = layout[layout.Count - 1];
    var width = (last.Count > 0) ?
    last[0].X + last.Width : 0; var height = (last.Count > 0) ? last[0].Y +
    last.Height : 0;
    return new SizeRequest(new Size(width, height));
}
```

It is therefore important to consider speed when implementing this function. Failure to implement this function will not always break your layout, particularly if it's always inside parents, which fix the child size anyway.

The `ComputeNiaveLayout` will return a list of **rows**. We then retrieve the last row from this list and use this for the max x-value and max y-value to determine the total width and height by calculating the difference between the first and last element on both the x-axis and y-axis. Finally, we return a new `SizeRequest` object with the calculated width and height, which will be used to resize the layout.

Let's add the missing functions `ComputeNiaveLayout` and `ComputeLayout` as follows:

```
public IEnumerable<Rectangle> ComputeLayout(double widthConstraint, double
heightConstraint)
{
    List<Row> layout = ComputeNiaveLayout(widthConstraint,
heightConstraint);
    return layout.SelectMany(s => s);
}
```

This function is used simply to perform the SelectMany query. The ComputeNiaveLayout layout is where all the work is done. This will iterate through all children; it will create one **row**, and one rectangle inside this row that will size to the height of the layout and the width will equal the total of all children widths. All children will be positioned horizontally next to one another to the right of the screen, as shown in the following screenshot:

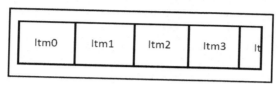

But only one child will be visible on screen at any one time as each child is sized to the full height and width of the layout:

```
private List<Row> ComputeNiaveLayout (double widthConstraint, double
heightConstraint)
    {
        var result = new List<Row>();
        var row = new Row();
        result.Add(row);
        var spacing = 20;
        double y = 0;
        foreach (var child in Children)
        {
            var request = child.Measure(double.PositiveInfinity,
            double.PositiveInfinity);
            if (row.Count == 0)
            {
                row.Add(new Rectangle(0, y, LayoutWidth, Height));
                row.Height = request.Request.Height; continue;
            }
            var last = row[row.Count - 1];
            var x = last.Right + spacing;
            var childWidth = LayoutWidth;
            var childHeight = request.Request.Height;
            row.Add(new Rectangle(x, y, childWidth, Height));
            row.Width = x + childWidth; row.Height = Math.Max(row.Height,
Height);
        }
        return result;
    }
```

Hold on! What if I have a lot of children? This means that they will be stacked horizontally past the width of the screen. What do we do now?

The idea of a carousel view is to only show one view at a time, when the user swipes left and right; the view on the left/right side of the current view will come onto screen while the current view will move out of view, as shown in the following screenshot:

Even though we have a custom layout that presents children horizontally, how are we going to handle the swipe events and scroll control?

We will achieve scroll control via a `ScrollView` and create a custom renderer for handling swipe events.

Adding scroll control to the CarouselView

Add a new file into the `Controls` folder called `CarouselScroll.cs` and implement the first part as follows:

```
public class CarouselScroll : ScrollView
{
    #region Private Properties
    private CarouselLayout _carouselLayout;
    #endregion
    public DataTemplate ItemTemplate
    {
        set
        {
            _carouselLayout.ItemTemplate = value;
        }
    }
    public CarouselScroll()
    {
```

```
        Orientation = ScrollOrientation.Horizontal;
        _carouselLayout = new CarouselLayout();
        Content = _carouselLayout;
    }
}
```

The `CarouselScroll` will inherit the `ScrollView` object as this will be the bounding view for the `CarouselLayout`. We are also going to create a `DataTemplate` variable for setting the `DataTemplate` object inside the `CarouselLayout`. Then, in the constructor, we instantiate a new `CarouselLayout` object as the `Content` of the `ScrollView`.

Now let's add a custom binding object for the `ItemsSource`. Like a `ListView`, we will bind an `ObserableCollection` of items to this property:

```
        public static readonly BindableProperty ItemsSourceProperty =
        BindableProperty.Create<CarouselLayout, IEnumerable<Object>>(o =>
        o.ItemsSource,
            default(IEnumerable<Object>), propertyChanged: (bindable, oldvalues,
        newValues) =>
            {
            ((CarouselScroll)bindable)._carouselLayout.ItemsSource = newValues;
            });
```

Take note of the `propertyChanged` event; when the binding changes, we will update the `ItemsSource` property of the `CarouselLayout`. Remember that the `CarouselLayout` is in charge of laying out a child for every item in the `IEnumerable`.

We also need another bindable property for data changes. This will be an `IObservable` object that will listen for any `DataChange` events. If an event occurs, the `CarouselLayout` will layout the children:

```
        public static readonly BindableProperty DataChangesProperty =
        BindableProperty.Create("DataChanges",
            typeof(IObservable<DataChange>), typeof(CarouselLayout), null,
        propertyChanged: (bindable, oldvalue, newValue) =>
            {
        ((CarouselScroll)bindable)._carouselLayout.SubscribeDataChanges((IObservabl
        e<DataChange>)newValue);
            });
```

Then we need to override the `LayoutChildren` function; so when the `ScrollView` updates its children, we want to update the height and width properties of the `CarouselLayout`, thus updating the layout of the children:

```
        protected override void LayoutChildren(double x, double y, double width,
        double height)
```

```
    {
        base.LayoutChildren(x, y, width, height);
        if (_carouselLayout != null)
        {
            if (width > _carouselLayout.LayoutWidth)
            {
                _carouselLayout.LayoutWidth = width;
            }
            _carouselLayout.ComputeLayout(width, height);
        }
    }
}
```

We also have one more function, `GetSelectedItem`, which simply returns a child from the `CarouselLayout` using an index:

```
public Object GetSelectedItem(int selected)
{
    return _carouselLayout[selected];
}
```

Our next stage into the `CarouselView` is creating a `CustomRenderer` that will allow swipe gestures.

Building a CustomRenderer for native gestures

Now we need to handle swipe left and right gestures for each mobile platform. Unfortunately, `Xamarin.Forms` doesn't offer a cross-platform feature for swipe gestures, so we need to implement this ourselves. In order to do this, we are going to build a `CustomRenderer`. Start by adding a new file to the `Controls` folder called `GestureView.cs` and implement the following:

```
public class GestureView : View
{
    public event EventHandler SwipeLeft;
    public event EventHandler SwipeRight;
    public event EventHandler Touch;
    public void NotifySwipeLeft()
    {
        if (SwipeLeft != null)
        {
            SwipeLeft (this, EventArgs.Empty);
        }
    }
}
```

```
public void NotifySwipeRight ()
  {
     if (SwipeRight != null)
       {
          SwipeRight (this, EventArgs.Empty);
       }
  }
public void NotifyTouch ()
  {
     if (Touch != null)
       {
          Touch(this, EventArgs.Empty);
       }
     }
  }
```

This view has an `EventHandler` for each gesture, we also require a gesture for tap events. Even though `Xamarin.Forms` offers this feature when we render over the top of the `CarouselView` at runtime, the `Xamarin.Forms` gesture will no longer work.

Now, inside the `FileStorage.iOS` project, let's add a new folder called `Renderers` and another folder inside this called `GestureView`. Then, inside the `GestureView` folder, add in a new file called `GestureViewiOS.cs` and implement the following:

```
[Register ("GestureViewiOS")]
  public sealed class GestureViewiOS : UIView
    {
       private UIView _mainView;
       private UISwipeGestureRecognizer _swipeLeftGestureRecognizer;
       private UISwipeGestureRecognizer _swipeRightGestureRecognizer;
       private UITapGestureRecognizer _tapGestureRecognizer;
       public GestureViewiOS ()
         {
           _mainView = new UIView ()
             {
               TranslatesAutoresizingMaskIntoConstraints = false
             };
           _mainView.BackgroundColor = UIColor.Clear;
         Add (_mainView);
         // set layout constraints for main view AddConstraints
         (NSLayoutConstraint.FromVisualFormat ("V:|[mainView]|",
          NSLayoutFormatOptions.DirectionLeftToRight, null,
          new NSDictionary ("mainView", _mainView)));
         AddConstraints (NSLayoutConstraint.FromVisualFormat ("H:|[mainView]|",
NSLayoutFormatOptions.AlignAllTop, null, new NSDictionary ("mainView",
_mainView)));
         }
```

```
    }
```

This view has an `EventHandler` for each gesture, we also require a gesture for tap events. Even though `Xamarin.Forms` offers these features when we render over the top of the `CarouselView` at runtime, the Xamarin.Forms gesture will no longer work.

```
public void InitGestures(GestureView swipeView)
    {
        _swipeLeftGestureRecognizer = new UISwipeGestureRecognizer
(swipeView.NotifySwipeLeft);
        _swipeLeftGestureRecognizer.Direction =
UISwipeGestureRecognizerDirection.Left;
        _swipeRightGestureRecognizer = new UISwipeGestureRecognizer
(swipeView.NotifySwipeRight);
        _swipeRightGestureRecognizer.Direction =
UISwipeGestureRecognizerDirection.Right;
        _tapGestureRecognizer = new
UITapGestureRecognizer(swipeView.NotifyTouch);
        _tapGestureRecognizer.NumberOfTapsRequired = 1;
        _mainView.AddGestureRecognizer (_swipeLeftGestureRecognizer);
        _mainView.AddGestureRecognizer (_swipeRightGestureRecognizer);
        _mainView.AddGestureRecognizer (_tapGestureRecognizer);
    }
```

This function will only be called once from the `OnElementChanged` function of the `GestureViewRenderer`.

Now let's add the renderer class. Add another file called `GestureViewRenderer.cs` and implement the following:

```
public class GestureLayoutRenderer : ViewRenderer<GestureView,
GestureViewiOS>
    {
        private GestureViewiOS _swipeViewIOS;
        private bool gesturesAdded;
        public GestureLayoutRenderer()
            {
                _swipeViewIOS = new GestureViewiOS ();
            }
        protected override void OnElementChanged
(ElementChangedEventArgs<GestureView> e)
            {
                base.OnElementChanged (e);
                if (Control == null)
                    {
                        SetNativeControl(_swipeViewIOS);
                    }
```

```
if (Element != null && !gesturesAdded)
    {
        _swipeViewIOS.InitGestures(Element);
        gesturesAdded = true;
    }
    }
}
```

Whenever a property from the `UI` object changes, the `OnElementChanged` function will be called. We only call the `SetNativeControl` once if the `Control` property of the renderer is null. The `Element` property of a renderer is usually the UI object from the `Xamarin.Forms` project (in our case the `FileStorage` project, `GestureView`). When we receive a reference to the `GestureView` object (inside the `OnElementChanged` function), we pass this into the `InitGestures` function in order to use the `EventHandlers` on the `GestureView` object. Now, when we swipe left and right or tap on the native `mainView` object, it will call the `NotifySwipeLeft`, `NotifySwipeLeft`, and `NotifyTouch` functions for the `GestureView` object.

Don't forget to add the following line above the namespace declaration:

```
[assembly:
Xamarin.Forms.ExportRenderer(typeof(FileStorage.Controls.GestureView),
typeof(FileStorage.iOS.Renderers.GestureView.GestureLayoutRenderer))]
    namespace FileStorage.iOS.Renderers.GestureView
```

We must always add the `ExportRenderer` attribute to a custom renderer class to specify that it will be used to render the `Xamarin.Forms` control.

The `GestureViewiOS` object will be the view displayed on top of the `GestureView` object in our `FileStorage` project. Wherever a new `GestureView` object is placed in our `ContentPage`, the `GestureViewRenderer` will render a new `GestreViewiOS` view in its place.

Now let's implement the same for Android. Add a new folder inside the `FileStorage.Droid` project called `Renderers` and another folder inside this called `GestureView`. Then, inside the `GestureView` folder, add in a new file called `GestureListener.cs` and implement the first part:

```
public class GestureListener : GestureDetector.SimpleOnGestureListener
    {
        private const int SWIPE_THRESHOLD = 50;
        private const int SWIPE_VELOCITY_THRESHOLD = 50;
        private GestureView _swipeView;
        public void InitCoreSwipeView(GestureView swipeView)
        {
```

```
            _swipeView = swipeView;
    }
}
```

A `GestureDetector` is used to respond to multiple types of press event for a particular view. We also pass the `Xamarin.Forms GestureView` object into this class so that we can fire the `NotifySwipeLeft`, `NotifySwipeLeft`, and `NotifyTouch` functions when a particular event occurs. The threshold values are used as a minimum swipe distance and touch pressure. When a user performs a swipe on this view, a certain amount of pressure and movement must be applied for an event to be fired.

 The `SimpleOnGestureListener` extension is a convenience class when you only want to listen for a subset of all the gestures.

Now we must override the following functions (we aren't going to be doing anything with these but they must be overridden):

```
public override void OnLongPress (MotionEvent e)
    {
        base.OnLongPress (e);
    }
public override bool OnDoubleTap (MotionEvent e)
    {
        return base.OnDoubleTap (e);
    }
public override bool OnDoubleTapEvent (MotionEvent e)
    {
        return base.OnDoubleTapEvent (e);
    }
public override bool OnDown (MotionEvent e)
    {
        return base.OnDown (e);
    }
public override bool OnScroll (MotionEvent e1, MotionEvent e2, float
distanceX, float distanceY)
    {
        return base.OnScroll (e1, e2, distanceX, distanceY);
    }
public override void OnShowPress (MotionEvent e)
    {
        base.OnShowPress (e);
    }
public override bool OnSingleTapConfirmed (MotionEvent e)
    {
        return base.OnSingleTapConfirmed (e);
```

```
}
```

Now for the functions that we are going to use. The `OnSingleTapUp` function will be responsible for handling touch events, called when a user applies a single tap gesture to the view:

```
public override bool OnSingleTapUp (MotionEvent e)
    {
      _swipeView.NotifyTouch();
      return base.OnSingleTapUp (e);
    }
```

The `OnFling` function is responsible for handling swipe events. The two `MotionEvent` items are the start and end points (*x*, *y*) when a user starts to swipe and when the finger is removed. We calculate the drag distance and make sure that the absolute value of `diffX` is greater than the absolute value of `diffY`. This ensures that we are dragging horizontally. We then make sure that the absolute value of `diffX` is greater than the `Swipe_Threshold`, and the `VelocityX` is greater than the `Swipe_Velocity_Threshold`. If all this is met, we then fire a swipe right if the `diffX` is positive; otherwise, it will fire a swipe left:

```
public override bool OnFling (MotionEvent e1, MotionEvent e2, float
velocityX, float velocityY)
    {
      try
        {
          float diffY = e2.GetY() - e1.GetY();
          float diffX = e2.GetX() - e1.GetX();
          if (Math.Abs(diffX) > Math.Abs(diffY))
            {
              if (Math.Abs(diffX) > SWIPE_THRESHOLD && Math.Abs(velocityX) >
SWIPE_VELOCITY_THRESHOLD)
                {
                  if (_swipeView != null)
                    {
                      if (diffX > 0)
                        {
                          _swipeView.NotifySwipeRight ();
                        }
                      else
                        {
                          _swipeView.NotifySwipeLeft ();
                        }
                    }
                }
            }
        }
      catch (Exception) { }
```

```
        return base.OnFling (e1, e2, velocityX, velocityY);
    }
```

Let's now build the `GestureViewRenderer` and integrate is with the `GestureDetector`. Add a new file into the `Gesture` folder called `GestureViewRenderer.cs` and implement the following:

```
public class GestureViewRenderer : ViewRenderer<GestureView, LinearLayout>
    {
        private LinearLayout _layout;
        private readonly GestureListener _listener;
        private readonly GestureDetector _detector;
        public GestureViewRenderer ()
            {
                _listener = new GestureListener ();
                _detector = new GestureDetector (_listener);
                _layout = new LinearLayout (Context);
            }
    }
```

We are now going to create an empty `LinearLayout` to use for the `Control`. This is the blank view that will receive the touch events. We then instantiate a new `GestureListener` from above and pass this into a new `GestureDetector`. The GestureDetector's `OnTouchEvent` function is called for all touch and motion events, and within this class we break down the events in more detail to determine the exact event that took place:

```
protected override void OnElementChanged
    (ElementChangedEventArgs<GestureView> e)
    {
      base.OnElementChanged (e);
      if (e.NewElement == null)
        {
          GenericMotion -= HandleGenericMotion;
          Touch -= HandleTouch;
        }
      if (e.OldElement == null)
        {
          GenericMotion += HandleGenericMotion;
          Touch += HandleTouch;
        }
      if (Element != null)
        {
          _listener.InitCoreSwipeView (Element);
        }
      SetNativeControl (_layout);
    }
    private void HandleTouch (object sender, TouchEventArgs e)
```

```
    {
        _detector.OnTouchEvent (e.Event);
    }
    private void HandleGenericMotion (object sender, GenericMotionEventArgs
e)
    {
        _detector.OnTouchEvent (e.Event);
    }
```

Notice the null checks on the `OldElemenet` and `NewElement` properties of the arguments?

If the `OldElemenet` is null, we must deregister touch events, and if the `NewElement` is null, we register the `GenericMotion` and `Touch` events.

Now that we have our `GestureView` and `GestureViewRenderers` ready, it's time to create the final control and add a new **Forms ContentView Xaml** file called `CarouselView.xaml`, as shown in the following screenshot:

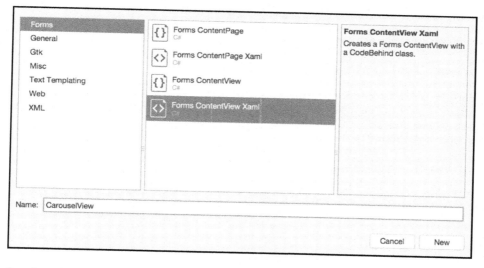

We also implement the following in `CarouselView.xaml`:

```xml
<?xml version="1.0" encoding="UTF-8"?>
<ContentView xmlns="http://xamarin.com/schemas/2014/forms"
    xmlns:x="http://schemas.microsoft.com/winfx/2009/xaml"
    xmlns:controls="clr-namespace:FileStorage.Controls;assembly=FileStorage"
    x:Class="FileStorage.Controls.CarouselView">
<ContentView.Content>
    <Grid x:Name="Container">
    <Grid.RowDefinitions>
```

```
        <RowDefinition Height="*"/>
      </Grid.RowDefinitions>
      <Grid.ColumnDefinitions>
        <ColumnDefinition Width="*"/>
      </Grid.ColumnDefinitions>
      <controls:CarouselScroll x:Name="CarouselScroll" ItemsSource="{Binding
    Cells}"
        ItemTemplate="{StaticResource CarouselTemplate}"
        DataChanges="{Binding DataChanges}" Grid.Row="0" Grid.Column="0"/>
      <controls:GestureView x:Name="GestureView" Grid.Row="0" Grid.Column="0"/>
      </Grid>
    </ContentView.Content>
  </ContentView>
```

The preceding code will create a Grid to overlay the GestureView on top of the CarouselScroll. This means that the GestureView will detect the swipe and touch events and pass these down to the CarouselScroll.

Now let's implement CarouselView.xaml.cs as follows:

```
public partial class CarouselView : ContentView
  {
      private bool _animating;
      public int SelectedIndex = 0;
      public static readonly BindableProperty SelectedCommandProperty =
    BindableProperty.Create<CarouselView, ICommand>(w => w.SelectedCommand,
    default(ICommand),
        propertyChanged: (bindable, oldvalue, newvalue) => { });

      public ICommand SelectedCommand
        {
          get
          {
            return (ICommand)GetValue(SelectedCommandProperty);
          }
          set
          {
            SetValue(SelectedCommandProperty, value);
          }
        }
      public CarouselView()
        {
            InitializeComponent();
            GestureView.SwipeLeft += HandleSwipeLeft;
            GestureView.SwipeRight += HandleSwipeRight;
            GestureView.Touch += HandleTouch;
        }
  }
```

The first part shows the event registration to the GestureView. We also have a custom binding for a Command, which will be invoked when a Touch event occurs. Let's add the EventHandler functions as follows:

```
public void HandleTouch(object sender, EventArgs e)
    {
      if (SelectedCommand != null)
      {
        var cell = CarouselScroll.GetSelectedItem(SelectedIndex);
        SelectedCommand.Execute(cell);
      }
    }
public async void HandleSwipeLeft(object sender, EventArgs e)
    {
      if (((CarouselScroll.ScrollX + CarouselScroll.Width) <
(CarouselScroll.Content.Width - CarouselScroll.Width)) && !_animating)
        {
          _animating = true;
          SelectedIndex++;
          await CarouselScroll.ScrollToAsync(CarouselScroll.ScrollX + Width +
20, 0, true);
          _animating = false;
        }
    }
public async void HandleSwipeRight(object sender, EventArgs e)
    {
      if (CarouselScroll.ScrollX > 0 && !_animating)
      {
        _animating = true;
        SelectedIndex--;
        await CarouselScroll.ScrollToAsync(CarouselScroll.ScrollX - Width
- 20, 0, true);
        _animating = false;
      }
    }
  }
}
```

The HandleTouch function will simply call the GetSelectedItem function from the CarouselScroll. This means we get the bound object from the view and we use this as a parameter that is passed into the execution of the SelectCommand. The HandleSwipeLeft function will increase the selected index by 1 and scroll to the left by the entire width amount of the view. Remember, each child takes up the entire width and height of the view, so in order to move to the next child, we have to scroll horizontally by the width.

Then we have the `HandleSwipeRight` function, which will perform the opposite to `HandleSwipeLeft` and scroll in the opposite direction. In each swipe function, we also perform a check to see if we are on the starting child or the last child.

Congratulations, you have just built your first custom layout. Now let's build the rest of the user interface and see how we can use it.

Building the user interface

It's now time to build the user interface screens; we are going to start by building the view-models. Inside the `FileStorage.Portable` project, add a new folder called `ViewModels`, add a new file called `MainPageViewModel.cs`, and implement the following:

```
public class MainPageViewModel : ViewModelBase
{
    #region Private Properties
    private string _descriptionMessage = "Welcome to the Filing Room";
    private string _FilesTitle = "Files";
    private string _exitTitle = "Exit";
    private ICommand _locationCommand;
    private ICommand _exitCommand;
    private ISQLiteStorage _storage;
    #endregion
}
```

We include the `ISQLiteStorage` object in this view-model because we will be creating the database tables when this view-model is created. Don't forget we need to implement the public properties for all `private` properties; the following are two properties to get you started:

```
#region Public Properties
public ICommand LocationCommand
{
    get
    {
        return _locationCommand;
    }
    set
    {
        if (value.Equals(_locationCommand))
        {
            return;
        }
        _locationCommand = value; OnPropertyChanged("LocationCommand");
```

```
        }
      }
  public ICommand ExitCommand
    {
      get
        {
          return _exitCommand;
        }
      set
        {
          if (value.Equals(_exitCommand))
            {
                return;
            }
          _exitCommand = value; OnPropertyChanged("ExitCommand");
        }
      }
  #endregion
```

Then we add the remaining properties. We call the `SetupSQLite` function from the constructor to set up the database as follows:

```
#region Constructors
public MainPageViewModel (INavigationService navigation, Func<Action,
ICommand> commandFactory,
IMethods methods, ISQLiteStorage storage) : base (navigation, methods)
  {
      _exitCommand = commandFactory (() => methods.Exit());
      _locationCommand = commandFactory (async () => await
Navigation.Navigate(PageNames.FilesPage, null));
      _storage = storage;
      SetupSQLite().ConfigureAwait(false);
  }
#endregion
private async Task SetupSQLite()
  {
    // create Sqlite connection _storage.CreateSQLiteAsyncConnection();
    // create DB tables await _storage.CreateTable<FileStorable>
    CancellationToken.None);
  }
}
```

The `SetupSQLite` function is responsible for creating the asynchronous connection to the local database and building the one table from the `FileStorable` object.

Now let's build the page for this view-model. Add a new folder called `Pages` inside the `FileStorage` project, add in a new file called `MainPage.xaml`, and implement the following:

```xml
<?xml version="1.0" encoding="UTF-8"?>
<ui:ExtendedContentPage xmlns="http://xamarin.com/schemas/2014/forms"
    xmlns:x="http://schemas.microsoft.com/winfx/2009/xaml"
    xmlns:ui="clr-namespace:FileStorage.UI;assembly=Xamarin.Forms"
    x:Class="FileStorage.Pages.MainPage"
    BackgroundColor="White"
    Title="Welcome">
<ui:ExtendedContentPage.Content>
    <Grid x:Name="Grid" RowSpacing="10" Padding="10, 10, 10, 10"
VerticalOptions="Center">
        <Grid.RowDefinitions>
            <RowDefinition Height="*"/>
            <RowDefinition Height="Auto"/>
            <RowDefinition Height="Auto"/>
            <RowDefinition Height="Auto"/>
        </Grid.RowDefinitions>
        <Grid.ColumnDefinitions>
            <ColumnDefinition Width="*"/>
        </Grid.ColumnDefinitions>
        <Image x:Name="Image" Source="files.png" HeightRequest="120"
            WidthRequest="120" Grid.Row="0" Grid.Column="0"/>
        <Label x:Name="DesciptionLabel" Text="{Binding DescriptionMessage}"
            TextColor="Black" HorizontalOptions="Center" Font="Arial, 20"
            Grid.Row="1" Grid.Column="0"/>
        <Button x:Name="LocationButton" Text="{Binding FilesTitle}"
            Command="{Binding LocationCommand}"
            Style="{StaticResource ButtonStyle}" Grid.Row="2"
Grid.Column="0"/>
        <Button x:Name="ExitButton" Text="{Binding ExitTitle}"
            Command="{Binding ExitCommand}" Style="{StaticResource
ButtonStyle}"
            Grid.Row="3" Grid.Column="0"/>
    </Grid>
</ui:ExtendedContentPage.Content>
</ui:ExtendedContentPage>
```

Remember our custom control `ExtendedContentPage`?

We are going to use this for all pages so that every page has alert functionality connected with its view-model. The following line gives the reference to our custom control:

```
xmlns:ui="clr-namespace:FileStorage.UI;assembly=Xamarin.Forms"
```

We have to declare a new `ExtendedContentPage` like the following:

```
<ui:ExtendedContentPage
```

The rest of the page is the same as previous projects. A simple **Grid** contains an image, label, and two buttons. Now implement the following for `MainPage.xaml.cs`:

```
public partial class MainPage : ExtendedContentPage,
INavigableXamarinFormsPage
    {
        #region Constructors
        public MainPage (MainPageViewModel model) : base(model)
        {
            BindingContext = model;
            InitializeComponent ();
        }
        #endregion
        #region INavigableXamarinFormsPage interface
        public void OnNavigatedTo(IDictionary<string, object>
navigationParameters)
        {
            this.Show (navigationParameters);
        }
        #endregion
    }
```

We are able to assign the `BindingContext` property through the constructor because we are registering this item inside the IoC container.

Now we move on to the next page, where we will be including the `CarouselView`. We will also be loading in our files that are saved locally in our database. Our first step is to create a new view-model for each view that is going to appear in the `CarouselView`. Add a new file to the `ViewModels` folder called `FileItemViewModel.cs` and implement the following:

```
public class FileItemViewModel : ViewModelBase
    {
        #region Private Properties
        private string _fileName;
        private string _contents;
        #endregion
        #region Public Properties
        public string FileName
        {
            get
            {
                return _fileName;
            }
```

```
        set
        {
            if (value.Equals(_fileName))
            {
                return;
            }
            _fileName = value; OnPropertyChanged("FileName");
        }
    }
    public string Contents
    {
        get
        {
            return _contents;
        }
        set
        {
            if (value.Equals(_contents))
            {
                return;
            }
            _contents = value; OnPropertyChanged("Contents");
        }
    }
    #endregion
    #region Public Methods
    public void Apply(FileStorable file)
    {
        FileName = file.Key ?? string.Empty;
        Contents = file.Contents ?? string.Empty;
    }
    #endregion
    #region Constructors
    public FileItemViewModel(INavigationService navigation, IMethods
methods) :
    base(navigation, methods) { }
    #endregion
}
```

It is very simple, just two properties to contain the filename and text contents of the file. These two items will be saved in a FileStorable object in our local database. We have an Apply function that will take a FileStorable object to load the properties of the view-model.

Now let's build the page. Inside the `ViewModels` folder, add a new file called `FilesPageViewModel.cs` and implement the following:

```
public class FilesPageViewModel : ViewModelBase
    {
        #region Private Properties
        private readonly Func<FileItemViewModel> _fileFactory;
        private readonly ISQLiteStorage _storage;
        private readonly SynchronizationContext _context;
        private ICommand _editFileCommand;
        private ICommand _createFileCommand;
        private bool _noFiles;
        #endregion
    }
```

We have two commands for editing a file, which will be bound to the custom binding `SelectCommandProperty` on the `CarouselView`. When a user touches the current child on the `CarouselLayout`, this command will be invoked.

Notice the `SynchronizationContext` property?

This will be used for threading purposes to ensure we update the `ObservableCollection` on the main UI thread.

Now let's add the public properties as follows:

```
#region Public Properties
public Subject<DataChange> DataChanges { get; private set; }
public ICommand EditFileCommand
    {
        get
        {
            return _editFileCommand;
        }
        set
        {
            if (value.Equals(_editFileCommand))
            {
                return;
            }
        _editFileCommand = value;
        OnPropertyChanged("EditFileCommand");
        }
    }
public ICommand CreateFileCommand
    {
        get
```

```
        {
            return _createFileCommand;
        }
    set
        {
            if (value.Equals(_createFileCommand))
            {
            return;
            }
        _createFileCommand = value;
        OnPropertyChanged("CreateFileCommand");
        }
    }
public bool AnyFiles
    {
        get
        {
            return _noFiles;
        }
        set
        {
            if (value.Equals(_noFiles))
            {
                return;
            }
            _noFiles = value;
            OnPropertyChanged("AnyFiles");
        }
    }
public ObservableCollection<FileItemViewModel> Cells { get; set; }
#endregion
```

Don't forget that we only need a `public` property for the properties that are going to be bound to the view.

We have an `ObservableCollection` of type `FileItemViewModel`; so, for every file we pull from the database, a new view-model will be created to show the details on the child view of the `CarouselView`. We also have an `IObservable` property called `DataChanges`; every time we update the `ObservableCollection`, we will publish a new event through the stream, and because we will be binding this property to the `CarouselView`, the list of children will be structured accordingly.

Now let's add the constructor as follows:

```
#region Constructors
public FilesPageViewModel(INavigationService navigation,
Func<Action<object>, ICommand> commandFactory,
    IMethods methods, ISQLiteStorage storage, Func<FileItemViewModel>
    fileFactory) : base(navigation, methods)
        {
            DataChanges = new Subject<DataChange>();
            // retrieve main thread context _context =
            SynchronizationContext.Current;
            _storage = storage;
            _fileFactory = fileFactory;
            Cells = new ObservableCollection<FileItemViewModel>();
            _editFileCommand = commandFactory(async (file) =>
              {
                await Navigation.Navigate(PageNames.EditFilePage,
                new Dictionary<string, object>()
                  {
                    {
                       "filename", (file as FileItemViewModel).FileName},
                         {
                          "contents", (file as FileItemViewModel).Contents}
});
                    });
            _createFileCommand = commandFactory(async (obj) =>
              {
                var fileName = await ShowEntryAlert("Enter file name:");
                if (!string.IsNullOrEmpty(fileName))
                  {
                    await Navigation.Navigate(PageNames.EditFilePage,
                    new Dictionary<string, object>()
                      {
                        {
                           "filename", fileName
                        }
                    });
                }
            });
        }
#endregion
```

Using a SynchronizationContext

In all `Xamarin.Forms` applications, when we update view-model properties that are bound to a view, they must be changed on the main UI thread.

This rule applies to any application. UI changes must happen on the main UI thread.

The `SynchronizationContext.Current` property is used to retrieve the current sync context of any thread.

How do we know this context is from the main UI thread?

We store a reference to this context in the constructor because all view-models are created on the main UI thread. This means we have the current sync context of the main thread.

Let's have a look at how we are going to use this sync context reference:

```
#region Private Methods
private void UpdateFiles()
    {
      _context.Post(async (obj) =>
        {
          Cells.Clear();
          var files = await
_storage.GetTable<FileStorable>(CancellationToken.None);
          foreach (var file in files)
            {
              var fileModel = _fileFactory();
              fileModel.Apply(file);
              Cells.Add(fileModel);
            }
          AnyFiles = Cells.Any();
          DataChanges.OnNext(new DataChange()
            {
              SizeChanged = true
            });
        }, null);
    }
#endregion
```

The `UpdateFiles` function is called every time the page appears. When we call `Post` on the context object, we have to pass an action that will be propagated to the main UI thread when it becomes available. Inside this action, we will use the `GetTable` function to retrieve all files from the table. Then, for every `FileStorable` object, we instantiate a new `FileItemViewModel` from the factory and add this to the `ObservableCollection`. After we do this for all files, we publish a new event to the `DataChanges` sequence.

Finally, we have to add the `OnAppear` function, which will be called every time the page appears; it doesn't matter if we push or pop to this page, this function will be called every time. This means that we will update the current files, every time the page appears, so the `CarouselView` will have the most current list of files in the database at all times:

```
#region Public Methods
public void OnAppear()
    {
        UpdateFiles();
    }
#endregion
```

Now let's build the page for this view-model. To do so, inside the `Pages` folder, add in `FilesPage.xaml` and implement the following:

```
<ui:ExtendedContentPage.Content>
  <Grid x:Name="Grid" RowSpacing="10" Padding="10, 10, 10, 10">
  <Grid.RowDefinitions>
  <RowDefinition Height="*"/>
  <RowDefinition Height="60"/>
  </Grid.RowDefinitions>
  <Grid.ColumnDefinitions>
  <ColumnDefinition Width="*"/>
  </Grid.ColumnDefinitions>
  <Label x:Name="NoFilesLabel"
      IsVisible="{Binding AnyFiles, Converter={StaticResource
notConverter}}"
      HorizontalTextAlignment="Center" VerticalTextAlignment="Center"
Grid.Row="0"
      Grid.Column="0">
  <Label.FormattedText>
  <FormattedString>
  <Span Text="{x:Static resx:LabelResources.NoFilesLabel}"
FontFamily="Arial"
  FontSize="24" ForegroundColor="Black"/> </FormattedString>
  </Label.FormattedText>
  </Label>
  <controls:CarouselView x:Name="CarouselView" SelectedCommand="{Binding
    EditFileCommand}" Grid.Row="0" Grid.Column="0"/>
```

```
    <Button x:Name="CreateFileButton" Command="{Binding CreateFileCommand}"
    Text="{x:Static resx:LabelResources.CreateFileLabel}"
Style="{StaticResource
    ButtonStyle}" Grid.Row="1" Grid.Column="0"/>
    </Grid>
</ui:ExtendedContentPage.Content>
```

Since we are including the `CarouselView` in this page, we have to add a new reference namespace at the top of the page as follows:

```
xmlns:controls="clr-namespace:FileStorage.Controls;assembly=FileStorage"
```

Notice our custom binding property on the CarouselView with the SelectCommand?

Every time we click the current child, this will execute the EditFileCommand from the view-model.

The page has also been set up to hide the CarouselView and display the NoFilesLabel if there are no files in local storage. Then, if we want to create a new file, we click on the CreateFileButton.

Building the EditFilePage

Now we move to the last page of the application. Add a new file called `EditFilePage.xaml` to the `Pages` folder and implement the following:

```
<ui:ExtendedContentPage.Content>
  <Grid x:Name="Grid" RowSpacing="10" Padding="10, 10, 10, 10">
    <Grid.RowDefinitions>
      <RowDefinition Height="60"/>
      <RowDefinition Height="*"/>
      <RowDefinition Height="60"/>
      <RowDefinition Height="60"/>
    </Grid.RowDefinitions>
    <Grid.ColumnDefinitions>
      <ColumnDefinition Width="*"/>
    </Grid.ColumnDefinitions>
    <Entry x:Name="FileNameLabel" Text="{Binding FileName, Mode=TwoWay}"
        BackgroundColor="Silver"
        Grid.Row="0"
        Grid.Column="0">
    <Entry.Behaviors>
    <beh:LowercaseEntryBehaviour/>
    </Entry.Behaviors>
    </Entry>
```

```
<Editor x:Name="ContentsEditor" Text="{Binding Contents, Mode=TwoWay}"
    BackgroundColor="Silver" Grid.Row="1" Grid.Column="0"/>
<Button x:Name="SaveFileButton" Command="{Binding SaveFileCommand}"
    Text="{x:Static resx:LabelResources.SaveFileLabel}"
    Style="{StaticResource ButtonStyle}" Grid.Row="2" Grid.Column="0"/>
<Button x:Name="DeleteFileButton" Command="{Binding DeleteFileCommand}"
    Text="{x:Static resx:LabelResources.DeleteFileLabel}"
    Style="{StaticResource ButtonStyle}" Grid.Row="3" Grid.Column="0"/>
</Grid>
</ui:ExtendedContentPage.Content>
```

We have an `Entry` property at the very top for editing the filename and we have an `Editor` for filling in the text contents of the file. We also have two buttons: one for saving the file and one for deleting it.

Now, turn our attention to the `Entry` item; we are going to introduce a new `Xamarin.Forms` feature called `Behaviours`.

Behaviours

Behaviours enable you to implement objects which can be concisely attached to events and behaviours of any control type. This means we can package and reuse behaviours between similar controls without having to write repetitive code behind our XAML sheets.

Let's create a new folder called `Behaviours`, add in a new file called `LowercaseEntryBehaviour.cs`, and implement the following:

```
public class LowercaseEntryBehaviour : Behavior<Entry>
{
    protected override void OnAttachedTo(Entry entry)
    {
        entry.TextChanged += OnEntryTextChanged;
        base.OnAttachedTo(entry);
    }
    protected override void OnDetachingFrom(Entry entry)
    {
        entry.TextChanged -= OnEntryTextChanged;
        base.OnDetachingFrom(entry);
    }
    void OnEntryTextChanged(object sender, TextChangedEventArgs args)
    {
        ((Entry)sender).Text = args.NewTextValue.ToLower();
    }
}
```

The `OnAttachedTo` and `OnDetachingFrom` methods get invoked when the behavior is attached/detached from parent UI element; so we subscribe to the `TextChanged` event, and when it triggers, we update the `Text` property by calling the `ToLower` function. This means that irrespective of the case of the text when it is entered into the `Entry` object, it will always be lowercase.

Now let's add the view-model for the `EditFilePage`. Inside the `ViewModels` folder, add another file called `EditFilePageViewModel.cs` and implement the `private` properties first as follows:

```
public class EditFilePageViewModel : ViewModelBase
{
    #region Private Properties
    private readonly ISQLiteStorage _storage;
    private ICommand _saveFileCommand;
    private ICommand _deleteFileCommand;
    private string _contents;
    private string _fileName;
    #endregion
}
```

We have to use the `ISQLiteStorage` object for saving and deleting files on the local database. We then have another two properties to record the contents of the file and filename. The two commands are used to invoke the SQLite functions for saving and deleting.

Let's go ahead and add the public properties as follows:

```
#region Public Properties
public ICommand SaveFileCommand
{
    get
    {
        return _saveFileCommand;
    }
    set
    {
        if (value.Equals(_saveFileCommand))
        {
            return;
        }
        _saveFileCommand = value; OnPropertyChanged("FileEditCommand");
    }
}
public ICommand DeleteFileCommand
{
```

```
        get
          {
            return _deleteFileCommand;
          }
        set
          {
            if (value.Equals(_deleteFileCommand))
              {
                  return;
              }
            _deleteFileCommand = value; OnPropertyChanged("CreateFileCommand");
          }
      }
  public string Contents
      {
        get
          {
            return _contents;
          }
        set { if (value.Equals(_contents))
          {
            return;
          }
        _contents = value; OnPropertyChanged("Contents");
      }
  }
  public string FileName
      {
        get
          {
            return _fileName;
          }
        set
          {
            if (value.Equals(_fileName))
              {
                  return;
              }
            _fileName = value; OnPropertyChanged("FileName");
          }
      }
  }
#endregion
```

Remember that we only want to publicize the variables that are going to be bound through the XAML.

Now we add the constructor as follows:

```
#region Constructors
  public EditFilePageViewModel (INavigationService navigation, Func<Action,
ICommand> commandFactory,
      IMethods methods, ISQLiteStorage storage)
        : base (navigation, methods)
          {
              _storage = storage;
              _saveFileCommand = commandFactory(async () =>
              {
                  await _storage.InsertObject (new FileStorable ()
                  {
                    Key = FileName, Contents = Contents },
CancellationToken.None);
                  NotifyAlert ("File saved.");
              });
              _deleteFileCommand = commandFactory(async () =>
              {
                  await _storage.DeleteObjectByKey<FileStorable>(FileName,
CancellationToken.None);
                  await Navigation.Pop();
              });
          }
#endregion
```

Then, finally, we add the remaining functions; we have the OnDisppear function, which will be used for clearing the filename and contents whenever the page disappears. Then we have the LoadAsync override, which is going to set the filename and contents from the navigation parameters that are passed in from the previous page. From the FilesPage, when a user selects a file from the carousel, the FileItemViewModel object details are passed into a dictionary for the navigation parameters that are passed into the EditFilePage:

```
#region Public Methods
public void OnDisppear()
  {
    FileName = string.Empty;
    Contents = string.Empty;
  }
protected override async Task LoadAsync (IDictionary<string, object>
parameters)
  {
    if (parameters.ContainsKey("filename"))
      {
        FileName = (parameters["filename"] as string).ToLower();
      }
```

```
        if (parameters.ContainsKey("contents"))
        {
            Contents = parameters["contents"] as string;
        }
    }
#endregion
    }
```

Fantastic! We have finished implementing the user interface.

Challenge

We have built everything in the `FileStorage.Portable` and `FileStorage` projects, but there are still pieces missing. Here is your challenge; fill in the missing pieces of the solution and compile it. The remaining files are exactly the same from all our other `Xamarin.Forms` solutions, but now it is your turn to finish off the project.

Building the Windows Phone version

If you are looking for an even bigger challenge, then try adding on the Windows Phone version. Don't be intimidated by this exercise, most of the code is shared for you. On the Windows Phone version, you will have to implement the following:

- `WinPhoneMethods`
- `GestureViewRenderer`
- `SQLiteSetup`
- `LoggerWinPhone`

You will also need to download a Visual Studio extension for SQLite from the following link `http://sqlite.org/download.html`.

Download the **sqlite-wp81-winrt-3130000.vsix** file:

Precompiled Binaries for Windows Phone 8	
sqlite-wp80-winrt-3130000.vsix (3.82 MiB)	A complete VSIX package with an exter development with Visual Studio 2012 ta (sha1: adc130245268ace3103eb1a761
sqlite-wp81-winrt-3130000.vsix (4.00 MiB)	A complete VSIX package with an exter development with Visual Studio 2013 ta (sha1: 785f53ce4a91085b86d6aa3238

Install the extensions and then reopen Visual Studio. Then, in your Windows Phone project, right-click on **References** and select **Add Reference....** Then select **Windows Phone 8.1 | Extensions** from the left-hand side and select **SQLite for Windows Phone 8.1**, as shown in the following screenshot:

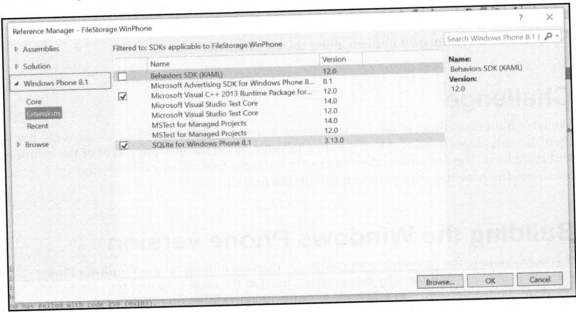

When you run this project, you must make sure that the **x86** configuration is set:

To help you get started, the implementation for the SQLiteSetup class is as follows:

```
public class SQLiteSetup : ISQLiteSetup
    {
        #region Public Properties
        public string DatabasePath { get; set; }
        public ISQLitePlatform Platform { get; set; }
        #endregion
        #region Constructors
        public SQLiteSetup(ISQLitePlatform platform)
        {
            DatabasePath =
Path.Combine(ApplicationData.Current.LocalFolder.Path,
            "mycaremanager.db3")
```

```
        Platform = platform;
    }
#endregion
}
```

To see the finished version, visit the following link: `https://github.com/flusharcade/chapter7-filestorage`.

Summary

In this chapter, we explored a walkthrough for integrating SQLite in a `Xamarin.Forms` application. We addressed the async-lock pattern and how to implement it with SQLite to make database connections thread-safe. In the final chapter, we will build a cross-platform camera application that will implement native control over camera hardware. We will also present camera video outlets via a `CustomRenderer` and build events to handle camera events in our portable library.

8

Building a Camera Application

We have reached the end of an era, learning the ins and outs of cross-platform development using the `Xamarin` platform.

In our last chapter, we are going to walk-through the final `Xamarin.Forms` project. We will introduce Effects, Triggers, and how they apply to UI elements. Then, we will build a `CustomRenderer` for each platform camera. The following topics will be covered in this chapter.

Expected knowledge:

- `Xamarin.Forms`
- XAML
- MVVM
- C# threading
- HashMap data structures
- CustomRenderers
- `INotifiedPropertyChanged` framework

In this chapter, you will learn the following:

- Solution setup
- Building the `MainPageViewModel`
- Improving the `INotifiedPropertyChanged` implementation
- Creating the custom UI objects
- Building the `FocusView`
- `Xamarin.Forms` animations
- `Xamarin.Forms` compound animations

- Building the `CameraView`
- Building a control for the iOS camera
- Building the iOS `CameraRenderer`
- Integrating the Android Camera2 framework
- Building the `CameraViewRenderer` in Android
- Handling native touch events through the `FocusView`
- Using RX to handle events
- Building a `VisualElementRenderer` for iOS
- Building the `CustomImageRenderer`
- Building the `UIImageEffect` class
- Building the `CustomImageRenderer` for Android
- Triggers
- Platform effects
- Building the `CameraPage`
- Adding native orientation events

Solution setup

Let's begin by creating a new `Xamarin.Forms` project and calling it `Camera`. We also want to create the `Camera.Portable` project. Now that we have built up several `Xamarin.Forms` applications, we have a lot of reusable parts that will be brought across to this application.

Starting with the `Camera.Portable` project, we want to copy in the `IoC`, `Extras`, and `Logging` folders used in `Chapter 7`, *Building a File Storage Application*. Make sure all the files contained in these folders are copied in accordingly.

 Don't forget to update namespaces in each code sheet.

Then we want to add the following NuGet packages for every project:

- Autofac
- Reactive extensions

Next, we want to create a folder called **Enums**. Add in a new folder called `PageNames.cs` and implement the following:

```
public enum PageNames
    {
            #region Properties

            MainPage,

            CameraPage,

            #endregion
    }
```

Like our other projects, this will be used in the navigation setup. In this folder, we also want to add another file called `Orientation.cs` and implement the following:

```
public enum Orientation
    {
            Portrait,

            LandscapeLeft,

            LandscapeRight,

            None
    }
```

This `enum` will be used with orientation settings on our `CameraPage`. Each different orientation setting will be handled for adjusting camera preview surface areas.

Our next step is to create a new folder called `UI` and copy in the `INavigationService.cs`. We also want to add another file called `AlertArgs.cs` and implement the following:

```
public class AlertArgs : EventArgs
    {
            #region Public Properties

            public string Message { get; set; }

            public TaskCompletionSource<bool> Tcs { get; set; }

            #endregion
    }
```

The preceding class will be used inside all alerts that are invoked inside our view-models. We use a `TaskCompletionSource` object to await the method that fires the alert, and the `Message` object for every alert message.

Building the MainPageViewModel class

Let's add the `ViewModelBase` class, which will contain the `AlertArgs` event. Create a new folder called `ViewModels`, add in a new file called `ViewModelBase.cs`, and implement the following:

```
public class ViewModelBase : INotifyPropertyChanged
    {
        #region Public Events

        public event PropertyChangedEventHandler PropertyChanged;

        public event EventHandler<AlertArgs> Alert;

        #endregion

        #region Public Properties

        public INavigationService Navigation;

        #endregion
```

The `ViewModelBase` class will be similar to the other `Xamarin.Forms` projects. We have the `INotifiedPropertyChanged` requirements, another `EventHandler` for alerts, and the `INavigationService` for navigation control.

Next, we have the constructor:

```
        #region Constructor

        public ViewModelBase(INavigationService navigation, IMethods
methods)
        {
            Navigation = navigation;

            _methods = methods;
        }

        #endregion
```

Improving the INotifiedPropertyChanged implementation

As you may have noticed from previous projects, our standard property implementation for handling property changes looks like the following:

```
private string _descriptionMessage = "Take a Picture";

public string DescriptionMessage
        {
            get
            {
                return _descriptionMessage;
            }

            set
            {
                if (value.Equals(_descriptionMessage))
                {
                    return;
                }

                _descriptionMessage = value;
                OnPropertyChanged("DescriptionMessage");
            }
        }
```

The repeated code in every public property makes our view-model code look much bigger than it actually is. In all your code sheets, a good coding practice to think about is how you can reduce the amount of lines of code and, especially repeated code. The following function `SetProperty` is an example of how we can turn 13 lines of code into just two:

```
        protected void SetProperty<T>(string propertyName,
        ref T referenceProperty, T newProperty)
        {
            if (!newProperty.Equals(referenceProperty))
            {
                referenceProperty = newProperty;
            }

            OnPropertyChanged(propertyName);
        }
```

In all properties, we always check first if the value being assigned is different to the current value before firing the `OnPropertyChanged` function. Since this is a generic type function, the same logic can be used for any property on all view-models. Now the `DescriptionMessage` property will look like the following:

```
public string DescriptionMessage
    {
        get { return _descriptionMessage; }
        set { SetProperty(nameof(DescriptionMessage),
            ref _descriptionMessage, value); }
    }
```

Let's add the rest of the `ViewModelBase` as follows:

```
        protected virtual void OnPropertyChanged([CallerMemberName]
        string propertyName = null)
        {
            PropertyChangedEventHandler handler = PropertyChanged;

            if (handler != null)
            {
                handler(this, new PropertyChangedEventArgs(propertyName));
            }
        }

        protected virtual async Task LoadAsync(IDictionary<string, object>
parameters)
        {
        }

        #endregion

        #region Public Methods

        public Task<bool> NotifyAlert(string message)
        {
            var tcs = new TaskCompletionSource<bool>();

            Alert?.Invoke(this, new AlertArgs()
            {
                Message = message,
                Tcs = tcs
            });

            return tcs.Task;
        }

        public void OnShow(IDictionary<string, object> parameters)
```

```
            {
                LoadAsync(parameters).ToObservable().Subscribe(
                    result =>
                    {
                        // we can add things to do after we load the view model
                    },
                    ex =>
                    {
                        // we can handle any areas from the load async function
                    });
            }

        #endregion
    }
```

The preceding functions are the same from previous implementations. Take note of how we fire the `Alert` event. Since we now have access to C# 6.0, we can turn a standard null check on an event like the following:

```
If (Alert != null)
{
Alert(this, new AlertArgs()
        {
            Message = message,
            Tcs = tcs
        });
}
```

Into this:

```
Alert?.Invoke(this, new AlertArgs()
        {
            Message = message,
            Tcs = tcs
        });
```

It looks much cleaner, meaning we can remove all the `if` statements.

Now let's add a new file called `MainPageViewModel.cs` and implement the following:

```
public class MainPageViewModel : ViewModelBase
    {
        #region Private Properties

        private readonly IMethods _methods;

        private string _descriptionMessage = "Take a Picture";
```

```
            private string _cameraTitle = "Camera";

            private string _exitTitle = "Exit";

            private ICommand _cameraCommand;

            private ICommand _exitCommand;

            #endregion
    }
```

Exactly like the other `MainPageViewModel` objects, the `MainPage` layout is the same, with two buttons, an image, and a label.

Now let's add the `public` properties. We are going to use the new `SetProperty` function for each `public` property:

```
        #region Public Properties

        public string DescriptionMessage
        {
            get { return _descriptionMessage; }
            set { SetProperty(nameof(DescriptionMessage),
                ref _descriptionMessage, value); }
        }

        public string CameraTitle
        {
            get { return _cameraTitle; }
            set { SetProperty(nameof(CameraTitle), ref _cameraTitle,
    value); }
        }

        public string ExitTitle
        {
            get { return _exitTitle; }
            set { SetProperty(nameof(ExitTitle), ref _exitTitle, value); }
        }

        public ICommand CameraCommand
        {
            get { return _cameraCommand; }
            set { SetProperty(nameof(CameraCommand), ref _cameraCommand,
    value); }
        }

        public ICommand ExitCommand
        {
```

```
        get { return _exitCommand; }
        set { SetProperty(nameof(ExitCommand), ref _exitCommand,
value); }
    }

    #endregion
```

Now for the constructor, we are going to use the `Command` factory again to instantiate our binded `Command`:

```
    #region Constructors

    public MainPageViewModel (INavigationService navigation,
Func<Action, ICommand> commandFactory): base (navigation, methods)
    {
        _methods = methods;

        _exitCommand = commandFactory (async () =>
        {
            await NotifyAlert ("GoodBye!!");

            _methods.Exit();
        });

        _cameraCommand = commandFactory (async () => await
Navigation.Navigate(PageNames.CameraPage, null));
    }

    #endregion
```

Now let's build the next view-model for the `CameraPage`. Add a new file called `CameraPageViewModel.cs` to the `ViewModels` folder and implement the private properties to begin with:

```
public sealed class CameraPageViewModel : ViewModelBase
    {
        #region Private Properties

        private Orientation _pageOrientation;

        private byte[] _photoData;

        private string _loadingMessage = "Loading Camera..."

        private bool _canCapture;

        private bool _cameraLoading;
```

```
        private bool _isFlashOn;

        private bool _photoEditOn;

        #endregion

    }
```

The `CameraPage` is going to include an `Orientation` property for adjusting `Grid` rows and columns using converters. The `_photoData` property will be used for recording the image taken as bytes, we will also be using these bytes to bind to an `ImageSource`. The `_loadingMessage` and `_cameraLoading` properties are used when displaying a view showing the native camera hardware is busy. The `_isFlashOn` will be used to control UI elements displaying the status of the flash. The `CameraPage` will also have a target image representing the focus target. Then finally, the `_canCapture` is used to determine whether the camera has loaded and we are ready to take photos, and the `_photoEditOn` is used to bind the visibility status of a view showing the photo just taken.

Next, we add the `public` properties; following are two to get you started:

```
    #region Public Properties

        public bool CanCapture
        {
            get { return _canCapture; }
            set { SetProperty(nameof(CanCapture), ref _canCapture, value);
    }
        }

        public string LoadingMessage
        {
            get { return _loadingMessage; }
            set { SetProperty(nameof(LoadingMessage), ref _loadingMessage,
    value); }
        }

    #endregion
```

Add the constructor as follows:

```
        #region Constructors and Destructors

        public CameraPageViewModel(INavigationService navigation,
    Func<Action, ICommand> commandFactory) : base (navigation, methods)
        {
        }
```

```
#endregion
```

Now for the `public` functions, we have the `AddPhoto` function, this will take the image as bytes from the native side, and the `PhotoData` is assigned for the `ImageSource` binding:

```
public void AddPhoto(byte[] data)
{
    PhotoData = data;
    PhotoEditOn = true;
}
```

We also have a function for resetting the variables used in the current photo taken. When the `PhotoEditOn` is `false`, this means we remove the view that is displaying the current photo taken. When the `PhotoData` property is assigned an empty byte array, this means we have freed the data of the image that is currently displaying:

```
public void ResetEditPhoto()
{
    PhotoData = new byte[] { };
    PhotoEditOn = false;
}
```

Finally, we have two more functions that are called when the page appears and disappears:

```
public void OnAppear()
{
    CameraLoading = false;
}

public void OnDisappear()
{
    CameraLoading = true;
    ResetEditPhoto();
}
```

The `OnAppear` function simply resets the `CameraLoading` property to `false`, and the `OnDisappear` function resets the entire view-model; when we return to this page, the state is the same as the starting point (that is, the camera is not loading, no photo is showing)

Excellent! Now that we have built our view-models, let's add the `PortableModule` for our IoC container as follows:

```
public class PortableModule : IModule
{
    #region Public Methods

    public void Register(ContainerBuilder builder)
```

```
    {
            builder.RegisterType<MainPageViewModel> ().SingleInstance ();
            builder.RegisterType<CameraPageViewModel> ().SingleInstance ();
    }


    #endregion
}
```

Let's begin building the user interface screens.

Creating the custom UI objects

Jump back in the `Camera` project and let's begin adding a new folder called `Controls`. Add in a new file called `OrientationPage.cs` and implement the following:

```
public class OrientationPage : ContentPage
    {
        #region Static Properties

        public static Orientation PageOrientation;

        public static event EventHandler<Orientation> OrientationHandler;

        public static event EventHandler<Point> TouchHandler;

        #endregion

        #region Static Methods

        public static void NotifyOrientationChange(Orientation orientation)
        {
            if (OrientationHandler != null)
            {
                OrientationHandler (null, orientation);
            }
        }

        public static void NotifyTouch(Point touchPoint)
        {
            if (TouchHandler != null)
            {
                TouchHandler(null, touchPoint);
            }
        }
```

```
        #endregion
    }
```

In our previous chapter, we created an `ExtendedContentPage` for handling alerts. This time, the `ExtendedContentPage` will inherit the `OrientationPage`, meaning it will be handling orientation events as well. The `CameraPage` is going to use this `OrientationPage` to track orientation events to resize camera preview areas, and rotate the camera view.

Our next control is the `FocusView`. It is going to be used for custom rendering purposes so that we are able to record touch point (*x, y*) coordinates on a view plane. These touch points will then be used to focus the camera at that particular (*x, y*) coordinate.

Our next custom control is an extension to the `Image` class. Add another file into the `Controls` folder called `CustomImage.cs` and implement the following:

```
public class CustomImage : View
    {
        public static readonly BindableProperty TintColorStringProperty =
BindableProperty.Create ((CustomImage o) => o.TintColorString,
string.Empty,
            propertyChanged: (bindable, oldvalue, newValue) =>
            {
                var eh = ((CustomImage)bindable).CustomPropertyChanged;

                if (eh != null)
                {
                    eh (bindable, TintColorStringProperty.PropertyName);
                }
            });

        public string TintColorString
        {
            get
            {
                return (string)GetValue(TintColorStringProperty);
            }
            set
            {
                this.SetValue(TintColorStringProperty, value);
            }
        }

        public static readonly BindableProperty TintOnProperty =
BindableProperty.Create ((CustomImage o) => o.TintOn, default(bool),
            propertyChanged: (bindable, oldvalue, newValue) =>
            {
```

```
            var eh = ((CustomImage)bindable).CustomPropertyChanged;

            if (eh != null)
            {
                eh (bindable, TintOnProperty.PropertyName);
            }
        });

    public bool TintOn
    {
        get
        {
            return (bool)GetValue (TintOnProperty);
        }
        set
        {
            SetValue (TintOnProperty, value);
        }
    }
}
```

These custom bindings will be used for tinting. Since this view will be used for a `CustomRenderer`, we will have access to native tinting features. This is where we will add some advanced techniques to our `CustomRenderer`.

Next, we are going to add two more custom bindings. The `Path` property will be used for the absolute path of the file, and the `Aspect` property will be used for the image aspect ratio so we can change the image aspect natively:

```
    public static readonly BindableProperty PathProperty =
BindableProperty.Create((CustomImage o) => o.Path, default(string),
        propertyChanged: (bindable, oldvalue, newValue) =>
        {
            var eh = ((CustomImage)bindable).CustomPropertyChanged;

            if (eh != null)
            {
                eh (bindable, PathProperty.PropertyName);
            }
        });

    public string Path
    {
        get
        {
            return (string)GetValue(PathProperty);
        }
```

```
        set
        {
            SetValue(PathProperty, value);
        }
    }

    public static readonly BindableProperty AspectProperty =
BindableProperty.Create((CustomImage o) => o.Aspect, default(Aspect),
        propertyChanged: (bindable, oldvalue, newValue) =>
        {
            var eh = ((CustomImage)bindable).CustomPropertyChanged;

            if (eh != null)
            {
                eh(bindable, AspectProperty.PropertyName);
            }
        });

    public Aspect Aspect
    {
        get
        {
            return (Aspect)GetValue(AspectProperty);
        }
        set
        {
            SetValue(AspectProperty, value);
        }
    }
```

Have a look at the delegate function passed in as the last parameter for each `Create` function. This will be called every time the property changes; the `bindable` object that comes from the first parameter of this delegate function is the object itself. We retrieve the `CustomPropertyChangedEventHandler` and fire a new event to signal that a property on this object has changed.

Let's add the following to the `CustomImage` class:

```
public event EventHandler<string> CustomPropertyChanged;

protected override void OnPropertyChanged (string propertyName)
{
    base.OnPropertyChanged (propertyName);

    if (propertyName ==
        CustomImage.TintColorStringProperty.PropertyName ||
        propertyName == CustomImage.TintOnProperty.PropertyName ||
```

```
            propertyName == CustomImage.AspectProperty.PropertyName)
        {
            if (CustomPropertyChanged != null)
            {
                this.CustomPropertyChanged (this, propertyName);
            }
        }
    }
}
```

That's all for the `CustomImage` class; let's move on to the next custom control.

Building the FocusView

The `FocusView` is going to be used as an overlay view with a target image for touching focus points. This will be a `CustomRenderer` as we have to use native libraries for retrieving specific (*x, y*) coordinates on touch points.

Start with adding a new file into the `Controls` folder called `FocusView.cs` and implement the following:

```
public sealed class FocusView : RelativeLayout
    {
        #region Constant Properties

        const int IMG_TARGET_BOUND = 100;

        #endregion

        #region Private Properties

        private bool _isAnimating;

        private bool _startingPointsAssigned;

        private readonly CustomImage _focalTarget;

        private Point _pStartingOrientation;

        private Point _pFlippedOrientation;

        #endregion

        #region Public Events
```

```
public event EventHandler<Point> TouchFocus;

#endregion
}
```

The first part we see here are two `Point` objects for specific (*x*, *y*) coordinates for portrait and landscape orientation starting points. These two points will be set when the view first loads. Both points will be set to the center of the view in both landscape and portrait orientations. We also have the `_startingPointsAssigned` Boolean to ensure we only set the starting focus points once.

The `CustomImage` object is used for the actual image of the target. We will be using the tinting properties each time a user touches to focus. The `_isAnimating` property is used for tracking progress of current animations (we will be animating the scale of the image each time a touch is detected). The constant property is used to hard set the height and width of the target image, and we have two events for detecting all user touch events.

Next, we have a single public property for the orientation:

```
#region Public Properties

public Orientation Orientation;

#endregion
```

Xamarin.Forms animations

`Xamarin.Forms` has multiple functions for animating views. We have access to the following functions:

- `FadeTo`: This is used to animate opacity (that is, fade in/out).
- `RotateTo`: This is used to animate rotations.
- `ScaleTo`: This is used to animate size.
- `TranslateTo`: This is used to animate (*x*, *y*) positions.
- `LayoutTo`: This is used to animate *x*, *y*, width, and height.

Stay away from the `LayoutTo` function. Jason Smith (the creator of `Xamarin.Forms`) recommends you stick with the `TranslateTo` instead. The issue with `LayoutTo` is the parent of the view you are calling `LayoutTo` on will not be aware of the translation/resize that happened and will simply overwrite it at the next layout cycle (like when you rotate the device). This is because `LayoutTo` is calling the same method Layouts call to position children.

We are now going to use a few of these animation functions to animate our target image when a use touches to focus. The `AnimateFocalTarget` function will be responsible for performing the animations every time a user touches the view. At first, it will change the tint color of the image to green, then translate the (x, y) coordinate to the starting position, expand the scale, fade the image, contract the scale, and wait a second until the tint color changes back to white:

```
#region Private Methods

private async Task AnimateFocalTarget(Point touchPoint)
{
    _focalTarget.TintColorString = "#007F00";

    await _focalTarget.TranslateTo(touchPoint.X - (IMG_TARGET_BOUND
/ 2),
                                   touchPoint.Y - (IMG_TARGET_BOUND / 2),
0).ConfigureAwait(false);

    await _focalTarget.ScaleTo(1, 0);

    // fade in
    await _focalTarget.FadeTo(0.7f, 25);

    await _focalTarget.ScaleTo(0.5, 250);

    _focalTarget.TintOn = true;

    await Task.Delay(1000);

    _focalTarget.TintColorString = "#FFFFFF";

    _isAnimating = false;
}

#endregion
```

All these await functions, is there a cleaner way?

In a lot of cases, you will need to combine multiple transitions at any one time. Let's replace the preceding combination of animations with a compound animation.

Xamarin.Forms compound animations

Compound animations give you the ability to combine multiple animations as a storyboard. Let's replace the preceding function with our new implementation using a compound animation as follows:

```
private async Task AnimateFocalTarget(Point touchPoint)
    {
        _focalTarget.TintColorString = "#007F00";

        var storyboard = new Animation();

        var translationX = new Animation(callback: x
         => _focalTarget.TranslationX = x,
                                    start: touchPoint.X,
                                    end: touchPoint.X -
(IMG_TARGET_BOUND / 2),

                                    easing: Easing.Linear);

        var translationY = new Animation(callback: y
         => _focalTarget.TranslationY = y,
                                    start: touchPoint.Y,
                                    end: touchPoint.Y -
(IMG_TARGET_BOUND / 2),

                                    easing: Easing.Linear);

        var scaleFirst = new Animation(callback: o =>
_focalTarget.Scale = o,
                                        start: 0.5,
                                        end: 1,
                                        easing: Easing.Linear);

        var fade = new Animation(callback: o => _focalTarget.Opacity =
o,
                                        start: 1,
                                        end: 0.7f,
                                        easing: Easing.Linear);

        var scaleSecond = new Animation(callback: o =>
_focalTarget.Scale = o,
                                        start: 1,
                                        end: 0.5f,
```

```
                                          easing: Easing.Linear);

            storyboard.Add(0, 0.01, translationX);
            storyboard.Add(0, 0.01, translationY);
            storyboard.Add(0, 0.01, scaleFirst);
            storyboard.Add(0, 0.5, fade);
            storyboard.Add(0.5, 1, scaleSecond);

            var tcs = new TaskCompletionSource<bool>();
            storyboard.Commit(_focalTarget, "_focalTarget", length: 300,
    finished: async (arg1, arg2) =>
            {
                _focalTarget.TintOn = true;

                await Task.Delay(500);

                _focalTarget.TintColorString = "#FFFFFF";

                _isAnimating = false;

                tcs.TrySetResult(true);
            });

            await tcs.Task;
        }
```

Each `Animation` object has the property we are animating, a start point and an end point, and `easing` (linear, bounce in, bounce out). All `Animation` objects are then added to the storyboard. The first two parameters of the `Add` function are the start time and finish time of that particular animation. Finally, we call the commit, and instead of awaiting the `Commit` function, we will use a `TaskCompletionSource` object to await the commit until it is finished. The `finished` action is called after the length of 300 milliseconds.

Isn't that much nicer than our previous implementation?

We should use this approach when we have multiple animations to commit at any one time.

Now let's add the `Reset` functions to our `FocusView`. This will be called whenever an orientation has occurred, we will use the assign the focus point to the correct orientation starting point:

```
        #region Public Methods

        public void Reset()
        {
            switch (Orientation)
            {
```

```
        case Orientation.Portrait:
            NotifyFocus(_pStartingOrientation);
            break;
        case Orientation.LandscapeLeft:
        case Orientation.LandscapeRight:
            NotifyFocus(_pFlippedOrientation);
            break;
    }
}
```

The NotifyFocus function is responsible for controlling the entire touch animation; this is where we will set the starting state of the _focalTarget image, call the AddFocualTargetImg function, and then fire the TouchFocus event. This event will be used to focus the CameraView through the custom renderer:

```
public void NotifyFocus(Point touchPoint)
{
    if (_isAnimating)
    {
        return;
    }

    _focalTarget.Opacity = 0.0f;
    _focalTarget.TintOn = false;
    _isAnimating = true;

    Device.BeginInvokeOnMainThread(async () => await
AnimateFocalTarget(touchPoint));

    TouchFocus?.Invoke (this, touchPoint);
}
```

Finally, we have the SetFocusPoints function to assign the starting focus points in each orientation (landscape and portrait). These starting points will always be the center of the CameraView. This is to ensure that the _focalTarget image is centered inside the CameraView on every change in orientation:

```
public void SetFocusPoints(Point pStart, Point pFlipped)
{
    _pStartingOrientation = pStart;
    _pFlippedOrientation = pFlipped;
}


#endregion
```

That's everything for our `FocusView`. Let's add our next custom UI element, the `CameraView`.

Building the CameraView

Our next custom element is the UI object for rendering the native camera. Let's add a new file into the `Controls` folder called `CameraView.cs` and implement the first part:

```
public sealed class CameraView : ContentView
{
    #region Events

    public event EventHandler<Orientation> OrientationChange;

    public event EventHandler<Point> Focus;

    public event EventHandler<bool> AvailabilityChange;

    public event EventHandler<bool> OpenCamera;

    public event EventHandler<bool> Busy;

    public event EventHandler<bool> Flash;

    public event EventHandler<bool> Torch;

    public event EventHandler<bool> Loading;

    public event EventHandler<byte[]> Photo;

    public event EventHandler<float> Widths;

    public event EventHandler Shutter;

    #endregion
}
```

There are many events to manage because we have to handle events coming from the `Xamarin.Forms` object in order for the native object to respond to, and vice-versa.

Next, we add the public properties:

```
    #region Public Properties

    public bool CameraAvailable;
```

```
public Orientation Orientation;

public float CameraButtonContainerWidth = 0f;

#endregion
```

The first `bool` is set when we receive events for the `AvailabilityChangeEventHandler`. The `Orientation` property is assigned every time the screen orientation changes.

> Screen orientation changes will come from the native side, these events will come from the `AppDelegate` (iOS), `MainActivity` (Android), and `MainPage.xaml.cs` (Windows).

Then we have the `CameraButtonContainerWidth`, this will only be relevant for iOS as we need to resize the preview layer for the iOS camera when the orientation changes.

Our next functions are all for notifying the preceding events:

```
#region Public Methods

public void NotifyShutter()
{
    Shutter?.Invoke(this, EventArgs.Empty);
}

public void NotifyOpenCamera(bool open)
{
    OpenCamera?.Invoke(this, open);
}

public void NotifyFocus(Point touchPoint)
{
    Focus?.Invoke(this, touchPoint);
}

public void NotifyBusy(object sender, bool busy)
{
    Busy?.Invoke(this, busy);
}

public void NotifyOrientationChange(Orientation orientation)
{
    Orientation = orientation;

    OrientationChange?.Invoke(this, orientation);
}
```

```
    public void NotifyAvailability(object sender, bool isAvailable)
    {
        CameraAvailable = isAvailable;

        AvailabilityChange?.Invoke(this, isAvailable);
    }

    public void NotifyPhoto(object sender, byte[] imageData)
    {
        Photo?.Invoke(this, imageData);
    }

    public void NotifyFlash(bool flashOn)
    {
        Flash?.Invoke(this, flashOn);
    }

public void NotifyTorch(bool torchOn)
    {
        Torch?.Invoke(this, torchOn);
    }

    public void NotifyLoading(object sender, bool loading)
    {
        Loading?.Invoke(this, loading);
    }

    public void NotifyWidths(float cameraButtonContainerWidth)
    {
        CameraButtonContainerWidth = cameraButtonContainerWidth;

        Widths?.Invoke (this, cameraButtonContainerWidth);
    }

    #endregion
```

Then, we have the constructor:

```
    #region Constructors

    public CameraView()
    {
        BackgroundColor = Color.Black;
    }

    #endregion
```

Excellent! Now we have the final custom control to build. Add a new `ContentView.xaml`, as shown in the following screenshot:

Call the `LoadingView.xaml` file and implement the following:

```xml
<?xml version="1.0" encoding="utf-8" ?>
<ContentView xmlns="http://xamarin.com/schemas/2014/forms"
    xmlns:x="http://schemas.microsoft.com/winfx/2009/xaml"
    x:Class="Camera.Controls.LoadingView"
    xmlns:controls="clr-namespace:Camera.Controls;assembly=LogIt.XamForms"
    xmlns:converters="clr-
namespace:Camera.Converters;assembly=LogIt.XamForms"
    BackgroundColor="White">

    <Grid x:Name="MainLayout" BackgroundColor="Black">
        <Grid.RowDefinitions>
            <RowDefinition Height="*" />
        </Grid.RowDefinitions>

        <Grid.ColumnDefinitions>
            <ColumnDefinition Width="*"/>
```

```
            </Grid.ColumnDefinitions>
            <StackLayout Orientation="Vertical" HorizontalOptions="Center"
    VerticalOptions="Center"
                     Grid.Row="0" Grid.Column="0">
                <ActivityIndicator x:Name="ProgressActivity" Color="White"
    IsRunning="true"  />
                <Label x:Name="LoadingLabel" Text="{Binding LoadingMessage}"
    TextColor="White"/>
            </StackLayout>
        </Grid>
</ContentView>
```

The layout of the FocusView consists of a Grid containing another StackLayout, which is centered both horizontally and vertically inside the Grid. The StackLayout contains an ActivityIndicator, which will be running every time this view is shown, and a Label to display a loading message.

Then, expand the LoadingView.xaml.cs and implement the following:

```
    public partial class LoadingView : ContentView
    {
        public LoadingView()
        {
            InitializeComponent();
        }
    }
```

This view will be used on the CameraPage. When the camera is loading or processing an image, the entire screen will be cast black, displaying the ActivityIndicator and loading message, to show the user that the camera is processing.

Building a control for the iOS camera

Now that we have built the CameraView object in the Xamarin.Forms PCL, we are going to build the CustomRenderer for iOS. Jump into the **Camera.iOS** project and add a new folder called Renderers, and then add a new file called CameraiOS.cs and implement the following private properties:

```
    public sealed class CameraIOS : UIView
    {
        #region Private Properties

        private readonly string _tag;
```

```
        private readonly ILogger _log;

        private readonly AVCaptureVideoPreviewLayer _previewLayer;

        private readonly AVCaptureSession _captureSession;

        private UIView _mainView;

        private AVCaptureDeviceInput _input;

        private AVCaptureStillImageOutput _output;

        private AVCaptureConnection _captureConnection;

        private AVCaptureDevice _device;

        private bool _cameraBusy;

        private bool _cameraAvailable;

        private float _cameraButtonContainerWidth;

        private float _imgScale = 1.25f;

        private double _systemVersion;

        private nint _width;

        private nint _height;

    #endregion
    }
```

The _tag and _log properties will be used for all logging that occurs when an exception occurs. The _previewLayer is used to display the video input from the camera; this will be set to the entire width and height of the CameraView. The _captureSession is used in conjunction with an AVCaptireVideoPreviewLayer object for capturing an image from the video input. The _input object is used in conjunction with an AVCaptureDevice and CaptureSession; this provides the video stream input, which the CaptureSession will use to capture an image. We also have an AVCaptureStillImageOutput object called _output; this is used to capture high-quality still images with accompanying metadata.

An `AVCaptureStillImageOutput` object also contains `AVCaptureConnections`, which we use for controlling the video stream orientation. Then finally, we have the `_device` property, which is the object that represents a physical capture device. In our example, we are going to use the rear camera. We will see how the remaining properties are used through the other functions.

Next we have to add three events that will be notified when the camera is busy, when the camera is available, and when a photo is taken:

```
#region Events

public event EventHandler<bool> Busy;

        public event EventHandler<bool> Available;

        public event EventHandler<byte[]> Photo;

        #endregion
```

Then we have the constructor:

```
        #region Constructors

        public CameraIOS()
        {
            _log = IoC.Resolve<ILogger>();
            _tag = $"{GetType()} ";

            // retrieve system version
            var versionParts = UIDevice.CurrentDevice.SystemVersion.Split
('.');
            var versionString = versionParts [0] + "." + versionParts [1];
            _systemVersion = Convert.ToDouble (versionString,
CultureInfo.InvariantCulture);

            _mainView = new UIView () {
TranslatesAutoresizingMaskIntoConstraints = false };
            AutoresizingMask = UIViewAutoresizing.FlexibleMargins;

            _captureSession = new AVCaptureSession();

            _previewLayer = new AVCaptureVideoPreviewLayer(_captureSession)
            {
                VideoGravity = AVLayerVideoGravity.Resize
            };

            _mainView.Layer.AddSublayer (_previewLayer);
```

```
            // retrieve camera device if available
            _cameraAvailable = RetrieveCameraDevice ();

            Add (_mainView);

            // set layout constraints for main view
            AddConstraints
(NSLayoutConstraint.FromVisualFormat("V:|[mainView]|",
NSLayoutFormatOptions.DirectionLeftToRight, null, new
NSDictionary("mainView", _mainView)));
            AddConstraints
(NSLayoutConstraint.FromVisualFormat("H:|[mainView]|",
NSLayoutFormatOptions.AlignAllTop, null, new NSDictionary ("mainView",
_mainView)));
        }

        #endregion
```

The constructor will start with retrieving the `ILogger` object from the `IoC` container and assigning the `_tag` to the type name using C# 6. Then we retrieve the system version information and create a new `UIView`. Setting the `AutoresizingMask` to `UIViewAutoresizing.FlexibleMargins` ensures that the `CameraiOS` view adjusts to the entire bounds of the `CustomRenderer`. Then we instantiate a new `AvCaptureSession` and an `AVCaptureVideoPreviewLayer`, we pass the `AVCaptureSession` object into the new `AVCaptureVideoPreviewLayer`, and add this layer to the `mainView` layer. We then retrieve the physical camera device using the `RetrieveCameraDevice` function.

Let's add this function in below the constructor:

```
public bool RetrieveCameraDevice()
        {
            _device =
AVCaptureDevice.DefaultDeviceWithMediaType(AVMediaType.Video);

            if (_device == null)
            {
                _log.WriteLineTime(_tag + "\n" + "RetrieveCameraDevice() No
device detected \n ");
                return false;
            }

            return true;
        }
```

On this line, add the following:

```
_device = AVCaptureDevice.DefaultDeviceWithMediaType(AVMediaType.Video);
```

This is used to retrieve the physical rear-view camera.

Now let's get back to the constructor. After we retrieved the physical device, we simply add the `mainView` to the `CameraiOS` view and set the layout constraints of the `mainView` to fill the bounds of the `CameraiOS` view.

Next, we add the `private` functions. Our first function `AdjustPreviewLayer` is responsible for setting the bounds of the layer to fill the `CameraiOS` view when an orientation change occurs:

```
#region Private Methods

/// <param name="orientation">Orientation.</param>
private void AdjustPreviewLayer(Orientation orientation)
{
    CGRect previewLayerFrame = _previewLayer.Frame;

    switch (orientation)
    {
        case Orientation.Portrait:
            previewLayerFrame.Height =
UIScreen.MainScreen.Bounds.Height - _cameraButtonContainerWidth;
            previewLayerFrame.Width =
UIScreen.MainScreen.Bounds.Width;
            break;

        case Orientation.LandscapeLeft:
        case Orientation.LandscapeRight:
            if (_systemVersion >= 8)
            {
                previewLayerFrame.Width =
UIScreen.MainScreen.Bounds.Width - _cameraButtonContainerWidth;
                previewLayerFrame.Height =
UIScreen.MainScreen.Bounds.Height;
            }
            else
            {
                previewLayerFrame.Width =
UIScreen.MainScreen.Bounds.Height - _cameraButtonContainerWidth;
                previewLayerFrame.Height =
UIScreen.MainScreen.Bounds.Width;
            }
            break;
    }

    try
    {
```

```
        _previewLayer.Frame = previewLayerFrame;
    }
    catch (Exception error)
    {
        _log.WriteLineTime(_tag + "\n" +
            "AdjustPreviewLayer() Failed to adjust frame \n " +
            "ErrorMessage: \n" +
            error.Message + "\n" +
            "Stacktrace: \n " +
            error.StackTrace);
    }
}
```

We also need a function for setting the starting orientation:

```
private void SetStartOrientation()
{
    Orientation sOrientation = Orientation.None;

    switch (UIApplication.SharedApplication.StatusBarOrientation)
    {
        case UIInterfaceOrientation.Portrait:
        case UIInterfaceOrientation.PortraitUpsideDown:
            sOrientation = Orientation.Portrait;
            break;
        case UIInterfaceOrientation.LandscapeLeft:
            sOrientation = Orientation.LandscapeLeft;
            break;
        case UIInterfaceOrientation.LandscapeRight:
            sOrientation = Orientation.LandscapeRight;
            break;
    }

    HandleOrientationChange(sOrientation);
}
```

Then we have the `SetBusy` function, which will invoke the `Busy` EventHandler and set the `private` variable to keep the busy status locally:

```
private void SetBusy(bool busy)
{
    _cameraBusy = busy;

    // set camera busy
    Busy?.Invoke(this, _cameraBusy);
}
```

Next, we have the `CaptureImageWithMetadata` function. This is called every time the user clicks to take a picture (this function will be called from the public method `TakePhoto`). When we call the `CaptureImageWithMetadata` function, we must pass in an `AVCaptureStillImageOutput` object and an `AVCaptureConnection`. From the `AVCaptureStillImageOutput` object, we call the `CaptureStillImageTaskAsync` function on the `AVCaptureConnection`. The connection we pass in is linked to the `_previewLayer` connection. After this call is successful, we retrieve the raw image as a JPEG and retrieve the raw bytes to invoke the `Photo` EventHandler. We also use the `RotateImage` function for rotating the original `UIImage` image to the correct orientation:

```
        private async Task
CaptureImageWithMetadata(AVCaptureStillImageOutput captureStillImageOutput,
AVCaptureConnection connection)
        {
        var sampleBuffer = await
captureStillImageOutput.CaptureStillImageTaskAsync(connection);
        var imageData =
AVCaptureStillImageOutput.JpegStillToNSData(sampleBuffer);
        var image = UIImage.LoadFromData(imageData);

        RotateImage(ref image);

        try
        {
            byte[] imgData = image.AsJPEG().ToArray();

            if (Photo != null)
            {
                Photo(this, imgData);
            }
        }
        catch (Exception error)
        {
            _log.WriteLineTime(_tag + "\n" +
                "CaptureImageWithMetadata() Failed to take photo \n " +
                "ErrorMessage: \n" +
                error.Message + "\n" +
                "Stacktrace: \n " +
                error.StackTrace);
        }
        }

        #endregion
```

Let's add the `RotateImage` function:

```
private void RotateImage(ref UIImage image)
    {
        CGImage imgRef = image.CGImage;
        CGAffineTransform transform = CGAffineTransform.MakeIdentity();

        var imgHeight = imgRef.Height * _imgScale;
        var imgWidth = imgRef.Width * _imgScale;

        CGRect bounds = new CGRect(0, 0, imgWidth, imgHeight);
        CGSize imageSize = new CGSize(imgWidth, imgHeight);
        UIImageOrientation orient = image.Orientation;

        switch (orient)
        {
            case UIImageOrientation.Up:
                transform = CGAffineTransform.MakeIdentity();
                break;
            case UIImageOrientation.Down:
                transform = CGAffineTransform.MakeTranslation
(imageSize.Width, imageSize.Height);
                transform = CGAffineTransform.Rotate(transform,
(float)Math.PI);
                break;
            case UIImageOrientation.Right:
                bounds.Size = new CGSize( bounds.Size.Height,
bounds.Size.Width);
                transform =
CGAffineTransform.MakeTranslation(imageSize.Height, 0);
                transform = CGAffineTransform.Rotate(transform,
(float)Math.PI / 2.0f);
                break;
            default:
                throw new Exception("Invalid image orientation");
        }

        UIGraphics.BeginImageContext(bounds.Size);
        CGContext context = UIGraphics.GetCurrentContext();

        if (orient == UIImageOrientation.Right)
        {
            context.ScaleCTM(-1, 1);
            context.TranslateCTM(-imgHeight, 0);
        }
        else
        {
```

```
                    context.ScaleCTM(1, -1);
                    context.TranslateCTM(0, -imgHeight);
            }

            context.ConcatCTM(transform);

            context.DrawImage(new CGRect(0, 0, imgWidth, imgHeight),
    imgRef);
            image = UIGraphics.GetImageFromCurrentImageContext();
            UIGraphics.EndImageContext();
        }
```

In the preceding function, we use the UIGraphics context for rebuilding and rotating the UIImage image. We start with a new CGImage, gather the orientation from the original UIImage, and transform this image, then redraw using the UIGraphics.GetImageFromCurrentImageContext() method.

Now we add the public methods. Start with overriding the Draw function so that we can assign the most recent frame on the _previewLayer. The Draw function is called every time the screen rotates. We want to ensure the _previewLayer frame fills the bounds of the screen:

```
            public override void Draw(CGRect rect)
            {
                _previewLayer.Frame = rect;

                base.Draw(rect);
            }
```

Next, we have the TakePhoto function. This will retrieve the current AVCaptureConnection from the AVCaptureStillImageOutput, set the connection orientation to the _previewLayer orientation, and pass the connection and output to the CaptureImageWithMetadata function:

```
            public async Task TakePhoto()
            {
                if (!_cameraBusy)
                {
                    SetBusy(true);

                    try
                    {
                        // set output orientation
                        _output.Connections [0].VideoOrientation =
    _previewLayer.Orientation;
```

```
        var connection = _output.Connections[0];

        await CaptureImageWithMetadata(_output, connection);

        SetBusy(false);
    }
    catch (Exception error)
    {
        _log.WriteLineTime(_tag + "\n" +
            "TakePhoto() Error with camera output capture \n "
 +
            "ErrorMessage: \n" +
            error.Message + "\n" +
            "Stacktrace: \n " +
            error.StackTrace);
        IoC.Resolve<ILogger>().WriteLineTime   ("CameraIOS:
Error with camera output capture - " + e);
    }
        }
    }
```

 Don't forget to look at the exception handling occurring for all functions. Sometimes, bizarre errors can occur (null connections, device retrieval fails) when dealing with camera hardware, so we must handle all exceptions that may occur.

Next, we have the `SwitchFlash` function, which is used to turn the flash on/off using the `AVCaptureDevice` configurations:

```
public void SwitchFlash(bool flashOn)
{
    NSError err;

    if (_cameraAvailable && _device != null)
    {
        try
        {
            _device.LockForConfiguration(out err);
            _device.TorchMode = flashOn ? AVCaptureTorchMode.On :
AVCaptureTorchMode.Off;
            _device.UnlockForConfiguration();
        }
        catch (Exception error)
        {
            _log.WriteLineTime(_tag + "\n" +
                "SwitchFlash() Failed to switch flash on/off \n " +
                "ErrorMessage: \n" +
```

```
                                 error.Message + "\n" +
                                 "Stacktrace: \n " +
                                 error.StackTrace);
                         }
                 }
         }
```

Then we have the `SetBounds` function. This is called from the
`OnElementPropertyChanged` method of the `CustomRenderer`, on any height and with
property changes:

```
        public void SetBounds(nint width, nint height)
        {
            _height = height;
            _width = width;
        }
```

The `ChangeFocusPoint` function is used for focusing the camera to the touch point
received from the user. First, we must lock the `AVCaptureDevice` configurations before
making any changes.

 When we make changes to the `AVCaptureDevice` configurations, we
must first call `LockForConfiguration` to notify the device that we are
making changes and then, once we are finished, call
`UnlockForConfiguration` for the changes to take effect.

Then we check to see if the `FocusPointOfInterestSupported` is `true` and set the
`FocusPointOfInterest` to a new `CGRect` point. We also do the same with exposure by
first checking the `ExposurePointOfInterestSupported` is `true` and setting the
`ExposurePointOfInterest` to a new `CGRect` point:

```
        public void ChangeFocusPoint(Point fPoint)
        {
            NSError err;

            if (_cameraAvailable && _device != null)
            {
                try
                {
                    _device.LockForConfiguration(out err);

                    var focus_x = fPoint.X / Bounds.Width;
                    var focus_y = fPoint.Y / Bounds.Height;

                    // set focus point
                    if (_device.FocusPointOfInterestSupported)
```

```
            _device.FocusPointOfInterest =
                new CGPoint(focus_x, focus_y);
        if (_device.ExposurePointOfInterestSupported)
            _device.ExposurePointOfInterest =
                new CGPoint(focus_x, focus_y);

        _device.UnlockForConfiguration();
    }
    catch (Exception error)
    {
        _log.WriteLineTime(_tag + "\n" +
            "SwitchFlash() Failed to adjust focus \n " +
            "ErrorMessage: \n" +
            error.Message + "\n" +
            "Stacktrace: \n " +
            error.StackTrace);
    }
  }
 }
```

Our next function is `InitializeCamera`, which we use to set up the `AVCaptureDevice`. We set the focus mode to `ContinuousAuto` and create a new `AVCaptureDeviceInput` using the instance of the `AVCaptureDevice`. We then create a new `AvCaptureStillImageOutput` object. Both the `AVCaptureDeviceInput` and `AvCaptureStillImageOutput` objects are assigned to the input/output of the `AVCaptureSession`, respectively. After this, the new `NSDictionary` is created with a key to set the video CODEC to JPEG (all still images taken will be in this format). Finally, the `Connection` object from the `_previewLayer` is retrieved, the starting orientation is set accordingly, and we call the `StartRunning` method on the `AVCaptureSession`:

```
public void InitializeCamera()
{
    try
    {
        NSError error;
        NSError err;

        _device.LockForConfiguration(out err);
        _device.FocusMode = AVCaptureFocusMode.ContinuousAutoFocus;
        _device.UnlockForConfiguration();

        _input = new AVCaptureDeviceInput(_device, out error);
        _captureSession.AddInput(_input);

        _output = new AVCaptureStillImageOutput();
```

```
            var dict = new NSMutableDictionary();
            dict[AVVideo.CodecKey] = new NSNumber((int)
AVVideoCodec.JPEG);
            _captureSession.AddOutput (_output);

            InvokeOnMainThread(delegate
               {
                   // capture connection used for rotating camera
                   _captureConnection = _previewLayer.Connection;
                   SetStartOrientation();
                   // set orientation before loading camera
                   _captureSession.StartRunning ();
               });
        }
        catch (Exception error)
        {
            _log.WriteLineTime(_tag + "\n" +
                "InitializeCamera() Camera failed to initialise \n " +
                "ErrorMessage: \n" +
                error.Message + "\n" +
                "Stacktrace: \n " +
                error.StackTrace);
        }

        Available?.Invoke(this, _cameraAvailable);

        _log.WriteLineTime(_tag + "\n" + "RetrieveCameraDevice() Camera
initalised \n ");
    }
```

Our next function is `SetWidths`, which will assign the local
`_cameraButtonConatinerWidth` property accordingly. This `local` property is used as an
extra reduction on the camera stream width to ensure that the camera stream does not fall
behind the black button panel on the `CameraPage`:

```
    public void SetWidths(float cameraButtonContainerWidth)
    {
        _cameraButtonContainerWidth = cameraButtonContainerWidth;
    }
```

Next, the last function is `HandleOrientationChange`, which will be called from the
`CustomRenderer` every time an orientation occurs because we must update the
`VideoOrientation` property of the `AVCaptureConnection` object.

Even though `Xamarin.Forms` automatically handles the orientation changes of the views for you, with this `CustomRenderer` view, the video stream from the `AVCaptureVideoPreviewLayer` does not rotate unless we change the underlying `CALayers`.

```
public void HandleOrientationChange(Orientation orientation)
{
if (_captureConnection != null)
{
switch (orientation)
{
case Orientation.Portrait: _captureConnection.VideoOrientation =
AVCaptureVideoOrientation.Portrait;
break;
case Orientation.LandscapeLeft: _captureConnection.VideoOrientation =
AVCaptureVideoOrientation.LandscapeLeft;
break;
case Orientation.LandscapeRight: _captureConnection.VideoOrientation =
AVCaptureVideoOrientation.LandscapeRight;
break;
}
}
AdjustPreviewLayer(orientation);
}
```

Finally, we have the `StopAndDispose` method. This will be called from the `Dipose` method of the `CustomRenderer`. It is responsible for freeing up all the resources involved with the camera stream, and switching off the flash if it is on:

```
public void StopAndDispose()
{
if (_device != null)
{
// if flash is on turn off if (_device.TorchMode == AVCaptureTorchMode.On)
{
SwitchFlash(false);
}
}
_captureSession.StopRunning();
// dispose output elements _input.Dispose();
_output.Dispose();
}
#endregion
}
```

Well done! Now we have built the native camera control, we are going to use this as the control for our CustomRenderer.

Building the iOS CameraRenderer

Now let's create the actual `CustomRenderer` that will use this custom iOS object. Add a new file into **Renderers | CameraView**, call it `CameraViewRenderer.cs`, and implement the following:

```
public class CameraViewRenderer : ViewRenderer<CameraView, CameraIOS>
    {
        #region Private Properties

        private CameraIOS bodyshopCameraIOS;

        #endregion

        #region Protected Methods

        protected override void
OnElementChanged(ElementChangedEventArgs<CameraView> e)
        {
            base.OnElementChanged(e);

            if (Control == null)
            {
                bodyshopCameraIOS = new CameraIOS();

                bodyshopCameraIOS.Busy += Element.NotifyBusy;
                bodyshopCameraIOS.Available += Element.NotifyAvailability;
                bodyshopCameraIOS.Photo += Element.NotifyPhoto;

                SetNativeControl(bodyshopCameraIOS);
            }

            if (e.OldElement != null)
            {
                e.NewElement.Flash -= HandleFlash;
                e.NewElement.OpenCamera -= HandleCameraInitialisation;
                e.NewElement.Focus -= HandleFocus;
                e.NewElement.Shutter -= HandleShutter;
                e.NewElement.Widths -= HandleWidths;

                bodyshopCameraIOS.Busy -= Element.NotifyBusy;
                bodyshopCameraIOS.Available -= Element.NotifyAvailability;
                bodyshopCameraIOS.Photo -= Element.NotifyPhoto;
            }

            if (e.NewElement != null)
            {
```

```
e.NewElement.Flash += HandleFlash;
e.NewElement.OpenCamera += HandleCameraInitialisation;
e.NewElement.Focus += HandleFocus;
e.NewElement.Shutter += HandleShutter;
e.NewElement.Widths += HandleWidths;
    }
}

#endregion

}
```

The first part of our `CustomRenderer` shows the `OnElementChanged` override. In all custom renderers, the `OnElementChanged` function may be called multiple times, so care must be taken to avoid any memory leaks that can lead to performance impact. Following is the approach that should be taken:

```
protected override void OnElementChanged
(ElementChangedEventArgs<NativeListView> e)
{
base.OnElementChanged (e);

if (Control == null) {
// Instantiate the native control
}

if (e.OldElement != null) {
// Unsubscribe from event handlers and cleanup any resources
}

if (e.NewElement != null) {
    // Configure the control and subscribe to event handlers
    }
}
```

Now back to the `OnElementChanged` implementation, we instantiate a new `CameraiOS` and register the EventHandlers to the `Xamarin.FormsCameraView` functions. This will fire another event that will be handled on our `CameraPage`. We then call `SetNativeControl` to assign the `CameraiOS` object to the `CustomRenderer` control, so when `CameraView` object is displayed on a `ContentPage`, a `CameraiOS` view will appear on top. We then register events and unregister events in both the if blocks to correctly dispose and assign the `CameraView` EventHandlers.

Let's add the next override for `OnElementPropertyChanged` as follows:

```
protected override void OnElementPropertyChanged(object sender,
System.ComponentModel.PropertyChangedEventArgs e)
{
        base.OnElementPropertyChanged(sender, e);

        if (Element != null && bodyshopCameraIOS != null)
        {
            if (e.PropertyName ==
VisualElement.HeightProperty.PropertyName ||
                e.PropertyName ==
VisualElement.WidthProperty.PropertyName)
            {
                bodyshopCameraIOS.SetBounds((nint)Element.Width,
(nint)Element.Height);
            }
        }
}
```

This function will be called for every property change on the `CameraView`. We will call the `SetBounds` method on the `CameraiOS` object so that our `AVCapturePreviewVideoLayer` always retains the latest height and width update.

Now we must add the `EventHandler` functions as follows:

```
#region Private Methods

private void HandleWidths (object sender, float e)
{
    bodyshopCameraIOS.SetWidths (e);
}

private async void HandleShutter (object sender, EventArgs e)
{
    await bodyshopCameraIOS.TakePhoto ();
}

private void HandleOrientationChange (object sender, Orientation e)
{
    bodyshopCameraIOS.HandleOrientationChange (e);
}

private void HandleFocus (object sender, Point e)
{
    bodyshopCameraIOS.ChangeFocusPoint (e);
}
```

```
private void HandleCameraInitialisation (object sender, bool args)
{
    bodyshopCameraIOS.InitializeCamera();

    Element.OrientationChange += HandleOrientationChange;
}

private void HandleFlash (object sender, bool args)
{
    bodyshopCameraIOS.SwitchFlash (args);
}

private void HandleFocusChange (object sender, Point args)
{
    bodyshopCameraIOS.ChangeFocusPoint (args);
}

#endregion
}
```

All these functions will respond to events fired from the `CameraView` and call their respect native functions to handle control on the native camera.

Now that we have implemented control over the iOS camera, let's do the same for Android.

Integrating the Android Camera2 framework

The new `Camera2` framework was introduced in API 21 (5.0 Lollipop) and provides a wide featured framework for controlling camera devices connected to any Android device.

Start by setting up the folder structure **Renderers** | **CameraView** inside the `Camera.Droid` project. Inside the `CameraView` folder, add a file called `CameraCaptureListener.cs` and implement the following:

```
public class CameraCaptureListener : CameraCaptureSession.CaptureCallback
{
    public event EventHandler PhotoComplete;

    public override void OnCaptureCompleted(CameraCaptureSession
session, CaptureRequest request,
            TotalCaptureResult result)
    {
        PhotoComplete?.Invoke(this, EventArgs.Empty);
    }
}
```

All we need to do is fire an event every time the `OnCaptureCompleted` function is called. This function is called after all the image capture processing is completed.

Next, we have to create a callback for receiving updates about the state of a camera capture session. We will listen for both the `OnConfigured` and `OnConfigureFailed` and fire two different events so that we can handle any errors that may occur with the configuration of the capture session:

```
public class CameraCaptureStateListener :
CameraCaptureSession.StateCallback
    {
        public Action<CameraCaptureSession> OnConfigureFailedAction;

        public Action<CameraCaptureSession> OnConfiguredAction;

        public override void OnConfigureFailed(CameraCaptureSession
session)
        {
            if (OnConfigureFailedAction != null)
            {
                OnConfigureFailedAction(session);
            }
        }

        public override void OnConfigured(CameraCaptureSession session)
        {
            if (OnConfiguredAction != null)
            {
                OnConfiguredAction(session);
            }
        }
    }
```

Our next class is another callback for receiving updates about the state of the camera device. Here we will be firing events for camera availability so that we can pass down the availability state of the native camera to our `CameraView` view in the `Xamarin.Forms` project:

```
public class CameraStateListener : CameraDevice.StateCallback
    {
        public CameraDroid Camera;

        public override void OnOpened(CameraDevice camera)
        {
            if (Camera != null)
            {
                Camera.cameraDevice = camera;
```

```
                    Camera.StartPreview();
                    Camera.OpeningCamera = false;

                    Camera?.NotifyAvailable(true);
                }
            }

            public override void OnDisconnected(CameraDevice camera)
            {
                if (Camera != null)
                {
                    camera.Close();
                    Camera.cameraDevice = null;
                    Camera.OpeningCamera = false;

                    Camera?.NotifyAvailable(false);
                }
            }

            public override void OnError(CameraDevice camera, CameraError
error)
            {
                camera.Close();

                if (Camera != null)
                {
                    Camera.cameraDevice = null;
                    Camera.OpeningCamera = false;

                    Camera?.NotifyAvailable(false);
                }
            }
        }
    }
```

 All the new Camera2 callback objects provide excellent control with error handling.

The CameraDroid class will be rendered on top of the CustomRenderer, which is equivalent to the CameraiOS object. We want to pass an instance of the CameraDroid class to the CameraStateListener, when the state of the camera changes, we update the availability status on the CameraDroid instance.

Next, we must add another callback instance for handling image availability. This is where the raw image bytes will come from. Add a new file called `ImageAvailableListener.cs` and implement the following:

```
public class ImageAvailableListener : Java.Lang.Object,
ImageReader.IOnImageAvailableListener
    {
        public event EventHandler<byte[]> Photo;

        public void OnImageAvailable(ImageReader reader)
        {
            Image image = null;

            try
            {
                image = reader.AcquireLatestImage();
                ByteBuffer buffer = image.GetPlanes()[0].Buffer;
                byte[] imageData = new byte[buffer.Capacity()];
                buffer.Get(imageData);

                Photo?.Invoke(this, imageData);
            }
            catch (Exception ex)
            {
            }
            finally
            {
                if (image != null)
                {
                    image.Close();
                }
            }
        }
    }
```

When the `OnImageAvailable` function is called, this means we have the raw image available. We call `AcquireLatestImage` on the `ImageReader` object to acquire the last image taken, pull the raw bytes into a `ByteBuffer`, and convert the `ByteBuffer` into an array of bytes.

 A `ByteBuffer` comes from the `Java.Lang` framework, which we use when we want to implement fast low-level I/O.

Now it's time to implement the `CameraDroid` class. Add in a new file called `CameraDroid.cs` and implement the following:

```
public class CameraDroid : FrameLayout, TextureView.ISurfaceTextureListener
    {
        #region Static Properties

        private static readonly SparseIntArray ORIENTATIONS = new
SparseIntArray();

        #endregion

        #region Public Events

        public event EventHandler<bool> Busy;

        public event EventHandler<bool> Available;

        public event EventHandler<byte[]> Photo;

        #endregion

    }
```

The `CameraDroid` class inherits `FrameLayout` and `TextureView.ISurfaceTextureListener`. The static `ORIENTATIONS` property is a `SpareIntArray`, which works similar to a `HashMap`, but it can only map integers to integers. This will be used when a picture is taken. We must rotate images based upon screen orientation for the picture orientation to appear correctly.

We also have three event handlers like our `CameraiOS` these, are used to track whether the camera has taken a photo, is busy or is available.

Next, we have the following `private` properties:

```
#region Private Properties

        private readonly string _tag;

        private readonly ILogger _log;

        private CameraStateListener mStateListener;

        private CaptureRequest.Builder _previewBuilder;

        private CameraCaptureSession _previewSession;
```

```
        private SurfaceTexture _viewSurface;

        private TextureView _cameraTexture;

        private MediaActionSound mediaSound;

        private Android.Util.Size _previewSize;

        private Context _context;

        private CameraManager _manager;

        private bool _mediaSoundLoaded;

        private bool _openingCamera;

        #endregion
```

The _tag and _log properties are used for logging like our other classes. We are also going to include an instance of all our callbacks.

Then we have the public properties. Every time the OpeningCamera property is assigned, it will fire a Busy event. Now we can track the busy state of the camera inside the CameraPage containing the CameraView. We also have an instance of the CameraDevice, which represents the actual device:

```
        #region Public Properties

        public bool OpeningCamera
        {
            get
            {
                return _openingCamera;
            }
            set
            {
                if (_openingCamera != value)
                {
                    _openingCamera = value;
                    Busy?.Invoke(this, value);
                }
            }
        }

        public CameraDevice cameraDevice;

        #endregion
```

Next, we have the constructor. We must first pass in the context, since we will be using this locally through the class. Then the `LoadShutterSound` function is called, which will return a Boolean once the sound has been loaded. We then assign `_log` from the `IoC` container and set `_tag` using the C# 6 method `GetType`. Using the `LayoutInflator`, we create a new `CameraLayout` and set the local `_cameraTexture` object. The `SurfaceTextureListener` property of the `_cameraTexture` must be set to the `CameraDroid` instance itself. This is why the `CameraDroid` class implements the `TextureView.ISurfaceTextureListener` framework. We then instantiate a new `CameraStateListener` and set the `Camera` property to the `CameraDroid` instance using the `this` keyword, and, add the orientation to rotation mappings:

```
#region Constructors

public CameraDroid (Context context) : base (context)
{
    _context = context;
    _mediaSoundLoaded = LoadShutterSound ();

    _log = IoC.Resolve<ILogger>();
    _tag = $"{GetType()} ";

    var inflater = LayoutInflater.FromContext (context);

    if (inflater != null)
    {
        var view = inflater.Inflate(Resource.Layout.CameraLayout,
this);

        _cameraTexture =
view.FindViewById<TextureView>(Resource.Id.CameraTexture);
        _cameraTexture.SurfaceTextureListener = this;

        mStateListener = new CameraStateListener() { Camera = this
};

        ORIENTATIONS.Append((int)SurfaceOrientation.Rotation0, 90);
        ORIENTATIONS.Append((int)SurfaceOrientation.Rotation90, 0);
        ORIENTATIONS.Append((int)SurfaceOrientation.Rotation180,
270);

        ORIENTATIONS.Append((int)SurfaceOrientation.Rotation270,
180);
    }
}

#endregion
```

Now let's move on to the `private` methods. We are going to start with `UpdatePreview`. This is responsible for starting the video stream through the surface texture. If we have both a session and camera object in play, we use the `CameraRequest.Builder` instance to set the capture request mode to auto. The `Handler` object that is created is required to run the `CameraPreview` on the main UI thread:

```
#region Private Methods

private void UpdatePreview()
{
    if (cameraDevice != null && _previewSession != null)
    {
        try
        {
            // The camera preview can be run in a background
thread. This is a Handler for the camere preview
            _previewBuilder.Set(CaptureRequest.ControlMode, new
Java.Lang.Integer((int)ControlMode.Auto));
            HandlerThread thread = new
HandlerThread("CameraPreview");
            thread.Start();
            Handler backgroundHandler = new Handler(thread.Looper);

            // Finally, we start displaying the camera preview
_previewSession.SetRepeatingRequest(_previewBuilder.Build(), null,
backgroundHandler);
        }
        catch (CameraAccessException error)
        {
            _log.WriteLineTime(_tag + "\n" +
                "UpdatePreview() Camera access exception.  \n " +
                "ErrorMessage: \n" +
                error.Message + "\n" +
                "Stacktrace: \n " +
                error.StackTrace);

        }
        catch (IllegalStateException error)
        {
            _log.WriteLineTime(_tag + "\n" +
                "UpdatePreview() Illegal exception.  \n " +
                "ErrorMessage: \n" +
                error.Message + "\n" +
                "Stacktrace: \n " +
                error.StackTrace);

        }
    }
}
```

Our next function is responsible for loading the click sound. The `LoadShutterSound` method is used above in the constructor. When it returns `true`, this means we have successfully loaded the `MediaActionSoundType.ShutterClick`, so every time a user takes a photo, the shutter sound will play:

```
private bool LoadShutterSound()
{
    try
    {
        mediaSound = new MediaActionSound ();
        mediaSound.LoadAsync (MediaActionSoundType.ShutterClick);

        return true;
    }
    catch (Java.Lang.Exception error)
    {
        _log.WriteLineTime(_tag + "\n" +
            "LoadShutterSound() Error loading shutter sound  \n " +
            "ErrorMessage: \n" +
            error.Message + "\n" +
            "Stacktrace: \n " +
            error.StackTrace);
    }

    return false;
}

#endregion
```

Now we move on to the `public` methods. Our first function `OpenCamera` will be called when the `CameraPage` appears:

```
#region Public Methods

public void OpenCamera()
{
    if (_context== null || OpeningCamera)
    {
        return;
    }

    OpeningCamera = true;

    _manager =
(CameraManager)_context.GetSystemService(Context.CameraService);

    try
```

```
        {
            string cameraId = _manager.GetCameraIdList()[0];

            // To get a list of available sizes of camera preview, we
retrieve an instance of
            // StreamConfigurationMap from CameraCharacteristics
            CameraCharacteristics characteristics =
_manager.GetCameraCharacteristics(cameraId);
            StreamConfigurationMap map =
(StreamConfigurationMap)characteristics.Get(CameraCharacteristics.ScalerStr
eamConfigurationMap);
            _previewSize =
map.GetOutputSizes(Java.Lang.Class.FromType(typeof(SurfaceTexture)))[0];
            Android.Content.Res.Orientation orientation =
Resources.Configuration.Orientation;
            if (orientation ==
Android.Content.Res.Orientation.Landscape)
            {
                _cameraTexture.SetAspectRatio(_previewSize.Width,
_previewSize.Height);
            }
            else
            {
                _cameraTexture.SetAspectRatio(_previewSize.Height,
_previewSize.Width);
            }

            // We are opening the camera with a listener. When it is
ready, OnOpened of mStateListener is called.
            _manager.OpenCamera(cameraId, mStateListener, null);
        }
        catch (Java.Lang.Exception error)
        {
            _log.WriteLineTime(_tag + "\n" +
                "OpenCamera() Failed to open camera  \n " +
                "ErrorMessage: \n" +
                error.Message + "\n" +
                "Stacktrace: \n " +
                error.StackTrace);
            Available?.Invoke(this, false);
        }
    }
```

Before opening the camera, we first check if the _context is null and that we are not already opening the camera. We then flag OpeningCamera to true and retrieve the camera device from the context using the GetSystemService method.

The `GetSystemService` method can be used to retrieve all hardware services.

Now that we have our `CameraManager` object, we call the `GetCameraIdList` method and retrieve the first camera ID from the list. We use this camera ID to retrieve the camera's characteristics that will be used for retrieving camera output sizes. We first use the camera output size to set the aspect ratio of the `_cameraTexture` and then we call `OpenCamera`, where we pass in the `cameraId` and `CameraStateListener`.

Now we have to add a function for taking photos. We start by checking if the `_context` and `cameraDevice` is not null. We then invoke a `Busy` event to communicate to our `CameraView` and check if the shutter click sound has been loaded, then play if it has loaded successfully.. Then we use the camera's characteristics to retrieve JPEG output sizes.

On every Android device, a camera will have supported output sizes for video streams and picture sizes. When we assign height, width, and ratio properties of camera display, they must be mapped to supported sizes.

We then set the first output size to the function's `width` and `height` properties. If the characteristics fail to show any JPEG output sizes, we start with the default width and height (640, 480).

Next, we use an `ImageReader` to retrieve and image from the `_cameraDevice`. We start with creating a new instance of an `ImageReader` and pass in our required width and height properties. An `ImageRenderer` also requires a surface, which is mapped to the output of a camera. When we take a picture, the `ImageReader` knows it will be reading from the output of the camera. We create a new `CaptureRequest.Builder`, which is created from the `CreateCaptureRequest` method of the `_cameraDevice`. Then we set the surface target to the surface we created earlier. Now the builder knows we are mapped to the output of the camera. We also set the capture request to auto, so most of the setup is taken care of. We then get the current orientation of the window from the `WindowManager` property (this is another service pulled from the `_context` using the `GetSystemService` method), and using the current orientation, set the rotation of the image accordingly.

Why do we have to change the orientation of the image? If we take an image on the current orientation, why is the image in a different orientation?

This is something we cannot control; the current orientation of the camera display does not map exactly how the image is interpreted when we take a picture, so we have to apply some minor rotation to bring the image into the same orientation as the camera surface.

This is a lot of work for the camera to do to prepare for capturing an image,

It takes a lot of work to prepare a capture session

how do we know when an image is actually taken?

All the work we have done so far is all for preparing the camera to take an image. We use our `ImageAvailableListener` for letting us know when the image is ready. Since we set up an event to hand us the image bytes, we can assign a delegate that will fire the `CameraDroid` so that the image bytes are passed back to the `CameraView` object.

Notice the use of the Handler?

The handler is used to handle the resulting JPEG in a background thread.

We then create an instance of our `CameraCaptureListener` to let us know capture operations have completed and assign a delegate function to restart the camera stream when the `PhotoComplete` event has been invoked. A new `CameraCaptureStateListener` object is passed into the `CreateCaptureSession` method to start the capture session and we assign a delegate to the `OnConfiguredAction` that will store the current `CameraCaptureSession`. We call the `Capture` method on the session and then call the `Build` method on the `captureBuilder` we created earlier. This occurs every time the `Capture` method is called.

The `captureListener` object and the handler are passed into the `Capture` method so that all capture processing is done on a background thread.

This means that when a picture is taken, the processing time in between preparing a photo will not lock the UI thread.

```
public void TakePhoto ()
{
    if (_context != null && _cameraDevice != null)
    {
        try
        {
            Busy?.Invoke(this, true);

            if (_mediaSoundLoaded)
```

```
                        {
_mediaSound.Play(MediaActionSoundType.ShutterClick);
                        }

                        // Pick the best JPEG size that can be captures with
this CameraDevice
                        var characteristics =
_manager.GetCameraCharacteristics(_cameraDevice.Id);
                        Android.Util.Size[] jpegSizes = null;
                        if (characteristics != null)
                        {
                            jpegSizes =
((StreamConfigurationMap)characteristics.Get(CameraCharacteristics.ScalerSt
reamConfigurationMap)).GetOutputSizes((int)ImageFormatType.Jpeg);
                        }
                        int width = 640;
                        int height = 480;

                        if (jpegSizes != null && jpegSizes.Length > 0)
                        {
                            width = jpegSizes[0].Width;
                            height = jpegSizes[0].Height;
                        }

                        // We use an ImageReader to get a JPEG from
CameraDevice
                        // Here, we create a new ImageReader and prepare its
Surface as an output from the camera
                        var reader = ImageReader.NewInstance(width, height,
ImageFormatType.Jpeg, 1);
                        var outputSurfaces = new List<Surface>(2);
                        outputSurfaces.Add(reader.Surface);
                        outputSurfaces.Add(new Surface(_viewSurface));

                        CaptureRequest.Builder captureBuilder =
_cameraDevice.CreateCaptureRequest(CameraTemplate.StillCapture);
                        captureBuilder.AddTarget(reader.Surface);
                        captureBuilder.Set(CaptureRequest.ControlMode, new
Integer((int)ControlMode.Auto));

                        // Orientation
                        var windowManager =
_context.GetSystemService(Context.WindowService).JavaCast<IWindowManager>()
;
                        SurfaceOrientation rotation =
windowManager.DefaultDisplay.Rotation;

                        captureBuilder.Set(CaptureRequest.JpegOrientation, new
```

```
Integer(ORIENTATIONS.Get((int)rotation)));

                    // This listener is called when an image is ready in
ImageReader
                    ImageAvailableListener readerListener = new
ImageAvailableListener();

                    readerListener.Photo += (sender, e) =>
                    {
                        Photo?.Invoke(this, e);
                    };

                    // We create a Handler since we want to handle the
resulting JPEG in a background thread
                    HandlerThread thread = new
HandlerThread("CameraPicture");
                    thread.Start();
                    Handler backgroundHandler = new Handler(thread.Looper);
                    reader.SetOnImageAvailableListener(readerListener,
backgroundHandler);

                    var captureListener = new CameraCaptureListener();

                    captureListener.PhotoComplete += (sender, e) =>
                    {
                        Busy?.Invoke(this, false);
                        StartPreview();
                    };

                    _cameraDevice.CreateCaptureSession(outputSurfaces, new
CameraCaptureStateListener()
                    {
                        OnConfiguredAction = (CameraCaptureSession session)
=>
                        {
                            try
                            {
                                _previewSession = session;
                                session.Capture(captureBuilder.Build(),
captureListener, backgroundHandler);
                            }
                            catch (CameraAccessException ex)
                            {
                                Log.WriteLine(LogPriority.Info, "Capture
Session error: ", ex.ToString());
                            }
                        }
                    }, backgroundHandler);
```

```
        }
        catch (CameraAccessException error)
        {
            _log.WriteLineTime(_tag + "\n" +
                "TakePhoto() Failed to take photo  \n " +
                "ErrorMessage: \n" +
                error.Message + "\n" +
                "Stacktrace: \n " +
                error.StackTrace);
        }
        catch (Java.Lang.Exception error)
        {
            _log.WriteLineTime(_tag + "\n" +
                "TakePhoto() Failed to take photo  \n " +
                "ErrorMessage: \n" +
                error.Message + "\n" +
                "Stacktrace: \n " +
                error.StackTrace);
        }
    }
}
```

It takes a lot of work to prepare a capture session on an Android camera using the `Camera2` framework, but the advantage is we have is the ability to control every single step separately, and handle any exceptions that occur at any point during the capture operation.

Our next function will be responsible for changing the focus point of the camera, when a touch on the `CameraView` occurs, this function will be called to change the focus point of the native camera:

```
public void ChangeFocusPoint(Xamarin.Forms.Point e)
{
    string cameraId = _manager.GetCameraIdList()[0];

    // To get a list of available sizes of camera preview, we
retrieve an instance of
    // StreamConfigurationMap from CameraCharacteristics
    CameraCharacteristics characteristics =
_manager.GetCameraCharacteristics(cameraId);

    var rect =
characteristics.Get(CameraCharacteristics.SensorInfoActiveArraySize) as
Rect;
    var size =
characteristics.Get(CameraCharacteristics.SensorInfoPixelArraySize) as
Size;
```

```
            int areaSize = 200;
            int right = rect.Right;
            int bottom = rect.Bottom;
            int viewWidth = _cameraTexture.Width;
            int viewHeight = _cameraTexture.Height;
            int ll, rr;

            Rect newRect;
            int centerX = (int)e.X;
            int centerY = (int)e.Y;

            ll = ((centerX * right) - areaSize) / viewWidth;
            rr = ((centerY * bottom) - areaSize) / viewHeight;

            int focusLeft = Clamp(ll, 0, right);
            int focusBottom = Clamp(rr, 0, bottom);

            newRect = new Rect(focusLeft, focusBottom, focusLeft +
areaSize, focusBottom + areaSize);
            MeteringRectangle meteringRectangle = new
MeteringRectangle(newRect, 500);
            MeteringRectangle[] meteringRectangleArr = { meteringRectangle
};
            _previewBuilder.Set(CaptureRequest.ControlAfTrigger,
(int)ControlAFTrigger.Cancel);
            _previewBuilder.Set(CaptureRequest.ControlAeRegions,
meteringRectangleArr);
            _previewBuilder.Set(CaptureRequest.ControlAfTrigger,
(int)ControlAFTrigger.Start);

            UpdatePreview();
        }
```

The `ChangeFocusPoint` function starts with retrieving the `cameraId` from the `CameraManager`. We then call the `Get` method of the camera characteristics to retrieve a rectangle and size of the active region of the camera sensor (that is, the region that actually receives light from the scene). We then retrieve the right and bottom bounds of this region and get the width and height of the `_cameraTexture`. When a user touches to focus, the point coordinate (x, y) passed into this function is used as the center of the focus region. As we have the middle point, we calculate the left and bottom points and we also use the `Clamp` function to make sure these points are within the width and height bounds of the `_cameraTexture`. We then create a new `Rect` representing the new active region for the camera sensor. Then, to perform the actual focus on the camera device, we must first disable the autofocus by calling the line:

```
_previewBuilder.Set(CaptureRequest.ControlAfTrigger,
(int)ControlAFTrigger.Cancel);
```

Then assign the camera sensor's active region by calling:

```
_previewBuilder.Set(CaptureRequest.ControlAeRegions, meteringRectangleArr);
```

And finally, reset the autofocus by calling:

```
_previewBuilder.Set(CaptureRequest.ControlAfTrigger,
(int)ControlAFTrigger.Start);
```

The operation works by disabling the autofocus, setting the active region, and then recalling autofocus. When the autofocus is started again, we have a new focus point in which the camera will adjust its focus point too.

We also call the `UpdatePreview` function for resetting the camera control to auto.

Next, we have the `Clamp` function, which is responsible for forcing the value passed in to be between a range. We use the following function:

```
private int Clamp(int value, int min, int max)
{
    return (value < min) ? min : (value > max) ? max : value;
}
```

Now for the `StartPreview` function, this will be responsible for starting the camera stream through the `TextureView`. We won't call this unit the camera has been opened previously:

```
public void StartPreview()
{
    if (cameraDevice != null && _cameraTexture.IsAvailable &&
_previewSize != null)
    {
        try
        {
            var texture = _cameraTexture.SurfaceTexture;

            texture.SetDefaultBufferSize(_previewSize.Width,
_previewSize.Height);
            Surface surface = new Surface(texture);

                                _previewBuilder =
cameraDevice.CreateCaptureRequest(CameraTemplate.Preview);
            _previewBuilder.AddTarget(surface);

            // Here, we create a CameraCaptureSession for camera
preview.
```

```
                    cameraDevice.CreateCaptureSession(new List<Surface>() {
surface },
                    new CameraCaptureStateListener()
                    {
                        OnConfigureFailedAction = (CameraCaptureSession
session) =>
                        {
                        },
                        OnConfiguredAction = (CameraCaptureSession
session) =>
                        {
                            _previewSession = session;
                            UpdatePreview();
                        }
                    },
                    null);

            }
            catch (Java.Lang.Exception error)
            {
                _log.WriteLineTime(_tag + "\n" +
                    "TakePhoto() Failed to start preview \n " +
                    "ErrorMessage: \n" +
                    error.Message + "\n" +
                    "Stacktrace: \n " +
                    error.StackTrace);
            }
        }
    }
```

The function starts with configuring the size of the default buffer to be the size of the camera preview. Then we want to create a new `Surface` object for the output surface of the camera, which is then assigned to a new `CaptureRequest.Builder`.

Don't forget we have another function to control the flash of the camera. We simply adjust the flash mode through `CaptureRequest.Builder` object and, based upon the `flashOn` `bool` passed in, we assign either `FlashMode.Torch` or `FlashMode.Off`:

```
        public void SwitchFlash(bool flashOn)
        {
            try
            {
                _previewBuilder.Set(CaptureRequest.FlashMode, new
Integer(flashOn ? (int)FlashMode.Torch : (int)FlashMode.Off));
                UpdatePreview();
            }
            catch (System.Exception error)
```

```
    {
        _log.WriteLineTime(_tag + "\n" +
            "TakePhoto() Failed to switch flash on/off \n " +
            "ErrorMessage: \n" +
            error.Message + "\n" +
            "Stacktrace: \n " +
            error.StackTrace);
    }
}
```

Next we have a public function to invoke the `Available` event, which we need for the `CmaptureStateListener` callback so that we keep track of the camera availability during a capture session:

```
public void NotifyAvailable(bool isAvailable)
{
    Available?.Invoke(this, isAvailable);
}
```

Next we have the `ConfigureTransform` function, which is responsible for transforming the texture view. Here we are handling surface orientations and matrix rotations:

```
public void ConfigureTransform(int viewWidth, int viewHeight)
{
    if (_viewSurface != null && _previewSize != null && _context !=
null)
    {
        var windowManager =
_context.GetSystemService(Context.WindowService).JavaCast<IWindowManager>()
;

        var rotation = windowManager.DefaultDisplay.Rotation;
        var matrix = new Matrix();
        var viewRect = new RectF(0, 0, viewWidth, viewHeight);
        var bufferRect = new RectF(0, 0, _previewSize.Width,
_previewSize.Height);

        var centerX = viewRect.CenterX();
        var centerY = viewRect.CenterY();

        if (rotation == SurfaceOrientation.Rotation90 || rotation
== SurfaceOrientation.Rotation270)
        {
            bufferRect.Offset(centerX - bufferRect.CenterX() ,
centerY - bufferRect.CenterY());
            matrix.SetRectToRect(viewRect, bufferRect,
Matrix.ScaleToFit.Fill);
```

```
                        matrix.PostRotate(90 * ((int)rotation - 2), centerX,
    centerY);
            }

            _cameraTexture.SetTransform(matrix);
        }
    }
```

Then we have the functions that are required by every `TextureView`:

```
        public void OnSurfaceTextureAvailable (SurfaceTexture surface, int
    w, int h)
        {
            _viewSurface = surface;

            ConfigureTransform(w, h);
            StartPreview();
        }
```

The `OnSurfaceTextureAvailable` function will call configure the texture's transformation matrix based upon the current window's orientation and call `StartPreview` to start the video stream through the texture view:

```
        public bool OnSurfaceTextureDestroyed (SurfaceTexture surface)
        {
            return true;
        }

        public void OnSurfaceTextureSizeChanged (SurfaceTexture surface,
    int width, int height)
        {
            ConfigureTransform(width, height);
            StartPreview();
        }
```

We also want to configure the texture's transformation matrix when the surface size changes:

```
        public void OnSurfaceTextureUpdated (SurfaceTexture surface)
        {
        }
```

Wow! That was one huge implementation. Configuring the camera is not an easy task; it involves a lot of step-by-step procedures that must be taken correctly for starting the camera stream and creating a capture session. Those are the two most important operations of any camera implementation.

Building the CameraViewRenderer in Android

Now we must add the CustomRenderer for the Android camera. In the `Renderers` folder, add a new file called `CameraViewRender.cs` and implement the following:

```
public class CameraViewRenderer : ViewRenderer<CameraView, CameraDroid>
    {
        #region Private Properties

        private CameraDroid Camera;

        #endregion
}
```

Our renderer contains only one private instance of the `CameraDroid` class. Then we override the `OnElementChanged` method:

```
        #region Protected Methods

        protected override void
OnElementChanged(ElementChangedEventArgs<CameraView> e)
        {
            base.OnElementChanged(e);

            if (Control == null)
            {
                Camera = new CameraDroid(Context);

                SetNativeControl(Camera);
            }

            if (e.NewElement != null)
            {

                Camera.Available += e.NewElement.NotifyAvailability;
                Camera.Photo += e.NewElement.NotifyPhoto;
                Camera.Busy += e.NewElement.NotifyBusy;

                e.NewElement.Flash += HandleFlashChange;
                e.NewElement.OpenCamera += HandleCameraInitialisation;
                e.NewElement.Focus += HandleFocus;
                e.NewElement.Shutter += HandleShutter;
            }
        }
```

Inside Android `CustomRenderers`, there is a bug with disposal using the `OnElementChanged` method. In some cases, this method is not called when the view is disposed, so we are going to override the `Dispose` method.

Here we follow the correct structure in the `OnElementChanged` method and instantiate the new control when the `Control` property is null. We also register our events when the new element is not null (events are registered on both the `CameraDroid` and `CameraView` objects).

Now let's add the override to handle the disposal:

```
protected override void Dispose(bool disposing)
{
        Element.Flash -= HandleFlashChange;
        Element.OpenCamera -= HandleCameraInitialisation;
        Element.Focus -= HandleFocus;
        Element.Shutter -= HandleShutter;

        Camera.Available -= Element.NotifyAvailability;
        Camera.Photo -= Element.NotifyPhoto;
        Camera.Busy -= Element.NotifyBusy;

        base.Dispose(disposing);
}
```

Here we simply unregister the events for both the `CameraView` and `CameraDroid` objects. Next, we have the `private` event delegate methods for calling the native camera methods:

```
#region Private Methods

private void HandleCameraInitialisation (object sender, bool args)
{
    Camera.OpenCamera();
}
private void HandleFlashChange (object sender, bool args)
{
    Camera.SwitchFlash (args);
}

private void HandleShutter (object sender, EventArgs e)
{
    Camera.TakePhoto();
}

private void HandleFocus (object sender, Point e)
{
```

```
                Camera.ChangeFocusPoint(e);
    }

    #endregion
}
```

Great! We have completed our camera implementations for both iOS and Android. Now we have to create another renderer for the `FocusView`.

Handling native touch events through the FocusView

Since our camera implementation is handling focus changes from touch events, we are required to receive these touch events from the native side. `Xamarin.Forms` does not have touch events that give (x, y) coordinates, so we have to do some more custom rendering on the `FocusView`. Let's start with the Android implementation this time, inside the `Renderers` folder, add a new folder called `FocusView`, and add a new file called `FocusViewGestureDetector.cs`, and implement the following:

```
public class FocusViewGestureDetector :
GestureDetector.SimpleOnGestureListener
    {
        #region Events

        public event EventHandler<MotionEvent> Touch;

        #endregion

        #region Public Methods

        public override void OnLongPress(MotionEvent e)
        {
            base.OnLongPress(e);
        }

        public override bool OnDoubleTap(MotionEvent e)
        {
            return base.OnDoubleTap(e);
        }

        public override bool OnDoubleTapEvent(MotionEvent e)
        {
            return base.OnDoubleTapEvent(e);
        }
```

```
        public override bool OnSingleTapUp(MotionEvent e)
        {
            return base.OnSingleTapUp(e);
        }

        public override bool OnDown(MotionEvent e)
        {
            if (Touch != null)
            {
                Touch(this, e);
            }

            return base.OnDown(e);
        }

        public override bool OnFling(MotionEvent e1, MotionEvent e2, float
    velocityX, float velocityY)
        {
            return base.OnFling(e1, e2, velocityX, velocityY);
        }

        public override bool OnScroll(MotionEvent e1, MotionEvent e2, float
    distanceX, float distanceY)
        {
            return base.OnScroll(e1, e2, distanceX, distanceY);
        }

        public override void OnShowPress(MotionEvent e)
        {
            base.OnShowPress(e);
        }

        public override bool OnSingleTapConfirmed(MotionEvent e)
        {
            return base.OnSingleTapConfirmed(e);
        }

        #endregion
    }
```

The preceding class is very similar to the gesture detector we created for the CarouselView in the last chapter. We only use this object to retrieve the MotionEvent object from the OnDown method.

Let's add in another file called `FocusViewRender.c` and implement the following:

```
public class FocusViewRenderer : ViewRenderer<FocusView, LinearLayout>
    {
        #region Private Methods

        private FocusViewGestureDetector _gestureDetector;

        private GestureDetector _detector;

        private LinearLayout _layout;

        #endregion
    }
```

The `FocusViewRenderer` will contain an instance of our `FocusViewGestureDetector` and `GestureDetector` for handling touches on the `FocusView`. We also have a `LinearLayout`, which is going to be the control assigned to the `FocusView`. This `LinearLayout` will be blank and will only be used to receive the native touch events.

Then we add the override to the `OnElementChanged` function:

```
        #region Protected Methods

        protected override void
    OnElementChanged(ElementChangedEventArgs<FocusView> e)
        {
            base.OnElementChanged(e);

            if (Control == null)
            {
                SetGestureDetectorListener();
                _layout = new LinearLayout(Context);

                SetNativeControl (_layout);
            }

            if (e.NewElement != null)
            {
                _layout.Touch += HandleTouch;
            }
        }

        #endregion
```

When the `Control` is null, before we call the `SetNativeControl` method, we set up the gesture detectors.

Now we must handle disposal as follows:

```
protected override void Dispose(bool disposing)
        {
                _layout.Touch -= HandleTouch;

                base.Dispose(disposing);
        }
```

Then we add the remaining:

```
        #region Private Methods

        private int ConvertPixelsToDp(float pixelValue)
        {
                return (int) ((pixelValue)/Resources.DisplayMetrics.Density);
        }

        private void SetGestureDetectorListener()
        {
                _gestureDetector = new FocusViewGestureDetector ();
                _detector = new GestureDetector (_gestureDetector);

                Observable.FromEventPattern<MotionEvent> (_gestureDetector,
    "Touch")
                        .Window (() => Observable.Interval (TimeSpan.FromSeconds
    (0.7)))
                        .SelectMany (x => x.Take (1))
                        .Subscribe (e => Element.NotifyFocus (new Point
    (ConvertPixelsToDp (e.EventArgs.GetX ()), ConvertPixelsToDp
    (e.EventArgs.GetY ())))));
        }

        private void HandleTouch (object sender, TouchEventArgs e)
        {
                _detector.OnTouchEvent (e.Event);
        }

        #endregion
    }
```

Using RX to handle events

Have a look at the `SetGestureDetectorListener` function where we are using the `FromEventPattern` method from the `Observable` framework. The function must be typed with a particular object (that is, `MotionEvent`) that contains an `EventHandler` property, in this case `Touch`. Every time a `Touch` event is fired, using the `Window` method, we wait 0.7 seconds before doing anything (this ensures that we only respond to the first event taken every period set in the `Window` method). Once this period is reached, `SelectMany` is called and the first `Touch` event is retrieved from the observable sequence via the `Take` method. Then we call `Subscribe` to assign the `NotifyFocus` method, and pass in the `MotionEvent` object taken from the `SelectMany` method.

To summarize, the `FromEventPattern` method is very useful for controlling multiple events and responding with specific actions. We have applied this technique with touch events because we want to make sure only one touch event is processed every 0.7 seconds. If we used a simply delegate function, a user could very fast, and for every touch event, the camera would run through the `ChangeFocusPoint` operation every time before the previous has finished, eventually crashing the application.

Now turn attention to the `ConvertPixelsToDp` method. We have to translate the pixel points into DPI when translating position coordinates (*x*, *y*) between native Android and `Xamarin.Forms` views. This will be called for every touch event for both x and y before we pass the coordinate to the `CameraView`.

 1 DP equals 1.5 physical pixels.

Building a VisualElementRenderer for iOS

To handle native touch events on iOS, we are going to build a `VisualElementRenderer`. These work similar to CustomRenderers, but instead of rendering and replacing the entire control, we are able to render specific attributes, so we are able to attach native attributes to a `Xamarin.Forms` view.

Let's start with adding a new folder inside the `Renderers` folder called `FocusView`. Add in a new file called `FocusViewRendererTouchAttribute.cs` and implement the following:

```
public class FocusViewRendererTouchAttribute :
VisualElementRenderer<FocusView>
```

```
    {
        public override void TouchesBegan (NSSet touches, UIEvent evt)
        {
            base.TouchesBegan (touches, evt);

            FocusView focusView = ((FocusView)this.Element);

            UITouch touch = touches.AnyObject as UITouch;

            if (touch != null)
            {
                var posc = touch.LocationInView (touch.View);
                focusView.NotifyFocus (new Xamarin.Forms.Point(posc.X,
posc.Y));
            }
        }
    }
```

Don't forget to add the assembly line above the namespace like the following:

```
[assembly: Xamarin.Forms.ExportRendererAttribute
(typeof(Camera.Controls.FocusView),
typeof(Camera.iOS.Renderers.FocusView.FocusViewRendererTouchAttribute))]
```

When the element is rendered, we will now have the access to the TouchesBegan override.
Inside this function, we have access to the render object (FocusView), where we can call the
NotifyFocus function and pass the current touch (*x*, *y*) coordinate back to the FocusView.

That's all for our FocusView renderers. Let's now move on to the CustomImageRenderer
so that we can apply color tinting to an image.

Building the CustomImageRenderers

We are going to start with the iOS implementation of the CustomImage. Inside the
Renderers folder, add a new folder called CustomImage, add a new file called
CustomImageRenderer.cs, and implement the following:

```
public class CustomImageRenderer : ViewRenderer<CustomImage, UIView>
    {
        #region Private Propertie

        private readonly string _tag;

        private ILogger _log;
```

```
        private UIImageView _imageView;

        private int _systemVersion = Convert.ToInt16
(UIDevice.CurrentDevice.SystemVersion.Split ('.') [0]);

        #endregion

        #region Constructors

        public CustomImageRenderer ()
        {
            _log = IoC.Resolve<ILogger> ();
            _tag = string.Format ("{0} ", GetType ());
        }

        #endregion
    }
```

Looking at our `private` properties, we have the logging objects again, an integer property to hold the current system version (that is, iOS version), and an `UIImageView` to use as the native control. Next we have to override the `OnElementChanged` method:

```
        protected override void OnElementChanged
(ElementChangedEventArgs<CustomImage> e)
        {
            base.OnElementChanged (e);

            if (Control == null)
            {
                _imageView = new UIImageView ();

                SetNativeControl (_imageView);
            }

            if (e.OldElement != null)
            {
                e.OldElement.CustomPropertyChanged -=
HandleCustomPropertyChanged;
            }

            if (e.NewElement != null)
            {
                LoadImage ();

                e.NewElement.CustomPropertyChanged +=
HandleCustomPropertyChanged;
            }
        }
```

Remember we have to follow the same structure for instantiating the control, and registering and deregistering EventHandlers. In this renderer, we are going to apply event handling a little differently. Instead of registering multiple events in the `OnElementChanged` method, we only have to register and deregister the `CustomPropertyChanged` event. In our `CustomImage` view, with each custom binding, when a property is changed, we assigned a delegate that would fire this event with the property name for every property. Therefore, we add one delegate function on the renderer side called `HandleCustomPropertyChanged`, and in this function, we will check what property has changed and respond with an action:

```
private void HandleCustomPropertyChanged (object sender, string
propertyName)
    {
        switch (propertyName)
        {
            case "TintColorString":
            case "TintOn":
                UpdateControlColor();
                break;
            case "Path":
                InvokeOnMainThread(() => LoadImage());
                break;
        }
    }
```

Much cleaner than handling multiple events right?

Every time the `Path` property is changed, we call a new method called `LoadImage`. Before we add this function in, we are going to add a `private` method for setting the image aspect ratio:

```
private UIViewContentMode SetAspect()
    {
        if (Element != null)
        {
            switch (Element.Aspect)
            {
                case Aspect.AspectFill:
                    return UIViewContentMode.ScaleAspectFill;
                case Aspect.AspectFit:
                    return UIViewContentMode.ScaleAspectFit;
                case Aspect.Fill:
                    return UIViewContentMode.ScaleToFill;
                default:
                    return UIViewContentMode.ScaleAspectFit;
            }
        }
```

```
            }

        return UIViewContentMode.ScaleAspectFit;
    }
```

This will take a `Xamarin.Forms` image aspect ratio value and return the related native image aspect ratio. This value will then be used for the aspect of the `UIImageView`.

Let's now add the `LoadImage` method as follows:

```
        private void LoadImage()
        {
            try
            {
                if (Element != null)
                {
                    if (!string.IsNullOrEmpty(Element.Path))
                    {
                        _imageView.Image = ReadBitmapImageFromStorage
(Element.Path);

                        if (_imageView.Image != null)
                        {
                            if (_systemVersion >= 7 && Element.TintOn)
                            {
                                _imageView.Image =
_imageView.Image.ImageWithRenderingMode
(UIImageRenderingMode.AlwaysTemplate);
                            }

                            UpdateControlColor();

                            _imageView.ContentMode = SetAspect();
                        }
                    }
                }
            }
            catch (Exception error)
            {
                _log.WriteLineTime(_tag + "\n" +
                    "LoadAsync() Failed to load view model.  \n " +
                    "ErrorMessage: \n" +
                    error.Message + "\n" +
                    "Stacktrace: \n " +
                    error.StackTrace);
            }
        }
```

This function is responsible for using the `Path` property to load an image into the `UIImageView`. Inside this function, we also use the `systemVersion` property to handle backward compatibility with color tinting. Only if the iOS device is using an iOS version greater than or equal to iOS 7, we apply the following line:

```
_imageView.Image = _imageView.Image.ImageWithRenderingMode
(UIImageRenderingMode.AlwaysTemplate);
```

This tells the `UIImageView` that its `Image` should always draw as a template image, ignoring its color information. We have to do this before we can apply a tinted color.

Next we have to add the `ReadBitmapImageFromStorage` function:

```
private UIImage ReadBitmapImageFromStorage(string fn)
        {
            var docsPath = Environment.GetFolderPath
(Environment.SpecialFolder.MyDocuments);
            string filePath = Path.Combine(Environment.CurrentDirectory,
fn);

            try
            {
                using (Stream stream = File.OpenRead(filePath))
                {
                    NSData data = NSData.FromStream (stream);
                    return UIImage.LoadFromData (data);
                }
            }
            catch (Exception error)
            {
                _log.WriteLineTime(_tag + "\n" +
                    "LoadAsync() Failed to load view model.  \n " +
                    "ErrorMessage: \n" +
                    error.Message + "\n" +
                    "Stacktrace: \n " +
                    error.StackTrace);
            }

            return UIImage.FromFile (Path.Combine
(Environment.CurrentDirectory, "loading.png"));
        }
```

Using the `File.OpenRead` method, we retrieve the files stream and load it into a new `NSData` object, and then from this `NSData` we load this into a new `UIImage` and return it to the caller (that is, the `LoadImage` function).

We must also add the `UpdateControlColor` function for assigning the tint color to the `UIImageView`:

```
private void UpdateControlColor()
        {
                if (Element.TintOn &&
        !string.IsNullOrEmpty(Element.TintColorString))
                {
                        var color = UIColor.Clear.FromHex (Element.TintColorString,
        1.0f);

                        _imageView.Image =
        UIImageEffects.GetColoredImage(_imageView.Image, color);
                }
        }
```

Here we are using another `static` class, which will take a color and the image and return a new image tinted to the color passed in.

Building the UIImageEffects class

Our final part to the image tinting on iOS is implementing the class that will return a tinted image from a template image and color. Create a new folder in the iOS project called `Helpers`, add a new file called `UIImageEffects.cs`, and implement the following:

```
public static class UIImageEffects
    {
        public static UIImage GetColoredImage(UIImage image, UIColor color)
        {
            UIImage coloredImage = null;

            UIGraphics.BeginImageContext(image.Size);

            using (CGContext context = UIGraphics.GetCurrentContext())
            {
                context.TranslateCTM(0, image.Size.Height);
                context.ScaleCTM(1.0f, -1.0f);

                var rect = new CGRect(0, 0, image.Size.Width,
        image.Size.Height);

                // draw image, (to get transparancy mask)
                context.SetBlendMode(CGBlendMode.Normal);
                context.DrawImage(rect, image.CGImage);
```

```
                        // draw the color using the sourcein blend mode so its only
draw on the non-transparent pixels
                context.SetBlendMode(CGBlendMode.SourceIn);
                context.SetFillColor(color.CGColor);
                context.FillRect(rect);

                coloredImage =
UIGraphics.GetImageFromCurrentImageContext();
                UIGraphics.EndImageContext();
        }

        return coloredImage;
    }
}
```

The function starts with creating a new `UIImage` and setting it to null. We then create a new image context by calling `BeginImageContext` and passing in the image size from the `UIImage` we pass in to the function. We then wrap the current context in a using statement to make sure we free memory taken from image processing in the context. We use the current context to assign correct (*x*, *y*) translation and scale to match the `UIImage` passed in. After this, we create a new `Rect` to match the bounds of the `UIImage` we passed into the function. We then call `SetBlendMode` to assign the image's transparency and call `DrawImage` to draw the image. Now that we have drawn the image within the context, we then call `SetBlendMode` again to using the `CGBlendMode.SourceIn` so that it only draws on the nontransparent pixels. We then set the fill color of the context to the color we passed into the function, which will be the tint color. The image context will then fill the bounds of the `Rect` we created earlier. Finally, we end the image processing by calling `EndImageContext` and return the new `colouredImage` to the caller.

Fantastic! We have now used the native `UIGraphics` framework to perform image tinting for iOS; let's do the same for Android.

Building the CustomImageRenderer for Android

Add a new folder into the `Renderers` folder called `CusotmImage`, add a new file called `CustomImageRenderer.cs`, and implement the following:

```
public class CustomImageRenderer : ViewRenderer<CustomImage, ImageView>
    {
        #region Private Properties
```

```
private readonly string _tag;

private ImageView _imageView;

private CustomImage _customImage;

private ILogger _log;

private Bitmap _bitmap;

#endregion

#region Constructors

public CustomImageRenderer ()
{
    _log = IoC.Resolve<ILogger> ();
    _tag = string.Format ("{0} ", GetType ());
}

#endregion
```

We are going to use an `ImageView` as the native control. We also have a local `CustomImage`, which will reference the element we are rendering on. We also have a local `Bitmap`, which will be the image we are tinting. Then we have the `_log` and `tag` properties again for logging any exceptions.

Let's now add the `OnElementChanged` method:

```
#region Protected Methods

protected override void OnElementChanged
(ElementChangedEventArgs<CustomImage> e)
{
    base.OnElementChanged (e);

    if (Control == null)
    {
        _imageView = new ImageView(Context);

        SetNativeControl(_imageView);
    }

    if (e.NewElement != null)
    {
        _customImage = e.NewElement;
```

```
                    SetAspect();

                    Android.App.Application.SynchronizationContext.Post(state
    =>
                    {
                        UpdateControlColor();
                    }, null);

                    LoadImage().ConfigureAwait(false);

                    e.NewElement.CustomPropertyChanged +=
    HandleCustomPropertyChanged;
                }
            }

        #endregion
```

Here we create a new `ImageView` as the control. When the `NewElement` is not null, we assign it to `_customImage`, set the aspect ratio of the `ImageView`, add the tint color, and load the image.

Now we have to handle disposal by overriding the `Dispose` method:

```
    protected override void Dispose(bool disposing)
        {
            if (_bitmap != null)
            {
                _bitmap.Recycle();
                _bitmap.Dispose();
            }

            Element.CustomPropertyChanged -= HandleCustomPropertyChanged;

            base.Dispose(disposing);
        }
```

Then we add the `private` methods. We are going to start with the `SetAspect` function. Like our iOS implementation, we will map the `Xamarin.Forms` image aspect value to the native `ImageViewScaleType`:

```
        private void SetAspect()
        {
            if (Element != null)
            {
                switch (Element.Aspect)
                {
                case Aspect.AspectFill:
```

```
                _imageView.SetScaleType (ImageView.ScaleType.FitXy);
                break;
            case Aspect.AspectFit:
                _imageView.SetScaleType
(ImageView.ScaleType.FitCenter);
                break;
            case Aspect.Fill:
                _imageView.SetScaleType (ImageView.ScaleType.FitXy);
                break;
            default:
                _imageView.SetScaleType
(ImageView.ScaleType.FitCenter);
                break;
        }
    }
}
```

Then we have the `delegate` function for handling all our property changes:

```
        private void HandleCustomPropertyChanged (object sender, string
propertyName)
        {
            switch (propertyName)
            {
                case "TintColorString":
                case "TintOn":
Android.App.Application.SynchronizationContext.Post(state =>
                    {
                        UpdateControlColor();
                    }, null);
                    break;
                case "Path":
                    LoadImage().ConfigureAwait(false);
                    break;
            }
        }
    }
```

Our `LoadImage` is a bit better than the iOS version because it loads the image asynchronously:

```
        private async Task LoadImage()
        {
            try
            {
                _bitmap = await ReadBitmapImageFromStorage(Element.Path);

                if (_imageView != null && _bitmap != null)
                {
```

```
Android.App.Application.SynchronizationContext.Post(state =>
_imageView.SetImageBitmap(_bitmap), null);
                }
            }
            catch (Exception error)
            {
                _log.WriteLineTime(_tag + "\n" +
                    "LoadAsync() Failed to load view model.  \n " +
                    "ErrorMessage: \n" +
                    error.Message + "\n" +
                    "Stacktrace: \n " +
                    error.StackTrace);
            }
        }
```

We only call the `SetImageBitmap` on the `ImageView` if the `ImageView` and `Bitmap` is not null.

Next we have the `UpdateControlColor` function for tinting the image. Android offers a much simpler solution for tinting using the `SetColorFilter` function. We must pass in a `PorterDuff.Mode`, which the `SetColorFilter` will use to determine how to compose the image based on the alpha value:

```
        private void UpdateControlColor()
        {
            try
            {
                if (_customImage.TintOn &&
!string.IsNullOrEmpty(_customImage.TintColorString))
                {
                    var color =
Android.Graphics.Color.ParseColor(_customImage.TintColorString);
                    _imageView.SetColorFilter (color,
PorterDuff.Mode.SrcAtop);
                }
            }
            catch (Exception e)
            {
                _log.WriteLineTime ("CustomImageRenderer: " + e);
            }
        }
```

Next we have the `ReadBitmapImageFromStorage` function, where we will be loading a `Bitmap` from the `Path` property of the `CustomImage`. We use the `GetIdentifier` function from the `Resources` framework to retrieve the integer ID of the image resource we want to load.

Remember, the image must be inside our `drawable` or `mipmap` folder for the image to be found.

We then open the raw file as a stream using the `OpenRawResource` function, and using the `BitmapFactory` framework, we can use the raw resource stream to decode a `Bitmap` object that will be returned:

```
private async Task<Bitmap> ReadBitmapImageFromStorage(string fn)
{
    try
    {
        if (!string.IsNullOrEmpty(fn))
        {
            var file = fn.Split('.').FirstOrDefault();

            var id = Resources.GetIdentifier(file, "drawable",
Context.PackageName);

            using (Stream stream = Resources.OpenRawResource(id))
            {
                if (stream != null)
                {
                    return await
BitmapFactory.DecodeStreamAsync(stream);
                }
            }
        }
    }
    catch (Exception error)
    {
        _log.WriteLineTime(
            "MyCareManager.Droid.Renderers.CustomImageRenderer; \n"
+
            "ErrorMessage: Failed to load image " + fn + "\n " +
            "Stacktrace: Login Error  \n " +
            error);
    }

    return null;
}

#endregion
}
```

Great! We have now built all our `CustomRenderers` for the solution. Let's see how we use these with our user interface screens.

Triggers

The first page will consist of two buttons, an image, a label, and extra additional UI functionality known as **triggers**. Triggers are declarative objects used in XAML, which contain actions executed when certain conditions or events occur. The main advantage of triggers is we can box up these handle actions for as many UI elements that need to perform the same actions. We have the option of the following four different types of triggers:

- **Property trigger**: This is executed when a property on a control is set to a particular value.
- **Data trigger**: This is same as the property trigger but uses data binding.
- **Event trigger**: This is occurs when an event occurs on the control.
- **Multi trigger**: This is allows multiple trigger conditions to be set before an action occurs.

In our solution, we are going to add two event triggers for button click events.

Let's start with adding a new folder called `Triggers` into the `Camera` project, add a new file called `ButtonClickTrigger.cs`, and implement the following:

```
public class ButtonClickedTrigger : TriggerAction<Button>
{
    #region Protected Methods

    protected override void Invoke(Button sender)
    {
        sender.TextColor = Color.Blue;
        sender.BackgroundColor = Color.Aqua;
    }

    #endregion
}
```

Our first trigger is for handling the `Clicked` event on the `CameraButton`. When this button is clicked, the background and text color of the button will change. We must override the `Invoke` function to claim the `Button` performing the action.

Now let's add another folder for the `Pages`, add a new file called `MainPage.xaml`, and implement the following:

```xml
<?xml version="1.0" encoding="UTF-8"?>
<ui:ExtendedContentPage xmlns="http://xamarin.com/schemas/2014/forms"
    xmlns:x="http://schemas.microsoft.com/winfx/2009/xaml"
    xmlns:ui="clr-namespace:Camera.UI;assembly=Camera"
    xmlns:t="clr-namespace:Camera.Triggers;assembly=Camera"
    x:Class="Camera.Pages.MainPage"
    BackgroundColor="White"
    Title="Welcome">

    <ui:ExtendedContentPage.Content>
        <Grid x:Name="Grid" RowSpacing="10" Padding="10, 10, 10, 10"
VerticalOptions="Center">
            <Grid.RowDefinitions>
                <RowDefinition Height="*"/>
                <RowDefinition Height="Auto"/>
                <RowDefinition Height="Auto"/>
                <RowDefinition Height="Auto"/>
            </Grid.RowDefinitions>

            <Grid.ColumnDefinitions>
                <ColumnDefinition Width="*"/>
            </Grid.ColumnDefinitions>

            <Image x:Name="Image" Source="camera.png" HeightRequest="120"
WidthRequest="120"
                    Grid.Row="0" Grid.Column="0"/>

            <Button x:Name="CameraButton" Text="{Binding CameraTitle}"
                Command="{Binding CameraCommand}" Style="{StaticResource
BaseButtonStyle}" Grid.Row="2" Grid.Column="0">
                <Button.Triggers>
                    <EventTrigger Event="Clicked">
                        <t:ButtonClickedTrigger/>
                    </EventTrigger>
                </Button.Triggers>
            </Button>
            <Button x:Name="ExitButton" Text="{Binding ExitTitle}"
                Command="{Binding ExitCommand}" Style="{StaticResource
ButtonStyleWithTrigger}"
                Grid.Row="3" Grid.Column="0"/>
        </Grid>
    </ui:ExtendedContentPage.Content>
</ui:ExtendedContentPage>
```

We must include the namespace reference to location of the `Triggers` folder. Then turn attention to the `CameraButton`, where we will attach the `ButtonClickedTrigger`. When the button is touched, the `Invoke` method of the trigger will be called.

The next trigger we add will perform a nice warping animation to a button when it is clicked. Let's add another file called `VisualElementPopTriggerAction.cs` and implement the following:

```csharp
public class VisualElementPopTriggerAction : TriggerAction<VisualElement>
{
    #region Public Properties

    public Point Anchor { set; get; }

    public double Scale { set; get; }

    public uint Length { set; get; }

    #endregion

    #region Constructors

    public VisualElementPopTriggerAction()
    {
        Anchor = new Point(0.5, 0.5);
        Scale = 2;
        Length = 500;
    }

    #endregion

    #region Protected Methods

    protected override async void Invoke(VisualElement visual)
    {
        visual.AnchorX = Anchor.X;
        visual.AnchorY = Anchor.Y;
        await visual.ScaleTo(Scale, Length / 2, Easing.SinOut);
        await visual.ScaleTo(1, Length / 2, Easing.SinIn);
    }

    #endregion
}
```

The `Anchor` property is used for the point (*x, y*) in which the `ScaleTo` function will reference. Since the reference points `X` and `Y` are `0.5`, when animate an expansion on the button, it will expand evenly on both the left/right and top/bottom. The `Invoke` method will be called when the button is clicked to begin the animation. We are also using the Sin easing for each animation:

Easing.SinIn

Starts slow and speeds:

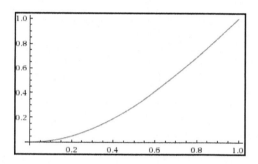

Easing.SinOut

Starts fast and slows down:

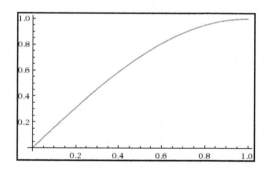

Let's have a look at how we will use the `VisualElementPopTriggerAction` inside a style. Add in the `App.Xaml` file and implement the following styles:

```
<Style x:Key="BaseButtonStyle" TargetType="Button">
    <Setter Property="TextColor">
```

```
        <Setter.Value>
            <OnPlatform x:TypeArguments="Color"
                Android="Navy"
                WinPhone="Black"
                iOS="Black">
            </OnPlatform>
        </Setter.Value>
    </Setter>
    <Setter Property="FontSize" Value="20" />
    <Setter Property="FontFamily" Value="Arial" />
    <Setter Property="BackgroundColor" Value="Silver" />
</Style>
<Style x:Key="ButtonStyleWithTrigger" TargetType="Button"
        BasedOn="{StaticResource BaseButtonStyle}">
    <Style.Triggers>
        <EventTrigger Event="Clicked">
            <t:VisualElementPopTriggerAction/>
        </EventTrigger>
    </Style.Triggers>
</Style>
```

Can you see what technique we are using here?

This is known as **style inheritance**. The `ButtonStyleWithTrigger` style inherits all the styling properties of the `BaseButtonStyle` by using the `BasedOn` property.

Wait! Aren't we missing the `DescriptionLabel` from the `MainPage`?

We still have one more element to add to the `MainPage`. But first we are going to talk about another object used in XAML known as **PlatformEffects**.

Platform effects

Platform effects are used to simplify native control customization, reducing the need to create `CustomRenderers` for small styling changes. This means we don't have to create a custom renderer every single time we want native customization. To implement a `PlatformEffect`, we first create a class that subclasses the `PlatformEffect` framework. Then we have to write platform-specific implementations for each.

Following is a small overview of how the rendering process will look among the different projects:

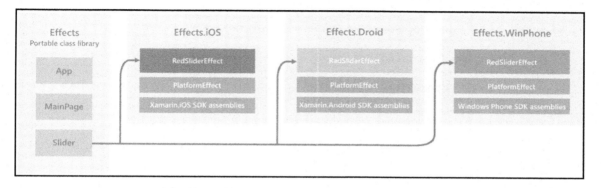

Let's add a new folder called `Effects` inside the `Camera` project, add in a new file called `LabelShadowEffect.cs`, and implement the following:

```
public class LabelShadowEffect : RoutingEffect
    {
        #region Public Properties

        public float Radius { get; set; }

        public Color Color { get; set; }

        public float DistanceX { get; set; }

        public float DistanceY { get; set; }

        #endregion

        #region Constructors

        public LabelShadowEffect() : base("Camera.LabelShadowEffect")
        {
        }

        #endregion
    }
```

Our `LabelShadowEffect` must inherit the `PlatformEffect` framework. The `Radius` property is responsible for the corner radius of the shadow. Then we have the `Color` property that will set the color of the shadow. Finally, we have the `DistanceX` and `DistanceY` properties for assigning the position of the shadow.

Now we must create the platform implementations. Let's start with iOS, add in a new folder called `Effects`, add in a new file called `LabelShadowEffectiOS.cs`, and implement the following:

```
public class LabelShadowEffectiOS : PlatformEffect
    {
        #region Protected Methods

        protected override void OnAttached()
        {
            try
            {
                var effect =
(LabelShadowEffect)Element.Effects.FirstOrDefault(e => e is
LabelShadowEffect);

                if (effect != null)
                {
                    Control.Layer.CornerRadius = effect.Radius;
                    Control.Layer.ShadowColor = effect.Color.ToCGColor();
                    Control.Layer.ShadowOffset = new
CGSize(effect.DistanceX, effect.DistanceY);
                    Control.Layer.ShadowOpacity = 1.0f;
                }
            }
            catch (Exception ex)
            {
                Console.WriteLine("Cannot set property on attached control.
Error: ", ex.Message);
            }
        }

        protected override void OnDetached()
        {
        }

        #endregion
    }
```

All `PlatformEffects` must override the `OnAttached` and `OnDetached` methods. The `OnAttached` method is where we set up all native shadow effects. We start with retrieving the first `PlatformEffect` from the `Effects` list of the `Element` object. Like our `CustomRenderers`, we have access to the original `Xamarin.Forms` element that we are customizing. In the `OnDetached` method, we would normally dispose any objects that are no longer required.

We must also add assembly lines above the namespace block like the following:

```
[assembly: Xamarin.Forms.ResolutionGroupName("Camera")]
[assembly:
Xamarin.Forms.ExportEffect(typeof(Camera.Droid.Effects.LabelShadowEffectiOS
), "LabelShadowEffect")]
```

We must add a `ResolutionGroupName` to specify the namespace for the effects; this prevents collisions with other effects of the same name. We also add the `ExportEffect` attribute to register the effect with a unique ID that is used by `Xamarin.Forms`, along with the group name, to locate the effect prior to applying it to a control.

Now let's add the equivalent for Android. Add a new folder in the `Camera.Droid` project, add a new file called `LabelShadowEffectDroid.cs`, and implement the following:

```
public class LabelShadowEffectDroid : PlatformEffect
    {
        #region Protected Methods

        protected override void OnAttached()
        {
            try
            {
                var control = Control as Android.Widget.TextView;

                var effect =
(LabelShadowEffect)Element.Effects.FirstOrDefault(e => e is
LabelShadowEffect);

                if (effect != null)
                {
                    control.SetShadowLayer(effect.Radius, effect.DistanceX,
effect.DistanceY, effect.Color.ToAndroid());
                }
            }
            catch (Exception ex)
            {
                Console.WriteLine("Cannot set property on attached control.
Error: ", ex.Message);
```

```
            }
        }

        protected override void OnDetached()
        {
        }

        #endregion
    }
```

In our Android implementation, we start with retrieving the control as a native `TextView`. We then retrieve the first `LabelShadowEffect` object from the list of effects from the `Element`. We then use the method `SetShadowLayer` to create native shadowing on the `TextView`.

Great! Now we have our native implementations, let's add the `DescriptionLabel` object to the `MainPage`:

```
<Label x:Name="DesciptionLabel" Text="{Binding DescriptionMessage}"
TextColor="Black"
                HorizontalOptions="Center" Font="Arial, 20"
Grid.Row="1" Grid.Column="0">
        <Label.Effects>
            <e:LabelShadowEffect Radius="5" DistanceX="5"
DistanceY="5">
                <e:LabelShadowEffect.Color>
                    <OnPlatform x:TypeArguments="Color" iOS="Black"
Android="Blue" WinPhone="Red" />
                </e:LabelShadowEffect.Color>
            </e:LabelShadowEffect>
        </Label.Effects>
    </Label>
```

Here we are able to attach the effect inside our XAML. We must also add the namespace to the `Effects` folder:

```
xmlns:e="clr-namespace:Camera.Effects;assembly=Camera"
```

This is how the `MainPage` will look once complete:

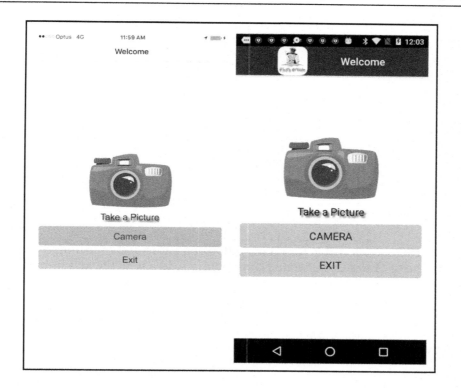

Building the CameraPage

Now for the final page of the solution, the `CameraPage` introduces some new tricks to handle orientation changes with `Grid` positions. We will be using `Converters` to change rows and columns on the `Grid` to reposition elements when we change orientation.

We are going to start with adding some converters to the project. Let's create a new folder in the `Camera` project, add a new file called `NotConverter.cs`, and implement the following:

```
public class NotConverter : IValueConverter
    {
        #region Public Methods

        public object Convert(object value, Type targetType, object
parameter, System.Globalization.CultureInfo culture)
        {
            var b = value as bool?;

            if (b != null)
```

```
        {
            return !b;
        }

        return value;
    }

    public object ConvertBack(object value, Type targetType, object
parameter, System.Globalization.CultureInfo culture)
    {
        throw new NotImplementedException();
    }

    #endregion
}
```

Our first converter is responsible for taking a Boolean value and returning the opposite. Next we have the `OrientationToBoolConverter`. Add a new file and implement the following:

```
public class OrientationToBoolConverter:IValueConverter
    {
        #region Public Methods

        public object Convert (object value, Type targetType, object
parameter, System.Globalization.CultureInfo culture)
        {
            try
            {
                var str = parameter as string;

                if (str != null)
                {
                    // split string by ',', convert to int and store in
case list
                    var cases = str.Split(',').Select(x =>
bool.Parse(x)).ToList();

                    if (value is Orientation)
                    {
                        switch ((Orientation)value)
                        {
                            case Orientation.LandscapeRight:
                            case Orientation.LandscapeLeft:
                                return cases[0];
                            case Orientation.Portrait:
                                return cases[1];
                            case Orientation.None:
```

```
                             return 0;
                        }
                    }
                }
            }
            catch (Exception error)
            {
IoC.Resolve<ILogger>().WriteLineTime("OrientationToBoolConverter \n" +
                    "Convert() Failed to switch flash on/off \n " +
                    "ErrorMessage: \n" +
                    error.Message + "\n" +
                    "Stacktrace: \n " +
                    error.StackTrace);
            }

            return 0;
        }

        public object ConvertBack (object value, Type targetType, object
parameter, System.Globalization.CultureInfo culture)
        {
            throw new NotImplementedException ();
        }

        #endregion
    }
```

This converter uses the `Orientationenum` we created at the start of the chapter. It will receive an `Orientation` value and a string as the parameter like the following:

```
'false, true'
```

> Converters can take parameters as well as values, so passing a string containing multiple cases allows us to use a set of specific return values to map to the values passed in.

We will then use the `Split` method to break up the string by the comma character, meaning we will have two strings that will be parsed in as a Boolean. These will be used as the return cases for the different orientations.

Now let's add another converter, which will convert a Boolean into a string:

```
public class BoolToStringConverter:IValueConverter
    {
        #region Public Methods
```

```
        public object Convert (object value, Type targetType, object
parameter, System.Globalization.CultureInfo culture)
        {
            try
            {
                var str = parameter as string;

                if (str != null)
                {
                    // split string by ',', convert to int and store in
case list
                    var cases = str.Split(',').Select(x => x).ToList();

                    if (value is bool)
                    {
                        return (bool)value ? cases[0] : cases[1];
                    }
                }
            }
            catch (Exception error)
            {
                IoC.Resolve<ILogger>().WriteLineTime("BoolToStringConverter
\n" +
                    "Convert() Failed to switch flash on/off \n " +
                    "ErrorMessage: \n" +
                    error.Message + "\n" +
                    "Stacktrace: \n " +
                    error.StackTrace);
            }

            return string.Empty;
        }

        public object ConvertBack (object value, Type targetType, object
parameter, System.Globalization.CultureInfo culture)
        {
            throw new NotImplementedException ();
        }

        #endregion
    }
```

We will use this on the camera page when the flash is turned on/off. If the flash is on, the string *on* will be returned. If the flash is off, we will return the string *off*. We use the same method as the `OrientationToBoolConverter` as we pass in a string value for the return cases.

Next, add another file called `BoolToPartialConverter.cs` and implement the following:

```csharp
public class BoolToPartialConverter:IValueConverter
{
    #region Public Methods

    public object Convert (object value, Type targetType, object
parameter, System.Globalization.CultureInfo culture)
    {
        try
        {
            var str = parameter as string;

            if (str != null)
            {
                // split string by ',', convert to int and store in
case list
                var cases = str.Split(',').Select(x =>
Double.Parse(x)).ToList();

                if (value is bool)
                {
                    return (bool)value ? cases[0] : cases[1];
                }
            }
        }
        catch (Exception error)
        {
IoC.Resolve<ILogger>().WriteLineTime("BoolToPartialConverter \n" +
                "Convert() Failed to switch flash on/off \n " +
                "ErrorMessage: \n" +
                error.Message + "\n" +
                "Stacktrace: \n " +
                error.StackTrace);
        }

        return 0;
    }

    public object ConvertBack (object value, Type targetType, object
parameter, System.Globalization.CultureInfo culture)
    {
        throw new NotImplementedException ();
    }

    #endregion
}
```

This will be used for updating opacity based upon the value being `true` or `false`. We use a string for the opacity values being returned for each Boolean value.

Our next converter `OrientationToIntConverter` is responsible for converting Orientation values into integers. This is the converter that will be responsible for changing the rows and columns numbers when the orientation changes:

```
public class OrientationToIntConverter:IValueConverter
    {
        #region Public Methods

        public object Convert (object value, Type targetType, object
parameter, System.Globalization.CultureInfo culture)
        {
            try
            {
                var str = parameter as string;

                if (str != null)
                {
                    // split string by ',', convert to int and store in
case list
                    var cases = str.Split(',').Select(x =>
Int32.Parse(x)).ToList();

                    if (value is Orientation)
                    {
                        switch ((Orientation)value)
                        {
                            case Orientation.LandscapeRight:
                            case Orientation.LandscapeLeft:
                                return cases[0];
                            case Orientation.Portrait:
                                return cases[1];
                            case Orientation.None:
                                return cases[0];
                        }
                    }
                }
            }
            catch (Exception error)
            {
IoC.Resolve<ILogger>().WriteLineTime("OrientationToIntConverter \n" +
                "Convert() Failed to switch flash on/off \n " +
                "ErrorMessage: \n" +
                error.Message + "\n" +
                "Stacktrace: \n " +
```

```
                    error.StackTrace);
            }

            return 0;
    }

    public object ConvertBack (object value, Type targetType, object
parameter, System.Globalization.CultureInfo culture)
        {
            throw new NotImplementedException ();
        }

        #endregion
    }
```

Again, we are using a string to contain the return cases, which we parse into a new integer using the Int32.Parse method.

Our last converter will be responsible for converting a byte array into an ImageSource. This is used for the binding created from the CameraViewModel in our Camera.Portable project. Since we don't have the ImageSource framework in our portable project, we will use byte arrays to hold the image data received from the camera:

```
public class ByteArrayToImageSourceConverter : IValueConverter
    {
        #region Public Methods

        public object Convert(object value, Type targetType, object
parameter, CultureInfo culture)
        {
            byte[] bytes = value as byte[];
            var defaultFile = parameter as string;

            if (bytes != null && bytes.Length > 1)
            {
                return ImageSource.FromStream(() => new
MemoryStream(bytes));
            }

            if (defaultFile != null)
            {
                return ImageSource.FromFile(defaultFile);
            }

            return ImageSource.FromFile ("loading.png");
        }
```

```
        public object ConvertBack(object value, Type targetType, object
parameter, System.Globalization.CultureInfo culture)
        {
            throw new NotImplementedException();
        }

        #endregion
    }
```

In the `Convert` method, we check to see if the byte array is not null and contains data, and if so, we use the `FromStream` method from the `ImageSource` framework to create a new `MemoryStream` from the byte array.

Now that we have all our converters, we must add these to the `App.xaml`:

```xml
<converters:NotConverter x:Key="notConverter"/>
        <converters:OrientationToBoolConverter
x:Key="orientationToBoolConverter"/>
        <converters:BoolToStringConverter
x:Key="boolToStringConverter"/>
        <converters:BoolToPartialConverter
x:Key="boolToPartialConverter"/>
        <converters:OrientationToIntConverter
x:Key="orientationToIntConverter"/>
        <converters:ByteArrayToImageSourceConverter
x:Key="byteArrayToImageSourceConverter"/>
```

Excellent! Let's build the interface for the `CameraPage`. We will see how these converters are used on each UI element.

Add a new file called `CameraPage.xaml` and implement the following:

```xml
<?xml version="1.0" encoding="utf-8" ?>
<ui:ExtendedContentPage xmlns="http://xamarin.com/schemas/2014/forms"
    xmlns:x="http://schemas.microsoft.com/winfx/2009/xaml"
    xmlns:controls="clr-namespace:Camera.Controls;assembly=Camera"
    xmlns:ui="clr-namespace:Camera.UI;assembly=Camera"
    x:Class="Camera.Pages.CameraPage"
    BackgroundColor="#F2F2F2">

    <Grid x:Name="MainLayout" BackgroundColor="Black"
            RowSpacing="0" ColumnSpacing="0">
        <Grid.RowDefinitions>
            <RowDefinition Height="*" />
            <RowDefinition Height="40" />
            <RowDefinition Height="*" />
            <RowDefinition Height="*" />
            <RowDefinition Height="*" />
```

```
            <RowDefinition Height="*" />
            <RowDefinition Height="60" />
        </Grid.RowDefinitions>

        <Grid.ColumnDefinitions>
            <ColumnDefinition Width="*"/>
            <ColumnDefinition Width="60"/>
            <ColumnDefinition Width="*"/>
            <ColumnDefinition Width="*"/>
            <ColumnDefinition Width="*"/>
            <ColumnDefinition Width="100"/>
        </Grid.ColumnDefinitions>

    </Grid>
</ui:ExtendedContentPage>
```

We start with an empty `Grid`, which has seven rows and six columns. The first element to add is the `CameraView`:

```
<controls:CameraView x:Name="CameraView" BackgroundColor="Black"
Grid.Row="0"
            Grid.RowSpan="{Binding PageOrientation,
Converter={StaticResource orientationToIntConverter},
ConverterParameter='7, 6'}"
            Grid.Column="0" Grid.ColumnSpan="{Binding PageOrientation,
Converter={StaticResource orientationToIntConverter},
ConverterParameter='5, 6'}"/>
```

Here we can see the use of the `OrientationToIntConverter`. The `PageOrientation` property from the view-model. When this property is set, and the `OnPropertyChanged` method is called. The `Convert` method will return a new integer, changing the number of rows the `CameraView` will take up. This is the same on the `ColumnSpan` property; the amount of columns taken by the `CameraView` will change when the orientation changes.

Next we add the `FocusView` as follows:

```
<controls:FocusView x:Name="FocusView"
        Grid.Row="0"
        Grid.RowSpan="{Binding PageOrientation, Converter={StaticResource
orientationToIntConverter}, ConverterParameter='7, 6'}"
            Grid.Column="0" Grid.ColumnSpan="{Binding PageOrientation,
Converter={StaticResource orientationToIntConverter},
ConverterParameter='5, 6'}"/>
```

This will match the entire space of the `CameraView`. The `FocusView` will lay on top of the `CameraView` to receive the touch events and pass the (x, y) coordinate down to the `CameraView` to perform a focus.

Next, we are going to add another `Grid` for containing the flash and photo buttons:

```
<Grid x:Name="CameraButtonContainerPortrait" ColumnSpacing="5"
        IsEnabled="{Binding PageOrientation, Converter={StaticResource
orientationToBoolConverter}, ConverterParameter='false, true'}}"
        Opacity="0" Grid.Row="6" Grid.Column="0" Grid.ColumnSpan="6">
    <Grid.RowDefinitions>
        <RowDefinition Height="*"/>
    </Grid.RowDefinitions>

    <Grid.ColumnDefinitions>
        <ColumnDefinition Width="35"/>
        <ColumnDefinition Width="45"/>
        <ColumnDefinition Width="*"/>
        <ColumnDefinition Width="45"/>
        <ColumnDefinition Width="35"/>
    </Grid.ColumnDefinitions>

    <ContentView BackgroundColor="Black"
        Grid.Row="0" Grid.Column="0" Grid.ColumnSpan="5"/>

    <controls:CustomImage x:Name="CameraButtonPortrait"
Path="photo_camera_button.png"
            TintOn="false" WidthRequest="50" HeightRequest="50"
            HorizontalOptions="Center" VerticalOptions="Center"
Grid.Row="0" Grid.Column="2">
        <controls:CustomImage.GestureRecognizers>
            <TapGestureRecognizer Tapped="HandleShutter"/>
        </controls:CustomImage.GestureRecognizers>
    </controls:CustomImage>

    <Label x:Name="FlashLabelPortrait"
        Text="{Binding IsFlashOn, Converter={StaticResource
boolToStringConverter}, ConverterParameter='On, Off'}"
        TextColor="#0ca6df" XAlign="Start" YAlign="Center"
        Grid.Row="0" Grid.Column="1">
        <Label.GestureRecognizers>
            <TapGestureRecognizer Tapped="HandleFlash"/>
        </Label.GestureRecognizers>
    </Label>

    <controls:CustomImage x:Name="FlashImagePortrait"
Path="photo_light.png"
            Margin="10, 0, 0, 0"
            VerticalOptions="Center"
            TintOn="false" WidthRequest="20"
            HeightRequest="35"
            Grid.Row="0" Grid.Column="0">
```

```
        <controls:CustomImage.GestureRecognizers>
            <TapGestureRecognizer Tapped="HandleFlash"/>
        </controls:CustomImage.GestureRecognizers>
    </controls:CustomImage>
</Grid>
```

Here we see the use of the `CustomImage` instead of a button because we want to be able to show a specific image for each button.

This panel is positioned under the `CameraView` like the following:

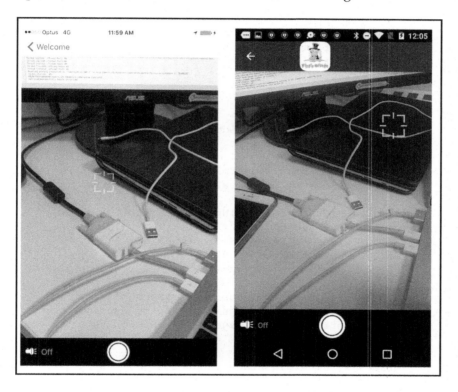

Next we have the `LoadingView` for displaying status of camera activity for initialization and taking photos:

```
<controls:LoadingView x:Name="LoadingView"
        Grid.Row="0" Grid.RowSpan="7" Grid.Column="0"
Grid.ColumnSpan="6"/>
```

We now need to add another element for the camera buttons in landscape mode:

```
<Grid x:Name="CameraButtonContainerLandscape" RowSpacing="5"
        IsEnabled="{Binding PageOrientation,
Converter={StaticResource orientationToBoolConverter},
ConverterParameter='true, false'}}"
        Opacity="0" Grid.Row="0" Grid.RowSpan="7"
        Grid.Column="{Binding PageOrientation,
Converter={StaticResource orientationToIntConverter},
ConverterParameter='5, 4'}">
    <Grid.RowDefinitions>
        <RowDefinition Height="45"/>
        <RowDefinition Height="40"/>
        <RowDefinition Height="*"/>
        <RowDefinition Height="40"/>
        <RowDefinition Height="45"/>
    </Grid.RowDefinitions>

    <Grid.ColumnDefinitions>
        <ColumnDefinition Width="*"/>
    </Grid.ColumnDefinitions>

    <ContentView BackgroundColor="Black"
        Grid.Row="0" Grid.RowSpan="5" Grid.Column="0"/>

    <controls:CustomImage x:Name="CameraButtonLandscape"
Path="photo_camera_button.png"
            TintOn="false" WidthRequest="50"
            HeightRequest="50"
            HorizontalOptions="Center" VerticalOptions="Center"
            Grid.Row="2" Grid.Column="0">
        <controls:CustomImage.GestureRecognizers>
            <TapGestureRecognizer Tapped="HandleShutter"/>
        </controls:CustomImage.GestureRecognizers>
    </controls:CustomImage>

    <Label x:Name="FlashLabelLandscape"
            Text="{Binding IsFlashOn, Converter={StaticResource
boolToStringConverter}, ConverterParameter='On, Off'}"
            TextColor="#0ca6df"
            XAlign="Center" YAlign="Start" Grid.Row="1"
Grid.Column="0">
        <Label.GestureRecognizers>
            <TapGestureRecognizer Tapped="HandleFlash"/>
        </Label.GestureRecognizers>
    </Label>

    <controls:CustomImage x:Name="FlashImageLandscape"
```

```
Path="photo_light.png"
                    Margin="0, 10, 0, 0" HorizontalOptions="Center"
                    TintOn="false" WidthRequest="30"
                    HeightRequest="30"
                    Grid.Row="0" Grid.Column="0">
               <controls:CustomImage.GestureRecognizers>
                    <TapGestureRecognizer Tapped="HandleFlash"/>
               </controls:CustomImage.GestureRecognizers>
          </controls:CustomImage>
        </Grid>
```

The following image shows the `CameraPage` in landscape:

The last element to add is another `Grid` that will appear when we take a photo:

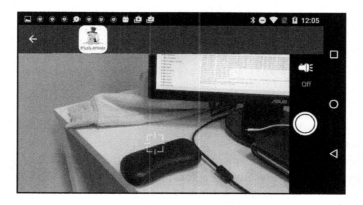

```
      <Grid x:Name="PhotoEditLayout" IsEnabled="{Binding PhotoEditOn}"
BackgroundColor="White"
               Opacity="{Binding PhotoEditOn, Converter={StaticResource
boolToPartialConverter}, ConverterParameter='1, 0'}"
```

```
            RowSpacing="0" Grid.Row="0" Grid.RowSpan="7"
Grid.Column="0" Grid.ColumnSpan="6">
        <Grid.RowDefinitions>
            <RowDefinition Height="*"/>
            <RowDefinition Height="60"/>
        </Grid.RowDefinitions>

        <Grid.ColumnDefinitions>
            <ColumnDefinition Width="10"/>
            <ColumnDefinition Width="*"/>
            <ColumnDefinition Width="*"/>
            <ColumnDefinition Width="*"/>
            <ColumnDefinition Width="10"/>
        </Grid.ColumnDefinitions>

        <Image x:Name="PhotoToEdit"
            Source="{Binding PhotoData, Converter={StaticResource
byteArrayToImageSourceConverter}}"
            Aspect="AspectFit"
            BackgroundColor="White"
            IsOpaque="true"
            Grid.Row="0" Grid.RowSpan="2" Grid.Column="0"
Grid.ColumnSpan="5" />

        <BoxView BackgroundColor="Black" Grid.Row="1" Grid.Column="0"
Grid.ColumnSpan="5"/>
        <controls:CustomImage x:Name="TrashImage"
Path="photo_trash.png"
                TintColorString="#FFFFFF" TintOn="true"
HorizontalOptions="Center"
                WidthRequest="40" HeightRequest="40"
                Grid.Row="1" Grid.Column="1">
            <controls:CustomImage.GestureRecognizers>
                <TapGestureRecognizer Tapped="HandleDelete"/>
            </controls:CustomImage.GestureRecognizers>
        </controls:CustomImage>
    </Grid>
```

The `Grid` contains the `Image` that will be bound to the `PhotoData` property on the view-model. This is where we use the `ByteArrayToImageSourceConverter`. Whenever the byte array is changed and the `OnPropertyChanged` method is called, a new image will be created from the byte array in the view-model. There is also a `CustomImage` that will add another button for closing the screen, deleting the image data, and returning to the camera to take another photo.

Adding native orientation events

Our next step is to add the notifications that are going to fire every time an orientation occurs. These events will come from the native side, so in order to have these pass down to our `Xamarin.Forms` project, we are going to use the static events on the `OrientationPage`.

Let's start with the iOS project. Open the `AppDelegate.cs` file and add the following function:

```
        public override void DidChangeStatusBarOrientation(UIApplication
    application, UIInterfaceOrientation oldStatusBarOrientation)
        {
            // change listview opacity based upon orientation
            switch (UIApplication.SharedApplication.StatusBarOrientation)
            {
                case UIInterfaceOrientation.Portrait:
                case UIInterfaceOrientation.PortraitUpsideDown:
    OrientationPage.NotifyOrientationChange(Orientation.Portrait);
                    break;
                case UIInterfaceOrientation.LandscapeLeft:
    OrientationPage.NotifyOrientationChange(Orientation.LandscapeLeft);
                    break;
                case UIInterfaceOrientation.LandscapeRight:
    OrientationPage.NotifyOrientationChange(Orientation.LandscapeRight);
                    break;
            }
        }
```

The `DidChangeStatusBarOrientation` function is contained in all `AppDelegate` objects. When we override this, we reference the exact orientation in the `UIApplication.SharedApplication.StatusBarOrientation` property of the `AppDelegate`. Every time an orientation occurs, this method will be called and we will then call the static method `NotifyOrientationChange` on the `OrientationPage` to fire the event back to the `Xamarin.Forms` page.

Let's do the same for Android. Open the `MainActivity.cs` file and add the following:

```
public override void
OnConfigurationChanged(Android.Content.Res.Configuration newConfig)
        {
            base.OnConfigurationChanged(newConfig);

            switch (newConfig.Orientation)
            {
                case Android.Content.Res.Orientation.Portrait:
```

```
OrientationPage.NotifyOrientationChange(Portable.Enums.Orientation.Portrait
);
                break;
            case Android.Content.Res.Orientation.Landscape:
OrientationPage.NotifyOrientationChange(Portable.Enums.Orientation.Landscap
eLeft);
                break;
        }
    }
```

Unfortunately for Android, we can only gather whether the orientation is in landscape or portrait. IOS has the ability to determine whether we are in landscape left or landscape right.

Like the `DidChangeStatusBarOrientation` function, the Android `OnConfigurationChanged` method will be called whenever the orientation changes. We use a switch statement again to call the static method on the `OrientationPage`.

Let's now add the logic behind the `CameraPage`. Here we will be responding to the native orientation events when they occur.

Open the `CameraPage.xaml.cs` file and implement the private properties:

```
public partial class CameraPage : ExtendedContentPage,
INavigableXamarinFormsPage
    {
        #region Private Properties

        private float CAMERA_BUTTON_CONTAINER_WIDTH = 70f;

        private CameraPageViewModel _model;

        #endregion
    }
```

We use the `CAMERA_BUTTON_CONTAINER_WIDTH` property when we render the camera stream on iOS, to make sure the stream bounds do not render behind the button container.

When the camera is rendered for iOS, we have to reduce the render bound width by a certain amount to make sure that the camera bounds don't render behind the button container. Every time the orientation changes, we will use this value to reduce the width of the render bounds.

We also have the `CameraPageViewModel` to keep locally when we retrieve it from the IoC container. Let's add the constructor as follows:

```
#region Constructors

public CameraPage(CameraPageViewModel model) : base(model)
{
    BindingContext = model;
    _model = model;

    InitializeComponent();

    Appearing += HandleAppearing;
    Disappearing += HandleDisappearing;

    CameraView.Photo += HandlePictureTaken;
    CameraView.AvailabilityChange += HandleCameraAvailability;
    CameraView.Loading += HandleLoading;
    CameraView.Busy += HandleBusy;

    FocusView.TouchFocus += HandleFocusChange;
}

#endregion
```

Here we retrieve the `CameraPageViewModel` from the IoC container. We also register event functions when the page appears and disappears. We also register event functions on the `CameraView` when we take a photo, when the camera initialization occurs, when the camera is loading, and when the camera is busy. Then, we register one event for the `TouchFocus` event on the `FocusView`. Every time a new point (x, y) is received, we pass this to the `CameraView` to perform a focus.

Let's add the `EventHandler` functions for page appearing and disappearing. Here we will register and deregister to the orientation `OrientationHandler` event:

```
private void HandleDisappearing(object sender, EventArgs e)
{
    OrientationHandler -= HandleOrientationChange;

    _model.OnDisappear();
}

private void HandleAppearing(object sender, EventArgs e)
{
    OrientationHandler += HandleOrientationChange;

    _model.OnAppear();
```

```
        }
```

Let's add the `HandleOrientationChange` method for updating the button container width by resizing the width of the `ColumnDefinition`. After we resize the `ColumnDefinition`, we then call `Reset` on the `FocusView` object; if the camera is ready to take a photo, we center the focus point of the camera to the middle of the screen. Then call the `NotifyOrientationChange` on the `CameraView` to update the renderer camera stream bounds and rotation:

```
public void HandleOrientationChange(object sender, Orientation arg)
    {
        FocusView.Orientation = CameraView.Orientation =
OrientationPage.PageOrientation = _model.PageOrientation = arg;

        switch (PageOrientation)
        {
            case Orientation.LandscapeLeft:
            case Orientation.LandscapeRight:
                MainLayout.ColumnDefinitions[5].Width = new
GridLength(CAMERA_BUTTON_CONTAINER_WIDTH,
GridUnitType.Absolute);
                break;
            case Orientation.Portrait:
                MainLayout.ColumnDefinitions[4].Width = new
GridLength(CAMERA_BUTTON_CONTAINER_WIDTH,
GridUnitType.Absolute);
                break;
        }

        if (_model.CanCapture)
        {
            FocusView.Reset();
        }

        CameraView.NotifyOrientationChange(arg);
    }
```

Next, we have the `HandleBusy` and `HandleLoading` functions, which simply set the `CameraLoading` property on the view-model:

```
    private void HandleBusy(object sender, bool e)
    {
        _model.CameraLoading = e;
    }

    private void HandleLoading(object sender, bool e)
    {
```

```
        _model.CameraLoading = e;
    }
```

Then add the `HandleShutter`, which will call the `NotifyShutter` method on the `CameraView`:

```
public void HandleShutter(object sender, EventArgs args)
    {
        CameraView.NotifyShutter();
    }
```

Then we have the `HandleFlash` function responsible for updating the `FlashOn` property of the view-model and calling the `NotifyFlash` method on the `CameraView`:

```
public void HandleFlash(object sender, EventArgs args)
    {
        _model.IsFlashOn = !_model.IsFlashOn;
        CameraView.NotifyFlash(_model.IsFlashOn);
    }
```

The `HandlePictureTaken` function is called every time the camera button is touched and data is received from the native camera. We then pass the byte array back to the view-model using the `AddPhoto` method:

```
public void HandlePictureTaken(object sender, byte[] data)
    {
        if (_model.CanCapture)
        {
            _model.AddPhoto(data);
        }

    }
```

Next we have the `HandleCameraAvailability` method, which is called when the native camera availability status changes. If the camera is available, we the set the view-model properties, assign the starting orientation, and set up `IsVisible` bindings on the camera button containers to the `PageOrientation` property of the view-model.

We must set up the `IsVisible` bindings after the camera has become available because a layout pass is not called on items that are invisible when the page is loaded. We need the height and width to be set on these items even if the items are invisible.

```
public void HandleCameraAvailability(object sender, bool available)
    {
        _model.CanCapture = available;
```

```
        if (available)
        {
            _model.CameraLoading = false;

            // wait until camera is available before animating focus
target, we have to invoke on UI thread as this is run asynchronously
            Device.BeginInvokeOnMainThread(() =>
            {
                // set starting list opacity based on orientation
                var orientation = (Height > Width) ?
Orientation.Portrait : Orientation.LandscapeLeft;
                // set starting orientation
                HandleOrientationChange(null, orientation);

                // these bindings are created after page intitalizes
PhotoEditLayout.SetBinding(VisualElement.IsVisibleProperty, new
Binding("PhotoEditOn"));

                // camera button layouts
CameraButtonContainerLandscape.SetBinding(VisualElement.OpacityProperty,
new Binding("PageOrientation", converter: new
OrientationToDoubleConverter(), converterParameter: "1, 1"));
CameraButtonContainerLandscape.SetBinding(VisualElement.IsVisibleProperty,
new Binding("PageOrientation", converter: new OrientationToBoolConverter(),
converterParameter: "true, false"));
CameraButtonContainerPortrait.SetBinding(VisualElement.OpacityProperty, new
Binding("PageOrientation", converter: new OrientationToDoubleConverter(),
converterParameter: "0, 1"));
CameraButtonContainerPortrait.SetBinding(VisualElement.IsVisibleProperty,
new Binding("PageOrientation", converter: new OrientationToBoolConverter(),
converterParameter: "false, true"));

                FocusView.Reset();
            });
        }

    }
```

Now we must add the `OnNavigatedTo` method. Here we will set a new binding on the
`IsVisible` property of the `LoadingView`.

 Remember, we must set the `IsVisible` binding after the page has done
the layout so that the `LoadingView` bounds are set correctly according to
the `Grid`.

We must also call the `SetFocusPoints` on the `FocusView` to set the starting focus points in both landscape and portrait. These starting points will be calculated from the height and width properties to get the center of the screen. Then we call `NotifyOpenCamera` to begin the process on the native camera to initialize it and open the camera. On only for iOS do we call the `NotifyWidths` method, so the widths of the button container are passed to the iOS native camera class:

```
        public void OnNavigatedTo(IDictionary<string, object>
navigationParameters)
        {
            _model.CameraLoading = false;

            LoadingView.SetBinding(VisualElement.IsVisibleProperty, new
Binding("CameraLoading"));

            _model.CanCapture = CameraView.CameraAvailable;

            switch (PageOrientation)
            {
                case Orientation.Portrait:
                    FocusView.SetFocusPoints(new Point(Width / 2, Height /
2),
                                            new Point(Height / 2, Width /
2));
                        break;
                case Orientation.LandscapeLeft:
                case Orientation.LandscapeRight:
                    FocusView.SetFocusPoints(new Point(Height / 2, Width /
2),
                                            new Point(Width / 2, Height /
2));
                        break;
            }

            CameraView.NotifyOpenCamera(true);

#if __IOS__
                CameraView.NotifyWidths (CAMERA_BUTTON_CONTAINER_WIDTH);
#endif

            this.Show(navigationParameters);
        }
```

Lastly, we have the `HandleDelete` method for removing the photo edit view and clearing the image bytes to free memory:

```
public void HandleDelete(object sender, EventArgs args)
{
    _model.ResetEditPhoto();
}

#endregion
}
```

Excellent! We now have implemented our entire `CameraPage` and native camera implementation for iOS and Android.

Challenge

We have built almost everything in the `Camera.Portable` and `Camera` projects, but there are still pieces missing. Here is another challenge. Fill in the missing pieces of the solution and get it compiling The remaining files are the exact same from all our other `Xamarin.Forms` solutions, but now it is your turn to finish off the project.

To see the finished version, refer to `https://github.com/flusharcade/chapter8-camera`.

Summary

In this chapter, we built complete control over the native camera hardware for iOS and Android. We looked at implementing Grid changes using Converters, and built `CustomRenderers` for accessing native tinting features and touch events. We also created event triggers for buttons and `PlatformEffects` for creating shadow on a Label on the `MainPage`.

Congratulations! We have made it to the end of our Xamarin journey.

Index

A

ALAssetLibrary class 30
Android navigation service
  building 280, 281
Android text-to-speech implementation 68, 69
Android
  IoC, setting up with 70
  MVVMCross, setting up with 160
architectural layers
  application/platform layer 250
  business layer (logic) 250
  common layer 250
  data access layer 250
  data layer 250
  service access layer 250
  user interface layer 250
asynchronous locking 334
audio player application
  Android SoundHandler, implementing with
    MediaPlayer framework 180, 181, 182
  AudioPlayerPageViewModel, creating 173, 176,
    178, 180
  bindings, creating 153, 154
  IoC, with MVVMCross 149
  iOS SoundHandler, implementing with
    AVAudioPlayer framework 162
  MVVMCross, setting up inside Portable Class
    Library 156
  MVVMCross, setting up with Android 159
  MVVMCross, setting up with iOS 157, 158
  Mvx IoC container 165
  MvxActivities 185, 187, 188, 191, 192
  NSLayout, using 169, 172
  NSLayoutConstraints 154, 156
  solution setup 148
  SoundHandler interface 161

user interaface, building to control audio 166,
  168
view-models, with Xamarin native 151
XML, and Mvx bindings 184
AuthenticationRepository
  AccountController, building 262, 264
  OAuth Authentication, configuring with Web API
    264
  setting up 259
  SignalR Hub, building 265, 267
  Web API, configuring 261, 262
authorization server
  creating, OWIN OAuth 2.0 used 256
Autofac
  using 57, 58
AVAudioPlayer framework
  used, for implementing iOS SoundHandler 162

B

Bearer tokens 254
behaviours 379
bindings
  about 65
  creating 153
bitmap functions 26, 27, 28

C

C# 6.0 syntax 341
camera application
  Android Camera2 framework, integrating 429,
    430, 432, 433, 435, 436, 437, 439, 440, 443,
    444, 445, 446, 447
  CameraPage, building 477, 479, 482, 483, 484,
    485, 488
  CameraView, building 408, 409, 410, 411, 412
  CameraViewRenderer, building in Android 449,
    450, 451

control, building for iOS camera 412, 413, 415, 416, 417, 418, 420, 421, 423, 424
custom UI objects, creating 398, 400
CustomImageRenderer for Android, building 462, 463, 464, 465, 466, 467
CustomImageRenderers, building 456, 458, 460, 461
Easing.SinIn 471
Easing.SinOut 471
event triggers, adding for button click events 468
FocusView, building 402
INotifiedPropertyChanged implementation, improving 391, 393, 394, 395, 396
iOS CameraRenderer, building 426, 427, 428
MainPageViewModel class, building 390
native orientation events, adding 491, 494, 495
native orientation events, building 493
native touch events, handling through FocusView 451, 452, 453, 454
platform effects 472, 474
RX, used for handling events 455
solution setup 388
UIImageEffects class, building 461, 462
VisualElementRenderer, building for iOS 455, 456
chat application
    Android ChatActivity, building 324, 327
    Android TableLayouts 323
    AuthenticationRepository, setting up 259, 261
    ChatPresenter, building 314
    ClientListViewController, creating 304
    clients, running 328
    ClientsListActivity, creating 308
    ClientsListPresenter, implementing 299, 301, 302, 303
    connection, creating between Presenter and View 289, 290, 292
    Hub proxy callbacks, handling 284
    iOS ChatView, building 316
    ListAdapter, building 311
    LoginActivity, building 294, 296, 297, 299
    LoginPresenter, implementing 286
    OnBackPressed() activity, overriding 310
    server, running 328
    TaskCompletionSource framework 307

UIColor framework, extending 320, 322
client message handlers 127
CLLocationManager library 90
commands 62
compound animations, Xamarin.Forms 405
core location 76
cross-platform development with Xamarin.Forms 42
custom elements
    styles, adding for 236
custom renderers 233

D

data contract 118
data trigger 468

E

event trigger 468
EventHandlers 282
Extensible Application Markup Language (XAML) 42

F

file storage application
    alerts, handling in view-models 346
    AsyncLock, creating 336
    AsyncSemaphore, creating 334, 337
    CarouselView, building with custom layouts 352, 354, 355, 356
    cross-platform logging, implementing 339, 340
    CustomRenderer, building for native gestures 358, 361, 364, 366
    data access layer, creating with SQLite 331, 332, 333
    EditFilePage, building 378
    ExtendedContentPage, building 351
    IMethods interface, building 348, 350
    IoC container, implementing 338
    ISQLiteStorage interface, building 333
    modules, implementing 338
    native setup requirements, implementing for SQLite 337
    project structure setup 330
    scroll control, adding to CarouselView 356
    SQLiteStorage class, implementing 341

SynchronizationContext, using 376, 377
user interface, building 368, 370, 371, 373, 375

G

gallery application
  ALAssetLibrary, using 29, 31, 32
  Android photo screen, adding 37, 38, 39
  Android project, creating 17
  bitmap processing 26, 27
  cells apperance, customizing 12, 15
  iOS photo screen, adding 33, 34, 36
  iOS project, creating 8
  ListView, creating 17
  row appearance, customizing 21, 22, 23, 24, 25
  shared projects, creating 19, 20, 21
  UITableView, creating 9, 12
  UIViewController, creating 9, 12
  XML interface, creating 18
Google API 119
GPS 76
GPS locator application
  Android, and LocationManager 101, 102, 104
  API key, creating for Android 107, 108, 110
  API key, creating for geocoding 120
  Application class 116, 117
  client message handlers 127
  CLLocationManager library 90, 91, 92, 93
  closest position, calculating 140, 143, 145
  core location services, with Windows Phone 114, 115
  core location, with iOS 90, 91, 92, 93, 109
  core location, with Windows Phone 112
  exit point, creating 105, 107
  GecodingWebServiceController, creating 121, 123, 124
  GeocodingWebServiceController, using 134
  Google Maps, integrating with
    Xamarin.Forms.Maps 87, 88
  JSON data, feeding into IObservable framework 130
  location updates, handling 94, 95, 96, 97, 98, 99
  Microsoft HTTP client libraries 126
  ModernHttpClient 127, 128, 130
  navigation control, building 80
  navigation with Xamarin.Forms 78

Newtonsoft.Json 125
OnNavigatedTo function 136
OnShow function 136
project, setting up 76
Pythagoras equirectangular projection 139
Reactive Extensions, importing 89, 132
Resource (RESX) files 132
view model navigation 82, 84, 86
Windows project, creating 110, 111
Grid 66
GZIP 129

H

HttpClientHandler 127
Hub 251
hub proxy 283
Hub proxy callbacks
  handling 284
HubConnection 251
HubProxy 251

I

IGeolocator 88
IoC container 56
IoC
  about 55
  implementing, with Windows Phone 72
  setting up, with Android 70
  with MVVMCross 149
iOS navigation service
  building 279
iOS text-to-speech implementation 59, 60, 61, 62, 65
iOS
  MVVMCross, setting up with 157, 158

L

ListView
  creating 17
locking 334
LoginPresenter
  implementing 286

M

Microsoft HTTP client libraries 126
mobile projects
  application state 278
  setting up 268
  SignalRClient, creating 269, 270, 271, 272,
    273, 274
  WebApiAccess layer, building 274, 276
Model-View-Presenter (MVP) pattern 249
Model-View-View-Model (MVVM) 42
Modules 58, 60
multi trigger 468
MVVMCross
  setting up, in Portable Class Library 156
  setting up, with Android 159
  setting up, with iOS 157, 158
Mvx IoC container 165

N

navigation service
  Android navigation service, building 280, 281
  iOS interface, building 282
  iOS navigation service, building 279
  setting up 278
Newtonsoft 125

O

Open Web Interface for .NET (OWIN)
  about 255
  authorization server, creating with OWIN OAuth
    2.0 256
  OAuthAuthorizationServerProvider 256
  UseOAuthBearerAuthentication 258
OWIN OAuth 2.0
  used, for creating authorization server 256

P

platform independent styling 73
Portable Class Library (PCL) 43
Portable Class Library
  MVVMCross, setting up in 156
Presenter 283
property trigger 468
Pythagoras equirectangular projection 139

R

race conditions 334
Reactive Extensions 89
RX framework 89

S

Shared C# App Logic block 43
SignalR
  about 251
  setting up 252, 253, 254
SignalRClient 277
Speech Talk application
  Android text-to-speech implementation 68, 69
  Autofac, using 57, 58, 59
  bindings, setting up 65, 68
  Inversion of Control (IoC), with Xamarin.Forms
    56
  IoC, implementing with Windows Phone 72
  IoC, setting up with Android 70
  iOS text-to-speech implementation 59, 60, 61,
    62, 65
  platform independent styling 73
  platform projects, setting up 44
  SpeechTalk.Droid project, setting up 49
  SpeechTalk.iOS project, creating 47
  Windows Phone Project, creating 50, 51, 54
  WinPhone text-to-speech implementation 71
SQLite 331
SQLiteStorage object 334
StockItemDetailsPageViewModel
  creating 236
Stocklist application
  API controller, building 198, 200
  ASP.Net Web API 2 project, creating 195, 196,
    197
  core mobile projects, building 201
  custom renderer, applying 233
  DataTemplate, adding to global resource
    dictionary 226, 227
  further optimization, with XAML 229, 230
  global App.xaml, creating 208
  ListViews, using 219, 220, 222
  MainPageViewModel, updating 214, 215
  mobile projects, setting up 200

native platform projects, setting up 239, 240
ObservableCollections, using 219, 220, 222
performance, improving 202, 203, 204, 206, 207
StockItemDetailsPage, creating 230, 231
StockItemDetailsPageViewModel, creating 236
Stocklist web service controller, creating 217, 219
styles, adding 227, 228
styles, adding for custom elements 236
theming, with ControlTemplates 210
value converters 225
Web API project, hosting locally 240, 241, 242
styles
adding, to custom elements 236

T

triggers
about 468
data trigger 468
event trigger 468
multi trigger 468
property trigger 468

U

UITableView
creating 11
UIViewController

creating 9, 10, 11
URIs 26

V

value converters 225
view-models
with Xamarin native 150

W

web service 118
Windows phone version
building 383
Windows Phone
IoC, implementing with 72
Windows Presentation Framework (WPF) 42
WinPhone text-to-speech implementation 71

X

Xamarin.Forms animations 403
Xamarin.Forms animations, functions
FadeTo 403
LayoutTo 403
RotateTo 403
ScaleTo 403
Translate.To 403
Xamarin.Forms
compound animations 405

Lightning Source UK Ltd.
Milton Keynes UK
UKOW04f1432270317

297627UK00001B/20/P

9 781785 887